The First Delaware Symposium
on Language Studies

The First Delaware Symposium on Language Studies

Selected Papers

Edited by
Robert J. Di Pietro,
William Frawley,
and Alfred Wedel

Newark: University of Delaware Press
London and Toronto: Associated University Presses

Associated University Presses, Inc.
4 Cornwall Drive
East Brunswick, N.J. 08816

Associated University Presses Ltd.
27 Chancery Lane
London WC2A 1NF, England

Associated University Presses
2133 Royal Windsor Drive
Unit 1
Mississauga, Ontario L5J 1K5, Canada

Library of Congress Cataloging in Publication Data

Delaware Symposium on Language Studies (1st : 1979 :
　　University of Delaware)
　　Selected papers.

　　　　1.　Language and languages—Congresses.　I. Di Pietro, Robert
J.　II. Frawley, William, 1953-　III. Wedel, Alfred.　IV. Title.
P106.D43　1979　　　　　　　　400　　　　　　　　80-71116
ISBN 0-87413-190-1

Printed in the United States of America

CONTENTS

Introduction

Linguistics continues to develop in diverse and unexpected directions. It is characterized by a great diversity of research interests and by a constant recasting of theoretical models. Of late, the applications of linguistics to bilingualism and second-language acquisition have attracted much attention among linguists and laypersons alike. The first Delaware Symposium on Language Studies (October 18-20, 1979) was organized to address such areas of interests and to bring together theoreticians and practitioners who otherwise might not have the opportunity to share their ideas and findings. Of the sixty-six papers read at the symposium, we have selected thirty as being representative of what was presented and discussed.

The six invited papers compose Part I of the volume. First is Robert Lado's defense of the significance of the native language in planning programs of second-language teaching ("The Language, Culture, and Thought of the Learner Cannot Be Ignored in Applied Linguistics"). Lado's commentary on contrastive analysis and error analysis must be confronted by any methodologist who would deemphasize the part played by the native language in the learning of a new language. The support for the significance of native competences is extended to include reading conventions, thought, and cultural patterns.

The address by Edward Stewart ("Talking Culture: Language in the Function of Communication") picks up the theme of culture and its relevance for the second-language teacher. Taking the Whorfian hypothesis as a point of departure, Stewart offers several languages as evidence for opposing stands on linguistic relativity. While French and Arabic speakers seem to tie their languages closely to their thought processes (therefore supporting Whorf), Japanese speakers rely more on images and nonverbal means to convey messages. In other words, the Japanese resist the temptation to summarize their thoughts with words while speakers of western languages search eagerly for just the right verbal expression to what they are thinking. These initial observations lead into Stewart's main intention, which is to offer a definition of culture applicable to the needs of the foreign-language teacher.

Richard Tucker's ("The Role of Language in Education") concern is twofold. First, he dispels several incorrect inferences drawn by American bilingual specialists from the research findings of Canadians on language switches between home and school. Second, he draws on a vast store of information about bilingual

1

education in Third World countries (specifically, Nigeria, Sudan, and the Philippines) in an effort to uncover evidence for the best selection and sequencing of languages in bilingual education. His conclusion is that uniform recommendations cannot be made to fit all situations. Each educational setting brings unique sociolinguistic factors into play in the choice and treatment of languages in bilingual schools.

In her paper ("Language beyond the Classroom"), Shirley Brice Heath advises linguists to gain professional occupations in noneducational institutions. Her recommendations stem from involvement in a network of communication among linguists already working in medicine, business, social work, and other nonacademic occupations. She describes several settings (federal credit unions, social service agencies, and banks) in which the analysis of discourse can help the administrators to operate more effectively with the public. The findings uncovered by linguists can be useful in restructuring curricula for language study, especially in the area of adult basic English. Conversational analysis has not been a central part of such curricula.

A. Julian Valbuena ("Verbal Strategies, Images, and Symbolic Roles in the Use of a Conventional Language by a Spanish Golden Age Playwright") applies several notions from linguistics to literary analysis. Taking several plays by Calderon, Valbuena demonstrates how a binary system of thematic features functions to advance plot structure. He also shows how repetition and redundancy in language use can serve as devices to enhance the clarity of messages conveyed in the text. Yet another insight is in how role types, such as the gracioso, are portrayed through the patterned distortions of language.

According to Lorraine Strasheim ("School Foreign-Language Programs: Reaching toward the Twenty-first Century"), the foreign-language-teaching profession has brought upon itself many of the difficulties it faces today. Many teachers are tenured and consequently are not interested in trying out new approaches to their subject matter. Foreign-language teachers also tend to be parochial, ignoring all languages but the one they teach. Opportunities to fit curricula to real communicative situations are missed on a regular basis. Strasheim offers several suggestions for remedying this situation. These include introducing languages that are not now part of the curriculum and launching ongoing projects in research, evaluation, and assessment. A number of different foreign language programs are shown how they might meet community needs.

The nine papers of the second part illustrate many of the ways in which linguistics is moving to new areas of interest. Wescott's paper ("Color Metaphors in Three Language Phyla") describes how metaphor operates across language boundaries. While many color references appear to be language-specific, Wescott argues that broad patterns of predictability underlie them. Drawing from a wide range of observations, he concludes that the metaphoric universals of color are basically iconic in nature.

Max Kirch ("Nonverbal Communication in Cross-Cultural Perspective") examines the ways in which nonverbal communication serves cultural systems. In Kirch's definition, nonverbal communication is of several types: paralinguistic (phonemically based but extraneous to the grammar), proxemic (distances maintained between speakers in various cultures), and kinesic (body movements, including gestures and gait). Multiple examples are provided for each type in which American nonverbal communication is contrasted with that of other cultures.

Although both linguists and psychiatrists have a vital interest in the use of language, there is a marked difference between the two groups in the interpretation of its function in conveying meaning. The main question for linguists is how people mean through language, and for psychiatrists, the concern is what people mean as opposed to what they say. In "Linguistics Looks at Psychiatry," Elaine Chaika draws comparisons between the two approaches to patient discourse. The critical issue for the analyst to resolve is when the "normal" rules affecting discourse give way to abnormal conditions in a patient's illness and when, in the remission stage, a patient should return to a normal usage.

Deborah Tannen ("When Is an Overlap Not an Interruption?") investigates the phenomenon of overlap in conversational language. Using two-and-one-half hours of transcribed spontaneous conversation, Tannen determines that overlap among some interlocutors is used as a cooperative strategy rather than as a simple interruption. Timing an overlap to cut off the end of the other speaker's sentences often shows interest and support for what is being said. The differences in the interpretation of overlap can be attributed to ethnic and cultural factors.

John Staczek's excursion into generative semantics ("Lexical Decomposition, Incorporation, and Paraphrase") provides a formal proposal about the workings of paraphrase. Quite possibly all languages use a process of stylistic restatement built around the properties of verb and noun units that permit certain recombined forms. The main body of Staczek's paper comprises illustrations of lexicalization and its opposite, decomposition, in English nouns and verbs.

In "Code-Switching in the St. John Valley of Northern Maine," Nancy Lee Schweda looks at the factors relevant to the choice of language use by the bilingual French-English inhabitants of that area. Code-switching among these people is not only situationally and thematically determined but also serves the purposes of goal-oriented interaction. Five language varieties are identified and located at different points on a linguistic continuum.

From Davis Lee ("Code-Switching as a Verbal Strategy among Bilingual Chinese") we learn that moving from one code to another is an important phenomenon among Chinese living in the United States but often goes unnoticed by them. For monolingual Chinese, switching between colloquial and classical forms of the language is a mark of cultural achievement. Lee lists four different strategic purposes for code-switching among bilingual Chinese and illustrates their uses. Since proverbs have prominence in Chinese conversations, proverbialized speech often involves code-switches from English to Chinese.

Rodney Moag ("The Language-Use Grid") constructs a framework within which the applied linguist can accommodate data useful to understanding several functions of language in a speech community. Not only are complex variables affecting language use and code switching accommodated, but through Moag's grid it becomes possible to foreground those variables that are most critical in specific instances.

Nancy Spekman ("Verbal Communication and Role-Taking") investigates the function of deictics in marking role-taking skill among young children. Although the children showed no difficulty in understanding the grammar of deictics, their ability to use such elements in communicating varied considerably. Spekman suggests that aberrancies in the use of deictics in children's speech may signal communicational difficulties even though their grammatical usage may show no deviancies.

Judy McInnis's paper, "A Computer-Assisted Study of Spanish-English Transfer," begins Part III. All nine papers in this section are centered about the research on second-language acquisition. McInnis's purpose is to determine whether any relationship exists between learners' knowledge of the grammar of their native language (English) and their performance in the target language (Spanish). The results of teaching grammar to an experimental group lead McInnis to refute the belief, prevalent in the 1960s and 1970s, that training in formal grammar is of little use in learning a second language.

Gerald Culley ("Two-Pronged Error Analysis from Computer-Based Instruction in Latin") describes a technique for error analysis through a set of Plato computer lessons. Computer-based programs of instruction provide large numbers of practice exercises with high efficiency. Since the computer can decline nouns in Latin, it can also identify the incorrect responses that the student makes while attempting to apply the rules of declension. The capacity of the computer to identify exactly where the error has been made is of great help to the teacher in evaluating the learning process and in making adjustments in the methodology.

Fred Eckman ("Some Empirical Evidence on the Nature of Interlanguages") finds support for the "interlanguage" hypothesis in the pronunciation of students of English from diverse language backgrounds. According to Eckman, sufficient parallels can be found in the errors made by these students to justify the positing of some rules that neither are transferred from the native language during the learning process nor are identifiable with rules of the target language.   Furthermore, interlanguage rules appear to be subject to the same constraints of rules belonging to first languages.

Marcel Danesi ("Contrastive Analysis Revisited") surveys the criticisms voiced against the usefulness for the methodologist and foreign language teacher of contrasting native and target languages.   The reasons why contrastive analysis has not fully predicted errors in second language learning, may be found in the inflexible application by practitioners or in the inadequacy of the linguistic framework employed.   Danesi views error analysis, which some see as a replacement for contrastive analysis, as a complement to the latter.   He concludes by advocating the extension of formal contrastive analysis to other areas than grammar, such as the verbal strategies of conversational language.

Alvino Fantini ("Transference in Child Speech: A Sociolinguistic Phenomenon") investigates the speech of bilingual children.   Such children display a wide variety of patterns in the ways they acquire their languages.   To answer some of the questions regarding the nature of linguistic systems in bilinguals, Fantini conducted case studies of two children.   His developmental evidence suggests that transference from one language to the other is a broad, socially motivated phenomenon that is responsive to the diverse contexts of language use.   Interference, on the other hand, seems much more limited to structural elements of language form.

Anna Uhl Chamot ("Contrastive/Error/Performance Analyses") selected six areas of predicted difficulty in second-language acquisition and tested them through three types of analyses.   Her conclusions were that five of the six areas did cause difficulty. Performance analysis provided insights into the subject's learning strategies that were unavailable through either contrastive or error approaches.   Chamot appeals to the teacher to pay more attention to the learner's correct production of target-language forms.

Susan Gass ("Second-Language Acquisition and Language Universals") investigates the ways in which evidence from second-language acquisition relates to the theoretical linguistic construct known as the "accessibility hierarchy."   Although this construct was formulated on the basis of a purely topological study of languages, the performance of learners of English from different language backgrounds support it in several ways.   Gass concludes with a plea for consideration by theoreticians of data from second-language studies.

Hector Hammerly ("Theories, Dichotomies, and Synthesis in L2 Teaching") argues that the field of second-language studies should work toward a synthesis rather than follow the theories of other disciplines.   The imitation of other fields has resulted in the proliferation of slogans (e.g., a language is a "set of habits" or language is "speech not writing").   These slogans have tended to obscure important findings that happen not to support them.   Such has been the case with interlingual similarities discovered at a time when the slogan "languages are different" was in vogue.   By the same token, contrastive and error analysis are complementary, rather than being oppositional.

In his paper entitled "The Competing-Plans Hypothesis Extended to Second-Language Speech Production," Hans Dechert adds a hitherto neglected dimension to the study of second-language acquisition. The execution of speech often displays pauses, errors, and self-corrections that can be traced to the speaker's indecision about the message to be conveyed. By investigating the performance manifestation of the speaker's mapping of speech in the second-language, we can gain an understanding of the underlying linguistic competence as it is developing in the learner.

Eugene Fong's "The Semantics of the French Subjunctive" begins the fourth and final part of the book. This section contains papers that deal specifically with techniques to be utilized in the foreign language classroom. Of the two principal ways of interpreting the subjunctive in French, Fong discusses the one that is derived from the speaker's intentions. A clear semantic distinction can be drawn between the use of the indicative and the subjunctive in sentential complements. Once this distinction is achieved, proper exercises can be formulated.

Using the example of relative pronouns in French textbooks, Jeannette Ludwig ("Defining the Need for a Pedagogical Grammar") illustrates the wide gap that separates present pedagogical treatments from the realities of what is needed by the student. Among the omissions in the textbooks is the treatment of the functions of grammatical forms. Functional/notional syllabi are yet to be implemented to fill this need. Moreover, textbook writers are yet to understand fully the psychological value of covering contrastively difficult matters at various times and in diverse forms. Procedures for grading according to difficulty remain to be found as well.

Jo Ann Crandall and Allene Guss Grognet ("The Notional/Functional Syllabus in Adult ESL") support the effort to make second-language teaching more communicational. Their focus is on the specific functions to which people put language and how they should affect a syllabus. An advantage to a notional/functional approach is its accounting of a variety of contexts and options for language use. The authors outline some of the problems faced by notional/functional syllabi. Among these problems must be included the placing of grammar in its proper perspective and the sequencing of functions through the course of instruction. Testing is another difficulty. With all its problems, however, the functional syllabi are the only ones that address the question of cultural coping skills needed by adult learners.

Louis Arena ("Accuracy Verses Fluency Revisited for the Advanced ESL Composition Class") finds that the imposition of the criterion of accuracy before fluency has an equally deleterious effect on native and ESL students attempting to learn English composition. Instead of subjecting the ESL student to sentence-bound grammatical exercises, Arena advocates use of a clause-analysis technique whereby the structural styles (expository, narrative, descriptive, and technical) are identified. The learner is led to write compositions in each style by utilizing the particular devices associated with them.

Bruce Barkman and Lise Winer ("The ESL Performance of Grade 10 Francophones in Quebec") report on part of a detailed study of the English-language development of French-speaking students. Learners' errors can be subclassified as extrinsic to English or due to transfer from the mother tongue, or as induced in the classroom. The authors conducted an analysis of student performance in English over a semester. Such a long time period was selected in order to override fluctuations in accuracy rates occurring in shorter time periods. The framework that evolves from the performance analysis is tested on the students' learning of the present progressive construction in English.

Beth Haslett ("Patterns of Teacher/Child Interaction in Preschool Settings") applies Flanders's interaction-analysis categories and Soskin and John's relational categories to the use of language in conversations between children and their teachers. Her analysis is directed toward understanding three factors: (1) functions in teacher-student dialogues, (2) differences in teacher talk across class levels, and (3) differences in children's responses to teachers. Among other things, Haslett found that teacher responses differed significantly across response categories. Children initiated conversation with teachers about twice as much as they responded to teachers. Requests for information were the most frequent utterances of children, regardless of age. As the children grew older, they initiated more talk with the teachers and used more communicative strategies. The parallel with mother/child interaction was evident.

In closing this introduction, the editors wish to acknowledge the help of Roberta Golinkoff and Deborah Tannen, who gave generously and graciously of their time in helping us select the papers appearing in this volume.

Robert J. Di Pietro
William Frawley
Alfred Wedel

University of Delaware

The First Delaware Symposium
on Language Studies

Part I
The Plenary Papers

1. The Language, Culture, and "Thought" of the Learner Cannot Be Ignored in Applied Linguistics

ROBERT LADO
Georgetown University

Introduction

Applied linguistics, which deals with practical problems in which language is an important component, adapts linguistic knowledge and the results of linguistic research to those practical problems. In the absence of adequate research, the applied linguist carries out ad hoc studies to obtain needed data or to test hypothetical solutions. The focus of such studies is the solution of the practical problem rather than exploration of theoretical questions. This focus on practical problems does not mean that the applied linguist may not contribute to linguistic theory, since language theories are put to the test in such practical problems and may have to be revised or abandoned and new hypotheses formulated to account for or explain the phenomena observed.

This testing of theory in field work, so to speak, is not peculiar to linguistics; it is true of all applied science. Early theories of fire, for example, awaited the test of applied science to be discarded and to yield to a new and more tenable theory.

A major component of most applied linguistic problems is learning—for example, learning a new language or dialect. Applied linguistics, then, involves language use and language learning.

In recent years we have witnessed an extended tug-of-war between two viewpoints. The first is that in teaching or establishing a new language or dialect the native language must be ignored or even suppressed until it is abandoned or forgotten altogether in favor of the new one. This view, though widely held and promoted, has seldom if even been fully successful, with the result that policies and educational practices change before the native language or dialect is abandoned or forgotten. The second and opposite tendency and view seeks to take into account the native language or dialect or even to capitalize on it. This viewpoint has also shown mixed results, probably because applied linguistic problems are not exclusively linguistic even in the wider perspective of socio-, psycho-, and pedagogical linguistics. Applied linguistic problems are complex matters whose solution depends on many factors besides those within the limits of linguistics and learning theories.

These underlying philosophies about the role of the language of the students continue to be ambivalent at present. In studies of 1st- and 2nd-language acquisition, there is a strong inclination to search for and find uniformity and universality in the sequence of acquisition and in learning strategies. Children of all languages and cultures are found to progress in similar ways and to use the same strategies. In studies of 2nd-language acquisition, data is sought that will show that contrastive analysis (CA), which gives major consideration to the native language, accounts for only a small proportion of the learning problems. On the other hand, error analysis (EA), which ignores the native language altogether, is vigorously pursued.

There is interest in direct methods that forbid or discourage the use of the native language without research evidence as a basis. Such is the case with The Silent Way and to some extent with audiovisual methods. And at the same time, incongruously, there is interest in cognitive methods that cannot be implemented adequately without recourse to the native language.

At the same time that the learner's language is relegated to the background or is ignored or suppressed altogether, there is increasing interest in bilingualism, biculturalism, and bidialectalism. And in the case of at least a handful of researchers, there is interest in early biliteracy as well. Bilingualism and biliteracy by definition give equal status and importance to the native and to the second or foreign language.

This paper attempts to show that ignoring, suppressing, or minimizing the language, culture, and thought of the learners is untenable in formulating any comprehensive applied linguistics rationale.

Language, "Languaging," Aptitude, and Teaching

To know a language presupposes a vast store of lexical items, grammar rules, pronunciation features, and rules in deep memory, so easily accessible that they can be used for communication at normal speed with primary attention on thinking. The process of using a language varies according to whether we are speaking, listening, reading, writing, or translating, but in every case it involves relating meaning and form to thinking. Since there is no generic global term to refer to the various uses of language, let me propose "languaging," which does not sound very elegant but will do for the moment. We can say that languaging is to language what thinking is to thought, instead of having to say speaking, listening, reading, and writing are to language, etc. Languaging is the process of referring language forms and meanings in texts and utterances to thinking within the system of a language, and thinking is the development of mental constructs within the systems of thought.

Language aptitude is supposedly an innate capacity to learn or acquire languages. John Carroll has demonstrated convincingly that it is distinct from other types of intelligence. The Carroll and Sapon Modern Language Aptitude Test (MLAT) can partially predict the success or failure of students in learning a foreign language. Pimsleur's Language Aptitude Battery (LAB), another well-known instrument to measure language aptitude, includes one subsection on attitude. Wallace Lambert demonstrated that attitude is also a factor in learning a language. Aptitude and attitude research is most interesting and useful, but it remains incomplete insofar as it ignores the native language and culture of the students.

An analysis of the problems measured in the sound-perception section of Pimsleur's LAB shows that the heaviest factor is the contrast between nasal and oral vowels. As a result, a student whose native language makes such a phonemic distinction, as does French, will perform better on the test than a speaker of English for whom nasalization is determined by phonetic environment. A student who has studied French or lived in France will also obtain higher scores on the test as a result of training and learning rather than aptitude. For similar reasons the MLAT has been found to be a better predictor in learning European languages than Asian ones.

Lambert's findings on attitude were based largely on English speakers from the United States learning French in Canada. The results cannot be generalized to Spanish speakers learning English in the United States or even to French speakers learning English in Canada. The students' native language and cultural identity were not threatened in Lambert's experiment; the students were learning French more or less voluntarily. The linguistic and cultural identity of the Spanish speaker in the United States may be perceived as threatened.

There is much informal evidence to support the view that the native language cannot be ignored in foreign-language learning and teaching. On a visit to the U.S. Naval Academy in Annapolis, I observed the performance of the top student in Russian, who was indeed a fine scholar. In conversing with him I learned that he spoke Polish at home with his family. Because Polish is a Slavic language, it was possible for him to excel in the study of Russian.

It is not unusual to find students from Italian-speaking families among the top performers in Spanish classes in the United States. The fact that Italian and Spanish are closely related Romance languages permits those students to use their talents effectively.

Similarly, students from Spanish-speaking homes usually do well in Portuguese, even though the teacher of Portuguese will object strenuously to Spanish interference in their Portuguese performance. Brazil is like a second home to me, partly because of the Spanish and Galician languages, both of which I spoke as a child in the northwest region of Spain. I also found myself quite at home on my first visit to Rome, even though I had not studied Italian formally. My Spanish helped linguistically, and the similarities between the Italian and Spanish cultures were also an aid. I had a more difficult time in Ankara, Turkey, as well as in Tokyo, Japan, and Jakarta, Indonesia, where I had to stay close to the hotel or go to places where English would be understood, except of course when friends who spoke English and the language of the country accompanied me.

Because of their native language, Spanish speakers have earned a reputation as good learners of Japanese in Japan—consider, for example, the five-vowel system of both languages—yet Spanish speakers have a reputation as poor learners of English in the United States, partly because of the dissimilarities between the two languages and partly because of the low sociolinguistic reaction to Spanish interference in English.

Of course, social scientists will say, "Your evidence is clearly impressionistic and anecdotal. You cannot support a theory on such soft evidence. Where is your hard evidence?"

There is some hard data, but before we consider it, let me appeal to your own experience as language teachers and learners and as humanists. Can you not duplicate the observations I have described, and indeed top them? They are almost self-evident to the experienced professional observer.

As for hard evidence, Carroll (1967) in his survey of the proficiency of foreign-language majors in the United States found that students who spoke the foreign language at home even only occasionally performed significantly better than those who did not. That finding was based on performance in the MLA Foreign Language Proficiency Tests. If the language of the home influences performance up to the college level, it must also be a factor in learning another foreign language.

With regard to evidence that knowledge of one language influences knowledge of another, I have data from the selection of subjects for an experiment in which it was required that they should not have studied Spanish previously. Even though none of the subjects had studied Spanish, we gave them a Spanish test and found that those who had previously studied a Romance language scored highest, those who had studied a foreign language other than one from the Romance-language family did next best, and those who had studied no foreign language were the weakest. I interpreted these data as supporting the view that study of one foreign language helps in the study of another and that use of the native language at home, which according to Carroll benefits performance in school, influences the study of another foreign language.

Contrastive Studies versus Error Analysis

Contrastive studies are intended to reveal similarities as well as differences between two languages. They show those elements and rules which the student will master easily and which the teacher may use to help the student understand and overcome the problems that result from various types of differences between the languages. Error analysis (EA) concentrates on the errors observed in the performance of the students and not on the resources that the native language provides. Because of this focus on errors, Charles Fries rejected a dissertation proposal that I submitted to him circa 1948 to study the errors in the written compositions of our foreign students at the University of Michigan. His view was that we should concentrate on the resources of the language rather than on errors. Some of the studies that showed small proportions of errors traceable to native-language transfer were conducted with young children in a target-language environment, and we all know that the younger the child, the more second-language will resemble acquisition of the first language.

Another factor that error analysis fails to take into account is the avoidance phenomenon (Schachter 1974), which is evidenced by the circumvention of troublesome constructions. Furthermore, the weaknesses and strengths that contrastive analysis (CA) reveals are bound to be of a nature and greater force than those resulting from the rules of the target language itself, since those revealed by CA have long been reduced to subconscious processing by extended use of the native language. This is shown by the fact that the native language of even advanced users of a second language can often be identified by some of their characteristic transfers to the target language.

And there are emotional and sociolinguistic dimensions to transfer problems that differ from problems of learning that are general for all learners. Einar Haugen referred to this with regard to native language influences in the English of Norwegian speakers in the United States. Who among those who speak a language other than English at home has not felt some concern for interference problems characteristic of our native language? And sociolinquistic research shows that there are strong differential reactions to different reactions to different native-language "accents". Thus we identify a further difference between the results of EA and CA.

EA complements CA since it identifies problems not caused by native-language interference and resolves indeterminacy when CA yields more than one possibility of transfer. As I pointed out in 1957, it can also serve to validate CA by observing the actual performance of the students:

> The list of problems resulting from the comparison of the foreign language with the native language will be a most significant list for teaching, testing, research, and understanding. Yet it must be considered a list of hypothetical problems until final validation is achieved by checking it against the actual speech of students. (Lado, 1957, p. 72)

CA is not the only way to look at the native-language factor, nor is it equally useful for every purpose, but whatever the technique or philosophy of considering the native language, we cannot ignore it in applied linguistics. CA may be only a useful fad that "has shown remarkable stamina under fire," according to Spolsky (1979), but the native language is not a fad; it is in the heart and mind of the learner.

Reading as Languaging

Reading is languaging in which we perceive a written text, grasp its meaning, think it through, and recall it according to our intentions, needs, knowledge, and abilities. National surveys show that Hispanic bilingual children and black bidialectals lag significantly in their English reading scores in the United States. This deficiency has a negative effect on academic success, and is a critical factor in the high drop-out rates of those children. I would also point out that it is a factor in the lower grade averages for those children that in turn keep them out of college and the professions.

In the case of Hispanic bilinguals, learning to read in Spanish is easier than learning to read in English—not only because they do not know English well, but also because Spanish shows fewer irregularities in its writing system than does English. Having learned to read by the easier route, the child transfers much of that knowledge to reading English. At the Spanish Educational Development Center in Washington, D.C., we are finding that all preschool children from lower-income Hispanic families are successfully learning to read their home language, and what is equally interesting, that they are learning to read English in half the time it takes them to learn to read Spanish. These findings contradict the widely held idea that bilinguals are poor readers because they are bilinguals, an explanation given to me because I was a poor reader.

In the case of Hispanic children we are able to capitalize on the native-language writing system and the children's knowledge of the language. The same strategy may or may not be appropriate with other native languages because of differences in writing systems. Learning to read Chinese requires mastering large numbers of logographs, or Chinese characters. It may or may not be advantageous to go that route if the children already know some English. But we cannot ignore the fact that their native language is Chinese, and if such children are to be taught to read in English it must be realized hat they have to learn to read as part of learning the language and not as if they were native speakers of English who already know it.

In the case of students who are literate in their native language we must still take into account that language and its writing system. This factor came to the surface in some early research on listening comprehension in English by foreign students at the University of Michigan. Comprehension was checked by means of pictures in one part of the test used and by written choices in the other. Farsi-speaking students who had the same average score on the picture part of the test as did Spanish speakers scored lower than the Spanish speakers on the written choices part. Since Farsi is written with the Arabic alphabet from right to left while Spanish uses the Latin alphabet from left to right, I interpret the result as evidence that the native-language writing system is a measurable factor beyond the beginning reading level.

A recent study of cross-cultural reading by Steffensen, Jogdeo, and Anderson (1979) shows that differences in speed, memory, and interpretation may persist into advanced levels of reading by college students, depending on whether the content of the reading passages is native or foreign. The reading matter was a description of an Indian and an American wedding, both written in English. The subjects were Indian students from India and American students. Both groups read faster, recalled more information, produced more culturally appropriate elaborations, and made fewer culturally based distortions when the passage dealt with the native culture of the students.

With regard to the study of foreign languages in the United States, we can assume that the students will have English as a common source language. The problem here is not one of ignoring the native language. In fact, all good language courses present and explain the foreign language in terms of English, whether this is admitted explicitly or not. For example, the subjunctive is treated extensively in texts for the Romance languages because the subjunctive has all but disappeared as a verb tense in English. Such extensive treatment would not be necessary when teaching one Romance language to speakers of another Romance language.

The problem in teaching foreign languages is more the tendency to ignore the need for languaging skills for communication at normal speed and to substitute instead word-for-word translation at practically no speed—an almost useless exercise for practical communication.

The Native Culture as a Factor

With the current interest in and prestige of ethnicity in the United States, it is easy to consider the native culture of the students. Every article or statement or legislation that mentions language mentions culture, affirming its importance and insisting that it be taken into account. This is commendable and beneficial.

The challenge is to go beyond superficiality and consider cultural traits that may affect learning—i.e., to go beyond exhibiting a Mexican sombrero or presenting a Philippine bamboo dance at a program. There is nothing wrong with presenting the folk dances and colorful customs of our neighbors. But we need to consider as well the differences in family structure and roles and many other differences that can be a factor in the performance of children in school.

The fact that a Korean child is expected to lower his eyes when talking to a teacher as a sign of respect should not be construed as sullenness or stupidity by an American teacher. Different concepts of loyalty across cultures may be misinterpreted as a lack of creativity. The idea that one must challenge the views of his teacher is not culturally universal. The rule that a child should not speak in the presence of adults may result in poor performance in the eyes of an examiner who considers it a virtue that the child speak spontaneously in his or her presence.

Different social classes have different expectations, and in many cultures the differences among social classes are very great. The performance of children from different cultural strata may differ markedly, depending on what they have been encultured to expect.

Finally, the very content of lexical items and categories may be culturally modified across cultures. Thus a mere translation of a text in terms of language will be insufficient if what is required is experience, perception, and conceptual grasp of the different content in the two cultures. The very meaning of father and mother, brother and sister, honor and shame, hero and villain, may be apprehended differently in the two cultures of the bilingual, and such differences will affect behavior, thought, and learning.

All cultures are worthy because they represent the rich variety in which communities develop their human existence. Only extreme practices that violate the natural law can be rejected universally. All cultures manifest in one way or another the universality of the human spirit. Yet that universality can be misinterpreted by the members of one culture in dealing with the members of another unless they strive not to ignore the native culture of the other.

Thought as a Factor

Within the general traits of a culture and the universal nature of human thought there are individual and group differences in thought and thinking. Not all Spaniards play the guitar and like bullfights and soccer. If teachers have an exalted position in a culture, we cannot assume that all the children without exception will show perfect respect for their teachers. We must not ignore the fact that an individual may think as a bully and behave accordingly toward his or her teachers. We should take into account the thought of the bully and try to change it.

All cultures are worthy, but not all thought is without error. If students in a physics class think that oil is heavier than water, their thought is in error and the teacher tries to change it. If a teacher thinks that bilingual children are poor readers because they are bilingual, we should try to change the thought of that teacher because it is based on inadequate information. Similarly, if low-income parents have been led to believe that their economic problems are due to the fact that they speak a language other than

English, they should be helped to correct that error in their thought. We should attempt to show them that their children need not forget, deny, or suppress their knowledge of the home language in order to succeed in society. They will gain by becoming fully bilingual, biliterate, and bicultural, rather than switching to mainstream monolingualism.

Richness of thought and thinking depends on age, cognitive development, experience, education, knowledge, capacity, and innate individual gifts. We should not make the naive mistake of assuming that because the members of one culture tend to think and act in a particular way, all the members of that culture think and act the same way. We cannot expect that because Polish speakers have the possibility of advancing rapidly in the study of Russian, all Polish speakers will master it equally well, and that only Polish speakers may do so. Cultural traits, tendencies, and features are important, but individual thought and individual experience also have to be considered. And this of course is our highest right and ultimate responsibility in applied linguistics.

Conclusion

I have pondered the bases for taking into account rather than disregarding the language, culture, and thought of the learner in applied linguistics, and I find myself reinforced in the view that they cannot be ignored, that any applied linguistic rationale will be incomplete without the native factor. In any social science, disregard for a significant factor such as the native language in the research design is considered a weakness or imperfection that renders the results suspect. Why is it that in applied linguistics and psycholinguistics some who do research and publish articles instead consider it a strength? The language, culture, and thought of the learner cannot be ignored in applied linguistics.

REFERENCES

Andersson, Theodore, and Boyer, Mildred. 1978. Bilingual schooling in the United States. 2d ed. Austin, Tex.: National Educational Laboratory Publishers.

Carroll, John B. 1967. Foreign language proficiency levels attained by language majors near graduation from college. FL Annals 1:131-51.

Carroll, John B., and Sapon, Stanley M. 1959. Modern language aptitude test. New York: Psychological Corporation.

Corder, S. Pit. 1967. The significance of learner's errors. International Review of Applied Linguistics 5:161-70.

_____. 1972. Describing the language learner's language. In CILT reports and papers, no. 6, pp. 57-64. London: Center for Information on Language Teaching.

Di Pietro, Robert J. 1971. Language structures in contrast. Rowley, Mass.: Newbury House.

Dulay, Heidi C., and Burt, Marina K. 1974. Errors and strategies in child second language acquisition. TESOL Quarterly 8:129-36.

Lado, Robert. 1949. Measurement in English as a foreign language with special reference to Spanish-speaking adults. Ph.D. diss., University of Michigan, Ann Arbor.

_____. 1957. Linguistics across cultures. Ann Arbor, Mich.: University of Michigan Press.

Lado, Robert, Aid, Frances, and Kruvant, M. 1970. Massive vocabulary expansion, phase II: the effect of oral and orthographic stimuli on the memorization and pronunciation of basic dialogues. Washington, D.C.: U.S. Dept. of HEW, Office of Education, Institute of International Studies.

Lado, Robert, and Andersson, Theodore, eds. 1976. Early reading. Georgetown University papers on languages and linguistics. No. 13. Washington, D.C.: Georgetown University Press.

Lambert, Wallace E.; Gardner, R. C.; Baird, H. C.; and Tunstall, K. 1963. Attitudinal and cognitive aspects of intensive study of a second language. Journal of Abnormal and Social Psychology 4:358-68.

Lee, Ok Ro. Early bilingual reading as an aid to bilingual and bicultural adjustment for a second generation Korean child in the U.S. Ph.D. diss., Georgetown University, Washington, D.C.

Pimsleur, Paul. 1966. Language aptitude battery. New York: Harcourt, Brace and World.

Schachter, Jacquelyn. 1974. An error in error analysis. Language Learning 24:205-14.

Schachter, Jacquelyn, and Celce-Murcia, Marianne. 1977. Some reservations concerning error analysis. TESOL Quarterly 11:441-51.

Spolsky, Bernard. 1979. Contrastive analysis, error analysis, interlanguage, and other useful fads. Modern Language Learning 63:250-57.

Steffensen, Margaret S.; Jogdeo, Chitra; and Anderson, Richard C. 1978. A cross-cultural perspective on reading comprehension. Urbana, Ill.: Center for the Study of Reading, University of Illinois.

2. Talking Culture: Language in the Function of Communication

EDWARD C. STEWART
George Washington University

The relationship between language and culture, the subject of this paper, is one that I come to as a psychologist who has for many years administrated, evaluated, or conducted cultural- and language-training programs. Typically, I work with Americans who are going to live in another society and who are to receive some cultural preparation and gain some command of the other language. This kind of work is often dissatisfying for those doing it. For many years training evaluations have shown that Americans are not learning foreign languages as well as they should be. There are many reasons for this deficiency and I am sure that many of you know them. I shall not burden you with them, since my intent is to focus on the fusion of language and culture as a learning strategy to improve training under prevailing conditions. I believe that if language instructors were to teach culture as well as language it would help to reduce the boredom, the exhaustion, and the emotional wallop of the new language. The interjection of culture would convey exotic, practical, and valuable information and would help to define language not only as code, but also as communication. For the cultural trainer, the infusion of language as communication imparts substance, rigor, and direction for a subject that often disintegrates into strings of anecdotes and exercises. In discussions on this subject with language teachers and with linguists as well, I am often told that teachers of language do convey culture in their teaching.

For example, recently I was speaking with an instructor of French, and I asked her if she taught culture along with the language. She said she did not always, but then she mentioned an advanced group that she was training in French and in glowing tones described discussions of Proust, Racine, and other French writers. What she meant by culture is not what I mean, and perhaps at this point one should mention a second meaning of culture often used by teachers, that being a country's customs and traditions, such as social conventions, verbal customs, food preferences, etc. Although literary heritage and traditional customs are valuable in training, they have concealed a different idea of culture, one which is more intimately tied to language and which has not been systematically used in language instruction. I refer to the view that language

guides may govern and at times even control our thinking. For free
thinkers, the "worst-case hypothesis" states that language
determines thinking. You will undoubtedly recognize in this strain
of thought the mind prints of Sapir and his famous student, Whorf,
but their views are not reserved for Americans only. The German,
Humboldt, 1767-1835, and the Frenchman, Condillac, even earlier in
1715-80, both held the idea that language to some degree influences
thinking. Those of us on the periphery of languages and linguistics
firmly believe in the Whorfian hypothesis, as it is sometimes called,
and are surprised to discover that Whorf does not preside at the
inner sanctum of linguistics. (Sapir has enjoyed a better fate.)
Whorf's low reputation deserves explanation since his work is so
powerful in the daily rounds of intercultural communication. This
requires the intervention of another controversial figure—
Chomsky. Whatever one's views of him may be, one aspect of his
work has become commonplace in the psychological marketplace,
and that is the distinction among cognitive theory, competence, and
performance (Stewart 1978). Psychology and education have
thoroughly assimilated this line of thought, sometimes distorting it,
and have applied it in theory and in practice. The threefold
breakout is useful in explaining the mixed reaction to the work of
Whorf. Linguists—Hoijer, for example (1976)—interpret Whorf in a
theoretical sense, and we are bound to agree with the conclusion
that whatever is said in one language can be translated into
another. The capability exists in any language to say whatever is
said in any other language. What I can say in English can be said in
French, Russian, Urdu, or Hindi. There are procedures of translation
and back translation, and specialists exist in these areas who can
demonstrate with exquisite skill that the capability of English is
precisely that of Urdu or Farsi. Given the formidable array of
specialists and techniques that can be brought to match precisely
the capability of any two languages, it seems professionally prudent
to agree that the Whorfian hypothesis is not accepted as a theory
that language to some degree determines thinking. I do not
completely wish to discard the Whorfian hypothesis, but a
theoretical position is irrelevant if we turn our attention away from
theory (capability) and instead consider competence (language
usage). Normally a speaker does not deliver the full capability of
the language on a given occasion. The speaker selects, forgets,
distorts linguistic features of language capability to create a
message. The filtering or the dislocation of theory is competence,
or language usage. I like to think of it as communication in the
talking place. When we consider the Whorfian hypothesis in the area
of competence, we discover a Catch-22. No practitioner
communicating in the talking place has the time or the skill to
analyze his use of language to prove that what he says can be put
precisely into the other language and understood without
distortion. I have never met any practitioner who cannot give
anecdotes and experiences that display the vitality of the Whorfian

hypothesis flourishing with hybrid vigor in the field of intercultural communication. The definition of language as communication in talking places clearly abides by Whorf.

I propose that languages themselves can be considered as more or less Whorfian. I have often had the impression that Arabic and, perhaps to a lesser degree, French are Whorfian languages, meaning that they exist more intimately with the thought of Arabic and French speakers.   On the other hand, Japanese offers a strong position for those who wish not to accept the Whorfian hypothesis, since the Japanese language seems to have less influence on Japanese thought than some other languages. The speculation is complex and has to be qualified. The structure of Japanese language seems to parallel the structure of Japanese thought but, at the same time, much of Japanese thought seems to rely on images, nonverbal communication, and observations rather than on the codified message embalmed in language. The structure of the language and of thought subscribe to parallels, but the relationship of semantics, or lexicon, to thought seems tenuous. Japanese language habits in communication do not bear out the Whorfian hypothesis in the way that the habits of westerners and Americans appear to.   The Japanese decline to summarize their thought with words. Compare that with our searches for the right term, label, or name. Remember how we feel compelled to defend our position once we have stated it. Once the word is out we try to stick by it, which brings Whorf to life.

I make these observations before treating more specifically the fusion of language and culture. I do not wish to raise arguments about either Whorf or Chomsky, but at the same time I want to establish a theoretical basis for the experience that I have had in using language in cultural training. It seems to me that the most fruitful position to take is that the language instructor should use cultural information to benefit the learning of a language. My experience, however, has been exactly the reverse. For many years I have been faced with the problem of how to introduce the concept of culture in a brief time period of one hour or less. A glance at the literature finds a multitude of methods, but I am convinced there are none that accomplish the task as well as language. There are two functions that language serves. First, the surface of language discloses some of the deep structure of culture. Second, linguistic communication reposes on what native speakers know about their world, and this knowledge functions as cognitive economies that need not be encoded directly in utterances, but serve as necessary assumptions for communication (Keesing 1979:14).   The second statement rephrases the Whorfian hypothesis, abandons determinacy, and replaces it with the complementarity of James or with the indeterminacy of Heisenberg. By implication, the structure of the experienced world is an open system that exists in equilibrium with culture, which is also an open system.   But when we turn to communication in the talking place, consider competence rather than theory, and examine interpersonal communication, we accept a modified Whorfian hypothesis and assume that the forms of communication govern or guide thinking.

These theoretical complexities do not clutter the instruction and training of businessmen, government officers, psychology students, and others who have learned difficult ideas in the domain of culture from linguistic examples. Success in these efforts requires that the teacher treat language as communication instead of code and then adopt a functional view of communicaion. Three categories will serve to collect useful examples for teachers and trainers:

1. Language structures disclose deep structure of culture.

The linguistic phenomenon of lexical markings (Clark 1969) in English reveals patterns of managing other people in American culture. It is not necessary to analyze or describe lexical marking. Let me only show it.

Notice the following adjectives and adverbs in English; they are paired, but that relationship does not imply that the adjectives are equal. Consider their features when used to ask questions. I can say, "How far is it to the window?" and "How far is it to Washington?" I do not say, "How near is it to the window?" and "How near is it to Washington?'

FAR	—	NEAR
HIGH	—	LOW
GOOD	—	BAD
WIDE	—	NARROW
LONG	—	SHORT
HEAVY	—	LIGHT

These examples reveal two qualities about the pairs. The ones listed in the left column are general; these words cover all possible qualities from one extreme to the opposite. The words in the right column are restricted in representation, covering only a narrow range of possible qualities on their side of the polarity. Second, these words are also negative in meaning, which of course is obvious with BAD, but consider the remaining adjectives as metaphors: they connote negative qualities. If this were not enough, they also possess different linguistic and psychological properties from the words in the left column. Note the last pair, HEAVY—LIGHT. "How heavy is the bag?" one may ask. But if the inquiry is aimed at an attractive young woman, custom requires that the question be phrased with a verb: "How much do you weigh?" The question is thus more neutral, but this exception, using a verb in the question, reminds us that English is an adjective language (Hall 1977:15). Not all other languages are, however. In Portuguese, nouns often anchor questions, which suggests that the linguistic structures and usages we have suggested for English are not necessarily replicated in all other languages. But consider now the use of lexical markings as a model to disclose patterns of managing in American society.

Notice how much more easily a speaker criticizes in English, while the more pleasant task of praise is quite difficult if the speaker wishes to appear intelligent. It takes brilliance to praise, to overcome mushy language, and not sound as if one gushes emotion; but only moderate intelligence is needed to find fault. Does this suggest the prevailing pattern among parents rearing children, teachers disciplining students, and managers administering those who report to them? I believe that it does. In American society the management of others is done by specifying negative features and by calibrating the punishments associated with these negative features. The language provides the precise vocabulary, which already carries the negative tone. Thus before long our students have learned to study to avoid bad grades, and managers, as well as others, learn to take problem-solving approaches. This brings us to the question, what is a problem? It is a difficulty or an obstacle that we must circumvent. If at some time the prototypal other, who has learned all actions to be avoided and who has mastered the punishments for their violations, were to ask, "Now that I know everything that I cannot do, please tell me what I should do." how do we answer this request? I suggest that the answer would resemble the following: "You should know what you ought to do; be yourself and be creative. Try." And with that observation we return full circle to the ambiguity of the positive in English and in American culture, the point with which we started this discussion of lexical markings.

With these observations of American culture, I do not intend to criticize, although it is difficult to avoid that implication since English is such a subjective language (Glenn 1976:182). The use of the negative case is essential in technology, where one speaks of the "worst case" as the basis for developing procedures for managing a nuclear power plant or for designing a bridge. The examples are numerous. I wish to stress that neither the surface of the language, English, nor the pattern of managing others is universal. I wonder if it would not be possible to develop other language examples that can be used to extricate cultural patterns from our webs of experience? Let us turn to a second category of examples of the connection between language and culture.

2. Language gives shape to and guides perception and thinking.

Above we have struggled with the nature of the relationship between language and linguistics on the one hand and cognitive processes on the other. Since both sides of the relationship can be considered open systems, it is possible to exploit the relationship without precipitating a debate on whether we speak of a mechanical joint, an inert link, an organic connection, or some other kind of relationship. The influence of language on both the shape and the substance of perception and thought can be illustrated with examples developed with word associations, which is a method developed by Carl Jung. The method relies on the idea that a message impinging on the listener acts like a trigger to mental activity. To understand the message, the listener's own cognitive processes and memory must contribute to the acquisition. The problem is how to tap into the process of thinking, remembering, and perceiving and how to describe it. Jung's answer to this question was direct and simple: present a stimulus word to the subject, who is asked to respond with whatever words come to mind. The experimenter controls the stimulus while the subject presumably signals with response words the flow of cognitive processes triggered by the stimulus word. Analysis of response words presumably reveals the nature of the cognitive processes—their shape and substance. Take the stimulus word fox. To me there come to mind the response words animal, red, eyes, alert, Reynard, bushy, and other words that literally describe a mental image of the animal sniffing the breeze until I remember that smells are better retained and conveyed by thick media, so the image shifts immediately. Reynard now sniffs the ground. My responses do not stand for purely linguistic meaning; the sound fox is largely arbitrary. If I repeat fox, fox, fox, indefinitely, the sound fox, is drained of meaning. The erosion can be blocked if I look at the word fox, but as I concentrate on the straight and curved lines that make up the letters of the word, the erosion of meaning recurs. It seems to me that this phenomenon illustrates that the sound and the written sign of the word stand for something other than linguistic features. It taps the perception, memory, and thinking of the subject.

Since the time of Jung many researchers have used the technique of word association to explore the mental qualities of people, and in many cases the method has been used to describe culture and cultural differences. Dr. Lorand Szalay has been one of the most avid researchers in this field (1975). Typically he selects representative samples of subjects from two cultures he is interested in. Then he selects stimulus words that he will use to collect response words; Szalay usually asks for six words or as many as the subject can provide during a stated period of time. Two hundred words carefully selected yield a reasonable profile of a culture. Here is an example taken from a comprehensive study of Anglo and Hispanic American groups that illustrates what can be done with the method. The stimulus word is me, which you see at the top of the chart (Table 1). The total scores reflect the fact that the Anglos (A) gave more word associations—2,180—than did the Hispanics (H)—1,531. The important results are conveyed by percentages. Note that the Anglos respond with I, myself 26 percent of the time to 5 percent for the Hispanics. The highest percentage for the Hispanics is with person, individual (18 percent), while the same category for the Anglos receives 10 percent of their responses. The remaining percentages fill out the different concepts of me, held by Hispanics and Anglo-Americans. On the chart for mental health (Figure 1), you can see a graphic display of the different views of mental health held by Hispanics and Anglo-Americans. The Anglos associate mental health with 'sickness' and 'illness' significantly more than the Hispanic Americans, for whom mental health connotes 'mad', 'crazy'. A study of the distribution of resources to mental health helps explain why the mental health clinics in this country have been significant failures for Hispanic Americans.

Table 1
ME
Perceptions and Evaluations by
Anglo and Hispanic American Groups

Main Components	Percentage of Total Score	
	A	H
I, Myself	26	5
You, We, They	22	17
Woman, Mother	7	3
Love, Friendship	6	4
Selfish, Confused, Sad	5	3
Person, Individual	10	18
Good, Loving, Happy	14	15
Work Responsibility	1	9
Student, Study	—	8
Man, Father	4	7
Am, To Be	1	6
Miscellaneous	3	4
Total Scores	2180	1531

I have found that the word-association method successfully communicates difficult cultural ideas to students and trainees. And it seems to me that the connotations of words, which are what the associations probe for, are extremely important for language learning. We do not need to go to the laboratory or to the products of research to discover the heavy burden that our words carry. Practitioners are full of stories about these, but perhaps one of the most important ones comes from the end of the war with the Japanese in the Pacific. In 1945, the Japanese cabinet was considering the Potsdam ultimatum to surrender issued by the Allies. The Japanese apparently were ready to accept it but wished to have more time to consider the terms. The press release announced a policy of mokusatsu, a word in Japanese with two

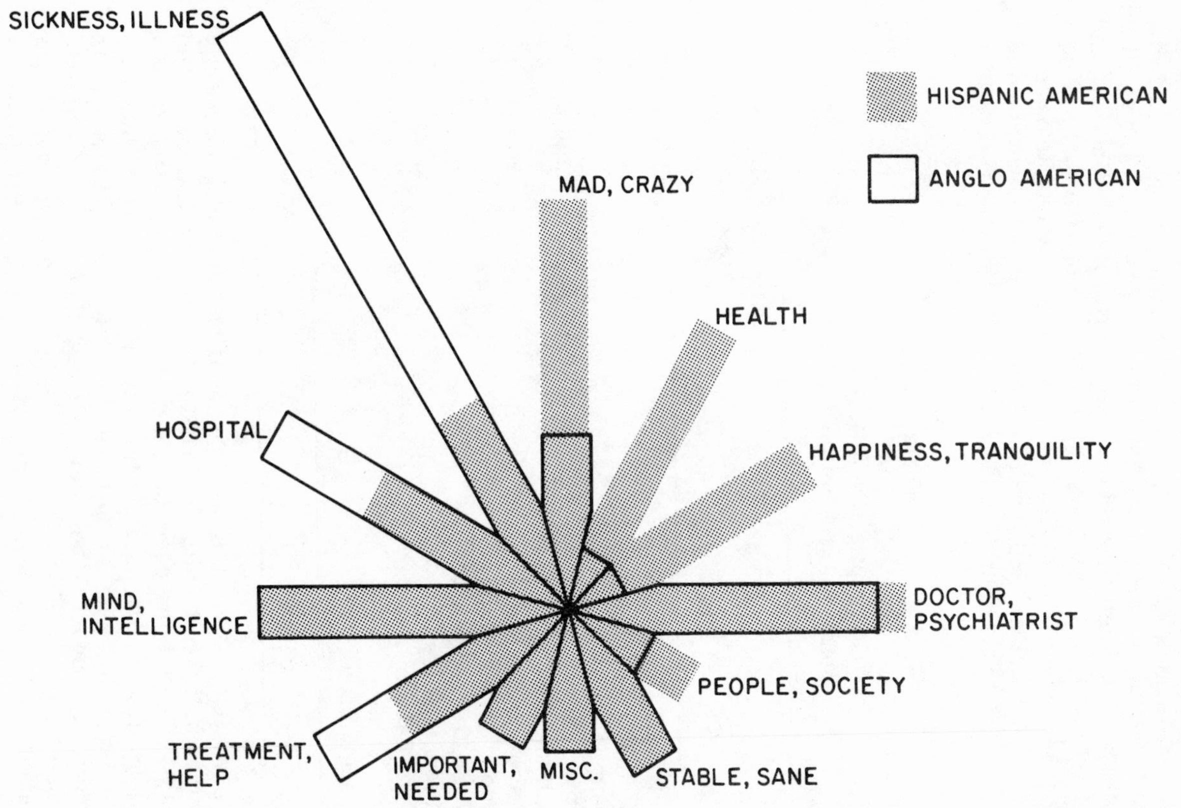

Fig. I MENTAL HEALTH

meanings: to ignore and to refrain from comment.   The press release was translated "to ignore" and an irreversible chain of events was precipitated that brought the end of the war with the atomic explosion. Fisher speculates as follows:

> The domestic situation in Japan was already delicate, and once the release had reached the public, it would have been too embarrassing to correct the error and, in effect, draw attention to the more compliant meaning. Had the Japanese cabinet not found itself out on this semantics limb, it is speculated, they might have backed up the Emperor's decision to surrender at that time; the atomic bomb might not have been used in Japan, Russian armies might not have come to Manchuria, and there might not have been a Korean war! (Fisher 1972:95)

Semantics supplies a rich harvest of problems in cross-cultural communication.   Backing away from the lexicon and considering syntactics and the general structure of language, we can again discover innumerable relationships between languages and culture that have been virtually untapped for either language or cultural training. Japanese and English provide some of the most interesting and important contrasts in both language and culture.   Kunihiro Masao discusses qualities of Japanese language and contrasts them with western language (1976). He concludes that Japanese language stresses "what" and omits "how" and "why" (273).   Western languages, claims Masao, embody process and logic. How do these qualities of language intrude into communication, if at all? First, it is often observed that Americans are much more likely than Japanese to draw causal relations when processing information for purposes of making decisions or planning. American culture has also been frequently preoccupied with process—features that are in contrast to Japanese culture.   These differences, I am convinced, were at the root of two experiences I had in Japan during the summer of 1979. I was speaking to Japanese nuclear authorities about work that I had done in the nuclear-power field. In the first experience, I had sat down to discuss with a Japanese physicist the attitude of Japanese scientists toward nuclear power, and by way of opening the conversation I mentioned that I had conducted interviews and participated in constructing a questionnaire on the subject of attitudes. I was a little taken aback when the physicists turned to me and asked, "What conclusions did you reach?" I did not believe that I had given him any leads to ask that question. In a very American way I had approached the work as something in progress, an activity, a process. His question was not isolated. A few days later I was present at a Science and Technology Agency meeting, convened for an exchange of views and experiences in the field of managing and regulating nuclear power. As with the physicists, the

first question addressed to me was "What were your recommendations?" Neither here nor with the physicist did I answer the direct
question, and there were no gaps in the conversation. I tend to
believe that in both cases I was in the middle of cross-cultural
communication. The Japanese wanted the what, and I was fixed on
the how and on the process.

Turning to English, we have already seen that it is an adjective
language. Consider the boarding passes issued by American Airlines
to its passengers. The pass is in English, Spanish, and French. The
English is rendered by an adjective, boarding, modifying a noun,
pass, but the Spanish requires a phrase: tarjeta de embarque.
French, like Spanish, builds meaning on a foundation of nouns: carte
d'accès à bord. Brief and adjectival English lacks the precision of
French, which prefers intentions and volition. English is a subjective
language that remains a stranger to the determinism and fatalism of
Russian (Glenn 1976:182-185). These features of language associate
with qualities in their relevant cultures, but at this point, the
discussion threatens to overburden and bring crashing down the
simple scaffolding of theory that we have built to accommodate
language and culture. For these purposes I have avoided specifying
the linkages between languages and behavior that can be found in
recent publications (Cummings and Renshaw 1979).

3. Language links the mind with the perceived world.

This final category, like the other two, is crude but serves as a
receptacle for examples. The link that is suggested between mind
and the perceived world is found with metaphors, which, in turn, can
be seen to represent transductive thinking by means of analogy. The
example that immediately comes to mind is the insistence in English
that a clock runs, while in Portuguese it walks, anda. The metaphor
for movement in timepieces can be associated with the quick tempo
of life in American society for runs, and with the more leisurely one
in Brazilian society for walks.   The initial interpretation can be
expanded to enclose features of time, business, and similar
considerations.   These aspects of culture revealed in languages
compose a rich lode of language fused with culture. Instructors of
languages use metaphors along with idiomatic examples as
testimonies for culture, so let us turn to an expressive metaphor of
the Russian poet Joseph Brodsky.

In a recent essay, Brodsky writes about his early life in
Leningrad (1979). In a digressive spirit, he develops a metaphor for
memory before commenting on language and culture. Brodsky
prepares for the ending of his essay by saying that

> Memory, I think, is a substitute for the tail that we lost
> for good in the happy process of evolution. (Brodsky
> 1979:49)

The Russian poet goes on to say that neither the tail nor memory is linear, since memory coils, recoils, digresses to all sides; just as a tail swishes around and explores the ground, so does memory explore the past. When Brodsky turns to consider the word, he remarks that

> to imitate on paper the subtlest fluctuations of the mind, the effort to reproduce the tail in all its spiral splender is still doomed, for evolution wasn't for nothing. The perspective of years straightens things to the point of complete obliteration. Nothing brings them back, not even handwritten words with their coiled letters. Such an effort is doomed all the more if this tail happens to lag behind somewhere in Russia. (Ibid.)

Brodsky continues, developing the thought that words are a mark of forgetfulness, and claims the sad truth that

> Words fail reality as well. . . . At least it's been my impression that any experience coming from the Russian realm, even when depicted with photographic precision, simply bounces off the English language leaving no visible imprint on its surface. . . . One gets done in by one's own conceptual and analytic habits-- e.g., using language to dissect experience, and so robbing one's mind of the benefits of intuition. . . . I merely regret the fact that such an advanced notion of Evil as happens to be in the possession of Russians has been denied entry into the consciousness of English-speaking people on the grounds of having a convoluted syntax (pp. 47-48)

The muscular statement is needed to sustain the elegaic air of the ending of the essay. The digressive swishing of language should not detract from the Whorfian implications sensed by Brodsky. Undoubtedly, the determinism and fatalism that Glenn finds in Russian (1976:182-84) sets the stage for Evil in Russian culture, which is averted by English syntax.
Samuel Johnson once said:

> Language is the dress of thought. Some may agree, while others may prefer Shelley's observations: He gave men speech and speech created thought.

Whether we are interested in well-dressed speakers, or streakers, or in speakers who think, all of us stand to gain from a close alliance between language and culture when language functions as communication.

REFERENCES

Brodsky, Joseph. 1979. Less than one. The New York Review of Books 26:32-48.

Clark, H. H. 1969. Linguistic processes in deductive reasoning. Psychological Review 76:387-404.

Cummings, H. W., and Renshaw, S. L. 1979. SLCA III: a metatheoretic approach to the study of language. Human Communication Research 5:291-300.

Fisher, Glen H. 1972. Public diplomacy and the behavioral sciences. Bloomington, Ind.: Indiana University Press.

Glenn, Edmund S. 1976. Meaning and behavior: communication and culture. In Intercultural communication: a reader, ed. L. A. Samovar and R. E. Porter. Belmont, Calif.: Wadsworth Publishing Company.

Hall, Edward T. 1977. Beyond culture. Garden City, N.Y.: Anchor Press/Doubleday.

Hoijer, Harry. 1976. The Sapir-Whorf hypothesis. In Intercultural communication: a reader, ed. L. A. Samovar and R. E. Porter. Belmont, Calif.: Wadsworth Publishing Company.

Keesing, R. M. 1979. Linguistic knowledge and cultural knowledge: some doubts and speculations. American Anthropologist 81:14-36.

Masao, Kunihiro. 1976. The Japanese language and intercultural communication. The Japan Interpreter 10:267-83.

Stewart, Edward C. 1978. Outline of intercultural communication. In Intercultural and international communication, ed. Fred L. Casmir. Washington, D.C.: University Press of America.

Szalay, Lorand B., and Bryson, Jean A. 1975. Subjective culture and communication: a Puerto-Rican-U.S. comparison. Washington, D.C.: American Institute for Research.

3. The Role of Language in Education: Evidence from North America and the Developing World

G. RICHARD TUCKER
Center for Applied Linguistics

A major purpose of this paper is to attempt to clarify for U.S. educators the background factors, methodology, findings, and implications of the research that has been conducted with Canadian programs involving a home and school language switch, since many of these educators have drawn incorrect and unwarranted inferences from the Canadian research. A secondary purpose is to describe briefly the methodology and preliminary findings from studies currently underway in several developing countries to see whether the accumulated evidence permits any generalizations concerning the optional selection or sequencing of languages for formal education.

During the past year or so it has become increasingly clear that despite explicit warnings to the contrary, many American educators have interpreted the Canadian research (summarized by Lambert and Tucker 1972; Swain 1974 1976 1978) as offering empirical support for the immediate submersion or mainstreaming of limited or non-English-speaking youngsters in monolingual English-medium classrooms. They have claimed that the Canadian research has demonstrated that any child, whether English Canadian, Mexican American, or ethnic Chinese, can learn simultaneously a second language and content material. Although this assertion in its most general form is in all probability correct, this does not mean that the most effective way to educate every child—regardless of the demographic, sociopolitical, or other circumstances—is by submersion in a second language.

The Canadian Experience

Let us consider for a moment the circumstances under which the Canadian immersion programs were undertaken and from which the data was collected.

1. The French-immersion programs were designed for anglophone youngsters in response to continued parental dissatisfaction with the level of French attainment by children participating in English instructional programs with a French as a Second Language component. The participants—for the most part,

English-speaking youngsters—spoke English as their mother tongue, the language of higher prestige and higher ascribed status. Within the North American setting, the target language French has relatively lower ascribed social and economic status even though it too is, of course, an important world language and even though benefits are likely to accrue to the individual who adds French to his repertoire, particularly in Canada.

2.   The participants in the immersion program throughout Canada have, for the most part, come from families of middle- to lower-middle socioeconomic backgrounds.

3.   Participation in such programs has always been voluntary and parents have always had the alternative of sending their children to traditional schools within the immediate neighborhood that offered instruction using English.

4.   Parents have, from the very beginning of the program, played an extremely strong, salient, and catalytic role in all aspects of program design, development, and implementation. In fact, it was parents—rather than school board officials, teachers, or university scholars—who relentlessly pressured school board officials to develop this innovative approach to second-language teaching.

5.   The early immersion approach most typically implemented and described involves introducing children to school in French, the second language from the very beginning. French is used for all initial readiness activities and is the language of initial reading instruction. For the most part, the language skills of entering children are uniform. All speak English as their mother tongue and live in neighborhoods populated by English-speaking playmates. They speak virtually no French upon entrance.

6.   Despite the fact that French is used as a major medium of primary instruction, an English language arts component is nevertheless added to the curriculum during grade two or grade three at the option of the principal. This addition serves to mark explicitly the continuing importance or status of English as a valued language and helps to solidify formal language skills.

7.   The federal government provides financial support for innovative second-language teaching. In fact, in FY 1979, it provided $170 million vs. approximately $150 million in the United States (for a Canadian population of 22 million vs. the United States population of 220 million). The important difference, however, lies not so much in the amount of the support but in the way the government of Canada allocates the funds. They do so on a per capita basis to the provinces, who then distribute funds to the local educational agency—a format quite different from that followed in the United States.

These general features characterize the programs that now exist in many communities throughout all ten Canadian provinces. It is not appropriate in this paper to reiterate in detail all of the research results reported to date. However, by way of summary, it can be noted that the consensus of researchers who have worked with large groups of different children participating over a long period of time in programs in different schools, school boards, and provinces is that, for these youngsters, an innovative approach to second-language teaching in which the target language is used as the sole or major medium of classroom communication facilitates second-language acquisition without causing any detrimental effects whatsoever to native language development. In addition, the youngsters perform as well as their English-taught peers on achievement tests in content areas such as math, science, or social studies (cf. Lambert and Tucker 1972; Swain 176; Cziko, Lambert, Sidoti, and Tucker 1978).

Conclusions from the Canadian Experience

On the basis of evidence such as this, we have argued (Lambert and Tucker 1972; Tucker 1977a 1977b) that in settings where the home language is highly valued by all members of the community, where parents do actively provide encouragement and support for the acquisition of the literacy in the mother tongue, and where it is "known" that the children will succeed, it would seem fully appropriate to begin schooling in the second language. These inferences also find support in the research and theorizing of Skutnabb-Kangas and Toukomaa (1976) and of Cummins (1978), who proposed that a child must attain a threshold level of competence in the target language to be able to profit from instruction in that language and that the development of second-language skills is dependent upon the adequate development of mother-tongue skills— something that, we believe, can occur in school or in a stimulating non-school environment.

We have not previously and we would not in the future recommend, on the basis of these careful, critical, and longitudinal studies, that Mexican-American, Franco-American, or other non- or limited English-speaking youngsters be submerged in English medium programs. We believe that the appropriate inference to be drawn is exactly the opposite. The implications of the Canadian research for United States educators will be discussed later. Let us first consider briefly a variety of other relevant experiences in selected Third-World countries.

The Nigerian Experience

In Nigeria, as in many other countries, there has arisen during the last decade an increasing concern with the development of curricula, the preparation of materials, and the implementation of instructional programs that (1) provide a relevant education for the child who will continue to secondary or higher education as well as for the child who will not; (2) foster the acquisition of lasting literacy skills, and that (3) provide a firm foundation for the child who must compete in a language of wider communication at secondary or tertiary levels with others who speak the target language as their mother tongue (see, for example, Afolayan 1978). For such children, it is often—but not always—the case that their home language has relatively low ascribed status when compared with the official language(s) of the country, that there does not exist pressure within the home to encourage literacy and language maintenance, and that the educational opportunities presently being developed for pupils far exceed those offered to their parents.

Prior to 1970, Yoruba for three years and then English for the next three years were used as media of instruction in the six-year primary education of all Yoruba-speaking children in the western part of Nigeria. The Yoruba Six-Year Primary Project (Fafunwa et al. 1974) was initiated in 1970 in an attempt to devise a program that would make the primary education of these children more effective and meaningful by using Yoruba as the sole medium of instruction for the first six years of school. To test the effects of the exclusive use of Yoruba as medium of instruction, a research project was begun. Experimental and control classes were set up at St. Stephen's "A" School in Ile-Ife, Western State, Nigeria. Early in the implementation of the project, however, the project administrators found what they believed to be serious defects in the primary school curriculum, and so took on the job of creating a new curriculum incorporating the subjects of Yoruba, English, science, social and cultural studies, and mathematics. Both the St. Stephen's experimental and control groups have made use of this new curriculum. In addition, a specialist teacher of English was used to provide English instruction for the experimental class, while the usual classroom teacher provided English instruction for the control class.

In 1973, the project was expanded to include ten additional "proliferation" schools, eight of which were to use Yoruba as the sole medium of instruction (the proliferation experimental group), while the remaining two were to follow the usual pattern of three years of Yoruba followed by three years of English (the proliferation control group). A comprehensive evaluatin of the Yoruba Primary Project began in 1976 with the testing of academic achievement, Yoruba- and English-language skills, and intelligence of Grade three children in the St. Stephen's and proliferation experimental and control classes, as well as children in selected traditional schools. This large-scale, longitudinal evaluation will continue until these children have completed primary school. It will attempt to determine the effects of using Yoruba as the exclusive medium of instruction, the impact of new curriculum materials, and the effectiveness of using a specialist teacher for the teaching of English.

The data that have been collected and reported to data (Cziko and Ojerinde 1976; Ojerinde and Cziko 178; Macauley 1979) indicate in general that children who have participated n the Yoruba-medium experimental program are performing as well as their control counterparts in terms of content mastery as well as in language arts. The children who are the object of this careful scrutiny have just completed their six-year primary education this past spring, and those data have not been analyzed; but anecdotal reports concerning these children as well as those in previous classes indicate that those who have received their primary education in Yoruba make the transition to an English-medium secondary school in the same numbers and with no more difficulties than their English-instructed counterparts (Macauley 1979). In addition, those who continue do as well as those who do not have a firm grasp on Yoruba literacy, as well as a solid grounding in basic science and social studies concepts.

One can argue, convincingly I think, that these children have profited by instruction in their mother tongue. This instruction solidified its development and resulted in a readiness to learn the second language to such a point where it was possible to effect a smooth transfer to instruction using the second language. We must draw inferences cautiously, of course, for the full story remains to be told.

The Sudanese Experience

The south of the Sudan, an administratively autonomous region, is, like Nigeria, a multilingual polity. Although there have been periodic fluctuations in medium of instruction, most recently Arabic has served as the principal medium of primary and secondary education in government schools. In 1977, a decision was taken for many of the reasons previously discussed to develop curricula, prepare materials, and train teachers in nine Sudanese vernacular languages that will serve in the south as the major languages of primary-cycle instruction, with Arabic and English taught as second languages. The Summer Institute of Linguistics (SIL) has agreed to assist the Ministry of Education in the curricula development, materials preparation, and teacher-training phases of the project. The Center for Applied Linguistics has agreed to assist the Ministry of Education and the SIL by conducting a critical, empirical, and longitudinal assessment of the relative efficacy of Arabic-medium versus vernacular-medium primary instruction for selected youngsters. This research will serve to replicate, in a general sense, the Yoruba Six-Year Primary Project in Nigeria and should strengthen the generalizations that can be drawn from those data.

The Philippine Experience

Passing attention should also be called to the fact that the Philippine government adopted in 1974 a national policy of bilingual education designed to capitalize on many of the factors already described. Their approach is slightly different from that found in Nigeria, the Sudan, Canada, or the United States inasmuch as Philippine vernaculars are used as auxiliary media in non-Pilipino

(Tagalog)–speaking areas during the early primary grades. English, for language arts and the natural sciences (including mathematics), and Pilipino, for language arts and social studies, serve as dual media of instruction throughout the government-supported primary and secondary cycles. Pascasio (1977) provides a comprehensive, current description of bilingual education activities in the Philippines.

The United States

Various facets of the contemporary American experience with bilingual education have been described, and it is not the intent of this paper to repeat those descriptions (see, for example, Andersson and Boyer 1978; Schneider 1976; Troike 1978b). It is relevant to note, however, that despite more than ten years of federal support for bilingual education, very little critical, empirical, and longitudinal research has been conducted. One notable exception is the evaluation of the Navajo-English bilingual program at Rock Point community school. Troike (1978) provides a good summary of the scanty but relevant research, as does Paulston (1977).

The intent of this section is not to bemoan the paucity of American research but rather to attempt to identify some of the salient characteristics of American bilingual education programs. In the final section, the implications of the Canadian and the international research for American bilingual education will be presented. Who are these children, then, who comprise the participants of American bilingual classes?

1. Present-day American Title VII or other government-supported bilingual programs have been designed, in a sense, as compensatory or remedial programs for limited or non-English-speaking youngsters who seem unable to profit from instruction in English. Separate programs have been designed for children from diverse ethnolinguistic backgrounds. In 1978-79, 547 Title VII projects were funded that provided bilingual education in more than forty languages plus English, the language of higher ascribed social status. Typically, but not always, the mother tongue of the participating child is a language of lower ascribed social or economic status.

2. Many of the participants in bilingual programs come from families in which the parents have not completed the local equivalent of the compulsory cycle of American education.

3. Despite the provision in Title VII legislation for parental advisory committees, many parents are sadly informed or misinformed about the purpose, structure, or content of bilingual education programs in their communities. A survey conducted by staff at the Center of Applied Linguistics during academic year 1978-79 revealed that many parents feel cut off from school happenings and that many schools make no attempt whatsoever to communicate with parents in their mother tongue—even though they

may speak no English whatsover.

4. The entry-level language skills of participating children are extremely heterogeneous. A Spanish-English class may include, for example, Spanish monolingual children, Spanish dominant children, children of questionable dominance in either language, English dominant, and English monolingual children. Needless to say, it is extremely difficult for any—even the most talented—teacher, to reach such a diverse clientele. Likewise, many of the children live in the linguistically heterogeneous communities. They often fail to receive encouragement or support from parents or peers to pursue extracurricular academic interests.

5. Unfortunately, in many communities it appears as though negative stereotypes characterize the minority-group child and it is "known" that a disproportionately high number will not be academically successful.

6. Federal legislation explicitly encourages transitional bilingual education. This legislation seems on the one hand designed to nurture the child's mother tongue and to encourage conceptual development through the strong language while introducing a second language but, on the other hand, it seems to withdraw abruptly recognition and credibility for the mother tongue as soon as possible—and, in most cases, before the building blocks of the mother tongue have been solidified.

7. To date, there continues to be a paucity of teachers trained explicitly to work in bilingual programs. Waggoner (1979) notes the discouraging fact that fewer than one half of teachers teaching through a non-English language, teaching ESL or doing both, had had even one bilingual education course, and only 14 percent had had relevant training for teaching non-English language arts, etc. Likewise, there exists a serious need for the continued development and improvement of curricula, materials, and testing instruments.

At this point, it is appropriate to reiterate that the scanty research evidence alluded to earlier (Rosier and Holm in press; Troike 1978a) does suggest that children will thrive when they are educated initially by their mother tongue and then later bilingually in carefully designed and well implemented programs by sensitive teachers working in communities where there exists widespread knowledge and support for bilingual education.

Implications for U.S. Bilingual Education

The information summarized above, including a description of some of the salient and criterial attributes of Canadian, selected third-world, and American bilingual programs, leads to the following general conclusion: in settings such as the various ethnic communities in the United States, in multilingual developing countries, and in parts of Canada where groups of non-English-non-French-speaking residents have congregated, and where the home language is one of lower ascribed social or economic status; where there does not exist uniformly high pressure within the home and community to encourage literacy and language maintenance; where many teachers in the educational system are unaware or insensitive to the values and traditions of the minority-group pupils, it would seem desirable to introduce children to schooling in their home language. This schooling should take the form of a carefully developed language arts program integrated into a general curriculum in which content material is also taught in the mother tongue. The purpose is to sustain and to nurture youngsters' linguistic and cognitive development while teaching English as a second language and while gradually introducing content material through English. This approach is consistent with the earlier suggestions of Lambert and Tucker (1972), Cummins (1978), Skutnabb-Kangas (1975), and Ojerinde and Cziko (1978). Furthermore, it should be added that there is no indication whatsoever from the research literature that transitional bilingual programs are pedagogically more effective than maintenance programs.

The claim that the results from studies of Canadian immersion programs lead to the conclusion that minority group youngsters in the United States (or in Canada) or that Third World pupils should be immersed or submerged in the target language is false. These results do, however, suggest that in settings where the home language is highly valued, where parents and peer group do actively encourage literacy and mother tongue maintenance, and where it is "known" that the children will succeed, schooling can appropriately and without detriment commence in the second language. In fact, it has been argued elsewhere that the central problem facing us is to reach the "dominant-group" American in an attempt to drive home sensitivity to cultural diversity for this large group of Americans who have never heard of TESL, much less bilingual education.

In conclusion, then, it seems as though the available data highlight the fact that the constellation of social and attitudinal variables interact in unique ways to diverse sociolinguistic settings to affecs the child's ultimate progress.

REFERENCES

Afolayan, A.   1978.   Toward an adequate theory of bilingual education for Africa. In Georgetown University round table on languages and linguistics 1978, ed. James E. Alatis, pp. 330-90. Washington, D.C.: Georgetown University Press.

Alatis, J. E., ed.   1978.   International dimensions of bilingual education. In Georgetown University round table on languages and linguistics 1978, ed. James E. Alatis. Washington, D.C.: Georgetown University Press.

Andersson, T., and Boyer, M.   1978.   Bilingual schooling in the

United States, 2d ed.   Austin, Tex.:   National Educational
Laboratory Publishers.

Cziko, G. A.; Lambert, W. E.; Sidoti, N.; and Tucker, G. R. 1978.
Graduates of early immersion: retrospective views of grade 11
students and their parents. Multilithed. Montreal: McGill
University.

Fafunwa, A. B., et al. 1974. Six-year primary project. Multilithed.
Ile-Ife, Nigeria: University of Ife, Institute of Education.

Lambert, W. E., and Tucker, G. R. 1972. The bilingual education of
children. Rowley, Mass.: Newbury House.

Macauley, J. I. 1979. Bilingual education in Nigeria: The Ife
Yoruba project. Paper read at the Conference on Foreign
Language Education and Bilingual Education, Arlington, Va.,
Center for Applied Linguistics.

Ojerinde, A., and Cziko, G. A. 1978. Yoruba six-year primary
project: the June 1977 primary 4 evaluations. Unpublished
research paper. Ile-Ife, Nigeria: University of Ife.

Pascasio, E. M., ed. 1977. The Filipino bilingual. Quezon City,
Philippines: Ateneo de Manila.

Paulston, C. 1977. Research. In Bilingual education: current
perspectives. Vol. 2, Linguistics, pp. 87-151. Arlington, Va.:
Center for Applied Linguistics.

Rosier, P., and Holm, W. Forthcoming. Saad Naaki Bee Na'nitin:
teaching by means of two languages (Navajo and English at
Rock Point community school). Arlington, Va.: Center for
Applied Linguistics.

Schneider, S. G. 1976. Revolution, reaction or reform: the 1974
bilingual education act. New York: Las Americas.

Skutnabb-Kangas, T. 1975. Bilingualism, semilingualism and school
achievement. Paper read at the 4th International Congress of
Applied Linguistics, Stuttgart, Germany.

Swain, M. 1974. French immersion programs across Canada:
research findings. Canadian Modern Language Review 31:117-
29.

_____. 1976. Bibliography: research on immersion education for
the majority child. Canadian Modern Language Review
32:592-96.

_____. 1978. Home-school language switching. In Understanding
second and foreign language learning: issues and approaches,
ed. J. C. Richards, pp. 238-50. Rowley, Mass.: Newbury
House.

Troike, R. C. 1978. Research evidence for the effectiveness of
bilingual education. NABE Journal 3:13-24.

_____. 1978b. Bilingual education in the United States: the first
decade. International Review of Education 24:401-5.

Tucker, G. R. 1977. Bilingual education: the linguistic
perspective. In Bilingual education: current perspectives.
Vol. 2, Linguistics, pp. 1-40.

_____. 1977b. Some observations concerning bilingualism and second-language teachng in developing countries and in North America.   In Bilingualism: psychological, social and educational implications, ed. P. A. Hornby, pp. 141-46.   New York: Academic Press.

Waggoner, D.   1979.   Teacher resources in bilingual education: a national survey. NABE Journal, 3:53-60.

4. Language beyond the Classroom

SHIRLEY BRICE HEATH
University of Pennsylvania

In the Golden Anniversary Symposium of the Linguistic Society of America held in 1974, Charles Ferguson made the statement, "Most trained linguists should be in careers of application outside the university." He pointed out that approximately 85 percent of employed linguistics were in academic positions and that only 15 percent were in other jobs. He argued for a reversal of these figures:

> Our society, and for that matter the rest of the world, is plagued with language problems which linguistics can help resolve, and I think the bulk of our output of linguists should be headed for careers outside the university. The smaller number of linguists needed for university programs should be recruited from those temperamentally suited to meet high professional standards, and most people trained in linguistics whether they regard themselves primarily as linguists or as attached somewhere else in the language sciences should be engaged in the application of linguistics. (Ferguson 1975:74)

Others have not urged so strongly that linguists find employment outside academe but desire that they at least move their research settings into "the real community." In 1965, Kenneth Clark stated:

> I believe that to be taken seriously, to be viable, and to be relevant social science must dare to study the real problems of men and society, must use the real community, the market place, the arena of politics and power as its laboratories, and must confront and seek to understand the dynamics of social action and social change. (Intro.)

Dell Hymes's views (e.g., 1977) on the applications of anthropology and linguistics, especially in the field of education, have been well known since the 1960s. He and an increasing number of other linguists and anthropologists have argued forcefully for the

45

study of language in its social context and for laying out the social as well as linguistic rules of language.

Some linguists and other social scientists have followed these recommendations and have given attention to the social contexts of language in the "real community." Public interviews, as well as marketplaces, courtrooms, hospital emergency rooms, counseling offices, and playgrounds are some of the settings linguists have used their studies of language. Their research reports have appeared in scholarly journals, such as Discourse Processes, in proceedings of the NWAVE conferences, and at the 1979 Georgetown Round Table on Languages and Linguistics. University students in linguistics courses now sudy with fascination these new lines of research in linguistic analysis.

It is clear that many linguists are now carrying their research into the "real world," but are they themselves seeking either part-time or full-time applied careers outside the university? The best example of the application of the skills and research findings of linguistics outside the university is, no doubt, in public education. Linguists, as either part-time consultants or as full-time directors of research (within school systems or independent firms), have prepared textbooks and other materials both for the training of teachers and for the teaching of language arts, reading, or foreign languages. They have constructed and evaluated tests of reading abilities, oral language proficiencies, and composition skills. Though there has been considerable debate about the effectiveness of this intrusion of linguists into public education, public schools and their administrative units have been the most frequent work environments for linguists outside the university.

The purpose here is to suggest other employment areas available for linguists, either as part-time consultants or as full-time employees. Obviously, linguists of different training have different resources for use in the worlds of law, business, human service delivery systems, etc. Mazzocco (1980) outlines opportunities for those whose training has been in computational linguistics. His focus is on linguistics whose training has been in discourse analysis, including conversational analysis and the study of narrative. Those whose primary interest is formal syntax with some exposure to semantics and pragmatics would also be prepared to move into the settings described here. In many of these areas, linguists will have to be the aggressors; that is, they will have to learn about other professions and discover and promote ways in which their own knowledge and skills are appropriate. In addition, institutions have to be willing to have linguists join them in the identification of language as a major factor in achieving institutional goals. The numbers of people involved, the extent of institutional disruption, and the intensity of federal, state, and general public pressures to identify and alleviate communication problems will determine how language rates in the order of priorities.

The recommendations made here are drawn from two major sources. The first is reports of linguists responding to publicity about a course, "Language in Professional Contexts," taught at the Linguistic Society of America Summer Institute in 1978. A network of communication has resulted among linguists working in medicine, business, social work, pharmacy, dentistry, law, and adult basic education. The second source is my fieldwork in two southeastern United States communities. Over a period of several years I worked at various times with local housing authorities, legal aid and health clinic officials, and adult basic education personnel. The recommendations focus attention on (1) the direct roles linguists can play in human service delivery systems, and (2) how the results of linguistic research can be used in such environments.

Types of Work Environments

<u>Federal Credit Unions</u>. This environment is drawn from my own work in textile mills of the Southeast. Ever since the mills opened in the South in the early twentieth century, the mills have in numerous ways provided financing services for their employees. However, in the past two decades, most mills have created credit unions that are strictly controlled by federal regulations. Employees of the credit unions are often new to the mill, while a majority of the employees or their families have had long associations with the mill. Some mills, especially those long established in particular communities, are managed by "old-timers" who want to maintain the image of the mill as a family-type community. Recreational areas for families of employees, a weekly newspaper, and numerous other personal touches are used to create the image that some of the familiarity and warmth of earlier mill days still remain.

Some mill executives have recently seen the credit union as a major barrier to maintaining this family metaphor. Employees have charged that credit union officials are insensitive, do not know what they are doing, mislead employees, and do not tell the entire truth about financing arrangements. On the other hand, credit union employees, many of whom have come to their jobs from other financial institutions, find the clients poor credit risks, inept communicators, and generally untrustworthy customers. Both sides named communication as a major problem; therefore, it was logical in their view and my own to look first at the communication exchanges that take place between credit union officers and mill employees. Most of the customers were white couples, both partners working in the mill, or single black males or females who were the only members of their families working in the mills. The most frequent requests were for loans to buy cars or household appliances or to pay off accumulated bills, though the credit union also financed purchases of homes and trailers.

The following exchange (Table 1) between a female credit union official and a black female client illustrates one type of information the linguist made available to mill executives about communication in the credit union. Throughout the interview, the black female client tries to accommodate to the purpose of the interview and to the special demands of this speech event. In her opening statement, she adopts some aspects of a formal interview register, using some specialized vocabulary and adding full endings to her words. She recognizes that a successful outcome of the interview is dependent on her stating an acceptable need for the money and providing accurate information of certain types. The interview is a speech event that is not normally used within her primary speech community, yet she shows her knowledge of the fact that in an interview situation, a particular register of language is needed to allow each party to play out a particular social role. The credit union official, however, does not notice these efforts on the part of the client and conducts the interview predominantly with the file of written information before her. The hurdle in the interview that the client cannot overcome is the credit union official's use of the written source as the basis of the speech event.

The interviewer enters the small room where the client is sitting; she offers no greeting, but her "okay" announces that the interview is open and that she is holding the floor to open the interview with a question. The client anticipates the question and interrupts it with her response (2). The client corrects here initial wanna to wanted and uses the term personal reserve, an expression not in her daily repertoire but one that is familiar from workshops on budgeting offered in her neighborhood center. To have a personal reserve is a desirable goal. The irony in this case is that as the interview proceeds, it is clear that the woman needs the loan because she has in fact no personal reserve, and the loan is to be used in place of such a reserve—i.e., to pay off accumulated bills. The credit union official pays no attention to the client's opening, cuts her off, and goes out to get the folder (which she should have picked up before she came to the office, because the client's name had been placed on her roster). When she reenters the office, she asks the client if she wants to increase "it" to seventeen (4), and again asks the purpose of the loan, indicating that she either did not hear or did not accept the earlier statement that the loan was needed for a personal reserve.

During the remainder of the conversation, the credit union employee flips through pages in the folder and directs her questions to the client primarily on the basis of what is on the written document before her. Her task is to reconcile the written document with the current oral request by the client. However, the client is asked to supply information as though she knew the contents of the written document. Referents for pronouns (it in (4), this in (7), this in (10), and they in (16)) are not clearly identified, and the client must play a constant guessing game, the goal of which is to determine without any visual cues the referents of these pronouns.

In (4) the credit union employee essentially introduces new

Table 1

Cl: Client
Off: Credit Union Official

(enters office where client is seated)

(1) Off: okay, hh, what kind of a loan did you⌐hh wanna see about now?
          └well, hh, I wanna   wanted it for my hhh personal reserve.
              (pause)
              (exits)

(2) Cl:

(3) Off: let me get your folder. I'll be right back.
    (reenters)

(4)   and you want to increase it to seventeen.
    (looking at folder)

(5)   (looking toward client)
    and your purpose?

(6) Cl: I hhh need a personal (pause) uh, I got some small bills.

(7) Off: because when I did this, I, hhh, didn't know, but you were telling both had to sign.
                (looking at folder)
    (looking at client)

(8)   what kind of bills?

(9) Cl: water, gas, clothes, hhh, water department.

(10) Off: (flips through folder, writing figures on pad)
    okay, now you're paying fifty a month, and you want, you, hh, ummmmm
    you want your payments to stay at that, okay, you live at 847 J.O. Connel,
              (pause)
    and you've been there three years, okay   um, let's see, we're gonna combine this,
    gross weekly salary is $146-46, forty-hour week

(11) Cl: └no, about $170

(12) Off: (looking at folder)
    you don't have a car and your rent is $120, and you still owe Sears, hhh   it's twenty=
              (pause)

(13) Cl: =no, it's more than that=
    (looking at client)

(14) Off: =what is it now?

(15) Cl: I think it's about $180 ⌐some

(16) Off: └is that everything, yea, all we've got to do is apply to the credit bureau,
    they decide, you can come back tomorrow.

Total units of discourse: 16
4 elicitations directed to Cl; 4 responses by Cl; 4 utterances directed to folder by Off; 2 responses
by Cl to folder information; 2 announcements of exits by Off.

information, unless she presupposes that the client will know the referent of it to be the amount of the current loan. However, the client has not said that it is the amount of the new principal she has in mind, and neither party has said anything about two individuals signing (7). This information is never explained in the interview; either it is something carried over from information in the folder, or the credit union official is engaging in seemingly unrelated reverie. The record apparently now shows that the client has a loan that is being repaid by having a certain amount deducted from her weekly paycheck; for individuals in her salary range, there is an upper lmit of $1,700 for a loan. The client must either figure this out herself or ask for clarification of the credit union official's comment/question. The official's basic purpose is to tell the client that her loan limit is $1,700 and that, in order to get this amount, she must give satisfactory reasons (4,5).

The client at this point moves away from the personal reserve idea and hesitantly says she has some small bills (6). The credit union official's next comment is never explained, but she follows it with "What kind of bills?" The official makes no comment on the listing of bills, nor does she take note of the fact that the client corrects water to water department in an effort to list kinds of bills and to adopt aspects of the interview register. The official instead gives the conventional signal okay to say that she is once again directing the interview (10). She makes a statement announcing that the client wants the payment to remain at $50 per month. The client is not asked about this. The official then calculates the period of time during which deductions will be made if the client gets approval for an additional loan to make the total principal equal to $1,700. A second okay signals a change in the conversation's direction; the official reads from the folder, but she does not ask for confirmation or denial of this information. Her third and fourth okays continue to hold her place in the conversation while she talks to herself throughout her calculations. In the last portion of (10), the official makes an ambiguous statement—"we're gonna combine this"—and this can only be assumed to be the current amount of the loan with the amount of the new loan—i.e., the two figures that will now equal the total of new principal—$1,700. The official has already made the decision that the client should not increase her monthly payments, and the client has not objected. The statement of gross weekly salary is $146.66 is, however, corrected by the client (11) but the official does not verbally acknowledge this correction; she continues writing. Whether she records the new figure and takes it into account in her calculations is not known. Since the amount of the loan is determined by the weekly salary, this figure is very important in the entire transaction, yet it is not admitted as evidence by the official. The official moves on to another series of statements, apparently reading or interpreting from the record (12). Again, the client corrects a figure, and this time the official stops to collect new information (14). Before that exchange is completely finished, she interrupts with a question in form, but a statement in purpose (16), announcing that she has all the information she needs to close the interview. The answer will be available for the client on the next day. No politeness formula closes the interview.

It is important to note that throughout this interview the client was questioned on the basis of written information to which she had no access. Following the interview, the credit union official was asked what she had learned from the client.

> I know she wants a loan. She's behind in payments—she must have had a clothes-buying spree at Sears. She can only get up to $1,700 total; she's now got one for $1,200. I checked over the information in her folder with her, and now it's up to the board to decide. I don't think they should go along with it.

The official asserts that she has checked the information with the client yet the client was never told that was the purpose of the reading in (10) and (12). The client was also not told that her new loan would be for only $500, not $1,700. The client, when asked "How did it go? Do you think you'll get the money?", gave a different version of the interview:

> They gonna let me have $1,700, if they let me have it at all. Couldn't tell about that woman—don't know—she may think I ought not to get it just to pay my bills off. She ain't talk a whole lot, sorta made it all up in her head as she went along. We see what happen tomorrow.

Considerable gaps existed between the facts understood by each party: the client believed she would get $1,700 and thought the interviewer was primarily interested in why she wanted the loan and was not much interested in other information. The client intuitively felt the interviewer's personal judgment of her cause would play a role in the decision. The interviewer knew the loan would not exceed $500, believed she had "checked" necessary information, and personally judged the purpose of the loan—irresponsible buying patterns and a poor record of keeping up with bills—adequate reason for not giving it.

Mill executives who had been distressed by complaints about the credit union were given transcripts of such interviews, and explanations were made of the erroneous assumptions being made by each party that led to later charges of ineptness, dishonesty, etc. An immediate change was a program to have available to each employee the written information from which questions were being asked. Thereafter, as the interviewers moved through the interview they related each oral question to a piece of information contained in the folder. They explicitly requested confirmation of the accuracy of each piece of information given in the file: "Has your address changed since you gave this as your address?" (pointing to the address on the form and reading it aloud).

Several other changes were made in the layout and language of the forms, as well as in the spatial arrangements for interviews. In one corner of the waiting room, automatic slide presentations explained the process of obtaining a loan, who made decisions on loans, and the bases for these decisions. The linguist as change agent in this situation enabled mill executives to understand how past communication practices resulted in misunderstandings and poor credit records for some employees. New practices tried to clarify the process of decision making behind granting a loan. Successful introduction of these changes led the mill management to consider other changes in communication strategies in different sections of the mill's operation.

Social Service Agencies. A second example of an area in which linguists can play a direct role is public services, such as social services and legal aid, where effective communication between those served and those who manage the paperwork is necessary. One example, drawn from an urban housing office, will illustrate how the knowledge of a linguist can be applied in these situations. Residents of urban housing who were cited for breaking rules of occupancy were asked to come into the housing office for conference. In these conferences, the officer's style was to ask a series of questions, all of which were basically charges or accusations (for a discussion of this question type, see Heath, 1979). "Why do you have all those people living with you when you know you can have only your immediate family living with you?" or "The rules about only members of your immediate family apply to you as well as everybody else, you know?" The client's response usually took the form of a narrative, into which he periodically inserted evaluations: "Well, my sister lives up north now, and she took her kids with her. They didn't like it up there, and come summer time, you know how kids are, they wanted to come back. They come to stay, but then my brother's got a kid out on Long Island, and he want to come too. You know how kids all like to get together in the summer."

Throughout such a narrative, the officer would nod his head, saying "okay," "I understand," or "Yes, go ahead." As the resident accounted for those actions that violated the housing rules, the official would continue to punctuate the narrative with nods and verbal signals. The resident interpreted these not as the conversational supports the official intended, but as consent to or approval of the events being recounted. When residents were later cited for violations or given eviction notices, they viewed the officials as dishonest, as approving of their actions when face-to-face, but citing them behind their backs. The officials were unaware that they had seemed to give tacit support to actions that violated the housing rules. They did not recognize that their "back channel signals" (Yngve 1970) for the narrative were more important to the clients than their pointed reminders about the rules of their redistribution and underlining of written regulations.

In this situation, the work of the linguist seems obvious, and the problems would seem to be those a perceptive social worker or housing official would notice. However, linguists, because of their study of details of language structure, are able to identify multiple causes of communication breakdown and to talk about these more effectively than individuals trained to focus on other aspects of client interviews. As a result of the detailing by the linguist of difficulties in communication in this urban housing office, a change in procedures as well as increased awareness of different communicative habits helped to improve efficiency and effectiveness of client relations. The roles of linguists in social services are in many ways similar to those some social scientists have assumed in industries (Radom 1970), where they not only play a direct role in bringing about changes in the communication patterns, but also provide recommendations for structural administrative changes based on local needs, rather than theoretical approaches to generalized problems.

Banks and Savings and Loan Associations. In a large metropolitan center of the Southeast, Boyd Davis, a linguist at the University of North Carolina at Charlotte, has in the past two years been requested by executives of financial institutions to offer their employees workshops on communication. Davis agreed to do so only if the executives would themselves also take part in the series of workshops with their employees. The sessions were held in the financial offices and materials of the institutions were used in the workshops. Topics covered were structural differences in dialects, varieties of questioning style, and ways of using written sources in an interview to the advantage of both the client and the customer. Simulations of transactions were videotaped and analyzed, and simulated telephone interviews or requests for specific types of information were taped for analysis. The goals of executives were to improve their communication with those they supervised and to enable their employees to communicate more effectively with customers from different social and cultural backgrounds. Simplification of forms and a general thrust for Plain English in their written documents had not achieved their goals. Since the initial workshops in the summer of 1978, the banks have repeatedly asked for more and have suggested new areas of attention for future simulations.

Preparation of Curriculum Materials. This method seems old and established, but it has been used by linguists primarily for primary school language arts and reading classes. There are, however, other areas of application, such as Adult Basic Education programs and new uses of linguistic research in English and social studies classes at the junior and senior high school levels.

Adult Basic Education programs traditionally focus on the teaching of reading. Materials are generally drawn from cultural events and populations unfamiliar to adult beginning readers in their daily lives. In addition, the reading materials contain forms rare in the active speaking repertoire of many of the readers (embedded questions, etc.). There is a growing dissatisfaction on the part of ABE instructors with these materials, and linguists acting as consultants in the rewriting of beginning materials at local levels can benefit these programs. It is critical that these materials be prepared locally by teachers and staff members. Such materials, which use photographs of local settings as illustrations and provide texts covering local topics, such as neighborhood centers and church festivals, have been much more successful than commercially prepared programs.

Another major benefit of the work linguists in ABE programs is provision of materials on verbal exchanges in social service settings. Linguists doing research on service encounters and exchanges in human services delivery systems, such as welfare offices, health clinics, hospitals, lawyers' offices, etc., have described the rules of interaction that operate in these situations. Such work almost always indicates that the individual who is not the professional and who does not know the rules of the exchange is at a considerable, and sometimes high-risk disadvantage. Videotapes of such exchanges, transcripts, and analyses of what took place and why could help meet the real needs of adults in ABE programs. The work of Cicourel (e.g., 1981) on interactions in emergency rooms between doctors and patients and their families is another example of information suitable for use in ABE programs. Analysis of such interactions enables ABE students to see where and how breakdowns in communication occur; most important, they can learn to reorganize points at which they can ask clarification questions and initiate such strategies as "Now let's see if I have this right," followed by a brief summary of what has occurred.

Of special importance in this situation is the explanation by linguists of the uses of literate sources by those who manage human services delivery encounters. The credit union official in Table 1 had the advantage of knowing what was on the written record and using that to direct her conversation. In a recent paper by Cicourel, the doctor's write-up of the medical history based on the interview bears little resemblance to what was said in the oral exchange. Yet patients and clients are victimized—not because they cannot read this information, but because they do not have access to it, and because it is used as the basis of a speech event, the rules of which are determined by the use of the written document. ABE programs desperately need such information, which currently is being collected by linguists and examined for their own purposes, but is rarely made available to those who could profit from understanding these rules.

A second use of research by linguists is providing units for

English and social studies classes in junior and senior high schools. Currently, in what are termed the "average track" English composition classes, students study American and/or British fiction and nonfiction. Students analyze style and content of the literature while investigating and defining the principles of good writing. Students are expected to cultivate "good taste" through their study of literature and the application of its techniques to their own writing. Such analysis often emphasizes not only the historical context out of which the literary piece evolved, but also the internal stylistic features of the piece, the vocabulary used, the juxtaposition of ideas, and stylistic devices used to achieve effect, etc. Students are given points for incorporating these devices into their own compositions as well as for being able to label and recognize them in test questions. Such work has a long and established tradition in the teaching of English in the United States. It is believed to teach critical thinking, to foster cultural awareness of "good" literature, and to help in the organization of thinking.

I suggest that as an addition to, but not as a replacement for, this analysis of literature videotapes of interactions in the "real community" be used for the same purposes. Doctor and patient in an interview for a health history or an exchange between a loan officer and customer could be analyzed with the same skills and transfer of stylistic and organizational devices now used only for literature. Students, with the help of a guide prepared by linguists, could come to understand the latching of details to the main idea, juxtaposition of facts and opinions, techniques of hedging (G. Lakoff 1972), and the interplay between written sources and oral language in such interviews. These skills are as justifiable and as transferable to good writing, clear thinking, logical organization, and critical analysis as are those used in analyzing a piece of literature. Moreover, these skills increase knowledge about the structure and pragmatics of discourse, which can be applied to conversations presented in literary works as well as to real-life exchanges.

The ramifications of this idea for other subject matters can only be suggested here. A civics unit in the ninth grade could use either a video or audio tape of interactions between policeman and accused at the scene of the crime, at the station, and in the trial. Students can see in these interactions: (1) the operationalization of concepts they learn in civics; (2) the shifts in interpretation of events that occur from place to place; and (3) the transfer from speech to writing of the events in each setting. Such an opportunity provides for acquisitions of skills, knowledge, and dispositions currently espoused as ideals of social studies instruction. The theoretical concepts and historically removed events of politics and social life are translated into current interactions in existing institutions. Moreover, the linguistic and social interactional analysis of such real life incidents can help increase "basic skills" such as understanding details, recognizing the main idea, identifying sequencing mechanisms, etc.

One other situation for the use of linguistic research in curriculum units is family life classes. In many inner-city schools, these are now being offered with the ostensible goal of teaching citizenship behaviors. These classes are generally offered for the lowest track, those individuals who will not pursue higher education and who may well be breadwinners and heads of households interacting in human services delivery systems sooner than their colleagues in the collegebound track. Indeed, many may already be breadwinners and/or parents. Family life courses generally give no emphasis to communication outside the home; the language of warranties, consumer contracts, medical recommendations, and health forms is not discussed. Yet these students will need to know how to interpret them and how to ask questions about their contents. In spite of the Plain English movement, many forms remain unitelligible to consumers. This is especially true for those who at an early stage in their academic career have been closed out of English classes, in which the goal is to take apart language in order to see how it works to say what it is the writer wants to convey.

Furthermore, because of the changing degree and focus of government intervention in the lives of many of these students and their families, new speech acts and events are being called for. Events such as interviews and explanation through specific questions rather than through narrative are not familiar speech events for many of these students. Through the linguistic research that records and interprets these events, their discourse structures, and their social settings, explanatory materials and data become part of the curriculum of a wide range of educational settings. The rules for accounting for what one has done differ from client to official, clarification and verification episodes introduced by clients depend on appropriate timing, use of politeness formulae, and structural formulation of questions. The ability to get what one needs in these encounters depend on the ability to handle these new speech events and to use the strategies necessary to disentangle meaning from them. Such skills are justifiable curricular content in both public education and adult basic education.

Some suggestions offered in these curricula will help the powerless to understand how the powerful communicate. Linguists and their research can reveal how institutional representatives organize information in oral discourse and how they use the written word to structure that discourse. English classes can learn how to analyze an interview and how to break in with clarification questions or verifying repetitions of the information just reviewed. Students can learn how to request explanation, to question decisions made by the interviewer for them, and to achieve access to the written materials from which they are being questioned. In other suggestions, the work of the linguists is with those who have the power, and the goal is to inform them of ways to change the communication patterns their institutional representatives use with customers. Institutions can and often will adapt their their methods of informing clients, to the advantage of both institution and client. Improved understanding brings improved performance by clients and less harassment by institutions; those who have had effective communication about what, when, and why they are paying are usually more inclined to pay bills than are those who do not understand how a total was reached or what the payment terms are. Thus, some institutions are recognizing the advantages of understanding the conventions of language use that each party brings to those public speech events through which goods and services are exchanged. Ironically, the focus of the institutional representative on a single task in an interview has been instilled through professional training (Heath 1979), and explicit analysis of performance in an interview may be necessary to stimulate recognition of the multiple perspective parties bring to such an event. The work of Gumperz (forthcoming) with industries in England and that of Erickson and Schultz (forthcoming) in interethnic counseling situations illustrate ways in which linguists analysis can raise the "sociolinguistic consciousness" of both the powerless and the powerful.

Ervin-Tripp (1979) describes conversational competence as requiring

> paying attention to what the partner says, and making appropriate replies. Evidence of reciprocity of attention can be gaze, minimal overlap while one is talking, and speech that is contingent on the partner's in form, in function, and in topic. An incompetent speaker would not gaze at or orient to partners, would display random gaps and overlaps in conversation, and would talk about objects and thoughts at whim without any regard to what has just been said. (1979:391)

The analysis of Table 1 indicates that the interviewer had none of the competencies enumerated; she paid little attention to what her conversational partner said, offered infrequent verbal and nonverbal reinforcement, allowed random gaps to enter the conversation, and seemed to introduce some thoughts at whim. Data from numerous public service encounters indicate similar incompetencies when the parties bring different assumptions about both the rules and the intentions of the encounter to such situations. Identification and clarification of such blatant breaches of conversational competence is an obvious task of the linguist. In addition, the work of linguists in such settings can supplement materials used in professional training programs, periodic evaluations of institutional effectiveness in meeting communication goals, and revamping of social services agencies to meet the needs of a diverse clientele. In short, linguists beyond the classroom can play a critical role in the renewal of attention not to the institutional structures society has produced, but to the people for whom they were produced.

REFERENCES

Cicourel, Aaron. 1981. Language in medicine. In Language in the USA, ed. Charles A. Ferguson and Shirley Brice Heath, pp 389-412. New York: Cambridge University Press.

Clark, Kenneth B. 1965. Dark ghetto. New York: Harper and Row.

Erickson, Frederick, and Schultz, Jeffery. Forthcoming. Talking to "the man": social and cultural organization of communication in counseling interviews. New York: Academic Press.

Ervin-Tripp, Susan. 1979. Children's verbal turn-taking. In Developmental pragmatics, ed. Elinor Ochs and Bambi B. Schieffelin, pp. 391-414. New York: Academic Press.

Ferguson, Charles A. 1975. Applications of linguistics. In The scope of American linguists, ed. Robert Austerlitz, pp. 63-76. Lisse, Netherlands: Peter de Ridder Press.

Gumperz, John. Forthcoming. The sociolinguistic basis of speech act theory. In Speech act ten years after, ed. Julian Boyd and Sandro Ferrara. Milan: Versus.

Heath, Shirley Brice. 1979. The context of professional languages: an historical overview for medicine. Language in public life. In Georgetown University round table on languages and linguistics, ed. James E. Alatis and G. Richard Tucker. pp. 102-18. Washington, D.C.: Georgetown University Press.

_____. 1981. Questioning at home and at school: a comparative study. In Educational Anthropology in Action, ed. George Spindler. New York: Holt, Richard and Winston.

Hymes, Dell H. 1977. Foundations in Sociolinguistics: an ethnographic approach. London: Tavistock.

Lakoff, George. 1972. Hedges: a study in meaning criteria and the logic of fuzzy concepts. Chicago Linguistic Society 8:183-228.

Mazzocco, Alexis. 1979. Opportunities for linguists in the field of computers. The Linguistic Reporter 22:6.

Radom, Matthew. 1970. The Social Scientist in American Industry. New Brunswick, N.J.: Rutgers University Press.

Yngve, Victor. 1970. On getting a word in edgewise. Chicago Linguistic Society 6:567-78.

5. Verbal Strategies, Images, and Symbolic Roles in the Use of a Conventional Language by a Spanish Golden Age Playwright

A. JULIAN VALBUENA
University of Delaware

After years of teaching and developing research, several scholars have reached the conclusion that literary critics and linguists should become more aware of the need to expand their knowledge to related fields. A number of linguists are trying to establish a bridge between language and literature, which, for a period of time, seemed to be going in different directions. Perhaps a training in philology will be a base for this understanding. It has become evident, in spite of the positions that were taken by Professor Leonard Bloomfield and his school, that a pleiad of linguists are working today to create new perspectives in literary criticism, as, for example, William O. Hendricks (Semiology of Literary Discourse), Iuri Tinianov (The Problem of Poetic Language), Vladimir Propp (Morphology of the Short Story), A. J. Greimas (Structural Semantics), and Eduardo Forastieri (A Structural Approach to the Theatre of Lope de Vega).

Roman Jacobson and Emile Benveniste have provided a revision of the impersonal approach developed by the influential Saussurean methodology. Di Pietro has written that "human creativity with language, taken in its larger sense, is tied immediately to our physical, psychic and social nature. ... No meaningful inquiry into the evolution of language can be made without seeing language as one of several communication systems."[1] One can therefore envision literature as a basic element in the science of communication.

The Spanish plays of the seventeenth century may be used to exemplify the semiotic theory. The comedia nueva is thus a linguistic structure of specific functions, which are grouped under a system of metaphors, strategies, and symbolic roles. These structures present a unique communication to the audience. The plays by Don Calderón de la Barca (1600-1681) can then be considered systems of functions, written in an elaborated code, whose representations provide a medium for divulging definite political, philosphical, and artistic beliefs.

The comedia nueva exhibits the dramatic formula promulgated by Lope de Vega (1562-1635), who explained his theories in a treatise, written in verse, entitled The New Art of Making Comedias in This Time, published for the first time in 1609. It includes a number of recommendations he put forward at a meeting of the Academy of Madrid, held under the auspices of Don Diego Gómez de Sandoval y Rojas, Count of Saldaña, probably in the autumn of 1607.

The comedia nueva was organized in three parts, called journeys or acts, whose total number of lines fluctuated generally between 2,400 to 3,300. The coordination of semic units and their correlated sequences depended on certain metaphors, verbal strategies, and symbolic roles that established a prepared communication between the author and the public. It is safe to say that the dramatists of the seventheenth century contributed, with their writing ability, to the development of a sense of cohesion within the country. This is in accord with Hayyim N. Bialik's (1873–1934) statement that "language is the key to a nation's heart." Both Lope and Calderón propagated patriotic principles and defended the interests of the Hapsburg dynasty.

The methodology followed in carrying out this investigation has Roman Jacobson's theories as point of departure. For Jacobson, linguistic expression is part of a system transmitted by a speaker in a context, or environment, that is addressed to a recipient. [2] Jacobson correctly gave a place of importance to Wilhelm von Humboldt, who had stated that "language is not only a simple means of communication, but the expression of the spirit and the conception of the world of the speaker; life in society is the auxiliary necessary for its development." [3] With this in mind, a number of functions can be observed in the act of speaking. Since a verbal sign points to a specific objectivity, it follows that language has a referential performance. There is an emotive expression that reflects the attitude of the speaker of a linguistic proposition. Language also possesses a conative, sometimes called injunctive, function, which connects the message with the receiver. The manuscript, the medium, studied on its own by the observation of the symbolization, and so forth, reveals its aesthetic or poetic value. Also the "phatic function" exists, which "affirms, maintains or halts the communication." [4] The written play is the medium emitted by our author and contains a message in a specific literary code, directed to a receiver. An analysis along these lines will help to delineate certain linguistic aspects of Calderón's works and to appreciate better the craftmanship of the author. We shall give special attention to Calderón's Life Is a Dream (ca. 1632). This famous play illustrates a very human and universal predicament: the search for what is real and what is illusory in man's experience. With an obvious social purpose, Calderón presents a philosophical problem and a solution that are applicable to Everyman.

The analysis of the sequence, or diégesis, a word coined by Souriau [5] brings about the transformation of Segismund, the protagonist, and with it a change in his social environment. The audience observes the transition from an initial state of discord to a balance of harmony. The change from confusion to order constitutes a structural pattern depicted in the comedias of Lope de Vega and his school, whose output comprises the Golden Age of Spanish drama.

Of interest here is the paradox, a word formation created to attract the attention of the public or the reader. Paradox has been used for this purpose since the times of the Romans. Cicero classified a number of similar anomalies in his Paradoxae Stoicorum. This collection added to the spread of Platonic thought that was present in the philosophical and educational discourse during the first century B.C. In another period, close to Calderón, Pico della Mirandola, one of the most talented exponents of Neoplatonism during the Renaissance, made extensive use of this rhetorical figure. The following statement is attributed to him: "Contradictoria in nature actuali se compatiuntur" (Opposites in nature admit each other).[6] The practice of dramatizing relational opposites increased during the Renaissance and Baroque epochs. The oxymoron, a rhetorical example of this style, is a figure of speech producing an effect by a seeming self-contradiction, as in cruel kindness. Use of the oxymoron gives the author a startingly original meaning to his message. Think about the intriguing and mystical expression of nature in a harmonious moment, "sonorous solitude," by San Juan de la Cruz (1542-91); or about the term liquid jaspers, authored by Góngora (1561-1627), designating the waves of the seas; or about the adored enemy, inscribed in a play by Guillén de Castro (1569-1631). We can observe, in these examples, the paradoxical meanings and realize their new connotations.

Calderón, on his part, when he titled his play La vida es sueño (Life Is a Dream) established a vivid semantic idea, and effective catchword. The maxim "life is a dream" was not his invention; in fact, it was used rather frequently in his epoch. Churchmen, intellectuals, and other playwrights expounded on the topic "sic transeunt gloriae mundi," which was closely related to his title. Antonio de Pereda, who painted the famous "Dream of the Gentleman," would illustrate this theme on canvas later on, circa 1660. Calderón himself, living in the center of Madrid, could easily have attended the Church of the Virgen del Carmen, where Father Augustine Núñez Delgadillo preached his sermons. These were collected for publication under the somewhat bombastic title of Celestial Mines Discovered in the New Testament for Lent (1629). The first sermon, for Ash Wednesday, carries some reflections on the topos "Memento homo quia pulvis es," which touches on the idea that life is a dream in a similar way to the general idea that Calderón would propagate in his play. The phraseology of Father Núñez interpreted dream to signify that man is asleep, or immersed in a dream, when he does not understand and practice Christian principles.

Calderón was a devout Christian with an intellectual Neoplatonic perspective. His writings show that he was familiar with Boscan's translation of Il Cortegiano by Castiglione, with the Dialoghi di amore, by León de Hebreo, and a number of treatises on love and philosophy. The Neoplatonic scholars had concluded that man's path goes through several stages of knowledge in an ascensional direction. It starts with the perception of the senses, comes to a period where reason separates good from bad, and finally reaches the stage of transcendental meditation where man can experience a feeling of universal harmony. When man misinterprets the spiritual objectives of the soul, he forgets about caritas (or altruism) and devotes himself to the enjoyment of senses.

Calderón uses an aesthetic design written with the techniques of chiaroscuro to dramatize this philosophy. He portrays good with light and evil with shadows, forces which, as we have seen, interact in Segismund's itinerary. The playwright adorns the sequence of the action with binary images that relate to the effects of illumination and darkness. The play begins in a thick mountainous area with the prince of Poland imprisoned in a secluded tower in which he has been living since his birth. Darkness covers this location, described by Calderón as a "blind labyrinth." The room in which he lives is where the "night is born." The arrival of Rosaura awakens an admiration and with it a hope. Later, his experience in the Polish court produces a blinding bewilderment; lights and colors kindle his senses and, when he wants to satisfy his material pleasures, his desires push him into violence. Back in the tower he is led to believe that everything he remembers is a dream, but nevertheless he enters a new state of discernment between the force of the senses and the light of illumination. Reflection will enable him to control his destiny. He begins to become a different person as he realizes that life holds responsibilities. When his chance comes again, he will know how to choose and to act more wisely. The underlying message is obvious: man may win over a dark and ominous fate when he reaches enlightenment and practices Christian virtues.

The metaphor in praesentia "life is a dream," the title of this play, enacts a functional, paradigmatic binary system of relational opposites whose syntagmatic correlations pervades this literary work. There are two fluctuating values designated with the terms life (X) and sleep $\approx$ dream (Y), which have a rich functional interplay. The two analogous words, sleep and dream, are translated from sueño, a word that is polysemous. One can apply componential analysis to the logical relationship between these two terms X and Y. Two conflicting forces, with different degrees of influence, operate on Segismund's conduct. His components life (X) and dream (Y) are relational opposites and they possess their respective moral-axiological connotation of good (A) and bad (B). The initial components, X and Y, have sets of associated correlates that are also relational opposites. Consociate to life (X) we allocate: reality (x_1), freedom of choice (x_2), cognizance (x_3) and spiritual values (x_4). Allied to dream (Y) we position the corresponding opposites: dormancy (y_1), slavery (y_2), illusion (y_3) and materialistic values (y_4). These relational opposites are ornamentally illustrated in baroque style with images derived from the dichotomy light (M) and shadow (N). This additional pair of symbolic quantities correlate with the initial antithesis life ⇌ dream. The dichotomy M ⇌ N serves to elaborate a chiaroscuro technique of an aesthetical function. The associated correlates accompany the sequence of events throughout the play.

The changes of the variables X and Y, along with their associated correlates, illustrates the flow of continuum through the episodes taking place within the three acts of the play. The pattern of the function of the components and their associated correlates can be demonstrated by a graphic life line (see Table 1) that begins

Table 1
Graphic Life Line of Segismund

	1 Discord	2 Fight & Discovery		3 Harmony
	Y N B	Y N B	X m a	X M A
Segismund (S) ――――――――――――――――――――――――――――――				(Z) Segismund
	1 x m a	2 x m a	3 y n b	4 y n b
	Initial State	Transformation		Balance

Act 1. 1. Initial State. To live without libery is to dwell in shadows, or to be asleep.

2. Transformation. To live without responsibility, dominated by one's emotions, is to exist in a dreamlike state.

Act 2. 3. To realize that life is as brief as a dream, or similar to representation, is to begin to understand the enigma of life.

Act 3. 4. Balance. To govern oneslf with love and prudence is to make one's life transcendent.

The path of enlightenment:
Philosophical level: X → A versus Y → B
The aesthetic elaboration: X ≈ M : Y ≈ N

Key: → Implications
         ≈ Similarity

with an unenlightened Segismund and the two paradigmatic components with the negative one (Y → B) overpowering the positive (X → A). The variables change to a neutral, equilibrious point that engenders the beginning of the transformation of the protagonist. This refers to the point in time when Segismund has been returned to the tower, again a prisoner, and he starts to reflect on his experiences at court. The component X proceeds to overcome Y as Segismund realizes that life is as short as a dream, and therefore, that materialistic values (y₄) are ephemeral and not worthy of pursuit. At the end of the life line, the equiponderance between the relational components has been reversed and X dominates Y. This coincides with the end of act 3 when Segismund, guided by prudence and moved by love for his subjects, instigates acts of charity. Harmony, the Neoplatonic ideal, is achieved when he, as the spiritual leader of Poland, enacts justice for all. Such behavior enlightens his soul and exemplifies to all mankind the path to transcendence. Calderón's didactial message conveys an elaborated code of behavior in tune with the treaties of the Renaissance and post-Renaissance.

The expression life is a dream is composed of a paradoxical metaphor. The juxtaposition establishes the mental transfer of meaning from one word into another. The relationship in itself embodies a function that presents a structural format correlating to different elements of the plot. The syntagmatic interrelations fall in the axiological catergories of B or A, respectively. We can see on the life line that Y is paramount at the point of departure but that its influence gradually decreases; on the other hand, X obtains more and more force and overpowers Y at the end of the play. The proportion changes little by little until the values of good surmount those of evil. Segismund, with the symbolic role of Everyman, progressively acquires the wisdom necessary for him to choose the correct path leading to the fulfillment of an optimum life.

This anaylsis of the metaphor life is a dream has enabled us to visualize in a new perspective the structure and functional relationships of this play. We have constructed a synthetic formulation bearing two opposing terms and united by a mental bridge or thought process. This may be outlined in a mathematical proportion: $(Y \approx N) \rightarrow B: (X \approx M) \rightarrow A.$ [7]

The Calderón comedia is well known for its use of antonyms and relational opposites that mold the structure of the written medium, but its complexity reveals a plurality of interests to the linguist. Repetition is a case in point since it is possible to state that the comedias are verbal structures built upon the rules of this figure of speech. Wherever the critic looks within the drama, he observes patterns of reiteration of sounds. Rhythm, rhyme, alliteration, parallelistic constructions and internal echoes express the variation of the signifiers. Scholars have begun to ascertain the numerical combinations of the different types of formal repetitions. Specific stanzas may be used to convey determined dramatic situations. [8] Lope de Vega offered some recommendations along these lines. [9] In a sense, it can be considered that repetition in the comedia has its distant origins in the magical effects of primitive incantation. [10] However, the seventeenth-century playwright has organized this technique for definite functions. He may try to impart a subjective and emotional impact, or he may motivate reactions of surprise and admiration. At times, his strategy in arranging reiteration of words may lead to the crescendo in intensity. In other occasions, the use of allusions and connotations that relate to objects out-of-text may have ornamental purposes. Finally, the interruption of a sequence of thought by the manipulation of bisemic terms can be produced for comical expectations. The play on words emphasizes or builds or complicates the syntagmatic segment and confers a definite tone and character to the style. Calderón makes use of repetition in his play, The Mayor of Zalamea (ca. 1636), in a variety of ways and shows mastership in applying rhetorical figures to his verse. Parallelistic constructions are abundant in Calderón's plays. John V. Bryans, in his chapter entitled "Verbal Structure" makes reference to the so-called parallel structures. [11] He understands this device to be a binary line with semantic similarity and written with the intention of decorative symmetry or amplification. The parallelistic construction can be used as stichomythia where there are one or two lines for each of the two characters in argumentative passages illustrated by contrasted statements, repetition of the opponents words, and angry retort. [12] This is very effective formula for presenting personae in an antagonistic scene. In The Mayor of Zalamea, Pedro Crespo, the wealthy farmer, is opposite to Don Lope de Figueroa, an army general in command of the troops temporarily lodged in the village. Both characters have pride in their honor, but Crespo represents the horizontal idea of this concept, appropriate to a commoner, while Don Lope has a vertical understanding of it in accordance with his nobility and high rank. [13] The contrast between them begins as an encounter when Pedro Crespo pronounces his famous lines:

> My life and property I render
> to the King; but honor is
> the heritage of my soul,
> and my soul belongs to God alone. [14]   (873-76)

Don Lope cannot deny the right of the common man to possess honor and so he exclaims, "I swear to God, there seems to be some truth in your words" (877-78), and Pedro Crespo replies, "Yes, I swear to God, and I've always been right." So an exchange of remarks begins in which Crespo strongly attempts to assert his independent point of view. This altercation ends the first act. In the second, the confrontation between the two characters develops into a crescendo in the famous garden scene. The proud farmer has ordered a meal for his illustrious guest. During the dinner, Don Lope suddenly swears because his wounded leg disturbs him: "Goddam it, it is killing me." Crespo answers: "Goddam it, I am sorry for you." The villager feels compelled to swear also since Don Lope's exclamation has breached the customary protocol. Calderón reveals the parallel and opposite idiosyncrasies of these two dramatic figures through these parallelistic dialogues.

The anaphora is frequently found in the verses of this play.[15] One of the best examples of this type of repetition is the declaration of Don Alvaro's passion for Isabel in act 2. The captain of the soldiers stationed in Zalamea introduces his thoughts with the reiteration "within a day/in a day. . . ." [16]

> Within a day the sun sheds light
> and fades away; kingdoms fall and rise
> within a day. In one day,
> the proudest building lies in ruin;
> in a day a losing battle's won.
> A ocean storms and stills within a day;
> in a day a man is born and dies.   (lines 969–78)

> And so, having come to know within
> one day an age of love's torment,
> why may it not still grant me time
> to know its bliss?   (lines 987–92)

The anaphoras create an atmosphere of intensity in a progressive graduation of Don Alvaro's emotions, illustrated by correlative images that serve to ornament his expression.

Calderón manifests his ingegnosità with numerous symmetrical repetitions. He uses anadiplosis, epanadiplosis and epiphoras, and also reduplications, among which the epimone has particular emphasis. These exercises of parallel arrangement have a conative function: they spotlight a particular idea on the mind of the spectator. All these devices constitute an evident display of Calderón's dramatic craftsmanship. However, the contemporary reader may prefer repetition when it is not limited to a rigid pattern. The effect is more striking in a free form. One of the most famous speeches in The Mayor of Zalamea occurs in act 3. The newly elected administrator to the Town Hall, Pedro Crespo, has implored Don Alvaro to marry his daughter whom Alvaro has abducted and raped. Don Alvaro responds disdainfully, saying he will answer only to a military court and that he and his soldiers should be dealt with respect. Crespo then orders his men to place the offender in prison and replies with these words:

> Right you are! I heartily agree;
> take him to his cell, with due respect.
> Then, with due respect, shackle him.
> With due respect, see to it
> he does not communicate
> with any of the soldiers.
> Then put the other two in jail
> as well, and, as it befits their case,
> keep them duly separated,

so that afterwards, with due respect,
they may each of them submit
their sworn depositions
whereupon if any two of them
evidence their culpability,
by God, I'll hang them one and all
at once—with due respect. [17]   (lines 2362-77)

The repeated expression contains a multiple purpose. It attempts to awaken the public's indignation, to show appreciation for the strength of Crespo's character, and to convey a feeling of satisfaction for revenge after having witnessed the arrogance of the captain.

With these examples it becomes obvious that Calderón used redundance for specific functions and stylistic reasons, bestowing distinction, splendor and poignancy to his verse.

The final linguistic convention to be considered in this essay is the use of dialectal vocabulary in the dialogue. This prerogative is given to the comic character. The gentleman and the lady were well versed in the socialities of language spoken in court, and they even took the liberty of playing with words, demonstrating their ingegnosità. On the other hand, the gracioso [18] could be a country bumpkin who speaks in Sayagués, or a morisco who converses in a regional jargon. He, then, does not enunciate properly, confuses words, and fails to impart the correct form of the signifiers. His dialect is an expression of his subculture, something looked down upon with mirth. Low motivation and primitive desires could give a particular tone to his enunciation. The mistakes in his pronunciation have been carefully planted to produce a comical reaction. A consideration of these strategies, which have aimed to arouse psychological impressions in the audience, gives pertinent insights into the language of the Spanish drama of the seventeenth century.

The humorous dialogues also have an aesthetic function. With them the author is able to establish an emotional balance with respect to the serious dramatic scenes. The sequence of events alternate between two planes, one serious and the other comic. This variation in tone and mood generates relief for the spectator when he sees the participation of the gracioso. It prepares him for feeling more deeply the dramatic effect of the next scene. The interplay also has been designated as a technique of chiaroscuro. [19] The name is descriptive. It refers, as has been pointed out, to the distribution of light and color. In a painting, light brings a direct perception of a section, while the dark color provokes an impression of depth. Similarly, in a play, the two planes, serious-comic, allow the author to convey the main aspects of his plot with more power and effect through contrasts and dual presentation.

Sayagués was the name applied to a colloquial form spoken in Sayago in the southwestern part of the province of Zamora, which is located in northwest Spain. [20] Later it was also used to refer to charro, a dialect spoken in the province of Salamanca. In the early Renaissance theater, the comic characters babbled in Sayagués to provide an element of distinctive humor. Their jargon stressed the rudimentary education of these persons and their laughable naivete. The public enjoyed seeing these stock characters. Lope de Vega and his school of playwrights wrote dialogues in Sayagués to portray uncouth villagers in general. The play Fuente Ovejuna by Lope is a good example. The stock character vacillates in the pronunciation of vowels. He says dimuño instead of demonio, quistion instead of cuestión, polidos for pulidos, soceso for suceso and so forth. He uses aphaeresis of the initial "A" (cademia for academia). A similar lack of security is observed in the pronunciation of the consonants. He goes into rhotacism, as in brando for blando. He replaces the "f" with an aspirated "h" (he for fe, huego for fuego; ahuera for afuera). He reduces the consonantic group "str" into "s" as in nueso for nuestro. The group "ni" is palatalized (dimuño for demonio). The command form is apocopated and he says entrá, mostrá, echá in lieu of entrad, mostrad, and echad. He resorts to rustic expressions such as voto a tal, tirte ahuera (get away), arre (giddap), a he, por Dios, pardiez, soncas (in truth), emberrincho (to be crossed), respingo (sign of disapproval), pringar (to have a bad time). These examples provide a glimpse of the linguistic richness of the Sayagués dialect.[21]

Calderón limits the use of Sayagués in his plays. Even in works where the action takes place in a rustic milieu, the playwright prefers to employ the standard and conventionals Spanish for his personae. However, some traits of Sayagués are placed in specific scenes to depict the comic characters. In these instances, a tendency to present buffoonish couples is apparent, such as Paulín and Locía in The Purgatory of St. Patrick, Gil and Menga in The Devotion to the Cross, Perote and Gileta in The Lady and the Maid, and Benito and Gila in The Last Duel in Spain. Calderón then resorts to using light touches in Sayagués to conform with the dramatic convention already established. The play The Devotion to the Cross has some good examples for our consideration.[22] Gil and Menga have the roles of graciosos and they speak several Sayagués words to illustrate their humorous parts in the play: dó for donde, ¡ho! arre (from the Arabic harr'giddap'). They use "r" instead of other consonants (an example of rhotacism as in diabro for diablo) and typically confuse their use of vowels (mijor for mejor etc.) These expressions are spoken in the starting scene when the two villagers have watched their donkey fall into a muddy ditch from which it does not want to move.

Gil, in another scene, returns to an apocopated form diz for dice and an archasim, plegue for plazca (I hope). He also mispronounces the word bandolero (bandit) by uttering buñolero, mixing his words with buñuelo (doughnut), which is very much on his mind, since the graciosos are always hungry. Gil also uses slang common to rowdy characters, as in soy de la carda, which can be translated as "this is my gang."

In the same manner that the Christian gentleman had his alter ego in the _gracioso_ the Morisco gentleman has his counterpart in the rustic Morisco. A prime example is Alcuzcuz, the Morisco servant who appears in Love after Death (ca. 1635) and The Great Prince of Fez (1669). His antecedents may be traced to the Moorish _comedias_ by Lope de Vega and Luis Vélez de Guevara.

Calderón carefully elaborated the dialectial speech pattern of the Moorish _gracioso_. Alcuzcuz, who bears the name of a Moorish dish and who is another hungry stock character, also carries traits typical of his role. He is a coward. He enjoys drinking. He lies when it is convenient and he has no sense of responsibility. But what makes him different from other comic figures are his Moorish customs and his Morisco dialect. One can observe abundant linguistic forms related to phonetics, morphology, syntax and lexicon in the two plays cited. There is a certain discriminatory strategy in the use of the Morisco dialect, which ridicules those who had not become assimilated into the Castilian culture.

As an illustration of Calderón's technique, consider the Morisco dialect of Alcuzcuz in the play Love after Death.[23] His speech contains several types of phonetic changes: vocalic vacillation (_proceto_ for _precepto_, _Alpujarro_ and _Alpojarra_ for _Alpujarra_, _crestiano_ for _cristiano_, _hoyendo_ for _huyendo_, _Gavio_ for _Gavia_, _voneno_ for _veneno_, _venagre_ for _vinagre_, _Altuza_ for _Alteza_, _excosar_ for _excusar_, etc.). The tonic, or accented, open "os" and "es" do not diphthongize (_portas_ for _puertas_, _nostra_ for _nuestra_, _bonas_ for _buenas_, _revente_ for _reviente_). The conjunction "y" is used in its archaic form of "e". There are cases of the loss of the initial vowel by aphaeresis (_casión_ for _ocasión_). The Moorish people found it hard to pronounce the voiceless dorso-alveolar sibilant "s"; consequently they changed its point of articulation so that it became a prepalatal "s" (_xanior_ for _señor_, _xastre_ for _sastre_). Instead of applying the palatals, "ñ" and "ll" they resorted to the forms "ni" and "li" (_astilias_ for _astillas_, espanolilio for _espaniolillo_, _lievarla_ for _llevarla_, _haliar_ for _haller_, _cristianilio_ for _cristianillo_, _caliar_ for _callar_, _senior_ for _señor_, _caniones_ for _cañones_). In addition, the liquids "l" and "r" are interchanged (_sel_ for _ser_).

Morphological changes and omissions are reflected in the speech patterns of _gracioso_ Alcuzcuz, who at times either excludes the definite article or uses it incorrectly (_el postas_ for _las postas_, _el leña_ for _la leña_, _el nuez_ for _la nuez_, _el cautela_ for _la cautela_, _el vida_ for _la vida_, _el yegua_ for _la yegua_, _el horas_ for _las horas_, _el lengua_ for _la lengua_, _el peor parte_ for _la peor parte_). One can notice examples of incorrect agreement between the adjective and pronoun and the noun (_malo es esta_ for _mala es esta_) and also between the pronoun subject and the verb (_me pensar_ for _yo pienso_, _me ser crestiano_ for _yo soy cristiano_). The practice of using the infinitive instead of the flexible forms in the case of the verb simplifies the conjugation to a minimum. One is not surprised to learn that Alcuzcuz, with very few exceptions, does not voice the subjunctive mood.

The reader may enjoy a translation of the galimatias spoken by Alcuzcuz. In this scene he has been asked to care for his master's horse. Alcuzcuz is sleeping and so in order to stay awake he talks to himself. The horse frees herself and Alcuzcuz considers his fate of being punished by death for misdemeanor and therefore decides to drink poison.

> Since it's fatal I must perish,
> Alcuzcuz, I better choose
> mode of death. Me to die by poison
> because the easiest be; then to be so
> since I don't like life anymore.
> Much better to perish this way;
> since I will not die uglily
> bathed and smeared all over with blood. (He drinks)
> How still I be feeling? Why, I am all right:
> the poison not to be strong:
> then if I have to die,
> more venom take, a good deal more.[24]

Alcuzcuz, of course, is drinking from a bottle of wine and proceeds to get very drunk.

The linguistic virtuosity of the Golden Age dramatists has endowed us with a literature based on the aesthetic usage of words; words that give a message and pleasure to the receptor, not only from what is said, but from the way in which it was said. As August Wilhelm von Schlegel repeated "Literature is the immortality of speech." The seventeenth-century dramatists have preserved for us the language of years gone by, the trophies of the past, and the armory of the human mind. The three linguistic inquiries presented in this paper represent a novel synthesis of the findings of linguistic methodology applied to literature.

NOTES

1. Robert Di Pietro, Language as Human Creation (Washington, D.C.: Georgetown University Press, 1976), p. 13.
2. Roman Jacobson, "Linguistique et pioétique," Essais de linguistique général (Paris: Minuit, 1963).
3. Wilhelm von Humboldt, Oeuvres Complètes (Berlin, 1907), 6:23.
4. Piere Guiraud, La sémiologie (Paris: Presses Universitaires de France, 1971), ch. 1.
5. E. Souriau, Les 200 000 situations dramatiques (Paris, 1950).
6. Pico della Mirandola, "Conclusiones paradoxe numero LXXI, 13," Conclusiones (Rome, 1486).
7. Table 1 for some of the mathematical signs used in this paper.
8. The following are very useful: Diego Marín, Uso y función de la versificación dramática en Lope de Vega (Valencia:

Castalia, 1962), and Vern G. Williamsen, "The Structural Function of Polymetry in the Spanish Comedia," in Perspectivas de la Comedia (Valencia: Estudios de Hispanófila, 1978).

9. See Lope de Vega, El arte nuevo de hacer comedias en este tiempo, ed. Juana de Prades (Madrid: Clásicos Hispánicos, C.S.I.C., 1971), pp. 192-204.

10. For this point see Marjorie Boulton, "The use of Repetition," in her The Anatomy of Poetry (London: Routledge and Kegan Paul, 1953).

11. John V. Bryans, Calderón de la Barca: Imagery, Rhetoric and Drama (London: Tamesis, 1977).

12. John Leonard Hancock, Studies in Stichomythia (Chicago: University of Chicago Press, 1917).

13. A useful study of this topic is Gustavo Correa, "El doble aspecto de la honra en el teatro del siglo XVII," Hispanic Review 26 (1958):99-107.

14. The English translation has been written by the poet Edwin Honig, Calderón 4 Plays (New York: Hill and Wang, 1961).

15. "La anáphora consiste in la repetición de una parte de la oración al comienzo de grupos de palabras sucesivos." Heinrich Lousberg, Elemente der literarischen Rhetorik (Munich: Max Hueber Verlag, 1963). Translated by Mariano Marín (Madrid: Gredos, 1972), p. 131.

16. I have accepted Professor Honig's translation for this passage, although it should be noted that the anaphora is consistently "en un día" in the original. The numerated lines correspond to the original in Spanish of my edition (Madrid: Cátedra, 1977).

17. Honig, Calderón 4 Plays.

18. For a discussion on the gracioso see Charles D. Ley, El gracioso en el teatro de la península (Madrid: Revista de Occidente, 1954).

19. For the concept of chiaroscuro see Helmut Hatzfeld, Estudios sobre el barroco (Madrid: Gredos, 1966), p. 286.

20. John Lihani, "A Literary Jargon of Early Spanish Drama: The Sayagués Dialect," in Linguistic Approaches to the Romance Lexicon, ed. Frank H. Nuessel, Jr. (Washington, D.C.: Georgetown University Press, 1978).

21. Lope de Vega, Fuente Ovejuna, ed. Francisco López Estrada (Madrid: Castalia, 1969). Also, for a glossary on Sayagués see John Lihani, El lenguaje de Lucas Fernandez (Bogotá: Instituto Caro y Cuervo, 1973).

22. Calderón de la Barca, La devoción de la cruz, ed. Sidney F. Wexler (Madrid: Anaya, 1966).

23. The first edition of this play appeared under the title of El Tuzani de las Alpujarras in the collection Quinta Parte de Comedias de Don Pedro Calderón de la Barca by Antonio Francisco de Zafra (Madrid, 1677). This is the text followed for this paper.

24. In rendering this English translation, I have tried to retain the awkwardness of the original Arabic-influenced Spanish.

6. School Foreign-Language Programs: Reaching toward the Twenty-first Century

LORRAINE A. STRASHEIM
Indiana University

Where Are We?

The pessimists among us—and even some of the realists—have to be wondering today, not about what kinds of foreign-language programs there will be in the schools of the twenty-first century, but whether there will be foreign languages at all in the schools then, because the troubles in foreign-language education in the schools are far more complex than the oft-cited enrollment declines. The bleak catalog includes a myriad of separate yet interrelated problems:

1. Only 15 percent of the total national student population is currently studying foreign languages, which causes extreme difficulties in justifying the staff and program costs.

2. The attrition rates between the first and second years of study in the high school and levels one and two in the lower schools have reached such heights that over half of those who begin foreign-language studies never reach the second stage.

3. Total school populations are declining, with the declines presently centered in the elementary and middle schools.

4. Faculties are being reduced and schools are being closed.

5. The vast majority of teachers are "tenured in"—licensed for life—and are without incentives to retrain or change their practices.

6. The enormous attrition rates between levels one and two and the overall decline in enrollments have forced ever-increasing numbers of schools to offer two or more years of a foreign language in a single class period in a phenomenon known as the "multilevel" or "combined" class.

7. Budget "crunches" and taxpayers' demands for spending "lids" have become commonplace.

8. Over half of the foreign-language teachers in the schools are burdened with multiple daily preparations in two or more subject-matter areas in the curriculum.

Despite these enormous challenges, however, to those optimists and even some realists not ready to yield to despair, it seems that if we but "transform" his verb tenses (an ancient and revered foreign-language practice), Charles Dickens's opening line to A Tale of Two Cities becomes the most appropriate description of

73

foreign languages in the schools today: "It is the best of times, it is the worst of times."

Those teachers who despair today are guilty of what Marshall McLuhan has dubbed "rear-view mirrorism"; they yearn for the halcyon days of NDEA, conveniently forgetting what the sixties were really like. These colleagues persist in perceiving global interdependence as a phenomenon predicted for some point in the mists of the future. They read but do not heed George W. Bonham.

America's young people face a set of new national and international circumstances for which they have only the faintest of notions. Globally speaking, they are blind, deaf, and dumb; and thus handicapped, they will soon determine the future directions of this nation. This country has developed mass communications and universal education to a point unprecedented in human affairs. We are, in many ways, the most informed nation of citizens, and yet we continue to live in a fool's paradise in believing that this is still the American Century, and that it is here to stay (Bonham 1979).

Only some kind of educational paralysis could ever delude us into believing that we can educate leaders and citizens for the twenty-five century by restoring the sixties, despite what some of us told the President's Commission on Foreign Language and International Studies in 1979.

The emergence of global education in the schools, under the leadership of the social studies, ought to fire every foreign-language teacher with renewed vigor, revitalized enthusiasm, and a real taste for activist involvement. As Robert Leestma has said, "Global education is a challenge that has the potential to rival Sputnik in re-invigorating American education with a sense of mission. Taken as a whole, it offers the closest thing in education to a moral equivalent of war. The concerns involved convey the full complexity and fascination of world reality as well as the imperative element of survival" (1979).

"The Future," C. S. Lewis said, "is something which everyone reaches at the rate of sixty minutes an hour, whatever he does, whoever he is" (The Screwtape Letters, 1942). It is for this reason that everyone of us has a personal stake in global interdependence and global education above and beyond our professional interests—as the present and future inhabitants of "Spaceship Earth."

The key to whether this is the best or worst of times—the key to the twenty-first century—lies, to a very great extent, in how we choose to use the present and the immediate future this decade.

How can we use the next ten years?

This decade will call upon us to use all of our skills in learning as well as in teaching. Leestma's challenge is clear.

Every teacher, journalist, and broadcaster, every leader in community, business, or government—indeed every student and every adult citizen—is a prospective Founding Father for the future. Among other competencies and sensitivities, each person needs to develop:

1. Some basic cross-cultural understanding, empathy, and ability to communicate with people from different cultures;

2. A sense of why and how mankind shares a common future—global issues and their dynamics and the calculus of interdependence;

3. A sense of stewardship in one's use of the earth and acceptance of the ethic of intergenerational responsibility for the well-being or fair chance of those who will come after us (Leestma 1979).

Responding to this challenge will demand interdisciplinary and even multidisciplinary cooperation and interaction, not only with all the other subject-matter areas represented in the curricula of the schools but among the languages.

Global education cannot be a monolingual offering in English, nor can it be a Western European bilingual offering. Can we now use that solidarity we tried to develop in addressing the President's Commission for some really professional purposes? Can we, for example, finally promote all foreign languages and not just French, German, and Spanish? Can we encourage and foster the entrance of Chinese, Japanese, Russian, the African languages, Portuguese, the Arabic languages—any and every language—into the curricula of our schools? In 1969, John H. Lawson, the superintendent of schools in Shaker Heights, Ohio, advised a symposium of school administrators and foreign-language teachers:

> Our course offerings must become more inclusive. Many school districts and other groups of communities must find new ways in which they can share human and financial resources. Higher levels of instruction in Western languages can be offered by cooperative efforts between public and independent school districts (1971).

Can we give up our belief that a foreign-language program must consist of separate classes for each level, each wholly teacher-led, each meeting five times a week? Can we give up our "territorial" definition of foreign-language teaching as a room in a school? Can we learn to think of every student in any language, be it Italian, Portuguese, Japanese, Swahili, or German, as one of "ours"? Can we devise foreign-language offerings that, as Neil Simon says on the Celebrity Tapes, "give your mind a change to travel" and that are, as I called for almost ten years ago to the day, "apprenticeships" to a society or a national community and worth of a student's "employment"? (Strasheim 1971)

Can we do these things? We can if we but will. The state of Michigan is concentrating its efforts on a developing global education in its schools as an "umbrella philosophy," that encompasses multidisciplinary cooperation and implementation. Indiana University is initiating plans for certifying middle, junior high, and high school teachers in the so-called less commonly taught languages.   Two school systems in Indiana are exploring the possibilities of adding Chinese to their curriculum as a complement and/or an outgrowth of their world culture courses.

But the new world demands more than an expansion and/or a realignment of the languages offered. Bonham, for example, calls for a "renaissance," and recommends that foreign-language "teachers should analyze the uses to which most students will put their foreign language knowledge and teach them accordingly." He warns us that the goal is "to turn out a generation of culture-aware Americans, not an army of philologists" (1979). In that regard, we need materials in both the commonly and less commonly taught languages that both fit the teaching situation and capitalize upon what we have learned in the seventies, the decade of education "innovative overchoice." These "teachable" materials should:

1. Be built around minimal learning outcomes defined for each level or state;

2. Provide a balance of skill-getting and skill-using learning activities;

3. Move much of the linguistic content "backward" into the advanced courses and much of the cultural content "forward" into the earlier levels or states;

4. Be one-third to one-half the present textbook size to make mastery possible in the instructional time available;

5. Build in self-instructional or individualized components for greater utility in multilevel classes; and

6. Include teachers' manuals complete with strategies for adapting the teaching materials to the multilevel class situation.

Textbooks and teaching materials, like teacher training in the languages, should be designed to fit the realities of the teaching world and not from the standpoint of an ideal that has never existed. We must stop focusing on what a language "major" should know and begin, at long last, to concentrate on preparing the teacher by giving him or her the language skills s/he is called upon to use and by training him or her for the classroom situations in which s/he will be called upon to use them. Teachers are not badly prepared today; they are simply not prepared for the language uses necessary today in our schools. And no matter what the professional literature says, make no mistake about it: whatever the evils, elementary schools offer the most creative and effective education in the country today and the quality of the teaching is lowered with each successive "higher" level.   One of the greatest adjustments education has to make as we are "dragged" into the future is that one cannot build from the top down, from graduate school down to kindergarten; we have to begin on the ground and build upward. And each successive level should be built on the one that precedes it, rather than by a "prescribing downward"; the second-grade teacher should be told by the first-grade teacher what the incoming students have done and can do before planning his or her year, the college teacher should be told by the high school teacher what language students have done and can do before decreeing what the entry-level courses will be. We must stop defining what student "should be"; for what we need to know is where they are.

As the popular dorm poster says, "When life gives you lemons make lemonade." Since multilevel classes and multiple daily preparations will not be eliminated in the forseeable future—certainly not in view of the realities of declining student populations and school funding—let us prepare programs, materials, and teachers for the world that is. We can help, not by struggling futilely to schedule separate classes for six or eight students, but by lobbying with professional organizations and teachers' unions to fight for more inschool preparation time, perhaps one preparation period for every three daily preparations, counting each segment of the multilevel class as a separate entity.

The less commonly taught languages are doomed to fail in the curricula of the schools, as are the common taught languages, if they persist in either or both of these expectations:

1. Teachers can be trained in only the language.

Teachers in the schools must be prepared to teach in at least two subject-matters in order to be employable. The best second discipline courses are those required—the social studies, mathematics, and English.

2. Separate classes for each level must exist.

Taxpayers have demanded minimal class sizes, often with fifteen to twenty students, meaning that programs with low enrollments (fifteen in first-year Latin, for example) are doomed to extinction unless those "selling" the program both publicize and plan the instruction for the multilevel offering.

These are the "givens." The realities are hard to accept, but it is well past the time for us to follow Sylvia Ashton-Warner's advice to "waste the old ideas."

We do not waste enough in school. We hoard our old ideas on charts to be used again and again like an old rag. Ideas are never the same again, even those of the masters—even if the only change is in our own mood of approach. Yet there is never a shortage of ideas if the stimulus is there. Waste the old paper and waste the old pictures—it is tidier and simpler (Ashton-Warner 1964).

We have to devise programs that will fit the school, the community, and the students; we must accept programs with varied scheduling patterns and varied approaches. In developing the criteria for the establishment and the maintenance of a program, we must consider what the school's resources—fiscal, staff, and student—can support.

We should, obviously, be trying to recruit some career teachers into the study of the less commonly taught languages. These are some of the finest people we can identify to launch and maintain a program; they know what works in the classroom and how to operate the administrative power structure. Some programs staffed by people without this kind of expertise will succeed, but Russian, for example, usually has not succeeded because the teachers either were unfamiliar with the age group or the inner workings of the school.

Whether the programs of the twenty-five century will be rare, "spotty" successes or whether they will grow rampantly depends on the extent to which we can adjust to the realities of the school and the extent to which we can "waste the old ideas." It should not be possible to say of us as a profession what Thomas Babington, Lord Macaulay, said of Dryden: "His imagination resembled the wings of an ostrich. It enabled him to run, though not to soar" (On John Dryden, 1828).

The futurists say that education has about ten years to prepare for the changed and ever-changing life that has become the pattern. What is clear about the immediate future of foreign languages in the schools is that:

1.   Any plan for the future of foreign languages must capitalize on the knowledge that the profession already has, especially that gained in the past decade of innovation and experimentation;

2.   Revitalized ways of inservice training and staff development must be found to address and motivate a teacher population that is, by and large, tenured and certified for life;

3.   Thinking must go beyond the commonly taught European languages to languages not historically part of foreign-language curricula in the schools, such as Chinese, Japanese, Russian, Arabic, and some of the African languages; and

4.   There must be continuing, ongoing efforts in research, in evaluation, and in assessment.

We have the wherewithal to face the ambiguities of our lives, present and future. Most of us are making valiant efforts to adjust to a life of working hypotheses rather than solutions or final answers. Some of us believed in the early seventies that we could never develop the flexibility required, but we are coping. It is as Samuel Clemens/Mark Twain pointed out: "A round man cannot be expected to fit in a square hole right away. He must have time to modify his shape" (More Tramps Abroad, 1897).

"Seeds of the future can be seen in emerging and planning programs. What do they bode for the twenty-first century? What programs are reaching toward the twenty-first century?

Whenever anyone attempts to project the future, s/he is assuming the "catbird" seat. Before defending the status quo to the death, the immediately defensive reactor should recall George Santayana's contention, "Fanaticism consists of redoubling your efforts when you have forgotten your aim" (The Life of Reason, 1:1905-6). The other point to keep in mind is that most of these programs exist, some in experimental stages, some in planning stages; overriding each are the realities of schools today.

A model, "Foreign-Language Programs: Reaching toward the Twenty-First Century," has been provided (see Figure 1). The model is designed to accommodate a variety of school and student-

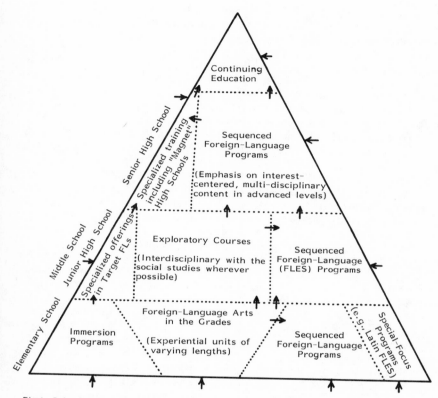

Fig. I School Foreign-Language Programs: Reaching toward the 21st Century

Key: ➔ = Entry

population needs as well as providing for flexibility and change. The general characteristics of the model as a whole are:

1. Language learning, in keeping with the futurists and the proponents of lifelong learning, is defined as a process to be engaged in at any stage of life and to a depth commensurate with the needs and interests of the learner.

2. Learner entry and/or reentry is possible at every stage of the model. The learner may also move laterally within a level as well as progress vertically through a sequence.

3. In keeping with the principles of local control, schools, communities and teachers retain options in the development of school-specific programs and offerings.

4. The model will accommodate changed priorities among the commonly taught languages—French, German, Latin, and Spanish—with other languages added or replacing them in a school

curriculum. The twenty-first century should see the curriculum offering Chinese, Japanese, Russian, Arabic, and some African languages, with provision, where appropriate, for the independent or individualized study of ethnic languages.

5. The model is built on the premise that the movement in foreign-language education, beginning in the early eighties, will be to deemphasize the development of skills in order to facilitate travel and will be toward the preparation of Americans with global perspectives, cross-cultural awareness, and second-language skills appropriate to life and work in the world community.

To earn—and hold—a place in the curricula of the twenty-first century education, foreign-language teaching has to be tailored to become the means toward learners' ends, rather than considering the acquisition of a second (or third) language as an end in itself. Options, the real contribution of the period of experimentation and innovation of 1965 to 1979 will be open to school corporations and to communities. They will be asked to examine, select, approve or disapprove from a range of possibilities rather than to vote positively or negatively on a single kind of program offering.

On the elementary level, the options are varied. No longer is the choice between no program at all or adopting a FLES (Foreign Language in the Elementary School) as the first stage in an extended sequence. The possibilities are these:

1. Immersion programs in which the second language is the medium of instruction, beginning with all instruction in the target language in kindergarten and diminishing to 50 to 60 percent in the second language by grade six. Cincinnati and Milwaukee, among other school systems, are working with immersion programs.

2. Standard FLES programs in which the elementary classes, often grades three or four through six, constitute the first stage (level one) in the system's sequence of foreign-language offerings. This is the best-known type of elementary offering and is usually built on mastery and skills objectives.

3. Special Focus programs in which the emphasis is on the second language as a vehicle for improving other skills of the students. The most familiar form of this type of program is the Latin FLES implemented in the Philadelphia, Indianapolis, and Los Angeles schools and designed to improve the pupils' reading and vocabulary skills in English and to develop cross-cultural awareness.

4. Foreign-Language Arts or Foreign Language Arts in the Grades (FLAG) offerings consist of occasional short-term units to be incorporated into the elementary language arts learnings. This new option offers foreign-language experiences to the widest possible audiences. The Indianapolis State Department of Public Instruction currently is developing such units to be piloted in the primary grades, kindergarten through grade three. The materials will be designed to be used by the classroom teacher horizontally as contrastive linguistic or cultural lessons or vertically as a single-language experience.

Elementary school immersion programs, for obvious economic, social, and political reasons and despite their worthy efforts to create a pseudo-natural environment for the acqusition of a second language, will probably never become the dominant form of elementary school foreign language. The standard FLES program, too, as the first stage of an extended sequence, will continue to occur only in select and random school systems because it is the rare child who is ready to commit himself or herself to a six- or nine-year course of study. The special-focus programs, like Latin FLES, will also be limited to select and random school districts or even to select schools within a district. The foreign-language arts or FLAG programs appear to be, within the constraints of fiscal and social realities, the only type of elementary approach that can become widespread. This latter approach places its prime emphases on the development of a readiness to learn other languages, the reduction of the inhibitions and fears usually appended to second-language study, the fostering of cross-cultural awareness, and the whetting of interest in studying some language in depth at a later stage. These aspects are closely in tune with the lifelong learning or continuing education thrusts emerging within the construct of education and can only serve to broaden and strengthen interest in the sequential foreign-language program in whatever grade it is initiated. Wisdom says, for a variety of reasons that we need not belabor, that the less commonly taught languages would be well served by a collaboration in the development of foreign-language arts units and materials.

While there are many school corporations across the country that will be able to offer one or more of the elementary foreign-language options, substantially more will find middle school or junior high school offerings more affordable. The options at this level are dependent upon what, if any, elementary foreign-language experiences have been offered, upon community interest and support, upon the size and resources of the district, and upon the attrition patterns from level to level. The following descriptions are of the various components of foreign-language programs as we reach toward the twenty-first century (see Figure 1):

1. Exploratory Programs

These programs, usually self-contained semester or year courses, sometimes required at a grade level, offer students a structured experience in several languages, usually either those taught in the high school or community ethnic languages. The courses are not merely the beginning to level one, but stress instead cross-linguistic and cross-cultural studies, developing a "readiness" to learn a second language, teaching students how to learn language, and giving them bases for the selection or nonselection of a second language to study in depth at a later point in their lives.

2. Sequenced Foreign-Language Programs

The so-called standard sequence is often begun in the middle or junior high school. The sequence, more often than not, begins in grade nine; when it originates earlier, grades seven and eight together often constitute level one.

3. Specialized Course Offerings in the Target Languages

The emergency of immersion programs have resulted in the planning—if not the current implementation—of courses taught in the varied languages. The courses go beyond the "maintenance of skills" courses once discussed, for contemporary planning stresses the language as a vehicle rather than an end. Courses taught in the languages can range from elective home economics and science courses to required offerings in the social studies.

The probable patterns are obvious: more schools will be able to offer only exploratory courses than any other type of pattern, but some schools will opt for only sequenced programs, some for both exploratory and sequenced offerings. Relatively few schools will ever be able to support offerings taught in the target languages, especially should the attrition rates at the end of elementary immersion programs follow the patterns prevailing for the immediate future in the standard programs.

The majority of school systems will continue to find it more possible to offer second languages in the high school rather than at lower levels. Two basic kinds of approaches will be evident.

1. Specialized Training or "Magnet" Schools

These will be schools, by and large, in sizable and comprehensive districts where students can receive in-depth training in one or more specific languages. Students from several high schools in a district, or even from several districts on a contract basis, will attend these schools on a full or part-time basis. These schools in particular will be where the less commonly taught languages will flourish.

2. Sequenced Foreign-Language Programs

Students will still be able to begin language study at this level, but we shall begin to see shifts in content emphases. There will be far more cultural or humanities material and a de-emphasis of the elementary topics of family, house, and food. Advanced levels will be multidisciplinary in content with much more focus on some of the problem-solving approaches utilized in global education.

3. Continuing Education

Schools, especially those in areas not served by nearby colleges or universities, should be alert to the continuing education possibilities in their communities. Conversation courses, courses on the arts, cooking courses, courses of every dimension are possible both in and built around a language and culture.

The seeds of these programs exist, some in beginning implementational stages, some in planning stages. We know enough to do these and much more imaginative programs if we will only unite our efforts and dare some bold new approaches.

Conclusion

Because, as Christopher Morley pointed out, "The enemies of

the future are always the very nicest people" (Kitty Foyle, 1939), the naysayers will persist in "rear-view mirrorism"; for those of sterner stuff, however, those who are convinced, like T. S. Eliot, that "every vital development in language is a development of feeling as well" (Philip Massinger, 1920), the prospects are challenging and exciting. Times like these, "the best of times. . . the worst of times" are, in Pogo's words, "insurmountable opportunities" for people who have mastered the phoneme-grapheme challenges of French, the inflections in Russian and German, or tone languages.

REFERENCES

Ashton-Warner, Sylvia. 1964. Teacher. New York: Bantam Books.
Becker, James M. 173. Education for a global society. Bloomington, Ind.: Phi Delta Kappa Educational Foundation.
Bonham, George W. 1979. Language and global awareness. ADFL Bulletin 10:5.
Hanvey, Robert G. 1975. An attainable global perspective. New York: Center for Global Perspectives.
Lawson, John H. 1971. Should foreign language be eliminated from the curriculum? In Foreign language in a new apprenticeship for living, ed. Lorraine A. Strasheim, pp. 11-12. Bloomington, Ind.: Indiana Language Program, Indiana University.
Leestma, Robert. 1979. Education for a global age: what is involved? Vital Issues, 28:1-7.
McLuhan, Marshall, and Fiore, Quentin. 1968. War and peace in the global village. New York: Bantam Books.
Michigan State Department of Education. 1978. Guidelines for global education. Lansing, Michigan.
Ryder, Frank G. 1976. Some declarations for 1976. ADFL Bulletin 8:33-37.
Shane, Harold G. 1977. Curriculum change toward the twenty-first century. Washington, D.C.: National Education Association.
Simon, Paul. 1978. What the people who know have to say about the importance of foreign languages. Tape recording by the Joint National Committee for Languages and distributed by Richard Klein, Holy Cross College, Worcester, Mass.
Strasheim, Lorraine A., ed. 1971. Foreign language in a new apprenticeship for living. Bloomington, Ind.: Indiana language program, Indiana University.
_____. 1979. The president's commission. Dialog 10:1-18.

Part II: Contributions toward Widening Linguistic Perspectives

7. Color Metaphors in Three Language Phyla

ROGER WESCOTT
Drew University

In this paper, the word <u>color</u> will be used in its broader sense, to refer both to shades, such as black and white, and to hues, such as red and green (Berlin and Kay 1969). The word <u>metaphor</u> will likewise be employed in its broader sense, to mean any figurative rather than literal usage. The word <u>phylum</u>, finally, will be used to designate the most inclusive kind of genetic or genealogical grouping recognized by polygenetic linguists (that is, linguists who do not regard all languages as derived ultimately from a single primordial language).

The colors considered here are roughly those treated by Berlin and Kay in their <u>Basic Color Terms</u> (1969). These authors deal with eleven lexemes, listed here in order of their postulated evolutionary development here as follows:

(1)   black
      white[1]

(2)   red
(3)   green
(4)   yellow[2]
(5)   blue
(6)   brown
(7)   purple
      pink
      orange
      gray[3]

The colors that we shall discuss number only ten (because terms for

---

I am grateful to the following colleagues who provided me with helpful information either orally or by mail: Paul Abolagba, George Bistis, Frank Oluyori, Hyung-Ki Rhee, Tadaaki Shimmyo, all of Drew Univ., Madison, N.J., Panos Bardis, University of Toledo, Toledo, Ohio; Ursula Bellugi, Salk Insitute, La Jolla, Calif.; Paul Friedrich, Univ. of Chicago; Sige-Yuki Kuroda, Univ. of California at San Diego; Adam Makkai, Univ. of Illinois at Chicago Circle; and Barry Mangus, Bronx, N.Y.

orange are not used metaphorically in any of the languages studied here) and occur in a slightly different order, reflecting the frequency of their figurative usage in our sample, as follows:

(1) black
(2) green[4]

(3) white
(4) yellow

(5) red
(6) blue[5]
(7) gray
(8) brown

(9) purple
(10) pink

The metaphors discussed are of four major types, according to whether they relate to (1) emotion, (2) character, (3) nonvisual sensory impressions, or (4) miscellaneous traits. Each of these types is in turn crosscut by three other categories, according to whether the metaphors in questions are (a) members of semantically and lexically paired antitheses, (b) members of semantically but not lexically paired antitheses, or (c) unpaired. An example of (1c), an unpaired metaphor of emotion, would be a color that represents anger. An example of (2a), a fully paired metaphor of character, would be two colors that represent virtue and vice, respectively. And an example of (3b), a semantically but not lexically paired metaphor of synesthesia, would be a color that represents tartness without a logically corresponding color that represents sweetness.

The phyla, families, and languages from which the exemplificatory material in this have been drawn are these:

(I) Indo-European

   (A) Germanic
      (1) English
      (2) Dutch
      (3) German
      (4) Danish
      (5) Norwegian
      (6) Swedish

   (B) Romanic
      (1) French
      (2) Portuguese
      (3) Spanish
      (4) Italian

      (5)   Latin

  (C)   Hellenic
      (1)   Modern Greek
      (2)   Classical Greek

  (D)   Indic
      (1)   Bengali

(II) Ural-Altaic

  (A)   Uralic
      (1)   Hungarian
      (2)   Estonian

  (B)   Turkish
      (1)   Osmanli

  (C)   Korean

  (D)   Japanese

(III) Congo-Kordofanian[6]

  (A)   Kwa
      (1)   Yoruba
      (2)   Edo[7]

  (B)   Bantu
      (1)   Ndembu

The reason for including non-Indo-European languages is, of course, the need to avoid the ethnocentricity involved in dealing solely with European languages that are not only genealogically close to one another but are subject to mutual typological influence as well. To be sure, languages like Hungarian and Osmanli Turkish may exhibit the effects of European linguistic influence, but it is unlikely that Korean or Edo do. (In order to maximize the universality of my sample, I would have liked, ideally, to include some Australian, Oceanian, or American languages. No informants or adequate lexicons for these languages, however, were available to me.)

    Not surprisingly, the color metaphors discussed here are drawn most abundantly from English, next most from continental European languages, less from Asian languages, and least from African languages. Although this seriation partially reflects the writer's cultural background, it also reflects the objective ethnolinguistic fact that the number of color terms in common use is smaller in Africa than in Asia and smaller in Asia than in Europe (Berlin and Kay 1969).

    In a lively and provocative article in a recent issue of

Verbatim, Sterling Eisiminger discusses "basic color terms and their associations . . . in a dozen mostly Indo-European languages." After devoting due attention to Berlin and Kay's thesis that color terminologies generally follow universal evolutionary laws rather than differing arbitrarily from language to language as most anthropologists and linguists previously assumed (Bloomfield 1933), he concludes that "the curious and usually inconsistent color associations in the twelve languages researched . . . are strong indications of linguistic relativism." The surrounding context makes it clear that he sees discrepant metaphors as evidence that each language expresses the idiosyncrasies of the culture of its speakers and that there are no discernible pan-human trends in the figurative use of color terms.

Eisiminger is certainly right that the same color can have quite different metaphorical meanings in different languages and that the same meaning can have quite different color representations in different languages. Thus green, for example, has the metaphorical meaning of infantile in Japanese, sexually aroused in Turkish, fearful in Polish, in debt in Italian, sour in Portuguese, entertaining in Spanish, alert in French, pretentious in Swedish, close by in Norwegian, sleep-inducing in Danish, well-disposed in German, dizzy in Dutch, and jealous in English.[8] Conversely, anger is chromatically represented as black, white, or green in German, as red in Yoruba and Italian, yellow in Polish, blue in Latin, and purple in English.[9]

Judging by these examples above, one would certainly say that there seems to be little carry-over of color metaphor from language to language. In fact, however, metaphoric discrepancies are almost as common within languages as between languages. Some of these intralingual discrepancies, to be sure, can be accounted for by substantial time-lapses, as in the case of the Elizabethan phrase "a blue eye," which today we call "a black eye." But most of them are synchronic, as in the case of "an obvious lie," which, in Japanese, can be either "a white lie" or "a red lie."[10] Moreover, the discrepancies are as common in literally used as in figuratively used color terms. Thus, what we call blue cabbage, the Swedes call brown cabbage.[11] Such discrepancies occur within languages, too, as in the case of dark wine, which, in Italian, can be called either black wine or red wine.[12] Etymology reveals an even greater number of discrepancies in literal color designation, as witness the following Indo-European cognations: Sanskrit syama 'black', Lithuanian syvas 'gray', Russian sinij 'blue', and English hoary 'white'; Russian zelenyj 'green', Irish geal 'white' and English yellow; and Czech modry 'blue', and English madder 'orange-red' (Buck 1949).

Returning to figurative usages, we find, furthermore, that many seemingly discrepant color representations are actually consistent in the sense that they form chromatic series whose intermediate terms link the otherwise contrastive extremes. Examples are: happiness, which is white in Latin, pink in French, and red in Russian;[13] or envy, which is blue in Latin, green in English, and yellow in German.[14]

In many cases, iconicity explains what symbolicity appears to leave paradoxical (Wescott 1975). The fact, for example, that green connotes good health in Latin and French but sickliness in German and Danish may be a matter of environmental context.[15] Although in all cases the green probably refers to the color of organisms, the organisms implied are undoubtedly plants in the case of healthy appearance and animals or human beings in the case of sickly appearance. And, in the few cases where green refers implicitly to vegetation but still has a negative connotation, it seems reasonable to assume that it is the fruits or products of the plants rather than stems or leaves that are referred to. Hence the use of green to mean tart in French or sour in Portuguese.[16]

The same kind of reasoning, I think, goes far to explain the seemingly indefinite number of colors that may be used metaphorically to indicate anger, as we observed above. For, although uninhibited anger does indeed make the skin red from the outward rush of blood (as English, Italian, and Yoruba metaphors suggest), inhibited anger makes it either white from muscular constriction (as a German metaphor suggests) or blue from shallow and underoxygenated breathing (as a Latin metaphor suggests). Anger that is respirationally only semi-inhibited, on the other hand, gives the skin a reddish-blue or purple hue (as an English metaphor suggests). Anger that makes the angered individual feel sick gives the skin a green or yellow tone (as a German metaphor suggests). Angry scowling, finally, puts parts of the face in shadow and so makes the skin look black (as another German metaphor suggests).

There are, furthermore, some apparent universals of color metaphor, even if most of them are negative rather than positive in nature. One of these universals is that, many as are the colors that can stand figuratively for anger, none of these colors are chromatically mixed (in the sense that brown is a mixture of red and green, gray of black and white, and pink of white and red). The presumptive reason for this fact is that anger, unlike boredom, agitation, and other characteristically ambivalent feelings, is felt to be a positive and unique passion, of which a mixed color would be iconically unrepresentative.

Another such universal is the apparent lack of metaphorical colors for such generally recognized virtues as courage, sobriety, and modesty (even though cowardice is represented by white or yellow, drunkenness by black or blue, and pretentiousness by green). While no obvious explanation of this lacuna comes immediately to hand, it does seem clearly related to the general leaning of color metaphors toward pejorative rather than laudatory connotations. This leaning is exemplified by the preponderance of derogation in both semantically unpaired tropes such as ghastly (expressed in Latin by yellow) and semantically paired tropes like sane versus crazy (the first of which is lexically unexpressed but the latter expressed in Danish by black). [17]

Yet another universal of color metaphor is the uniformly negative meaning of yellow as a figure of speech. Yellow is used metaphorically by most of the languages in our sample and has the following meanings:

    (1)   bruised (in Danish and Norwegian)
    (2)   sickly (in classical Greek)
    (3)   fainting (in Bengali)
    (4)   failing (in Korean)
    (5)   insane (in Russian)
    (6)   ghastly (in Latin)
    (7)   angry (in Polish)
    (8)   jealous (in German and Danish)
    (9)   cowardly (in English)
  (10)   treacherous (in French)
  (11)   insincere (in French)
  (12)   sensationalized (in Italian and English)
  (13)   shrill (in Japanese)
  (14)   trivial (in Turkish)
  (15)   inferior (in English) [18]

The reason for this seemingly global veto on yellow as a metaphor of quality is far from clear. The widespread taboo on urine is unconvincing as an explanation, since brown is metaphorically less pejorative despite the even stronger taboo on feces. A more likely explanation, I think, is one that draws on the earlier discussion of green as connoting health when its implied reference is to plants but sickliness when its implied reference is to people. Unlike greenness, yellowness is equally ill-favored in both contexts, suggesting a withered leaf in a horticultural setting and a jaundiced skin in a medical setting. And, in those cases where the pejoration does not refer overtly to physical health, it may be said to refer, by associative extension of meaning, to emotional or moral health.

In terms of our language sample, the qualitative order of metaphorical colors seems to be as follows, reading from most to least favored:

    (1) pink

    (2) purple
    (3) white

    (4) green
    (5) red

    (6) blue
    (7) brown
    (8) gray

(9)   black

(10) yellow

The spaces after pink, white, red, and black are meant to separate the five ordinal categories, which we may call "highly favored," "favored," "mixed," "unfavored," and "highly unfavored," respectively. The reader may have noticed that this sequence is negatively slanted by the greater number of unfavored than of favored colors. In fact, the negative slanting is even greater than appears from the above subgroupings, since pink (in the sense of 'socialistic') may be regarded as derogatory, whereas yellow has no laudatory meanings in any of the fourteen languages here cited: in other words, the derogatory colors tend to be more derogatory than the laudatory colors are laudatory.

The only universal of color metaphor that could be called intuitively obvious (in the sense that many investigators might have assumed it before they verified it) is that black and white are in fact a co-occurrent pair, semantically as well as chromatically polarized. The universal meaning of white, moreover, is 'good', 'virtuous', 'fortunate', and the like, while that of black is 'bad', 'evil', 'unfortunate', and the like. The fact that these meanings are as widespread in Africa as in Eurasia indicates strongly that it is not skin color that is being iconized here but something else. Since light and dark are among the meanings of this pair of colors, my guess is that the positive value placed on white reflects our species' diurnal phylogeny and the negative value placed on black reflects our consequent vulnerability to nocturnal hazards. This surmise is strengthened, I believe, by the fact that chimpanzees schooled in manual sign-languages use the sign for black, with apparent spontaneity, as a trope for 'repulsive' or the like (Linden 1975).

In addition to these global (or at least hemispheric) universals, there are some cross-linguistic peculiarities in the use of color metaphors that might be called local universals. One such is the frequency of the phrasal arrangement X + Y in North Sea languages — which is to say, all of the Germanic languages in our sample except Swedish. Examples are:

(1)   English black and blue 'bruised'
(2)   Dutch green and yellow 'dizzy'
(3)   German green and blue 'bruised'
(4)   Danish yellow and green 'sick' [19]
(5)   Norwegian yellow and blue 'bruised' [20]

The nearest equivalent to this that I can find elsewhere is in Spanish, where a green with two blues means great amusement or entertainment (Eisiminger 1979).

In summary, I find that, despite the great and apparently chaotic diversity of color metaphors in the world's languages, there are broad underlying patterns of predictability in them, both local and global.   Nonetheless, one must admit that some specific locutions can be fitted into these patterns only by rather ingenious semantic rationalization.   Such a locution is German in green, meaning 'repeatedly'.   My guess is that it first referred to foliage and meant initially 'florescent' and then 'abundantly increasing'. More paradoxical is Spanish black (or blackie), meaning 'darling'. Here there are at least two quite disparate lines of plausible semantic development.   One is historical and based on the assumption that when the Iberian powers began to explore Africa and enslave its inhabitants, mariners' concubines were most likely to have been Negroes. The other is synchronic and based on the playful use of disparagement as an expression of teasing affection, such as one encounters in English phrases like "you old rascal" for a close friend or "you little imp" for a favorite child.   Most difficult of all—for me, at least—is Hungarian white-livered, meaning nymphomaniacal.   The only clue that occurs to me is that the chromatically synonymous English compound lily-livered means 'timid' or 'cowardly'.   Here the semantic progression might have begun with 'easily intimidated', shifted to 'sexually compliant', and eventuated in 'erotically insatiable'.[21]

In any case, further exploration of puzzling metaphors like these should be high on the agenda of tropologists and linguists. To aid in this exploration, more historical studies of changes in chromatotropic usage in individual languages seem indicated. To make sure that our Old World sample does not misrepresent the world's languages, some color metaphors from Oceanian and American vernaculars must be included in any analysis that can be termed unquestionably global. No purely analytical survey of color metaphor, however, can be said to give one a full appreciation of the rich color of language art. To experience this color in its fullness, one must actually encounter it in conversation or literature. This point has never been more effectively expressed, I feel, than it was by Goethe when he wrote

> Grau, teurer Freund, ist alle theorie — Doch grün des
> lebens goldner Baum!
> (Gray, my dear friend, is all our theory — But green
> the golden tree of life!)

NOTES

1. According to Berlin and Kay, all languages have both black and white. They refer to languages having only these two colors as Stage 1 (i.e., chromatically minimal) languages.

2. The brace before green and yellow indicates Berlin and Kay's finding that neither color universally precedes the other. Their Stage 3 languages have (in addition to black, white, and

red) either green or yellow. Their Stage 4 languages have both green and yellow.

3. Berlin and Kay's Stage 7 languages have any or all of the four colors purple, pink, orange, and gray in any order. (They do not recognize any stage prior to Stage 1 or subsequent to Stage 7.)

4. The braces linking black with green, white with yellow, and purple with pink indicate that the linked colors occur as metaphors with equal frequency.

5. The space between red and blue here indicates a large gap in frequency between the first five colors, which figure in many metaphorical expressions, and the last five colors, which figure in few.

6. Congo-Kordofanian is Joseph H. Greenberg's revised name for the sub-Saharan African language phylum that he used to call Niger-Congo. Other names for this phylum are Guineo-Bantu and Congoid.

7. Strictly speaking, Edo is, like Chinese, the name not of a language but of a closely related group of separate languages or dialect chains. The specific Edo vernacular from which the color metaphors treated here were drawn used to be called Kukuruku or Ivbiosakon but is now called Aomah.

8. Japanese midori go 'green child' = infant
    Turkisk yesillenmek 'to be green' = to be sexually aroused
    Polish zielony ze strachu 'green with fear'
    Italian essere al verde 'be to the green' = be in debt
    Portuguese estão verdes 'they are green' = they are sour
    Spanish darse un verde 'give oneself a green' = amuse oneself
    French prendre sans vert 'take without green' = catch (someone) napping
    Swedish göra sig grön 'make oneself green' = put on airs
    Norwegian ved min grøne side 'with my green side' = close beside me
    Danish sove paa sit grønne øre 'sleep on one's green ear' = be fast asleep
    German jemandem grün sein 'to someone green be' = be well-disposed toward someone
    Dutch groen en geel voor de ogen 'green and yellow before the eyes' = dizziness
    English green with envy 'envious'

9. German sich schwarz ärgern 'oneself black irritate' = go purple with rage

German jemanden zur Weissglut bringen 'someone to the white
glow bring' = make someone white with anger
German grün und gelb 'green and yellow' = angry
Yoruba oju re kpo 'eye him reddened' = he got angry
Italian vedere rosso 'see red' = experience sudden anger
Polish wylać swa zolcić 'pour out one's yellow' = vent one's
spleen
Latin lividus 'bluish' = hostile
English purple with rage 'discolored with anger'

10. Japanese shirajirashii uso 'white white lie' = a transparent lie;
makka na uso (deep-red-of lie) = a blatant lie

11. Swedish brunkål 'brown cole' = dark cabbage

12. Italian vino nero 'wine black' = dark wine; vino rosso (wine red)
= dark wine

13. Latin candidus 'glowing' = felicitous
French en rose 'in rose' = rosey
Russian krasnij 'red' = gay

14. Latin lividus 'bluish' = envious
German gelb werden vor Neid 'yellow become for envy' = go
green with envy

15. Latin viridis 'green' = vigorous
French verte viellesse 'green age' = lively old age
German grun und blau schlagen 'green and blue strike' = to beat
black and blue
Danish aergre sig gul og grøn 'irritate oneself yellow and green'
= make oneself sick with annoyance

16. French vin vert 'wine green' = tart wine
Portuguese verdes 'green(s)' = sour (grapes)

17. Latin luridus 'yellowish' = horrid
Danish snakke sort 'talk black' = talk nonsense, rave

18. Danish gul og grøn 'yellow and green' = discolored by bruising
Norwegian gul og blå 'yellow and blue' = discolored by bruising
Greek ōkhros 'pale yellow' = sallow
Bengali šarše phul dekha 'yellow color see' = lose consciousness
Korean saksi nolahta 'budding yellow' = doomed to fail
Russian želtyj dom 'yellow house' = insane asylum
Latin luridus 'yellowish' = horrid
Polish wylać swa zolcić 'vent one's yellow' = to rage
German gelb werden vor Neid 'yellow become for envy' = go
green with jealousy

Danish gul og grøn af misundelse 'yellow and green from envy'
   = jaundiced with jealousy
English yellow-bellied 'cowardly'
French un jaune 'a yellow' = a traitor
French ris jaune 'laugh yellow' = forced smile
Italian un giallo 'a yellow' = a mystery novel
English yellow journalism 'lurid tabloid writing'
Japanese kiiroi koe 'yellow voice' = shrill voice
Turkish sarcizmeli 'yellow' = a nobody
English yellow dog 'worthless person'

19. The yellow and green collocation is a favorite in Danish, where
     it can mean bruised, envious, or annoyed.

20. Dutch groen en geel
     German grün und blau
     Danish gul og grøn
     Norwegian gul og blå

21. German dasselbe in grün 'the same in green' = the same thing
       over and over
     Spanish negro, negra, negrito, negrita 'black'; 'blackie' =
       beloved (one)
     Hungarian fehérmáju 'white-livered' = oversexed (of a woman
       only)

REFERENCES

Berlin, Brent, and Kay, Paul. 1969. Basic color terms: their
   universality and evolution. Berkeley, Calif: University of
   California Press.
Bloomfield, Leonard. 1933. Language. New York: Holt, Rinehart
   and Winston.
Buck, Carl D. 1949. A dictionary of selected synonyms in the
   principal Indo-European languages. Chicago: University of
   Chicago Press.
Eisiminger, Sterling. 1979. Colorful language. Verbatim 6:1.
Linden, Eugene. 1975. Apes, men, and language. New York:
   Dutton.
Turner, Victor W. 1967. The forest of symbols (ch. 3, Color
   classification in Ndembu ritual). Ithaca, N.Y.: Cornell
   University Press.
Wescott, Roger W. 1975. Tonal iconicity in Bini color terms.
   African Studies 34:3

Other Sources

Berry, Lester V., and Van Den Bark, Melvin. 1953. The American thesaurus of slang. New York: Crowell.

The compact edition of the Oxford English Dictionary.   1971. Oxford: at the University Press.

Gamez, Tana De. 1973. Simon and Schuster's international English-Spanish, Spanish-English dictionary. New York: Simon and Schuster.

Greenberg, Joseph H. 1963. The languages of Africa. Publication 25. Bloomington, Ind.: Indiana University Research Center.

Lewis, Charlton T., and Short, Charles. 1879/1966. A Latin dictionary. Oxford: Oxford University Press.

Liddell, Henry G., and Scott, Robert. 1940. A Greek-English lexicon. Oxford: Oxford University Press.

Novo Michaelis dicionario illustrado, Inglês-Português, Português-Inglês. 1961. São Paulo: Edições Melhoramentos.

Prick Von Wely, E. P. 1967. Cassell's Dutch-English, English-Dutch dictionary. New York: Funk and Wagnalls.

Ragazzini, Giuseppe. 1967. An Italian dictionary. Chicago: Follett Publishing Co.

Scavenius, H. 1945. McKay's modern Norwegian-English, English-Norwegian dictionary. New York: David McKay Co.

Stanislawski, Jan. 1968. The great English-Polish, Polish-English dictionary. Warsaw: The State Publishing House.

Taylor, Ronald. 1960. A German-English dictionary of idioms. Munich: Max Hueber Verlag.

Wentworth, Harold, and Flexner, Stuart B. 1975. A dictionary of American slang. New York: Crowell.

Wessely's English-Swedish, Swedish-English dictionary. n.d. New York: David McKay Co.

8. Nonverbal Communication in Cross-cultural Perspective

MAX KIRCH
University of Delaware

Culture is made up of a complex of systems, all of which are dependent upon communication. Without communication, every society would come to an immediate standstill. Although language is obviously important, especially for the transmission of information, nonverbal communication is at least as important in social interaction. According to Birdwhistell, "probably not more than 30 to 35 percent of the social meaning of a conversation or an interaction is carried by the words" (Birdwhistell 1970:158). The purpose of this paper is to compare American nonverbal communication with that of other cultures.

Paralanguage is one aspect of nonverbal communication that is close to language because it is based to a great extent on sounds. The difference, however, is that the basic units of sound of language are phonemes, which are rarely meaningful until they are combined into morphemes. Paralinguistic signals, on the other hand, are frequently morphemes without combination and usually express complete messages. The so-called "Bronx cheer" expresses derision. To stop a horse, Americans say "Ho-o-o," Germans "Hu-u-u," Frenchmen "O-o-o," and Spanish "So-o-o." Paralinguistic sounds are often nonphonemic in the language concerned. Several African languages have clicks as part of the regular phonemic system, but clicks, although nonphonemic in English, are part of our paralinguistic system. The alveolar click <u>tsk</u> is used in repetition by Americans for "That's a shame" or to express a moral judgment, whereas the Arabs and Greeks use it for negation. Germans use the alveolar click to call a dog, and Italians may employ the labial click or "kiss" for the same purpose. The glottal stop, which is phonemic in various Indian languages, is part of several paralinguistic utterances in American English: The exclamation <u>Oh? Oh</u>, the negation <u>Uh? Uh</u>, and the warning <u>Ah? Ah</u> (Key 1975:42).

Stress is phonemic at the word level in English, but not usually in French. The normal unemphatic pronunciation of <u>formidable</u> includes a lengthening of the vowel <u>a</u> in the last syllable. The "accent d'insistance" or emphatic accent increases the intensity on the first syllable. Another paralinguistic signal of French is represented by the tendency of many Frenchmen to lower the entire level of pitch of their voices when discussing a matter of importance.

Clapping the hands may be used for applause in America, but it is used to summon the waiter in Spain and the Orient (Rohrich 1967:13). German students drum their feet to applaud a professor and shuffle their feet to express disapproval. The Basuto hiss to applaud, whereas the Japanese hiss to express deference to a superior (La Barre 1947:56). Unfortunately, not enough research has been done on paralanguage across cultures.

Another aspect of nonverbal communication is proxemics, the study of distance. Hall established for Americans four distances corresponding to the various registers of speech described by Joos (Hall 1969:116ff). Latin Americans interact at much closer range. A North American working in Latin America barricades himself behind a huge desk to maintain distance from the Latin, who tries to clamber over the desk to attain the proximity he feels necessary for interaction. Watson tested subjects from various parts of the world to determine (1) how directly they faced each other in personal interaction, (2) how close they were to one another in conversation, (3) touching during interaction, (4) eye contact, and (5) loudness of voice (Watson 1970:74ff). He distinguished by means of the data two different groups: the "low contact" and "high contact" groups. In general, the North Europeans and Far Easterners faced each other less directly, maintained greater distance, touched significantly less, maintained less eye contact and were less loud than the Southern Europeans, Latin Americans, and Arabs. The Northern European subjects were all Germanic: British, Dutch, German, Norwegian, and American. Since the Southern Europeans included the French, the Italians, and Turks, the Latins were all included in the "high contact" group. The variations for individual members of each group were relatively minor.

Since I am fortunate enough to have daily contact with people of different cultures in our department of languages and literature, I undertook an unofficial experiment with my colleagues, informing them of what I had done only after the fact. Engaging each one in conversation on different occasions, I deliberately moved up to about half the proximity usual for Americans. Without exception the Germans immediately backed away. When I revealed to them later the nature of the experiment, each explained that he/she could not help him/herself. The Latins merely beamed more warmly, probably because they felt more comfortable in closer interaction.

Kinesics is the study of all communication by body movement, including gestures, which will be treated separately below. Kinesic movements other than gestures are produced by the subconscious, betraying the true feelings of the sender, even when he is trying to deny them in his verbal message. That we are not completely unaware of such discrepancies is revealed in the words of a song popular many years ago: "Your lips tell me 'No, no' but there's, 'Yes, yes' in your eyes." For the same reason we are frequently reluctant to discuss important matters on the telephone. We prefer a personal meeting, because we want to see whether our partner's body language confirms or refutes his verbal message.

Kinesics includes gaze, gait, posture, and facial movements, among other things. Gaze varies a great deal from culture to culture. When an American walks down the street, he waits until he is within a few feet of someone coming from the opposite direction, briefly glances in his or her face to determine whether it is someone he knows he should greet and, if it is not, immediately glances away. In France, however, men look at strange women on the street longer and more appreciatively. According to Edward Hall, many American women returning from Paris have felt sensually deprived because American men pay them so much less attention (Hall 1969:145). Most Americans believe that they maintain close eye contact in normal conversation, but research indicates that such contact is broken from 25 to 75 percent of the time. The Arab, on the other hand, maintains an intensity of eye contact so great that it causes uneasiness in the average American male. At the opposite end of the spectrum stand certain African cultures in which aversion of gaze is used to show deference to superiors. This attitude also exists in other parts of the world than Africa. Difference in habits of gaze may cause a failure in communication. Howard Fast recounts an anecdote about a Puerto Rican student in a New York high school who was accused by the vice-principal of lying because throughout his interview with her, she kept her gaze averted from his face (Fast 1971:136ff). Only later did a Puerto Rican colleague tell him that in this student's culture an aversion of gaze signaled deference.

The way one walks differs from culture to culture. Most American males swing their arms as if in limitless space when they walk, whereas Frenchmen keep their arms at their sides (Wylie 1977:xii). North Americans think that the Latin American swaggers, whereas the Latin American feels that the North American walk is authoritative (Hall 1977:248). All three groups walk "from the shoulders like bears," as Norman Mailer describes it, in contrast to blacks who walk "from the hips like cats."

Cultures differentiate themselves in sitting, too. Spanish males sit straight up on the base of the spine with legs together when they take part in a formal interaction with a superior, whereas American males usually sit with legs crossed in such situations. In casual or intimate interactions Americans relax by putting their feet on the table, whereas Hispanics sprawl.

American body movements have been investigated more by Birdwhistell than probably any other individual. He believes that body movements are similar to language in that they can be broken down into kinemes and kinemorphs, like phonemes and morphemes (Birdwhistell 1970:101). The cultural ties of kinemorphs are proven by films of the late Fiorello La Guardia, who was equally fluent in English, Italian, and Yiddish. According to Birdwhistell, when viewing the films with no sound, one can easily tell by the body movements which language the Little Flower was speaking.

Gestures differ from other body movements in that they are

more obvious. They are produced and registered more consciously, whereas other kinesic signals are produced largely beneath the level of awareness and are registered in the same way. Gestures often represent a complete communication, especially those that indicate contempt or mockery. They may supplement, complement, or replace verbal messages because they are more consciously controlled by the sender to produce an integrated, consistent communication.

Gestures are probably the most obvious form of nonverbal communication. Darwin thought all gestures had a common biological origin and therefore had universal meaning. Anthropological research seems to show that the same gesture may have different meaning in different cultures. For example, West Europeans and Americans are accustomed to nodding their heads up and down to indicate assent, whereas the Greeks, ever since Homer's day, have used the upward motion for dissent and the downward nod for assent. The Neapolitan upward toss of the head imitates the Greek gesture of negation. Americans stick out their tongues to signal contempt, insult, or mockery. In Polynesia it is used as a form of greeting.

Many of the gestures of Western Europe go all the way back to the ancient Greeks who brought the gestures with them to Southern Italy and, from there, spread them to the North and West. Many of the gestures have two or three different layers of meaning. They are used apotropaically—i.e., to ward off the evil eye, and also to express mockery or contempt, frequently with a sexual message. The meaning is made clear by the context. Examples are the "horns" (Fr. les cornes, Ger. die Hörner, It. le corna, Sp. los cuernos). This gesture, made by extending the index and little finger, while closing the other fingers, may be used to ward off the evil eye or to mock a cuckold. The "fig" (Fr. la figue, Ger. die Feige, It. la mano fica), made by inserting the thumb between the index and middle fingers is employed apotropaically or to show contempt for one's partner in interaction. Another gesture that represents insult with vulgar overtones is the digitus impudicus, publicized not too long ago by the late former vice-president Nelson Rockefeller. Americans make the gesture by pointing the middle finger upward, while clenching the other fingers to the palm held in the horizontal plane. The French point the finger horizontally, away from the speaker. The first historically documented use of this gesture is credited to Diogenes, who is said to have used it against Demosthenes.

Some gestures show more variation from one culture to another. The Italian gesture for "farewell" is made by holding the hand upright, palm facing the gesticulator, fingers moving toward his face, like the American gesture for "Come here." The same gesture, formerly popular in Spain, has been increasingly replaced by a gesture similar to the American gesture: hand raised in front of face, palm outward and moving from side to side in front of the face. The French hold the palm down and move the fingers horizontally as if to speed the departing one on his way (Mitton 1949:143). Knocking on doors also varies. The French and the Germans hold the palm toward the face with fingers clenched, whereas Americans turn the palm toward the door.

Gestures resemble language also in the different keys, levels, registers, or styles with which they are associated. If we think of the five registers Martin Joos described (1962), we rarely find gestures at the frozen or formal levels. Gestures are most often produced in the casual or intimate registers and are more often used by men than women. They are less often used by adults than by children, which is natural, since children rarely use registers of speech other than the intimate or the casual. Some gestures have been almost exclusively relegated to childhood use. One example is sticking out one's tongue. Another is "thumbing the nose" (Fr. faire un pied de nez, Ger. eine lange Nase machen), made by touching the thumb to the end of the nose and extending the fingers toward the other party. A third childish gesture is made by moving the first joint of the right index finger along the left index finger from the knuckle to the tip. The Germans call it Rübchen schaben. American children accompany the gesture with the words "pissmashame" or "sissmashame."

History provides evidence for the connection between gestures and informal styles of interaction. According to La Barre, "French courtiers, before the arrival of the Italian Catherine de Medici, made few gestures and thought them vulgar" (La Barre 1964:204). Obviously gestures were not deemed appropriate for the formal style of interaction of the court. However, Rabelais, who was an older contemporary of Catherine, did not shy away from gestures. The eighteenth chapter of his Pantagruel describes the contest between the Englishman Thaumastos and Panurge, who represents Pantagruel. The Gaul easily bests his Anglo-Saxon opponent. The esprit gaulois of Rabelais obviously characterizes a more informal level of interaction than that of the court.

Gestures are rarely used alone. Frequently they are accompanied by a verbal description. One may say "I'll cross my fingers for you," as he performs the gesture itself. More often one may use the verbalization as a surrogate without performing the gesture at all. In formal registers of interaction the verbalization is more to be expected than the movement. Many people use the words without ever having executed or perceived the gesture. Examples of such verbalizations are, for French: aller la tête levée, s'arracher les cheveux, faire la figue, faire un pied de nez, montrer les dents; for German: durch die Finger sehen, den Daumen halten, den Kopf hängen lassen , Hörner tragen, eine lange Nase machen, die Zahne fletschen, die Faust in der Tasche ballen; for Italian: far le fiche, far le corna, ristringersi nelle spalle; for Spanish: arrancarse los cabellos, mostrar los dientes, encogerse de hombros; for English: turn up one's nose, hold one's head high, tear one's hair, pull a long face, prick up one's ears, keep a stiff upper lip, bare one's teeth, keep one's chin up, and grasp at the wind. An example of a verbal surrogate appeared in the NBC Nightly News television interview of Senator Howard Baker on September 5, 1979, in reference to the Cuban crisis. Senator Baker said: "I think the Russians are thumbing their noses at us."

The different kinds of nonverbal communication have certain similarities to language. The varieties of change evident in language can be perceived in nonverbal communication, too. Over the centuries alterations appear in form or meaning in language. In discussing the digitus impudicus above, I noted variations in form similar to historical change in language. Changes in meaning are illustrated by the evolution of the significance of those gestures that seem originally to have apotropaic or magical meaning. They also had sexual meaning because magic and fertility rites were often related. The use of most of these gestures to express contempt, mockery, or insult today represents a change in meaning. Some of the changes in form and meaning result in geographical differentiation similar to dialect variation in language. In the use of space we also see evidence of geographical variation. Not only do North Europeans belong to the "low-contact group" while South Europeans belong to the "high-contact group", but a similar differentiation is evident in the individual countries. Northern Frenchmen, Germans, and Italians are used to less proximity than their respective southern compatriots.

Variations in keys, levels, registers, or styles are observable in nonverbal communication as well as in language. The use of avoidance of gesture depends on the register of interaction. We automatically choose kinesic signals, too, to fit the key of the interaction. In using space also we tailor the distance to the level of the communicational situation.

Another characteristic that nonverbal communication shares with language is the fact that the signals may have different meanings in different contexts. Birdwhistell points out that individual body movements cannot necessarily be assigned discrete meanings. Their meaning is determined by how they are combined and the situation in which they are used. Gestures likewise may have different meanings in different contexts.

All of these similarities between language and nonverbal signals exist because speech and the "silent language" are both parts of the complex of systems that we call communication.

REFERENCES

Birdwhistell, Ray L. 1970. Kinesics and context. Philadelphia: University of Pennsylvania Press.

Fast, Howard. 1971. Body language. New York: Pocket Books.

Hall, Edward T. 1959. The silent language. Greenwich, Conn.: Fawcett Publications.

_____. 1969. The hidden dimension. Garden City, N.Y.: Doubleday-Anchor.

_____. 1977. Beyond culture. Garden City, N.Y.: Doubleday-Anchor.

Joos, Martin. 1962. The five clocks. New York: Harcourt-Brace.

Key, Mary Ritchie. 1975. Paralanguage and kinesics. Metuchen, N.J.: Scarecrow Press.

La Barre, Weston. 1947. The cultural basis of emotions and gestures. Journal of Personality 16 (1947-48): 49-68.

_____. 1964. Paralinguistics, kinesics and culture anthropology. In Approaches to semiotics, ed. Thomas, Sebeok et al. The Hague/Paris: Mouton.

Poyatos, Fernando. 1975. Cross-cultural study of paralinguistic "alternants" in face-to-face interaction. In the organization of behavior in face-to-face interaction, ed. A. Kendon, R. Harris, and J. M. Key, pp. 285-314. The Hague: Mouton.

Rohrich, Lutz. 1967. Gebarde-metapher-parodie (Wirkendes Wort, Brochure 4). Dusseldorf: Schwann.

Watson, O. Michael. 1970. Proxemic behavior: a cross-cultural study. The Hague/Paris: Mouton.

Wylie, Laurence, and Stafford, Rick. 1977. Beaux gestes. Cambridge, Mass.: Undergraduate Press.

9. Linguistics Looks at Psychiatry: A Study in the Analysis of Discourse

ELAINE CHAIKA
Providence College

Understanding what patients mean as opposed to what they say has been considered vital to psychiatry since Freud. Understanding how people mean on the basis of what they say is the concern of linguistics and philosophers. This difference in orientation yields radical differences in interpreting language. Because psychiatrists, like all of us, respond to people according to what they think those people mean, the differences in interpreting language become an important area of investigation.

Psychiatry traditionally has assumed that schizophrenics know what they are saying and say what they wish, although it must be emphasized that all diagnosed schizophrenics do not do these things, and few do them all of the time. (Chaika 1974a,b; 1977; 1979 discusses the etiology of such productions.) If the schizophrenic produces gibberish such as gao, itivare, fooch, or theykraimz, it is so he or she can express publicly but in concealed fashion forbidden thoughts, or so listeners will be driven away, or so he or she can hold a conversation while disclaiming that any such conversation is taking place (Ferreira 1960; Haley 1963; Laffal 1965; Robertson and Shumsie 1958). If the schizophrenic's phrasing is puzzling and incomprehensible, it is labeled TD (thought disordered), not SD (speech disordered). The therapist's job—indeed, special skill—lies in imaginative interpretation that can uncover disordered thinking or perceptions. There are even those, such as Forrest, Laing, and Szasz, who feel that the occasionally incoherence in schizophrenic speech is a result of high creativity. Szasz (1976:14) insists that schizophrenics are political prisoners who persist in using metaphors unacceptable to their psychiatrists. Forrest (1965; 1976) feels that schizophrenics are poetical. He explains the strange associative character of some schizophrenic speech as a way of affirming "right of choice which exists in thought and language, "of" look[ing] for extra connections in words . . . to firm up the connection between ideas we feel are related" (Forrest 1976:296). That there are normal ways to do all of these things, ways not requiring unusual interpretive measures, is ignored. Generally, psychiatry downplays the public and social nature of language. Rather, language is treated as a private system that each person can and does use pretty much as he or she wishes. Typically, meaning is taken to be holistic, with little or no attempt to justify it on the basis of actual syntax or lexicon used, much less by reference to language use in general. Imaginative exegesis, as in literary analysis, is admired. Forrest (1976:296), for instance, says "all language is metaphor." In order to understand, the psychiatrist needs

> empathy . . . and the familiarity with a wide diversity of human situations . . . to be able to flesh out in his imagination the particular situation the schizophrenic patient is clasping and conveying so clumsily with his cognitive tongs. (Forrest 1976:297)

Here are two examples of psychiatric interpretation of abnormal, typically schizophrenic language use. Harold Searles, one of the most respected modern interpreters of psychotic speech, explains that a patient who addresses envelopes "Father, Daddy, Dad, Sugar Daddy . . ." (running to twenty or thirty titles on an envelope)

> attempts on her part, apparently, to collect together and integrate into one being, all those part-aspects of him (the stern Father, the proud Daddy, the sexually interested, indulgent Sugar Daddy . . .) which she experienced as a collection of different related whole persons. (Searles 1967:125)

Searles frequently considers the schizophrenic's fragmented perception of people as a guide to interpretation.

In the second example, Forrest reinterprets a passage originally offered by the psychologist Brendan Maher (1968):

> Doctor, I have pains in my chest and hope and wonder if my box is broken and heart is beaten for my soul and salvation and heaven, Amen.

Maher interprets this as meaning that the patient, having pains in his chest, is worried that something is wrong with his heart. The chaining at the end is caused by the chance association of "heart and soul." Forrest (1976:296) offers, in his own words, an exegesis of what the schizophrenic really meant. "Doctor, I am heartbroken and hopeless, and I pray you will save me." Forrest continues:

> The listener is told, if he has ears for it, what it is like to be schizophrenic . . . but as no one who is not schizophrenic can fully empathize with this experience, the message is redirected to God's ear.

Linguistics, in contrast to psychiatry, emphasizes the public and social nature of language, the rules and strategies that a speech community share that enable people to understand each other. John

Searle (1975:63, 73) says that one assumes that someone speaking to us is cooperating in the conversation, so that his/her remarks are intended to be relevant. This does not mean that speakers do not lie, do not use language metaphorically, or do not use one utterance to imply something different from what was actually said. Speakers do all of these things, but lying, metaphor, and implicature are all rooted in normal uses of language and the shared conventions of speakers of a particular language. For instance, when someone lies, he or she depends upon the hearer's understanding of the lie to mean what it normally does. That is, the lie does not consist of unusual uses of the words in the utterance. To the contrary, it depends upon a normal reading of the words. If Max says, "I didn't cut the meat with a cleaver" when in fact he did, the lie is not in the negative n't. The lie works only if the hearer interprets n't as the denial it usually is. Lies do not violate language rules. They violate the larger conversational rules, such as Searle's cooperation principle and Gordon and Lakoff's sincerity principle (1975:84). Similarly, the force of a metaphor resides in the hearer's understanding that the central or inherent meaning of a word does not fit the given context; hence, the hearer must take a minor meaning or an associated one (Weinreich 1966; Bickerton 1969; Chaika 1976). Grice (1975:50), Searle (1975:70), and Gordon and Lakoff (1975:87), among others, show that conversational implicature means what it says literally, as well as what it implies. Moreover, what it implies depends upon shared language and social systems (e.g., Austin 1962:26; Ervin-Tripp 1972:245; Phillips 1970). Meaning is not derivable on an ad hoc basis. It must be explicable by reference to regular rules of language comprehension and must be predictable enough so that one can say: In situation S, P can possibly mean or will mean M, but in situation S', P will not mean M (e.g., Labov and Fanshel 1977).

Deviant speech, when interpretable, is understood only if the hearer can match the deviation with the nearest possible rule(s) that would produce an utterance appropriate to the given context (see Clark and Clark 1977:211-15 for synopsis of experimentation on hearer adjustment). Indeed, children as young as two years old are beginning to be able to recognize some sentences as ungrammatical for their language, even though they can understand what is said (Gleitman, Gleitman, and Shipley 1972). Human beings appear to have built-in strategies for dealing with imperfect speech, but these strategies all depend upon the listener's assumption that the speaker is trying to use language as he or she does (Van Dijk 1977:99), even if the speaker falls short of the mark because of imperfect learning, speech impediment, brain damage, or extreme excitement or anger. Thus, "No I see truck" seems to be a negative, so we assume it means "I don't see a/the truck," the nearest grammatical sequence. We do not assume, as some psychiatrists do of schizophrenic speech, that it is a way of explaining an entirely new perception of the matter. Nor do we assume that gibberish, incomprehensible neologizing, or asyntactic word salads proceed

from orneriness or creativity.   One can be ornery or creative in
normal   speech.   Such   deviation,   when   it   appears   in
nonschizophrenics, is evidence of true pathology and should be so
considered in schizophrenics as well.
     The discourse in the Appendix is from a twenty-nine-year-old
diagnosed schizophrenic, Carrie.   The exegesis of it is by Mary
Seeman and Howard Cole, two psychiatrists at the Clark Institute of
Psychiatry.   The samples come from a series of talks Carrie had
with a medical student, John.   These were set up to prove that
"interpersonal intimacy" is threatening to schizophrenics, by showing
that the patient's speech becomes more and more disorganized as
intimacy increases.   They judge passage (c), for instance, as
"inscrutable. She [Carrie] switches topic constantly, talks in riddles
and ambiguities, abondons the rules of grammar so that it is
impossible to know what she is referring to" (Seeman and Cole
1977:289).   Seeman and Cole make no justification for their
judgment of Carrie's speech, nor for their analysis, beyond quoting in
a dozen displaced ways some dicta of Harold Searles (1967), who
says, "Most often, when not easily understandable he [the patient] is
asking 'Do you like me?' " Since they judge passage (c) as not readily
understandable, it then follows that by that whole passage Carrie
means "Do you like me?"   They justify their interpretation of
passage (a) by Searles's (1967:122) contention that "it is the
nonhuman roles which predominate, more than any other, in the life
of the child who eventually develops schizophrenia." Similarly, they
apply Searles (1967:125) to Carrie's comment about the landlady in
passage (b).
     Why Seeman and Cole found these passages inscrutable or
thought that Carrie abandoned the rules of grammar is a puzzle. If
one reads them aloud, supplying pauses and hesitations, they are
perfectly comprehensible.   Meaning is readily derived from the
words and syntax by using ordinary decoding strategies.   That is,
based upon what they know about English, hearers can fill in what
has been left out or delete false starts like "But I do get involved in
. . . with . . . and when someone tells me." Seeman and Cole, to be
sure, do not indicate such pauses.   My supplying them may be
unjustified, especially since one very noticeable feature of deviant
schizophrenic speech is the lack of pausing within sentences
(Rochester, Thurston, Rupp 1977).   However, their experience and
mine is that rapid, pause-free speech, when it occurs, accompanies
associational chains as in the Appendix. Compared to spontaneous
speech at, say, an academic seminar, Carrie's speech, as reported in
Seeman and Cole (1977), is remarkably lucid and well formed.
"Spontaneous speech in the raw can be very raw indeed," write Clark
and Clark (1977:260).   The more difficult the ideas to be encoded,
the rawer the speech, the more false starts, filled and unfilled
pauses, erroneous lexical choices, and assorted slips of the tongue.
If each phrase, so far as it goes, is of normal structure, if each slip
of the tongue is explicable in terms of that structure, and if all is

subordinated to an inferrable topic appropriate to the occasion, then the speech is normal (Chaika 1974a, 1976, 1977; Van Dijk 1977:121, 134.) As evidenced by her frequent use of pause fillers (Goldman-Eisler 1961), Carrie appears excited and embarrassed in (c) as she is telling a medical student in a psychiatric hospital that she doubts the worth of psychiatry. Not surprisingly, then, lines 4-13 do seem especially to have hidden meaning. To tell people who have authority by virtue of position and/or education that they do not know what they are talking about is supremely difficult for those of lower status, normal or not. There is even evidence that women have more difficulty in such situations than do men; therefore, they hedge their remarks more than men do (Lakoff 1975; Eakins and Eakins 1978:23-52; 66-72). Considering these factors, it is reasonable to expect Carrie to have many hesitations, false starts, and filled or unfilled pauses in the situation eliciting her speech. Although Seeman and Cole claim that she switches topics constantly, her adherence to a general topic and the movement within it seems normal in every instance they report. Reading this section with pauses makes it clear:

(c) . . . I'm beginning to think psychiatry is rather old-fashioned. You know, there are new—there are young people on Yonge Street selling books about--I don't even know how to label them, but there are new ways for man coping with the environment and the people in it. And I haven't got into that but—I don't know--I—I—just—like, you have your set ways of doing things and you're in control.

As she starts to explain why psychiatry is old-fashioned, Carrie stops after new. Apparently, a word like ideas was intended, or, as appears later, ways. The reason for the hesitation seems straight-forward enough. She is not sure of the label and, when she does get the notion coded, it is with a whole sentence, "there are new ways for man coping with the environment and the people in it." However, she cannot get this all out until she has invested these ways with the authority of other people—young people—and books. This gives them more sanction that if they were ideas that Carrie, a woman and a mental patient, had dreamed up. To have just continued talking about the new ideas or ways would have placed too much of the blame on Carrie herself. Besides, the appeal to authority is always more convincing.

Carrie herself explains why she stopped after about. She does not have a ready label for the concepts that in her opinion are rendering psychiatry old-fashioned. What is important is that the discourse strategy she employs, a false start followed by "I don't even know how to label them," is entirely usual, one we have all probably used at one time or another. Common paraphrases are: "I forget its/his/her/name," "I don't know the word for it," and even,

"You know what I mean," and "whatchamacallit."

The next set of false starts is especially interesting. As a set, they imply that she disagrees with the student and the psychiatrists he is representing. Again, this is a normal strategy, a way of letting the other person know that you disagree without actually doing so in overt words. It is significant that the hesitations and false starts cluster at the point at which one would expect Carrie to be stating that she is disillusioned with psychiatry. "I haven't got into that but ..." seems like a normal entry into "the new approaches might be better than psychiatry," or some paraphrase thereof. Instead, Carrie stops after the but, the word that leads one to expect a disclaimer. Then she demurs with the feminine "I don't know" (Lakoff 1975:15-17), which has the effect of softening any following assertion. She starts to give her opinion again, saying "I", then starts all over still again, with "I just." This just is similar in force to the preceding but that caused this string of false starts. It announces that she holds an opinion different from that of the establishment, as in "I just don't believe in you anymore." This is not to say that those were necessarily her next words, but that the just in the given context does have the force of a disclaimer and she has previously voiced doubt about the efficacy of psychiatry. She stops short of having to put herself overtly on the line, although she has signaled enough for us to infer what she is "getting at." The like following the false start "I just" is often used in precisely the way Carrie uses it, to mean "what follows is not a direct expression of what I mean, but I'm finding it difficult to say exactly what I mean." What Carrie does is quite skillful. She has set her listener up for a criticism of psychiatry; then, without ever really giving that criticism, she tells John, "You have your set ways of doing things. That is, even if other things are better, you'd not be likely to change your mind." And, "you're in control" seems to mean just that. He is in control of the situation and of himself. Interestingly, the authors themselves stress the businesslike air of the student (p. 284), confirming Carrie's perceptions.

The thesis of the Seeman and Cole paper is to show how Carrie's speech becomes more disorganized as she feels the "intimacy of the daily meetings" (p. 289). In a large sense, that may be true. Intimacy makes Carrie dare to question her therapists, but the daring does not extend to speaking her mind openly. Surely, there is veiled meaning in her words, but the kind of veiled meaning and the way she expresses it seem wholly usual and normal, conforming to regular discourse strategies. She is cognizant of social situation, and, contrary to expectation (Rochester and Martin 1977; Rochester, Martin, and Thurston 1977) gives the listener ample information to know what she is referring to.

The rest of Carrie's speech is quite straightforward, if one decodes it as one would normal speech. The topic of (c) is the experiment in which Carrie is a participant. She is correct that this experiment is to see if her speech becomes disorganized as topics become more personal. Seeman and Cole (1977:284) had told her this. In other words, as Carrie says, the experiment is designed to see how vulnerable she is. She is also correct in assuming that the experiment has something to do with psychiatry. This is the lead-in to her indirect, but recoverable critique of psychiatry. As part of this critique, she complains that the previous day's session left her devoid of feeling, as with a release of tension—a common enough aftermath of a talk session—but she still does not see the purpose of the sessions. She continues the monologue with the unfortunately common plaint that she is always the loser in human relations. This does not seem to be an inappropriate topic switch since she is talking about the relations with John. The previous night, after the pointless (to her) "gab fest," she could not get anything done, nor does she feel that her talking that day has any purpose. She wants to aid the experimenters by participating. Also, being older than John, she feels as if she should be giving him insights, but she does not know if that would be appropriate, nor, actually, does she know what they are supposed to be talking about. Here I must point out that Carrie is not being particularly obtuse. Nowhere in the transcription is there any indication that John has responded to anything she has said. Apparently, he just lets her ramble on. This constitutes a highly abnormal situation. Normal conversation consists of turn-taking (e.g., Sacks 1967-72 & MSS; Jefferson 1978). Even very normal, confident people find it upsetting to be in a situation where they are supposed to carry on a conversation and the other person does not "carry the ball." If one adds to this normal discomfort the social convention that it is up to the female to "draw the male out" and "to keep the ball rolling" in social situations, especially in one-on-one occasions like dates, Carrie's speech is all the more normal. The situation she finds herself in with John is the same as if she were his girlfriend. In short, John's failure to take his rightful turns in the conversation, such as answering Carrie's questions, forces her to fill up the silence (Malinowski 1923) with a monologue. She is obeying normal, everyday conventions when she does so.

The passages above, when viewed again as spontaneous speech, also are amenable to quite ordinary meaning, rather ordinarily phrased, with one exception. And that exception Seeman and Cole do not point out. The segment in question occurred in passage (a) while Carrie was trying to teach John a foreign language (Seeman and Cole 1977:287)—hence, her comments about the dictionary. She, like many people, has ambivalent feelings about buying books. While talking about her feelings, for no apparent reason, Carrie mentions the color of the dictionary. One should note that there are two important rules of discourse, what Grice (1975:44-45) calls the Maxims of Quantity and Relation. The first says "Do not make your contribution more informative than is required" and the second, "Be relevant." Van Dijk (1977:109) claims that "constraints against over particularization are greater than those on generalization."

Grice explains why (1975:46): ". . . overinformativeness may be confusing in that it is liable to raise side issues; and there may also be an indirect effect, in that the hearers may be misled as a result of thinking that there is some particular point in the provision of the excess of information." One is reminded immediately of the clever trial lawyer who tries to fog the issues by introducing irrelevant evidence and of the fact that our judiciary, therefore, has stringent rules about information not leading to a relevant point. Grice (1975:51-55) goes on to show that violations of the Maxims of Quantity and Relation lead to certain kinds of implications— implications, I add, that could not be achieved if speakers did not share these maxims and understand conversation in terms of them. For instance, if someone gives too much information, the hearer suspects that the speaker is protesting too much, that the speaker is not certain of what he/she is saying, or that the speaker is implying that the proposition under discussion is controversial. Since Carrie's mention of the colors of the dictionary does not lead to any of these implications, nor does it seem to be a "red herring," I assume that it reflects a true discourse error.

It is puzzling that John could not comprehend the vehemence with which (b) was spoken (Seeman and Cole 1977:287). Even normal people get angry if they feel that they are being snubbed for no good reason and even they are jealous of friendships between people who exlude them. Carrie's feeling that the landlady and the other tenant are talking about her may be paranoid, but the structure of the language she uses to express that feeling is perfectly normal.

Seeman and Cole's explanation of Carrie's speech depends on their supposition that, because she is a schizophrenic, her speech must be interpreted differently from that of normal persons. In essence, they are claiming that there is a schizophrenic language and that they are among those with a key to it. In contrast, my interpretations of Carrie's speech depend upon the assumption that anyone using English is using it in much the same way as normal persons do (Austin 1962; Lyons 1977:735). There may be deviant schizophrenic speech (e.g., Chaika 1974a,b; 1977), just as there is deviant aphasic speech, or heavily accented speech, or imperfect toddler speech. However, all such speech must be tested against the crucible of normal speech.

Psychiatry and its sister disciplines, clinical psychology and psychiatric social work, are the only ones with which I am acquainted that assume that the incredibly complex sets of rules that enable us to handle human language, both as a system in itself and as a social system, can be wholly altered by one class of persons, the mentally ill. As John Searle (1975:67) said, in a somewhat different context, ". . . an ordinary application of Occam's razor places the onus of proof on those who wish to claim that these sentences are ambiguous. One does not multiply meanings beyond necessity." Nor, I hasten to add, does one claim idiosyncratic meaning when conventional meaning is retrievable by conventional means and fits the social context. Finally, to assume that schizophrenics abandon the usual meaning of words raises some very sticky questions. If the schizophrenic's meanings can be so very far removed from those of normal persons, how does anyone know what the schizophrenic means? At what point in a patient's illness does one suspend the normal rules of decoding and substitute the schizophrenic ones? At what point in remission does one abandon the schizophrenic interpretations and go back to the ones shared by other speakers? In sum: to ignore normal language use in interpretation allows no check on the validity of that interpretation.

REFERENCES

Austin, J. L. 1962. How to do things with words. J. Urmson and Marina Sbisa, eds. 2d ed. Cambridge, Mass.: Harvard University Press.

Bickerton, Derek. 1969. Prolegomena to a linguistic theory of metaphor. Foundations of Language 5:34-52.

Boomer, Donald S. 1965. Hesitation and grammatical encoding. In The psychosociology of language, ed. Serge Moscovici. Chicago: Markham Publishing Co.

Chaika, Elaine. 1974a. A Linguist looks at "schizophrenic" language. Brain and Language 1:257-76.

_____ . 1974b. Linguistics and psychiatry. Paper read at Linguistic Society of America, July 1974, at Amherst, Mass.

_____ . 1976. The possibility principle in semantics. Interfaces 6:9-12.

_____ . 1977. Schizophrenic speech, slips of the tongue and jargonaphasia, a reply to Fromkin and to Lecours and Vaniers-Clement. Brain and Language 4:464-75.

Clark, Herbert, and Clark, Eve. 1977. Psychology and language. New York: Harcourt Brace Jovanovich.

Eakins, Barbara, and Eakins, R. Gene. 1978. Sex differences in human communication. Boston: Houghton Mifflin Co.

Ervin-Tripp, Susan. 1972. On sociolinguistic rules: alternation and co-occurrence. In Directions in sociolinguistics: the ethnography of communication, ed. John Gumperz and Dell Hymes. New York: Holt, Rinehart and Winston.

Ferreira, A. J. 1960. The semantics and the context of the schizophrenic's language. Archives of General Psychiatry 3:128-38.

Forrest, David. 1965. Poiesis and the language of schizophrenia. Psychiatry 28:1-18.

_____ . 1976. Nonsense and sense in schizophrenic language. Schizophrenia Bulletin 2:286-98.

Gleitman, Lila; Gleitman, Henry; and Shipley, Elizabeth. 1972. The emergence of child as grammarian. Cognition 1-2/3:137-64.

Gordon, David, and Lakoff, George. 1975. Conversational

postulates. In Syntax and semantics, ed. Peter Cole and Jerry Morgan. Vol. 3, Speech Acts. New York: Academic Press.

Grice, H. Paul. 1975. Logic and conversation. In Syntax and semantics, ed. Peter Cole and Jerry Morgan. Vol. 3, Speech acts. New York: Academic Press.

Haley, J. 1963. Strategies of psychotherapy. New York: Grune and Stratton.

Jefferson, Gail. 1978. Sequential aspects of story-telling. In Studies in the organization of conversational interaction, ed. Jim Schenken. New York: Academic Press.

Laffal, Jules. 1965. Pathological and normal language. New York: Atherton Press.

Lakoff, Robin. 1975. Language and woman's place. New York: Harper and Row.

Lashley, K. A. 1951. The problem of serial order in behavior. In Cerebral mechanisms in behavior, ed. L. A. Jeffress. New York: John Wiley and Sons.

Lyons, John. 1977. Semantics. New York: Cambridge University Press.

Maclay, H., and Osgood, Charles. 1959. Hesitation phenomena in spontaneous English speech. Word 15:19-44.

Maher, Brendan. 1968. The shattered language of schizophrenia. Psychology Today. November.

Malinowski, B. 1923. Phatic communication. In Communication in face to face interaction, ed. John Laver and Sandy Hutcheson. Baltimore, Md.: Penguin Books, 1972.

Phillips, Susan U. 1970. Acquisition of rules for appropriate speech usage. In Georgetown University round table on languages and linguistics, ed. James Alatis. Washington, D.C.: Georgetown University Press.

Reich, Peter, and Dell, Gary. 1977. To err is (no longer necessarily) human. Interfaces 7:6-10.

Robertson, J., and Shamsie, S. 1958. A systematic examination of gibberish in a multilingual schizophrenic patient. In Language behavior in schizophrenia, ed. H. Vetter. Springfield, Ill.

Rochester, Sherry, and Martin, James. 1977. The art of referring: the speaker's use of noun phrases to instruct the listener. In Discourse production and comprehension, ed. Roy Freedle. Norwood, N.J.: Ablex Publishing.

Rochester, Sherry; Martin, James; and Thurston, Sharon. 1977. Thought process disorder in schizophrenia: the listener's task. Brain and Language 4:95:114.

Rochester, Sherry; Thurston, Sharon; and Rupp, Judith. 1977. Hesitations as clues to failures in coherence: a study of the thought disordered speaker. In Sentence production: developments in research and theory, ed. S. Rosenberg. Hillsdale, N.J.: Lawrence Erlbaum Associates.

Sacks, Harvey. 1967-72. Lecture notes. Mimeo.

_____. c. 1970. Untitled manuscript on discourse analysis Mimeo.

Sacks, Harvey; Schegloff, Emanuel; and Jefferson, Gail. 1978. A simplest systematics for the organization of turn taking for conversation. In Studies in the organization of conversational interaction, ed. Jim Schenken. New York: Academic Press.

Searle, John. 1975. Indirect speech acts. In Syntax and semantics. ed. Peter Cole and Jerry Morgan. Vol. 3, Speech Arts. New York: Academic Press.

Searles, Harold. 1967. The schizophrenic's experience of his world. Psychiatry 30:119-31.

Seeman, Mary, and Cole, Howard. 1977. The effect of increasing personal contact in schizophrenia. Comprehensive Psychiatry 18:283-92.

Sharrock, W. W., and Turner, Roy. 1978. On a conversational environment for equivocality. In Studies in the organization of conversational interaction, ed. Jim Schenken. New York: Academic Press.

Szasz, Thomas. 1976. Schizophrenia. New York: Basic Books.

Van Dijk, Teun A. 1977. Text and contest. explorations in the semantics and pragmatics of discourse. New York: Longmans.

Weinreich, Uriel. 1976. Explorations in semantic theory. In Current trends in linguistics, ed. Thomas Sebeok. Vol. 3. The Hague: Mouton.

APPENDIX

Carrie's discourse*	Seeman and Cole's Comments
(a) Yeah, I don't like this book, uhm, there's a dictionary that I was thinking of buying. It's seventy-five cents. I might buy it just for my own use but it's very compact and it's just, it's yellow and red, you know, it's very compact and precise. It's too bad in a way. I was, I was thinking of buying it but I you know, I kind of resented it having to pay out money you know.	This means: I could be like the dictionary, bright, compact and precise, but why should I put out such an effort? I don't know if you're worth it. The displacement and identification with an inanimate object is characteristic of Carrie (cf. Searles p. 122): "... it is nonhuman roles which predominate, more than any ... human ones in the life of the child who eventually develops schizophrenia."

Carrie's discourse and the comments by Seeman and Cole are reprinted by permission of Mary Seeman and Grune & Stratton, Inc. (Mary Seeman and Howard Cole. 1977. The effect of increasing personal contact in schizophrenia. Comprehensive Psychiatry 18:283-92.)

(b)

time when I first moved into the house, my landlord and landlady had me down to dinner and I was using the living language course which is different and I was, I was using the words of (Italian) and going along with it. But that was when I first moved in. They haven't invited me down for dinner for a while so, and I, when I get angry at someone I just shut their language out the way I shut them out, you know, and it's reflected in the way I'm learning it. . . . I think I became of the relationship the landlady has with the lady on the second floor. They seem to be really good friends, you know, and I feel kind of out of it. Sometimes I get awfully mad in my room listening to them talk, you know, and I was sure she, they were talking about me one day, that much I know, I can pick up when I'm being talked about.

Both passages . . . [c] . . . seemed out of context to John, and he could not comprehend the vehemence with which they were spoken. Carrie seems preoccupied by the question of how important John is to her. As in the dictionary segment she seems to be wondering whether he is worth the effort. This makes the suspiciousness of the latter two segments understandable. To quote Searles again (p. 125): "That the paranoid individual experiences the plot . . . as centering upon himself is in part a reaction to his being most deeply threatened lest he be as insignificant, as outside of everyone else's awareness, as he himself, with his severe depression of his own dependent feelings, tends to regard other individuals as being."

(Seeman and Cole 1977:287-88)

(c)

You know what the experiment is geared to find is how vulnerable, I guess, and, you know, if you get close to this person and how you feel about it and some pretty basic questions like it may have something to do with psychiatry, I don't. I'm beginning to think psychiatry is rather oldfashioned, you know there are young people on Yonge Street selling books about, I don't even how to label them, but there are new ways for man coping with the environment and the people in it. And I haven't got into that but, I don't know I, I just, like, you have your set ways of doing things and you're in control. You know and you're talking about yourself personally

The whole segment can be taken to mean: Do you like me, and if you do, that puts me in an intolerable position. And if you don't, that's unbearable. There seems to be no solution.

yesterday, you know, and I walked
out of there yesterday and I didn't
really have any feeling at all. It
was kind of like a release. I like
people to confide in me, but, like,
where is it going? What, it must
serve some purpose, I don't have
any theories about it. All I know
is that I do get involved with
people and it usually ends the
same way I, I become very angry
and you know something, well not
always, but I always get taken, I
get sucked in, you know, and I, I
was just immobilized last night I
didn't accomplish anything and
here again today I, I haven't
accomplished anything and I think
it's a hang-up I have got with you
but I, I don't think I'm alone
maybe maybe it's your hang-up
too, I, I really don't know. But I
do get involved in, with and when
someone tells me I want to help
out, and I want also to give
something of myself like I'm older
than you like I would like to give
you some of my own insights and
I, I don't know if it's appropriate
what are we talking about, what is
it we're talking about? We're just
talking about relationships and
they're different, you're a man
and I'm a woman and I guess I
identified a bit with your
girlfriend because I've done that
with my boyfriend.

10. When Is an Overlap Not an Interruption? One Component of Conversational Style

DEBORAH TANNEN
Georgetown University

"As I was saying when I was so rudely interrupted . . ."
"Excuse me for talking while you were interrupting . . ."
Or, as the caption of a cartoon read, "If you're going to interrupt me, Leroy, you might at least wait until I'm finished."

Formulaic expressions (and jokes) reflect cultural values and concerns (Matisoff 1979; Tannen and Oztek 1977). It is clear from the above and other common sayings that according to American conventional wisdom interruption is bad, something to be avoided. Such demands as "Let me finish" or "Don't interrupt" are heard as claims of an inalienable right.

In a scholarly vein, ethnomethodologists have made similar assumptions. Schegloff and Sacks (1974:236) propose as one of "two basic features of conversation," "at least, and no more than, one party speaks at a time in a single conversation." Sacks, Schegloff, and Jefferson have described a model of conversation in which each party seeks to begin speaking at "transition relevance places." In this system, interruption is seen as evidence of a malfunction: a speaker has mistakenly identified a transition relevance place. Sacks, Schegloff, and Jefferson observe:

> The lore and practices of etiquette concerning "interruption" and complaints about it, the use of interruption markers such as "excuse me" and others, false starts, repeats or recycles of parts of a turn overlapped by others, as well as premature (i.e., before possible completion) stopping by parties to simultaneous talk, are repair devices directed to troubles in the organization and distribution of turns to talk. (1978:39)

Bennett (1978) notes that these researchers differentiate between overlap and interruption on structural grounds, as seen in Schegloff (1973):

> By overlap we tend to mean talk by more than a speaker at a time which has involved that a second one to speak given that a first was already speaking, the second one has projected his talk to begin at a possible completion

point of the prior speaker's talk. If that's apparently
the case, if for example his start is in the environment
of what could have been a completion point of the prior
speaker's turn, then we speak of it as an overlap. If it's
projected to begin in the middle of a point that is in no
way a possible completion point for the turn, then we
speak of it as an interruption.

Thus, speakers are seen as intending to achieve turn-taking when
another speaker has finished; an overlap represents a tactical error
in this system, an interruption a violation of it.

Bennett points out that overlap and interruption are in fact
categories of logically different types. Whereas overlap is a
descriptive term referring to the observable coincidence in time of
contributions by two speakers, interruption is an interpretive
category, reflecting speakers' interpretations of "prevailing rights
and obligations" in the interaction. Thus, the question of whether an
overlap is an interruption—i.e., whether it is an obstructive device,
evidence of a conflict of conversational interests—is not merely a
matter of determining its relation to some structural feature of
talk.

I shall propose here that speakers differ with regard to when
they expect overlap, how much they expect, and how they interpret
and intend overlaps—i.e., the rights and obligations attached to
these phenomena. I will demonstrate, moreover, that there are
many speakers who regard overlap as a cooperative device in certain
conversational settings.

The cooperative use of overlap will be shown in a segment
taken from two-and-one-half hours of tape-recorded and transcribed
conversation that occurred naturally over Thanksgiving dinner in
1978 among six native speakers of English.[1] That these instances of
overlap are not interruptions for these speakers can be seen (1) in
the effects of their use in conversation as well as (2) in participants'
interpretations as expressed upon hearing a tape recording of the
conversation (the process called "playback" by Labov and Fanshel
1977).

Expectations and practices with regard to overlap constitute
an element of conversational style; in other words, they are among
an array of linguistic and nonverbal devices that co-occur to give
each person's speech a distinct and recognizable character (Lakoff
1979).

Analysis of the entire Thanksgiving conversation (Tannen,
1979b) indicates that cooperative overlap is an element in a
repertoire of devices used by three of the six participants. Other
features of their style include expressive phonology; sharp shifts in
amplitude and pitch, resulting in exaggerated intonation contours;
fast rate of speech as well as fast pacing with respect to turn-
taking; frequent and expressive back-channel responses; preference
for personal topics; frequent and abrupt topic switching; propensity

to tell personal narratives; and use of direct quotation and even role-playing in narration. Thus overlap is one feature of a style whose cumulative effect is a feeling of intensity and rapid pace that led those who used it to experience the conversation as "great" but struck others present as "frenetic" and "dominating." As Bateson (1972) has pointed out, every utterance has both a message and a metamessage. At the same time that the words impart information (the message), the fact of their utterance and the way they are uttered carry a metamessage—a statement about the relationship between speaker and hearer. To those who favor this style, the very fact of overlap is a vehicle for a metamessage of interpersonal rapport. This hypothesis will be discussed further after the data are presented.

Cooperative Overlap in Action

In the transcribed Thanksgiving conversation, overlap often did not lead to obstruction of conversational flow. Although there were clearly individual differences among them, three of the six participants evidenced far more use of overlap than did the three others. The transcript shows numerous interchanges among these speakers in which overlaps abound, yet conversation proceeded in an animated and rhythmically smooth manner that participants later reported having found satisfying. [2] Therefore I shall refer to these three speakers as "overlap-favoring."

I shall describe three distinct functions of cooperative overlap as used in the speech of the overlap-favoring speakers: K (Kurt), P (Peter), and D (myself).

The following brief excerpt is representative of much of the conversation at this dinner, which took place at the home of Kurt, a native of New York City living in Oakland, California. The following segment shows Kurt's attempt to explain the location of a building in New York that he has referred to. The talk was occasioned by mention of New York by another guest who had recently visited the city. Kurt directed a question to him, but soon after that the three participants who were from New York launched a rapid and animated discussion in which the three other guests did not participate. Peter (P) is Kurt's brother; I (D) am his friend. [3]

This short segment is characterized by much overlap, including at least three different types: (1) cooperative sentence-building, (2) requesting and giving verification, (3) choral repetition. [4]

Cooperative Sentence-Building

Cooperative sentence-building is a device by which a listener participates in what is clearly someone else's sentence, as in (11)–(12).

. . . .

(1) K Remember where ⌈W I N S used to be?

(2) D No⌉

(3) K   ⌊Then they built a big huge skyscraper there?

(4) D No. Where was that.

(5) K Right where Central Park West met Broadway. That
     acc
     ⌈building shaped like that. ⌈Makes a pyramid with hands.⌉

(6) P ⌊Did⌈I give you too much? ⌊re turkey⌋

(7) D   ⌊By Columbus Circuit? . . . 'that Columbus Circle?

(8) K   ⌊Right on Columbus Circle. Here's

     Columbus Circle, ...⌈here's Central Park West,

                   ⌊Now it's ⌈the Huntington Hartford

     Museum.

(10) P   ⌊That's the Huntington

     Hartford, right?

(11) K Nuhnuhno. ... Here's Central Park West, here's

     Broadway. We're going north, this way? ... and
     D Yeah.   D uhuh

     here's this building here. The Huntington Hartford

     is ⌈on the South Side.

(12) D   ⌊on the other⌉ across. Yeah, rightrightrightrightright . .

     ⌈And now that's a new building with uh--⌉

(13) K ⌊And there was ...   ⌊and ⌋   ⌊there was

     a⌉ stores here, and the upper second floor was

     W I N S.   ... And we listened to--⌉
     D oh --

                           ⌊Now it's a round

     place with a--movie theater.

(15) K Now⌉ there's a roun⌉ No. The next ... next

     block is but ... but ... this is a huge skyscraper
              D Oh

     right there.
           D Oh, yeah.

               . . . . . .

(11)   K   The Huntington Hartford is ⌈ on the South side.

(12)   D   ⌊ on the other? across.

This generally occurs at the end of a sentence, so that the listener "chimes in" to complete the sentence together with the speaker. The overlap is not turn-claiming; the speaker is entitled to continue speaking, as Kurt does in the present example in (13),[5] despite my continuing overlap, which is an example of the type to be considered next. By testimony of those who practice cooperative sentence-building, the metamessage lies in the overlap: "I understand you so well that I know what you are going to say." Those who do not share a preference for this device, however, do not understand the metamessage. They are the people who are likely to complain, "Don't put words in my mouth," or, "Don't tell me what I'm going to say."

Requesting and Giving Verification

At times, for some speakers, the preferred way to request or give verification is through use of overlap, as in (5)-(10).

(5)   K   Right where Central Park West met Broadway. That
            acc

       ⌈ building shaped like that. ⌈ Makes a pyramid with hands.⌉

(6)   P   ⌊ Did⌈I give you too much? ⌈ re turkey⌋

(7)   D   ⌊ By Columbus Circuit? . . .   that Columbus Circle?
                        ⌊
(8)   K   ⌊ Right on Columbus Circle. Here's
            Columbus Circle, ... here's Central Park West,

(9)   D   Now it's ⌈ the Huntington Hartford
            Museum.   ⌈
                                               ⌈
(10)   P   ⌊ That's the Huntington
            Hartford, right?

My (7) verifies the location of "where Central Park West met Broadway" in (5), and is timed to begin smack in the middle of Kurt's continuing talk. (Peter's overlap in [6] is concerned with food-serving, which can always come as an overlap during dinner conversation, as Sacks has noted.)   Then Kurt ratifies my verification by repeating in (8) my offering ("Columbus Circle") and working it into his own talk. (I call this a "ratifying repetition"—a common phenomenon in the cooperative enterprise of talk. The strength of the impulse to ratify an offering in this way—for Kurt at least, in this setting—is elegantly demonstrated in [13-14], where Kurt begins to repeat a preceding phrase that he in fact thinks is wrong.)

Similarly, my (9) and Peter's (10) are offered as verification of the building Kurt attempts to describe in (5). As has already been noted, (12) also contains a verification about the building location that overlaps with (13).

For these speakers in this setting, it is not only permissible to seek to verify information by overlap (as Sacks, Schegloff, and Jefferson have noted); it is preferable, if not required. The quick pace of the question or comment, together with its timing as an overlap, serves to signal, "This is not central to our talk; I don't want you to stop for my comment; but I really am interested and want to let you know that I'm with you thus far." By the same means, the quick pace and overlap of the answer serve to signal, "Got you; here's your answer; and don't worry, your question/comment didn't stop me." If the speaker, upon hearing the overlapped question or comment, stopped the flow of her/his talk, the overlapper would be surprised and disconcerted; it would seem like an overreaction, as if the speaker were trying to make the cooperative overlapper look like an interrupter—which s/he does not intend to be. This happens, in fact, in interactions between cooperative overlappers and others at the Thanksgiving dinner.

Choral Repetition

Sometimes two speakers say the same thing at the same time in the same or slightly different form. This phenomenon is associated with what Jane Falk (1979) has identified as a conversational duet, by which two speakers (usually spouses, relatives, or close friends) jointly hold one conversational role.

In the present example, Kurt is trying to explain where a certain building used to be; hence, he is playing the role of teacher. Peter and I are trying to follow his explanation; hence we are playing the role of students. In (9) and (10) Peter and I say nearly the same thing at the same time (both overlapping with Kurt, since our comments function as verifications).

(9)   D   ⌐Now it's ⌐the Huntington Hartford Museum.

(10)   └That's the Huntington Hartford, right?

Peter says (10) almost simultaneously with my (9), and his question gave all those present the impression that he too had some familiarity with the geography of New York. During playback, however, Peter commented that he felt insecure in this interchange and was trying to "hold his own" with some difficulty. He remarked that he does not know New York very well, since he never lived there as an adult. What he did was to piggyback a verification question on mine, taking advantage of our joint role as students in the geography lesson. He was able to use his familiarity with the rhythms and devices of the conversation to participate by echoing my comment. In fact, the "student" he chose to copy from hadn't much more knowledge than he did; Kurt corrected us both. Nonetheless Peter was perceived as a full participant in the conversation by all those present. His success is a striking testament to the fact that knowledge of a topic is not necessary for participation in a conversation, whereas familiarity with conversational control devices is not only necessary but sometimes sufficient. His choral repetition was not only acceptable; it was the means for his participation in the interchange.

Persistence

A concomitant of the overlap-favoring style, one which is presupposed if the overlap strategy is to work at all, is that speakers will persist in their attempts to make a conversational contribution. In this system, it is not the business of listeners to make sure that others have "room" to talk. It is their business to show interest and enthusiasm.[6] Finding room to talk is up to speakers. Indeed, it is incumbent upon speakers, if they are observing this system, to find things to say and places in the conversation to say them. A person who gives up after a single try is perceived by overlap-favoring speakers as being uncooperative, withholding, even sulking.

Persistence can be seen in the present example in (12) and (14). I begin to suggest in (12) that the site Kurt has in mind is now a round building with a movie theater in it, but Kurt does not stop his own recollection for me to do so. Therefore I make this contribution at the next possible time in (14)--probably occasioned by the slight elongation of the vowel in "to--" which constitutes a slight but perceptible slowing down of his talk. During the Thanksgiving conversation, Kurt, Peter, and I persist with our conversational contributions for from three to as many as seven turns without receiving responses from other participants. Two of the other speakers never persist beyond two tries if their topic are not picked up.

Discussion and Conclusion

Overlap-favoring speakers not only accept but expect overlap in a casual and friendly conversation. The failure to overlap is perceived by these speakers in these settings as lack of interest or dullness. I have hypothesized that overlap, like other features of this style that contribute to its "animated" character, represents conventionalized ways of honoring the quest for overt show of rapport. Robin Lakoff (1973 and in 1979) points out that speakers may be "polite" by following either the injunction "Don't impose" or the conflicting injunction "Be friendly." Drawing on Lakoff's work, Brown and Levinson (1978) have identified two overriding goals of conversation: positive and negative face. Positive face is the need to be approved of by others (what I like to think of as the need for community); negative face is the need not to be imposed upon (in other words, the need for independence). Overlap-favoring speakers, then, honor above all positive face. They find it better to risk imposing than to risk showing too little rapport. Theirs is a style, moreover, that always prefers talk to silence. Overlap and latching (i.e., beginning to talk immediately after a prior speaker) are necessary to avoid the ultimate evil—silence—which seems in this system to be evidence of lack of rapport.

The use of devices in service of these broad strategies is conventionalized. Speakers who use these devices do not necessarily feel a greater need for rapport; nor do they make conscious choices of how to achieve it. Rather, they habitually use devices that they have learned in previous interaction and that are, for them, self-evident and natural ways to have conversation. Problems arise only when the devices are used with others who have different conversational habits that are to them equally self-evident and natural.

The activity being engaged in in the example analyzed above is an identifiable activity that one commentator dubbed "New York geography." This activity has been recognized by numerous informants who have lived with native New Yorkers but are not themselves from New York; their responses to it range from amusement to feeling rejected or offended by it. New York geography is an activity they are not able to participate in, not only because they lack appropriate information but more because they are not familiar with the appropriate conversational control devices. One participant in the Thanksgiving dinner who was not able to participate in the geography talk, Dave, commented during playback, "I'm amazed at how you guys talk over each other, saying the same thing at the same time." Another one, Sally, commented, "I find it incredibly funny. I love it. It's ultimate New York." She said she could not distinguish between what was important and what was not in such a discussion: "I would never talk so intensely about something so insignificant." Sally remarked, furthermore, that when she was first exposed to conversation of this sort she found it offensive.

Sally is not the only one who may have found (or may find) an overlapping style offensive. A recent article in New West magazine (Esterly 1979) tells of the work of a psychologist at UCLA who believes that fast talkers are a conversational menace. He calls them "crowders" and offers a training course (at a price) designed to help them learn patience.

Indeed, it might be useful for some overlap-favoring speakers to learn patience for the purpose of interaction with others who do not share their style, especially if the others are likely to judge them—for example, in a job interview—just as speakers of nonstandard dialects may choose to adopt a standard idiom for interaction in public settings.   However, the present study indicates—and the larger study of which it is a part amply demonstrates—that cooperative overlap is an effective device for establishing rapport among those who share expectations about its use.

Afterword: Ethnic and Cultural Basis of Conversational Style

Throughout this discussion I have avoided direct consideration of the correlation between the style I have described as overlap-favoring and ethnicity, although I have made reference to the association of this style with speakers from New York City. It is impossible to make statements about ethnicity or geographical background based on a sample of six speakers. The present study seeks only to prove that some speakers use overlap cooperatively. It is clear, however, that in the minds of the participants as well as the others present at this dinner (and countless commentators), that such a style is associated with speakers from New York City. One thinks, for example, of the split-screen segment of Woody Allen's Annie Hall that juxtaposed for the purpose of contrast a dinner scene at the home of the New York Jewish hero with a dinner scene at the home of the midwestern WASP heroine. It seems clear, moreover, that it is the exercise of just such conversational devices that led Dave, for example, to recall that this dinner "was dominated by the New York Jewish element," and that has led to the stereotyping of speakers of this background as "pushy."   In the present discussion, furthermore, it does not seem coincidental that the topic of talk was "New York geography."   It has been the experience of numerous informants that they find themselves exercising the most exaggerated forms of a particular style when they are talking to others who share the style and in contexts associated with the one in which they learned the style.

Clearly, however, more research is needed to determine the ethnic, geographical, and other cultural correlates of this and other features of conversational style.

NOTES

1.   The entire conversation is the subject of a lengthy study (Tannen 1979b) of conversational style in which features making up participants' styles are analyzed in detail. In conducting that study, I incurred lasting debts to all my informants, pseudonymously called here Kurt, Peter, Sally, Dave, and Chad, as well as those who read and commented on my work, discussed it with me at various stages, and inspired me throughout:

Wallace Chafe, John Gumperz, and Robin Lakoff.
2. The alternate situation, in which styles are not shared and interaction is indeed obstructed, is beyond the scope of the present paper but is amply demonstrated in Tannen 1979b.
3. Transcription conventions:

⌐ indicates raised pitch.

acc indicates accelerated rate of speech.

∕ .indicates primary stress.

∖ indicates secondary stress.

__ indicates emphatic stress.

ʔ is the standard linguistic symbol for glottal stop.

-- indicates that preceding vowel sound was lengthened.

⌐ Brackets indicate simultaneous speech.

⌐ indicates utterance latched onto preceding utterance.

. each dot represents a half second of measured pause.

4. Two other types of cooperative overlap not evidenced here are questions as prompts and repetition/coda.
5. A speaker can ignore the contribution, incorporate it into her/his talk tacitly, or repeat it and incorporate it; this last would constitute a ratifying repetition.
6. I believe this phenomenon is related to a pattern I found in a study of expectations of indirectness by Greeks, Americans, and Greek-Americans (Tannen 1979a). In that study, it emerged that whereas American informants tended to expect casual conversation between spouses to reflect direct expression of preferences, Greek informants, and to some extent Greek-American informants as well, doubted the veracity of terse expressions of preference. They expected enthusiasm to be shown if a preference was sincere.

REFERENCES

Bateson, G. 1972. Steps to an ecology of mind. New York: Ballantine.
Bennett, A. 1978. Interruptions and the interpretation of conversation. Proceedings of the 4th Annual Meeting of the Berkeley Linguistics Society. Linguistics Department, University of California, Berkeley.
Brown, P., and Levinson, S. 1978. Universals in language usage: politeness phenomena. In Questions and Politeness, ed. E. Goody. Cambridge: Cambridge University Press.

Esterly, G. 1979. Slow talking in the big city. New West magazine, May 21.

Falk, Jane. 1979. Conversational duets. Ph.D. diss., Princeton University, Princeton, N.J.

Labov, W., and Fanshel, D. 1977. Therapeutic discourse. New York: Academic Press.

Lakoff, R. 1973. The logic of politeness, or minding your p's and q's. Papers from the 9th regional meeting of the Chicago Linguistics Society, Department of Linguistics, University of Chicago, Chicago, Illinois.

_____. 1979. Stylistic strategies within a grammar of style. Annals of the New York Academy of Science, vol. 327.

Matisoff, J. 1979. Blessings, curses, hopes, and fears: psycho-ostensive expressions in Yiddish. Philadelphia: Institute for the Study of Human Issues.

Sacks, H.; Schegloff, E.; and Jefferson, G. 1978. A simplest systematics for the organization of turn-taking for conversation. In Studies in the organization of conversational interaction, ed. J. Schenkein. New York: Academic Press.

Schegloff, E. 1973. Recycled turn beginnings. Public lecture, Summer Institute of the Linguistic Society of America, Ann Arbor, Mich.

Schegloff, E., and Sacks, H. 1974. Opening up closings. In Ethnomethodology, ed. R. Turner. Baltimore, Md.: Penguin.

Tannen, D. 1979a. Ethnicity as conversational style. Sociolinguistic working paper #55. Austin, Tex.: Southwest Educational Development Laboratory.

_____. 1979b. Processes and consequences of conversational style. Ph.D. diss., University of California, Berkeley.

Tannen, D., and Oztek, P. Comert. 1977. Formulaic expressions in Turkish and Greek. Proceedings of the 3d Annual Meeting of the Berkeley Linguistics Society. University of California, Berkeley.

11. Lexical Decomposition, Incorporations, and Paraphrase

JOHN J. STACZEK
Florida International University

That language permits an idea to be expressed in any of several syntactic patterns is an essential concept in any study of paraphrase. If we understand paraphrase to be a restating process whereby meaning is preserved and reference is made to the same objective situation, we have recourse to the insights of generative and lexical semantics that show that there are semantic, lexical, and morphological links between nouns and verbs. In other words, the sentence is considered to be a proposition, the constituent parts of which are a verbal unit and one or more nouns. Each proposition will "describe a state or action—spelled out in a verbal unit—and one or more entities involved in that state or action—spelled out in the nouns" (Clark and Clark 1977:11-12). This paper discusses the contributions of such generative semanticists as McCawley, Lakoff, and Binnick and other semanticists such as Miller and Gruber, who have identified a process in the grammar of language whereby the noun units can be lexicalized into verbal units, a process called incorporation by some, or its converse, lexical decomposition, wherein noun entities might be extracted from verb forms, leaving what is called here primary lexical matter or verbal lexical primes. That three simple and basic verbs such as give, make, and put combine with certain noun forms used as objects or locatives allows a flexibility for paraphrase. An understanding of the paraphrastic process requires an analysis of some syntactic underlying changes.

Paraphrase as defined here is a restative process with reference to the same objective situation. It is to be understood that while any two expressions or statements may indeed be synonymous when they refer to the same entity or situation there are cases in which meaning is not preserved. In sentences (1a) and (1b), the native speaker of English would argue, correctly, that the sentence are not totally synonymous.

(1a)   John put glue on the table.
(1b)   John glued the table.

The research presented here deals only with those decompositions and incorporations in which there is an isomorphism with respect to the meaning or interpretation of the sentences, as in (2a) and (2b):

(2a)   Romeo gave Juliet a kiss.

(2b)   Romeo kissed Juliet.

If we look to such linguistic models of grammar as generative semantics, lexical semantics, case grammar, and componential analysis, we find that the notions of surface structure, underlying representation or deep structure, proposition, lexical insertion, and paraphrase play a role in speaking and listening and, consequently, in the way the learner interprets the grammar. As the learner comes to an awareness of the structure of a simple proposition with give, make, and put (and in his native language this may truly be the only alternative open to him), he may then proceed to become conscious of the process of lexicalization whereby the noun role is incorporated into the primary verbal units, thus producing a new verbal lexical unit that may be in other ways syntactically different from the original. In the work of Charles Fillmore (1968) in case grammar, each sentence is analyzed as consisting of a verb surrounded by a number of roles with specific semantic functions. Those functions are that of deep-structure object (or surface direct object) and that of deep-structure locative (or surface object of a preposition, such as in or on). Later in this paper I will deal with incorporations of two other potential primes—have and go—and some instruments.   The sentence as proposition may be represented schematically as in Figure 1.

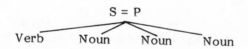

Figure 1.   Sentence as Proposition

As the noun, at the lexical level, is inserted into the structure it may remain in its original form as noun or may combine in many instances with give, make, and put, to produce new verbal lexical items with syntactic properties different from those of the original lexical primes. At times, however, the syntactic properties are the same. As we continue to describe the verbal lexical primes, we will refer to the verbal entity as capable of being a two- or three-place predicate. In the case of give, there is potential for three noun roles, namely, AGENT, EXPERIENCER, or BENEFACTOR, and OBJECT (Fillmore 1971a); in the case of make, a potential for the same three, although AGENT and OBJECT alone are more common; and, in the case of put, a potential for AGENT, OBJECT, and LOCATIVE.   Sentences (3a-b), (4a-b), and (5a-b) illustrate this potential.

(3a)   The highway patrolman gave me a ticket for speeding.
(3b)   The highway patrolman ticketed me for speeding.
(4a)   Elton John made an appearance at the Hollywood

Bowl.

(4b)   Elton John appeared at the Hollywood Bowl.
(5a)   John put a saddle on his horse.
(5b)   John saddled his horse.

It should be observed that the three lexical primes do not all have the same combinatory potential, that is, that give and make appear to lexicalize objects, whereas put, however, will combine with objects and locatives.   In examples (6-9), the process of lexicalization or incorporation can be observed:

(6a)   Pete gave me an answer to my question.
(6b)   Pete answered my question.
(7a)   William made a payment on VISA and Master Charge.
(7b)   William paid VISA and Master Charge.
(8a)   The intruder put a gag on his victim.
(8b)   The intruder gagged his victim.
(9a)   The carryout put the groceries in bags.
(9b)   The carryout bagged the groceries.

A comparison of (6a) and (6b) should reveal that as paraphrases, (6b) may indeed preserve the meaning of (6a). As the listener looks at the constituents of the sentences, they both seem to fit the semantic requirements of the verbal units. There is no question that under a different set of circumstances, (6a-b) might not be synonymous. In (7a) and (7b), there also appears to be synonymy, as is the case in (8a-b) and (9a-b). In sentences (6a-b), it should be observed that as an object is lexicalized into the lexical prime, the resulting newly lexicalized root is also transitive. In (7b), on the other hand, the new surface object derives from a former deep-structure locative.   The consequences of lexicalization or incorporation, it will be shown, are varied and complex. As speakers creatively incorporate or delexicalize, they are aware of the unconscious processes that require necessary syntactic changes in the resulting paraphrase.

Within the give class of verbal lexical primes, the decomposed verbal units exhibit several characteristics, namely: (1) that give is a three-place predicate of the type give (x, y, z); (2) that, upon lexicalization of the noun root, the surface structure continues to be that of a transitive verb; and (3) that several newly lexicalized verbal roots require surface objects that are sentence embeddings. Sentences (11-14a-b) illustrate the above characteristics:

(10a)   Mom gave me permission to go to the movies.
(10b)   Mom permitted me to go to the movies.
(11a)   The Chamber of Commerce gave him an award of a gold watch for his long years of service.
(11b)   The Chamber of Commerce awarded him a gold

watch for his long years of service.

In the case of (11a-b), the object of the preposition of, gold watch, becomes a direct object after lexicalization.

(12a)   The bank president gave him authorization for
         the withdrawal.
(12b)   The bank president authorized the withdrawal
         for him.

The bitransitive authorize in (12b) is allowed only with the above word order.

(13a)   The young man gave the woman a quick glance.
(13b)   The young man glanced quickly at the woman.

Sentences (13a-b) illustrate a change from adjectival modifier to that of verbal adverbial modifier, as does (14a-b)

(14a)   Sara gave a loud sigh.
(14b)   Sara sighed loudly.

Sentence (14b), although exhibiting the characteristics of (13b), deletes two of the three predicates. The following sentences show more or less common qualities of the lexicalization process with give.

(15a)   I gave my son a spanking.
(15b)   I spanked my son.
(16a)   My wife gave me a hug.
(16b)   My wife hugged me.
(17a)   He gave me a loan of $500.
(17b)   He loaned me $500.
(18a)   The young mother gave the infant a bath.
(18b)   The young mother bathed the infant.
(19a)   When Dracula walked in, he gave me a scare.
(19b)   When Dracula walked in he scared me.

Other syntactic consequences of the lexicalization require the sentence embedding in the object, as in sentences (20a-b).

(20a)   He gave me a recommendation to leave.
(20b)   He recommended that I leave.

Until now, no mention has been made of prohibitive lexicalization, in which the lexicalization process, for some reason, is not allowed to occur, either because the speakers have not found the need for the new root or because, morphologically, the process cannot occur.

(21a)   The sheik gave his youngest son a gift.
(21b)   *The sheik gifted his son.

The lexical item gifted does indeed occur but not as a verbal unit.
One other explanation is that the newly lexicalized form may have
taken on another meaning in the language. Sentence (22a-b) is
similar:

(22a)   Jason gave me a lift to the movies.
(22b)   *Jason lifted me to the movies.

Although give a lift might be interpreted as an idiom in (22a-b),
some idioms allow the lexicalized process to occur, as in sentence
(23a-b)

(23a)   Eric gave me a ride to class on his bicycle.
(23b)   Eric rode me to class on his bicycle.
or even
(23b)   Eric bicycled me to class.

Later, in the discussion of go lexicalizations, it will be shown that
instrumentals are potentially lexicalizable. In the case of (23),
however, the lexicalization derives from a different verbal prime
and also involves an animate object.

Table 1
Sample Primes and Potential Lexicalizable Elements

Give	Make	Put	
		object	locative
permission	claim	saddle	bottle
authorization	assertion	accent	can
donation	accusation	nail	box
sigh	promise	shoe	package
award	contribution	roofing	carton
reward	drawing	siding	crate
toast	comparison	paper	shelf
promise	sacrifice	paint	drawer
glance	promise	oil	closet
help	wish	wax	house
assistance	presentation	grease	garage
gift	toast	carpet	storage
kiss	bow	board	binding
hug	error	wire	pocket
advice	agreement	entry	refrigerator
recommendation	choice	glue	freezer

praise	plan	icing	frame
caress	attempt	frosting	
bath	demand	salt	encase
scare	request	pepper	enchant
examination	decision	spice	encipher
order	suggestion	line	encode
applause	proposal	wrap	encircle
punishment	visit	sole	enclasp
assignment	journey	heel	encyst
	report	trust	enfranchise
	confession	shroud	enlace
	investigation		enregister
	description		enlist
	connection		ensconce
	objection		entrench
	generalization		envelop
	impression		
	assumption		
	prediction		
	discovery		
	gesture		
	purchase		
	payment		

Within the make class of verbal lexical primes, the decomposed units exhibit several similar characteristics, though with some modification, namely, (1) that make is a potential three-place predicate of the type make (x, y, z), although it is more often a two-place type, (2) that, upon lexicalization of the noun root, the surface structure continues to be that of a transitive verb effecting no change in the surface structure other than the simple lexicalization and (3) that several newly lexicalized verbal units required surface objects that are sentence embeddings. These characteristics are illustrated in sentences (24–28a-b):

(24a)   He made a comparison of the two drawings.
(24b)   He compared the two drawings.
(25a)   He made a drawing of a still life.
(25b)   He drew a still life.
(26a)   The office staff made a fifty-dollar contribution.
(26b)   The office staff contributed fifty dollars.
(27a)   He made a report after his investigation.
(27b)   He reported after his investigation.
(28a)   He made a toast to the newlyweds.
(28b)   He toasted the newlyweds.

In sentences (28a-b), a surface and deep indirect object becomes a surface direct object upon lexicalization of the verbal unit.

Other make-class lexicalizations are morphologically complex in that many are of the -tion type as noun units, which then simplify morphologically upon lexicalization, as in sentences (29–35a-b):

(29a)   James made an assertion that he was now independent.
(29b)   James asserted his independence.
(30a)   The lawyer made a decision that I should go.
(30b)   The lawyer decided that I should go.
(31a)   He made a confession of guilt.
(31b)   He confessed his guilt.
(32a)   He made a presentation of his case.
(32b)   He presented his case.
(33a)   The jury made an assumption that the defendant was guilty.
(33b)   The jury assumed the defendant's guilt.
(34a)   I made an objection to his statement.
(34b)   I objected to his statement.
(35a)   The plaintiff made a false accusation of the defendant.
(35b)   The plaintiff accused the defendant falsely.

Sentences (35a-b) illustrate a similar syntactic consequence to that of the give type with the adjective changing to a verbal unit modifier or adverb. And sentences (36a-b) show at least one sentence embedding in the lexicalization:

(36a)   I made him a promise that I would go.
(36b)   I promised him that I would go.

The make group of verbal lexical primes also appears to inhibit the process of lexicalization, much for the same reasons as with the give group. Sentences (37a-b) and (38a-b) illustrate this kind of lexical gap in the process:

(37a)   We made an appointment with the optometrist.
(37b)   *We appointed with the optometrist.
(38a)   The kids made a hole in the wall.
(38b)   *The kids holed the wall.

One justification for the apparent impossibility of lexicalizing certain noun units with make is that with affected objects—those already in existence—the process occurs; but with effected objects—or those that are created, thus providing a slightly different semantic reading of make—the process does not occur. Otherwise the same rationale of historical accident or imperfect morphology or extension of range of meaning applies.

The put class of verbal lexical primes is unique as a single class inasmuch as put allows either a noun object or noun locative unit to be lexicalized into the existing prime. The characteristics of the <u>put</u> class are (1) that <u>put</u> is inherently, and apparently exclusively, a three-place predicate, of the type <u>put</u> (x, y, z) where the third argument or noun entity is always locative in nature; (2) syntactically the noun unit is totally absorbed into the verbal prime, thereby reducing the newly formed predicate to two places; and (3) that <u>put</u> types of lexicalizations are often more ambiguous than the <u>give</u> and <u>make</u> types.

The <u>put</u> group plus noun object unit yields a variety of new lexicalizations, many of them very common and specialized, as will be observed from the following examples.

(39a)   Put a saddle on the horse.
(39b)   Saddle the horse.
(40a)   Put shoes on the horse.
(40b)   Shoe the horse.

Sentence (40a), uttered out of context, would surely be ambiguous and give the listener pause. However, if <u>horseshoes</u> were used in place of <u>shoes</u> there would be no objection.

(41a)   I will put frosting on the cake later.
(41b)   I will frost the cake later.

Other noun units that fit this same pattern are <u>icing</u>, <u>salt</u>, (powdered) <u>sugar</u>, and even <u>pepper</u> and <u>spice</u>. <u>Cinnamon</u> and other condiments do not fit the pattern, as seen in sentence (42a-b):

(42a)   Don't forget to put cinnamon on the crumb cake.
(42b)   ?Don't forget to cinnamon the crumb cake.

There is every reason to believe that as the language continues to develop, (42b) and others like it could very well come into existence.

In the case of noun object units such as <u>wax</u>, <u>grease</u>, <u>paper</u>, and <u>tile</u>, as in sentences (43-46a-b), a certain lack of isomorphism in the paraphrase is noted.

(43a)   Put wax on the floor.
(43b)   Wax the floor.
(44a)   They are putting carpets on the floors.
(44b)   They are carpeting the floors.
(45a)   The workmen will put paper on the walls.
(45b)   The workmen will paper the walls.

In the case of (45a-b), <u>wallpaper</u> would help the paraphrase.

(46a)   The workmen put tile on the floors.
(46b)   The workmen tiled the floors.

In the case of (46a-b), there are obviously other contexts that would disambiguate the paraphrase, such as (47a-b).

(47a)　　We had the contractor put tile on the floors.
(47b)　　We had the contractor tile the floors.

Another noun unit, wire, for example, in the lexicalization is unusual or anomalous as in (48a-b)

(48a)　　I put wire in the house for the stereo.
(48b)　　I wired the house for stereo.

One other minor characteristic regarding the put verbal prime should be mentioned, namely, that certain noun units, once lexicalized, are morphologically simpler as in (49-51a-b):

(49a)　　We put new upholstery on the sofa.
(49b)　　We reupholstered the sofa.
(50a)　　I am planning to put new roofing on the house.
(50b)　　I am planning to roof the house.

The second class of put verbal lexical primes incorporates a noun locative into the existing prime.　This is a departure from the previous lexicalizations, which have been noun objects in nature.　In all cases the lexicalized noun locative unit is morphologically identical to the newly formed verbal unit, as seen in (51-60a-b):

(51a)　　In Vermont they don't put maple syrup in bottles, they put it in cans.
(51b)　　In Vermont they don't bottle maple syrup, they can it.

Bottle and can as verbal units are exclusive in nature, which means that although the grammar might produce a sentence such as (52a), it is quite illogical semantically:

(52a)　　*Hunt's catsup is now bottled in cans.

(52b)　　We'll have to put the engine in a shipment.
$$\begin{bmatrix} \text{box} \\ \text{crate for} \\ \text{carton} \\ \text{package} \end{bmatrix}$$

(52c)　　We'll have to shipment.
$$\begin{bmatrix} \text{box} \\ \text{crate} \\ \text{*carton} \\ \text{package} \end{bmatrix}$$ the engine for

Carton carries an asterisk because it is as yet unattested, but it is certainly quite possible as a new verbal lexical unit.

(53a)   Please do not put the books back on the shelves.
(53b)   Please do not reshelve the books.
(54a)   Where shall we put the car? In the garage?
(54b)   Shall we garage the car?
(55a)   I'll put the picture in a frame later.
(55b)   I'll frame the picture later.
(56a)   He put the $10 he found in his pocket.
(56b)   He pocketed the $10 he found.

Other morphological dissimilarities would include (57a-b) and (58a-b):

(57a)   For best results, do not put the cheese in the refrigerator.
(57b)   For best results, do not refrigerate the cheese.
(58a)   Eric, don't put the beer in the freezer.
(58b)   Eric, don't freeze the beer.

The set of anomalous paraphrases might include sentences like (59a-b) and (60a-b):

(59a)   We'll have to put the students in a house in the dormitory.
(59b)   We'll have to house the students in the dormitory.

In (59a-b), in the dormitory appears to narrow the specification or semantic reading of in the house or house.

(60a)   Don't forget to put the receipts in the drawer.
(60b)   *Don't forget to drawer the receipts.

Anomalous though (60b) is, it is nonetheless possible.
There are also some put class verbal units that are morphologically complex for different reasons, namely, that the new root takes on a remnant of the lexicalized noun locative in the form of the prefix en-, which surfaces as a bound prefix attached to the verbal roots as, for example, in the following list of incorporated verb forms:

encase	enfranchise
*enchant	*enlace
encipher	*enregister
encircle	enlist
*enclasp	ensconce
encode	*entrench
encrust	envelop
entrust	enclose

Those forms marked with an asterisk seemingly do not appear in modern English as decomposed verbal units with put. Several of the more common that do appear are found in the sentences (61a-b) and (62a-b):

> (61a)   The enemy put the message in code.
> (61b)   The enemy encoded the message.

Encode and encipher, it is interesting to note, in their negative paraphrases of decode and decipher, lose the morphological prepositional remnant in, a fact that is not the case with circle or encircle.

> (62a)   You must put a circle around your choice.
> (62b)   You must circle (encircle) your choice.

At this point it is worth mentioning several other examples of put lexicalizations that, because of their existence, are somewhat unusual. Relamp, for example, has no attested decomposition, that is, there is a gap at the primary lexical level of *"put a lamp." The example is taken from the RITTER lamp often found in a dentist's office; it is illustrated in (63a-c).

> (63a)   *Put a lamp in the RITTER.
> (63b)   *Lamp the device.
> (63c)   Relamp with RITTER 604B.

More research needs to be done on this particular type of lexicalizations and others of the re- prefix type.

Although in the introduction to this paper no mention was made of the following class of lexicalizations, it is important because propositionally and semantically, it is different from the give, make, and put classes. This class was described briefly in the work of Binnick (1968) in his discussion of motion verbs and consists, at this writing, of a single lexical prime, namely, go. Its propositional structure is three place, namely, go (x, y, z), where x is an AGENT, y a LOCATION, and z a MEANS or INSTRUMENT. The verbal lexical unit is intransitive. All cases listed are modes of conveyance and are illustrated in (64-66a-b):

> (64a)   The Indians went across the river in a canoe.
> (64b)   The Indians canoed across the river.
> (65a)   The kids went to the store on a skateboard.
> (65b)   The kids skateboarded to the store.
> (66a)   We'll go to the beach by bicycle.
> (66b)   We'll bicycle to the beach.

Other modes of conveyance include the following:

punt	canoe	sailboat
walk	foot	motorboat
skate	glide	surfboard
dinghy	scooter	trek

Computer programmers often speak of debugging a program or removing from the program any inappropriate instructions. Debug, in the process described in their paper, is a complex lexicalization that also includes negation, which is interpreted then at process reversal.

(67a)   I inadvertently put two bugs in the program.
(67b)   I have to remove the bugs from the program.
(67c)   I have to (NOT) (put the bugs) in the program.
(67d)   I have to debug the program.

Other verbs of the de- prefix type are: deform, decrystallize, decentralize, debark, disembark, and deplane. This area, too, suggests further productive research.

There is one other potentially lexicalizable prime that warrants serious investigation, namely, have. Although have is apparently a two-place stative predicator, usually BENEFACTIVE and OBJECTIVE, its nature in lexicalizations seems to change. In (68a-b) and (69a-b), at least in a particular style of English, that is, "bureaucratese," have exists as a former stative verb that, upon lexicalization, takes on the meaning of "cause."

(68a)   The gasoline shortage will have a profound impact on the economy.
(68b)   The gasoline shortage will impact the economy profoundly.
(69a)   We no longer have access to that information.
(69b)   We no longer can access that information.

It was proposed at the outset of this paper that paraphrase or the restatement of an objective situation in another syntactic form could indeed be shown to have a basis in generative semantics and lexical semantics. The procedure whereby lexicalization and its converse—decomposition—take place, can be employed to restate the objective situation in a meaning-preserving or synonymous way and to fill potential gaps in the system. The primes that have been shown as primary verbal lexical units are of high frequency in English and can be used to demonstrate the properties of verb units and noun units that can be used subsequently in simple stylistic restatement. Other languages besides English also avail themselves of the process and the set of strategies for searching for constituents and for recombining them in new and sometimes subtle ways.

REFERENCES

Binnick, Robert. 1968. On the nature of the lexical item. Chicago
    Linguistic Circle 4:1-11.
Clark, Herbert H., and Clark, Eve V. 1977. Psychology and
    language. New York: Harcourt Brace Jovanovich.
Cook, Walter A. 1974. Case grammar and generative semantics. In
    Georgetown University Papers on Languages and Linguistics,
    Number 8. Washington, D.C.: Georgetown University Press.
Fillmore, Charles. 1968. The case for case. In Universals in
    linguistic theory, ed. Emmon Bach and Robert T. Harms. New
    York: Holt, Rinehart and Winston.
_____. 1971. Some problems for case grammar. In Georgetown
    University round table on languages and linguistics, ed.
    Richard J. O'Brien. Washington, D.C.: Georgetown University
    Press.
Kirschner, Carl. 1976. Generative semantics and Spanish. Ph.D.
    diss., University of Massachusetts, Amherst.
Lakoff, George. 1970. Irregularity in syntax. New York: Holt,
    Rinehart and Winston.
McCawley, James D. 1971. Prelexical syntax. In Georgetown
    University round table on languages and linguistics, ed.
    Richard O'Brien. Washington, D.C.: Georgetown University
    Press.
Staczek, John J. 1976. La descomposición léxica en español. In
    Thesaurus 31:523-35.
_____. 1978. Degapping the lexicon of Spanish verbs. In
    Approaches to the Romance lexicon, ed. Frank Nuessel.
    Washington, D.C.: Georgetown University Press.
_____. 1979. Lexical decomposition, incorporation and paraphrase
    and the ESOL student. Paper read at 1979 International
    TESOL Convention, March 1-4, 1979, Boston, Mass.

12. Code-Switching in the St. John Valley of Northern Maine

NANCY LEE SCHWEDA
University of Delaware

To date, studies of multilingual speech communities have not included a unified theory of goal-oriented verbal interaction. I am interested in what Hymes 1974 and others have called the "ethnography of speaking." This viewpoint not only makes comparative analyses of speech events, but looks also to their functions and the social consequences of language varieties.

In my approach, I distinguish between verbal artifact (grammar) and verbal tool (Di Pietro 1976). The verbal tool can be further divided into strategy and protocol. A protocol is a speech ritual—i.e., something that is said almost invariably in a particular situation ("How are you?"—"Fine"). A strategy is more variable: its use is tied to the desire of a speaker to achieve a particular personal goal; i.e., one may compliment someone in the hope of receiving a favor.

The notion of continuum, as presented by Bickerton (1969) and others, relates solely to the artifact and not to the tool aspect of language. Accepting the notion of continuum, one may hypothesize that variations in the use of language in a multilingual society will be identified with speakers in accordance with their placement at various points on the proposed continua. My continua, however, in addition to representing linguistic varieties, deal with socially acceptable and situationally conditioned domains of language use among members of a speech community.

As there exists a grammar system for every language, do there not also exist functional systems that are dependent on sociological variables and situational factors? This paper proposes some possible answers to this question.

Results of my research in northern Maine lead me to hypothesize that the language or code-switch employed by speakers is dependent upon four factors:

1. the personal language capabilities of the subject in question; at which point/s does the subject fall on the continuum of locally spoken linguistic varieties?;
2. the setting of the particular interaction;
3. the subject under discussion;
4. the social and economic status of the speakers involved.

The Linguistic Continuum.   Before one can posit trends in sociolinguistic behavior, especially goal-oriented strategic interaction, one must first be aware of the linguistic continuum that characterizes the speech community in question.   Research data indicate the existence of a continuum (see Fig. 1):

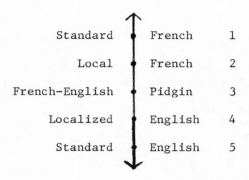

Standard	French	1
Local	French	2
French-English	Pidgin	3
Localized	English	4
Standard	English	5

Fig. 1.   Linguistic Continuum

Standard French.   Standard French is the language of the educated and is used by those who have studied French or have been educated with French as the language of instruction.   Even though a certain percentage of the local citizenry have a Standard French capability, it is rarely used in the St. John Valley.

Local French.   The Local French most often dominates the speech of elderly and rural people.   It is characterized by certain phonological and morphological forms that are considered archaic in Modern French.   For example, it uses nautical terms that, originally, had very specific meanings; these terms have been generalized to signify many actions in the same semantic domain as the original word (e.g., embarquer 'to set sail', 'to go off on a boat', now generalizes to 'to get into' [a car], 'to get on' [a horse]).

French-English Pidgin.   The English language exerts a very formidable influence on the Local French of the area.   Many English words have been lexicalized.   The English influence is so strong that a French-English pidgin language has evolved out of this particular language contact.   The pidgin is one in which verbs especially have been affected.   My data are particularly characterized by English verbs that have taken on French infinitive form features:

driver un truck   checker les spark plugs

Moreover, some have combined with propositions to form characteristically English compound verbs:

ringer in ('to ring in')
checker up ('to check up')

An example of a pidginized verb expression in the traditional French past participle form is

un tomato and lettuce, toaste (past participle 'toasted')

Of all the language varieties, I heard this pidgin language most often during my stay in the area. It appears to dominate everyday usage and is characteristic of virtually all age groups, except the very young and the very old.

Localized English. The Localized English has imprints of French, most often exhibited by its syntactic structure of emphatic pronoun use:

Me, I'm going there.
I went by there to see John, him.
Where my coat, me?

Standard English. The language of the educated, Standard English is the variety most often spoken by the average man on the street. It may also be the language of those who have left the area for a considerable time and have subsequently returned. Moreover, many monolingual Anglo families have moved into the region from outside areas, and one would hypothesize that they would be Standard English speakers.

To review, then, the five points listed give a comprehensive linguistic overview of the language varieties used in this region. My research shows that most people who live in the area fall at points 2, 3, and 4. (Note that the language variations are represented as points on the continuum; however, this is not to say that they are necessarily discrete points. Variations of and capabilities in linguistic varieties are widely diversified among community members, and people may fall at more than one point, or at an intermediate point between two or more different varieties.)

Setting Continuum. In addition to one's personal language capabilities, an important factor in any language situation is its setting. The following continuum has, at its extremes, formal and informal settings. I cite Fishman's Five Hypothesized Domains of Language Use (1971:255, 352) as general points of reference (see Fig. 2).

The most common informal settings are (1) within the home, (2) among friends in the neighborhood, and (3) some business dealings among local people who are previously acquainted. The informal settings would most likely be characterized by the use of points 2, 3, and/or 4 on the Linguistic Continuum (see Fig. 1).

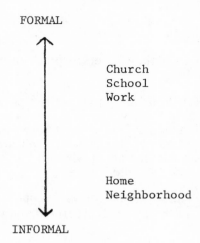

FORMAL

Church
School
Work

Home
Neighborhood

INFORMAL

Fig. 2.   Domains of Language Use

The most common formal settings are (1) church, (2) school, (3) work, (4) business dealings with strangers, (5) public speaking, (6) meeting new people, and (7) professional consultation.

Sometimes an informal language is used in what would normally be characterized as a formal situation. A good example of this is professionals with their patients and clients. Almost all of those interviewed who are bilingual told me that they converse in the language that is most comfortable for their patron. Furthermore, some people have a tendency to address the professional in a vernacular while the professional addresses them in a standard variety.

Moreover, the use of Standard English as an informal as well as a formal language is expected among those basically monolingual English speakers who speak, say, the French-English pidgin in their work only. The monolingual is limited to style shifts within the language he speaks, whereas the bilingual may switch from one language to another according to the particular circumstances of each unique situation.

The use of Standard French in formal situations appears to be limited to rituals or protocols, which are already written and merely recited (such as prayers and church services), or forms that are characteristically used in a particular situation. The spoken Standard French, as a language of communication and everyday conversation, is rarely encountered.

Subject under Discussion. The setting and subject under discussion are most definitely interrelated. Fishman's Five Domains may apply to both variables; moreover, we can also establish a formal/informal

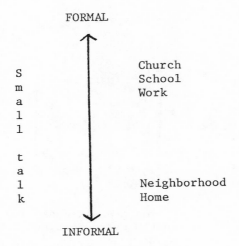

Fig. 3.   Continuum with Settings

continuum for the topics involved (see Fig. 3).

Certainly there are innumerable subjects one can talk about (just as there are innumerable settings); however, most would probably fall under one of these categories. Another category that I have added is making "small talk." Often people discuss inconsequential matters during the course of a conversation, whether it takes place in a formal or an informal setting. My data shows that very often the language of small talk among bilinguals of this region is either the Local French or the French-English pidgin whereas, when the subject changes to a more businesslike or professional one, the language very often selected is English. This is especially seen in the linguistic behaviour of professionals in the region. I have represented small talk as stretching the entire length of the continuum because of its generalized usage.

Status of Speaker. The continuum dealing with Status of Speaker (see Fig. 4) may be viewed in several ways. First of all, for any number of strategic reasons, those at the lower ends of the continuum will usually demonstrate an approach or accommodation strategy in order to approximate the speech patterns of a high-status speaker. He/she may wish to identify with the speaker who lies at a higher point on the continuum than he/she does, so he/she models the other's speech. This strategy may also be characteristic of one striving for upward mobility. The attempt to bring oneself closer to the high-status speaker may be considered as an identification strategy. However, if approximation attempts are unsuccessful, the lower-status speaker may be ridiculed.

This upward strategic use of language may be matched by its

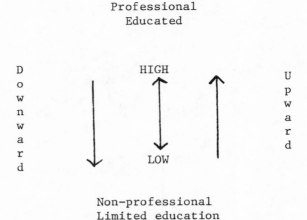

Fig. 4.   Continuum with Speaker Status

opposite.   Those who fall at the upper levels of the continuum strategically may alter their language patterns to approximate the speech of one who lies below them on the socioeconomic ladder. One of the most prevalent examples of this phenomenon is evidenced when a professional speaks a language variety that lies at another point on the continuum than his normally employed language in order to accommodate a patient or a client.   He/she interacts in this way to minimize the distance between the opposite extremes that characterize the continuum and, therefore, to achieve a common ground for satisfactory interaction.   This is also an accommodation strategy, but one which is accomplished by moving down the continuum from the top, whereas the first strategy described was characterized by an upward move from the bottom ranges of the continuum toward the top.   Of course, I do not wish to imply that only low- and high-status speakers exist.   Certainly, there are those who fall at intermediate levels on the status continuum.

In positing the existence of four separate continua, I have attempted to demonstrate the factors that play a key role in language use.   An endless number of possibilities exists; however, each instance of linguistic interaction is characterized by the interplay of these continua.

The idea of applying a continuum format to code-switching as a verbal strategy is not an unreasonable one because I have learned through the course of my research that certain subjects characteristically are discussed in one of the linguistic varieties involved.   Moreover, the setting, whether formal or informal, tends to further influence one's language choice.   Finally, the language of expression is, of course, dependent upon one's linguistic capabilities, which, in turn, are usually influenced and/or determined by one's socioeconomic status.

In light of the interaction of the continua, consider some examples (gathered anonymously) of code-switching by St. John Valley residents with regard to their strategic conversational value.

Episode One. I was interviewing a local physician when he was interrupted by a telephone call, which he took in the office where we were both seated. It was evident that he was speaking to a patient (they spoke of how a particular medication had helped this person). He conversed strictly in English. Toward the end of the conversation, however, the doctor said "C'est bon, c'est bon" ("It's good"). He then switched back to English to conclude the conversation.

Analysis of Episode One. I believe the significance of the interjection of this French phrase can be viewed in two ways. One interpretation is that it is used as a speech "protocol" (Di Pietro 1976:6, 7); in this instance, it is an expression that is used to indicate the completion of business, signaling the end of the conversation. However, I believe that its use may be more deeply interpreted as a strategy. It is expressed, not in the language of the conversation but, rather, in French. It is supposed that the other conversant is bilingual, therefore, the employment of "c'est bon" may serve to establish a camaraderie, a common ground between the doctor and his patient. Even though the entire preceding conversation is in English, the physician employs this identification strategy as a means of exhibiting understanding and concern. It has a cathected use in this sense. I observed this same use of "c'est bon" on numerous other occasions during the course of my stay.

(Note: "C'est bon," although grammatically correct as a French expression, is not correct in the sense in which it is used in the above example; "c'est bien" would have been more appropriate.)

Episode Two. A type of accommodation is evidenced in the following episode. One day when I was interviewing local high school teachers on their opinions of the bilingual education program in their school system, I was sitting with an interviewee in a group office, waiting for an appointment with another teacher. A young woman (also a teacher) walked in and began to address the interviewee about a school-related subject in what was a mixture of the Local French and the French-English pidgin. She did not take note of my presence in the office immediately. Soon after she began speaking, she noticed me and, at once, switched to English.

Analysis of Episode Two. Looking first at the teacher's use of French when addressing her colleague, one might think that because she spoke of a school matter she would have chosen English.

However, this gentleman appeared to be a friend as well as colleague. One can assume, then, that their friendship and ease with one another overrode the formal topic of school business with regard to her language choice. She selected an informal variety of language.

I asked this woman about her language switch to English when she noticed me. She explained that she recognized me as a stranger and, because of that, was not sure whether I would understand her. She began to speak English so as not to exclude me from their conversation. Interestingly enough, this young woman was not directly accommodating her speech to my language, because I said nothing. Rather, she switched to the language she perceived I would understand. One might refer to this as an indirect accommodation. Even though my status was unknown to her, she may have assumed that I was a visiting colleague, possibly from my appearance and the fact that I was carrying a briefcase. Moreover, we were in a school, which is traditionally classified as a formal setting. This may also have affected her code-switch to English.

Episode Three.   One afternoon I entered the Town Office in Fort Kent, Maine, hoping to locate some demographic information. The office was crowded and, while I was waiting, I overheard two employees conversing. A young woman about twenty years old was speaking English; the other conversant, a woman of about fifty-five, was addressing the young woman in Local French, although I noticed some code-switching. However, when the older woman approached me to ask if she could be of some service, she switched to English.

Analysis of Episode Three. I am a young woman; moreover, I was a stranger to the older woman. Both factors would indicate the use of English.   Furthermore, as a government office where official business is conducted, one would most probably choose English as the language of address when dealing with people who have come in for a business or professional reason.

Episode Four. I observed two middle-aged women shopping together in a supermarket in Madawaska, Maine. I first heard them speaking Local French; they were discussing what one woman's daughter does for a living and where she lives. However, they came upon a product they wanted to buy and switched their language to English, since one woman explained to the other why it was more economical to purchase a particular size. As they continued their shopping, I also heard instances of the French-English pidgin, in which code-switching reflected the use of English nouns in reference to product names and pidginized verbs.

Analysis of Episode Four. These women are obviously friends, and so status does not appear to play a critical role in this episode. Two friends shopping in a supermarket constitutes an informal situation.

They code-switch frequently. A family situation is most often and most comfortably discussed in Local French (their chat about one woman's daughter). The switch to English to discuss a particular product may have been triggered by the fact that it is more easily talked about in English. Moreover, the nature of the conversation (which size is more economical) may trigger a switch to English because it involves money management in a business sense. The return to a local language variety and subsequent code-switching is logical in this informal situation.

Conclusion. Even though the episodes cited in this paper were gathered at random, anonymously, and with no control whatsoever over the situation, they do exhibit certain similar characteristics, and some demonstrate recurrent strategies. It appears that the use of continua as factors in language selection constitutes a valid and practical approach. It is through the discussion of the continua's role and their application to actual events that I have attempted to present various underlying factors and linguistic goal orientations that manifest themselves overtly as code-switching.

REFERENCES

Bickerton, Derek. 1969. On the nature of a creole continuum. Language 49:640-69.
Di Pietro, Robert J. 1976. The strategies of language use. In The Second LACUS forum, ed. P. A. Reich, pp. 462-67. Columbia, S.C.: Hornbeam Press.
Hymes, Dell. 1974. Foundations in sociolinguistics: an ethnographic approach. Philadelphia, University of Pennsylvania Press.

13. Code-Switching as a Verbal Strategy among Bilingual Chinese

DAVIS L. LEE
George Washington University

Verbal interaction not only provides for the exchange of information but also, and perhaps more importantly, achieves certain psychological and social ends. To put it briefly, individuals use language for a wide range of goals.

According to Di Pietro (1976b), verbal strategies exist for "the attainment of success in dealing with other human beings. Among other things, they have to do with avoiding accusations of guilt, seducing, misleading, excusing one's self for a transgression, and making disclaimers." If we apply an approach to language learning that is based on verbal strategies, we extend an invitation to both linguists and language teachers to take a fresh view of the study of second-language learning.

The use of code-switching manifests itself among monolingual Chinese in the use of classical language versus the colloquial forms. This type of code-switching is a very important part of conversation in Chinese culture. Also prevalent is the use of words with two meanings (deliberate ambiguity). An episode from a Peking opera called <u>Black Dragon</u> demonstrates the latter point.

When Sung Jiang, a petty official, went to see his concubine Yen Hsichiao in his residence called Black Dragon, Yen treated him as an unwanted guest. Her lover, who had come before Sung, had hid himself and awaited Sung's departure. Yen tried every trick she knew to send Sung away, but she failed. Finally, Yen showed Sung a pair of red slippers that were to be a birthday gift for her elderly mother. She asked Sung for his opinion about them. The conversation went as follows:

> Y: Zheli you yishuang gei wo muqin de tuo xie. Ni juede zenmayang?
> (Here is a pair of slippers for my mother. What do you think of it?)
> S: Hua er ye hao, yang er ye hao, zhen shi hao, hao, hao.
> (The floral pattern is good, the design is also good. It's good.)
> Y: Yidiar buhao dou meiyou ma?
> (It's flawless, isn't it?)
> S: Ah, jiu shi yiyang bu tai hao.
> (Well, only one thing is not so good.)

Y: Neiyiyang?
    (What's that?)
S: Zhege yanse bu dui.
    (The color is not right).
Y: Yanse zenme bu dui?
    (Why is the color not right?)
S: Nide muqin zheme da de nianji, ta bu yingdang
    chuan hongde.
    (Your mother is advanced in age. She shouldn't
    wear the color red.)
Y: Yanse yaoshi bu dui, ni zao jiu bu gai lai.
    (If the color isn't right, you shouldn't come in the
    first place.)

The English equivalent of yanse is 'color'. Actually the color to which Sung referred was directed to Yen's uneasiness, as reflected in her facial expressions. At first, Yen did not get the meaning of what Sung was saying. Then, suddenly, she construed the clear message from him. The context produced an extension of the original meaning to its extended meaning, or, in more technical terms, an extension from denotational to connotational meaning.

Another example of extended meaning is taken from a Peking opera called The Meeting of Heroes, or in Chinese Chun Ying Hui. In one episode Ts'ao Ts'ao, the Premier of Wei State on the upper Yangtze, sends his special envoy Chiang Kan to persuade his classmate Chou Yu, who is the garrison commander of the Wu State on the lower Yangtse, to surrender. Chou entertains his former classmate and invites him to have a drink. The dialogue goes as follows:

Chou: Duo ri wei jian, wu deng zai gan yibei, ruhe?
         (I haven't seen you for such a long time, why
         don't we empty another cup?)
Chiang: Laoxiung zhi wo liang qian, buneng feng pei.
         (You know I can't drink. I've had enough.)
Chou: Bei zhan ruci zhi xiao, wu xiung dang neng yin
         zhi.
         (The cup is so small, I'm sure you can do it.)
Chiang: Ruci yin jiu, you ru shun liu er xia, kuai de jin
         ne.
         (When one drinks, it goes down very fast as if
         one were sailing downstream.)

The original meaning of kuai is fast. But here Chiang alludes to other meanings of kuai: sharp and vigorous. The implication is that Ts'ao's navy could easily destroy Wu's navy should there be a war between the two powers.

The third example concerns a sharp-tongued college coed who enjoys intimidating her male suitor. In one dialogue of a play, she portrays a lady of easy virtue. After the performance, a male student comes to congratulate her and says:

Ni yande feichang hao. Wei miao wei qiao.
(You acted very well. So skillfully imitated as to be indistinguishable from the original.)

The use of the proverb wei miao wei qiao was intended to convey an insult to the coed in a form generally construed as a compliment.

Motives for code-switching are many. The following are some general observations I have made on this matter.

1. Posturing (Showing Off)

From time to time, young Chinese immigrants or new students studying in this country are likely to use an English word in a Chinese sentence, such as Wo yao cong Route #1 zou 'I want to take Route #1'. Such an expression could be said by an educated person who wishes to show his relatives and friends that he recognizes the American way. One may say that this switch represents a quick assimilation to the new culture.

Once I asked an American-born Chinese woman whether she liked to eat blue cheese. She answered, "I don't care for it, because it is wei tong jiao la (as tasteless as chewing wax)." By using a Chinese proverb, she not only accentuated the fact that she did not care for blue cheese, but also reinforced her ethnicity by code-switching. Chinese who have been in this country for two or three decades may sometimes mix English grammar with Chinese word order. However, they never forget the correct usage of a Chinese proverb. It appears that a commonly shared proverb will remain with the speaker longer than the grammar of his mother tongue.

2.   Terms Lacking in Describing a Situation in One's Own Language

In a sentence like Wo yao chi yige cheeseburger 'I want to eat a cheeseburger', the use of English word cheeseburger stems from the fact that there is no such thing as cheese in China, let alone a cheeseburger.

In another example, if a student of economics is asked what is the topic that the professor covered in class, the answer is likely to be oligopoly in English because there is no Chinese equivalent for the term. Occasionally a speaker will not stop a flow of a discourse just for a word he cannot think of at the moment; instead, he will code-switch. Therefore it seems that not all instances of code-switching are for the purpose of verbal maneuvering, but instead are nonvolitional.

3.   Pleasing a Friend Who Knows the Language by Producing an Amusing Effect (Expression of Solidarity with Another Who Knows the Language)

The literal translation of an expression may be entirely

different from its actual meaning. For instance, the American expressions You sold me and I don't buy that can be used to show conviction or the lack of it. Both expressions may be interpreted as 'it must be a commercial deal' or 'a commodity must be involved'. The result is usually laughter when we code-switch spontaneously from English to Chinese even in a serious discussion. Ni ba wo mai le 'You sold me' in the sense that I am an object or a piece of commodity, and Wo bu mai neige 'I don't buy it' meaning that there is no transaction being made are often heard in business negotiations among Chinese in the United States.

In Madison, Wisconsin, during the summer of 1958, a Peking opera was performed by a local amateur group to entertain the participants of a two-day conference. The opera, Shih Yu Chuo (Picking up the Jade Bracelet), dealt with an episode about a rich young man who was out strolling one day and saw a pretty young lady sitting at the door embroidering silk slippers. Immediately smitten by the girl's charms, the young man began to flirt with her. In accordance with Chinese etiquette the girl went indoors. Not to be outdone, the would-be suitor placed a jade bracelet on the ground outside the door and retired to watch what would happen. Unable to contain herself any longer, the girl peeped out to see where the admirer had gone. Spying the bracelet, she hastily grabbed it and placed it on her wrist. Pleased with what he saw, the young man went off announcing to the world that he was going to ask his mother to arrange a formal betrothal with the girl.

During the performance, at the scene when the young lady picks up the jade bracelet, the actress remarked to the audience: Zheige bu shi yu de 'This is not jade', and then suddenly switched to English, saying: It's a cheap souvenir from Chinatown. The code-switch to English almost brought down the house.

4.   Keeping a Secret

American-born Chinese children who do not speak Chinese often have receptive competence in the language. However, they are usually not familiar with Chinese proverbs or common sayings. When discussing the behavior or conduct of a child, Chinese parents ordinarily use proverbs in their conversations. This technique is similar to the one American parents use when they spell a taboo word in front of the children instead of pronouncing it.

I once overheard a conversation between a couple whose child was at their side. One parent noticed that his son (around the age of four) somehow had learned the trick of being evasive. The youngster was accustomed to turning a deaf ear to them whenever the subject was unpleasant. The father said: This child now has learned . . . and then switching to a Chinese proverb Huan gu zuo you 'to look around, i.e., without answering the question'. I wonder where he learned that? The child was evidently confused and did not know what his parent was talking about because he did not understand the proverb.

The use of a Chinese proverb in the above conversation

demonstrates one way in which Chinese people attempt to gain an advantage in their verbal encounters by using commonly shared proverbs. These proverbs are expressed through language, which is a part of Chinese culture. By aligning Chinese culture on one's side against others in a conversation, one greatly increases the chances for achieving his strategic goals successfully.

I conclude that in language contact situations, forms may change (in the adoption of words from a second language) but the content, or meaning, can remain the same. From my personal observations, I have come to believe that code-switching for bilingual Chinese functioning in American culture fulfills strategic needs similar to those of monolingual Chinese interacting with each other in Chinese culture.

REFERENCES

Arlington, L. C. and Action, H. 1963. Famous chinese plays. New York: Russell and Russell.

Di Pietro, Robert J. 1971. Language structures in contrast. Rowley, Mass: Newbury House.

_____. 1976a. Code-switching as a verbal strategy among bilinguals. Paper read at the Linguistic Symposium on 27 March 1976, University of Wisconsin, Milwaukee.

_____. 1976b. The strategies of language use. In The second LACUS forum 1975, ed. P. A. Reich, pp. 462-67. Columbia, S.C.: Hornbeam Press.

_____. 1976c. Contrasting patterns of language use: a conversational approach. Canadian Modern Language Review 33, (October 1976):49-61.

_____. 1977. Verbal strategies in language 2. Lecture given at the University of Wisconsin, Milwaukee, 4 November 1977.

Goffman, Erving. 1971. Relations in public, microstudies of the public. New York: Harper and Row.

Lee, Davis L. 1978. Chinese proverbs: a pragmatic and sociolinguistic approach. Ph.D. diss., Georgetown University, Washington, D.C.

Liang, S. C. 1971. A new practical Chinese-English dictionary. Taipei: Far East Book Company.

Wong, S. M. 1977. Chinese idioms and phrases. Hong Kong: Shang-wu Book Company.

14. **The Language–Use Grid: A Versatile Tool for the Applied Linguist**

RODNEY F. MOAG
University of Michigan

The plotting of the interaction of two dimensions on the vertical and horizontal axes of a graph is a well-known technique. It is also possible to plot the progress of a single variable through a number of categories, or dimensions, by making each column along the horizontal axis stand for a separate condition through which the dimension on the vertical axis is traced. Such notational methods are often inadequate for the sociolinguist or applied linguist wishing to represent graphically some of the more complex relationships between linguistic behavior and the context in which it takes place, particularly in bi- or multilingual societies where accuracy necessitates representing the interdependence of half a dozen or so significant variables simultaneously.

This paper will show how the Language Use Grid (LUG) meets this need. Previous work on the LUG as a means of representing language use patterns in multilingual societies will be reviewed and its relative merits over other notational devices in print will be treated. Finally, the further potential of the LUG will be explored as a means of providing a framework for the representation of more complex interactions with respect to code-switching and of linguistic variables.

1. Representing Language Use and Language Choice

The first LUG (see Table 1) was worked out by Louisa Moag and was designed to represent the language use patterns of the two main speech communities, Fijians and Indians, in the multilingual South Pacific nation of Fiji. Considerations of both space and .topicality precluded a meaningful discussion of the merits of this new device when originally published (Moag 1978).

The original LUG (Table 1) plotted the interaction of five variables in a two-dimensional framework as follows:

1. Language/variety (on the vertical axis)
2. Group membership of addressee (on the horizontal axis)
3. Setting (also on the horizontal axis)
4. Community of speaker (within boxes on the grid)
5. Degree of use of each code or subcode (within boxes)

157

Table 1
Language Use Grid for Fiji According to Addressee and Speaker

Speaker's Key

F — Urban Fijian of 45 with Regional Origin
I — Urban Indian of 45 with Regional Origin

Usage Key

1 — Infrequent Use
2 — Moderate Use
3 — Extensive Use

ADDRESSEE → / LANGUAGE POOL ↓	(Regional) Formal Regional	(Regional) Informal Regional	(Communal) Formal Communal	(Communal) Informal Communal	Formal Intercommunal	Informal (I.I.) Intercommunal with Fijians	(Intercommunal) I.I. with Indians	(Intercommunal) I.I. with Chinese	(Intercommunal) I.I. with Other Islanders	(Intercommunal) I.I. with Europeans
Standard Fiji English	F1 I2		F1 I2		F3 I3					
Colloquial Fiji English		F1 I2		F1 I2		I3	F3	F3 I3	F3 I3	F3 I3
Standard Fijian (Bauan)			F2							
Chiefly Fijian (Bauan)			F1							
Colloquial Fijian (Bauan)				F3						
Ritual Regional	F1		F1							
Chiefly Regional Fijian	F1									
Colloquial Regional Fijian		F3								
Pidgin Fijian						I2	F2	F2 I1		
Standard Hindi	I2		I3							
Fiji Hindi		I3		I3						
Standard Regional South Indian	I1									
Colloquial Regional South Indian		I1								
Pidgin Hindi						I1	F1	I2		

I am indebted to Louise Moor for the ...

Variables 1 and 2 need little explanation. Variable 3 was achieved by subdividing each category of addressee into formal versus informal settings. These two commonly accepted categories for social context may be taken as composites of role, setting, and topic. Inclusion of variables 4 and 5 is achieved through the convention of multiple entries within individual boxes of the grid. Values for the coded letter and number symbols must, of course, be given in a key, as in Tables 1 and 2.

The specific categories for each of the five variables may vary from society to society. Whatever these might be in individual cases, each entry in the LUG makes a statement that would require two or more lines in print to express. Examining the bottom row of Table 1, for example, shows that Indians use Pidgin Hindi to a moderate extent in informal interactions with Fijian and Chinese outgroup members, but that Fijians only use Pidgin Hindi to an infrequent extent, and then only with Indian outgroup members. In addition to this succinctness of statement, the LUG makes apparent the contrasts between various entries and interactions of multiple variables that would be buried within a textual rendition of the data. It is further possible to follow each of the five variables through its intersection with all others, whereas text can be organized according to the categories of a single dimension.

Leaving textual representation aside, the LUG goes beyond previous graphic devices for plotting language use/choice such as Stewart 1968, Rubin 1968, and Platt 1977. Stewart's well-known system for describing multilingual societies (1968) encompasses four variables: degree of use, language, language type, and language function. Degree of use and language are listed in adjacent columns on the left with type and function appearing in an unbroken line of abbreviations to their right. The first two are the only variables easily traceable through the charts. It is not easy to trace specific functions such as education, wider communication, or the like since they do not have clearly demarcated columns of their own. I have worked out a modified system based on Stewart's typology allowing for the inclusion of more complete information on both language type and function (Moag unpublished), but the resulting charts are not only limited to the representation of only four variables, but are difficult to read because of the fact that all information except the names of languages or varieties is in coded symbols.

These same two problems occur in the representations of language use among the Chinese community of Singapore in Platt (1977:376). Though only two dimensions are plotted—domains on the vertical axis and language on the horizontal axis—categories for each are coded into numbers and lower case letters respectively—1 representing the friendship domain, c representing Colloquial Singapore English, etc. Platt states that choice of language "will be determined by the speaker's own verbal repertoire, his interlocutor's verbal repertoire and to what extent the speaker is prepared to accommodate to his interlocutor" (Platt 1977:377), but he makes no

Table 2
Language Use Grid for Fiji According to the Domain and Speaker

Speaker's Key

F — Urban Fijian with Regional Origin
I — Urban Indians with Regional Origin

Usage Key

1 — Infrequent Use
2 — Moderate Use
3 — Extensive Use

LANGUAGE POOL / DOMAIN	(Informal) HOME	SHOPPING Marketing, Bus., Post Office, etc.	SOCIAL Friendship	SCHOOL Playground	(Formal) SCHOOL Classroom	GOVERNMENT	RELIGION	POLITICS	MEDIA Print	MEDIA Aural
Standard Fiji English	F1 I1	F1 I2	F2 I2	F3 I3	F3 I3	F3 I3	F1 I1	F2 I2	F2 I3	F1 I2
Colloquial Fiji English	F1 I1	F2 I1	F2 I2		F1 I1			F1 I1		
High Bauan (Fijian)					F1	F1	F3	F2	F2	F3
Chiefly Bauan (Fijian)						F1				
Colloquial Bauan (Fijian)	F1	F2	F2	F1		F1				
Colloquial Regional Fijian	F3	F2 I2	F1	F1						
Pidgin Fijian		F2 I2		F1						
Standard Hindi					I1	I1	I3	I2	I1	I3
Fiji Hindi	I3	I2	I3	I2	I1	I1				
Colloquial Regional South Indian	I1									
Pidgin Hindi		F1 I1								

This LUG was prepared for a workshop presented at the TESOL Convention in Mexico City, 1978 (Moag and Moag 1978).

attempt to incorporate these three additional variables into his plot. The Language Repetoire that he plots on the horizontal axis is that of the speech community as a whole from which the repertoires of individual speakers and interlocutors vary considerably (Platt 1977:377).

A widely known chart showing language choice in the bilingual setting of Paraguay is found in Rubin (1968:518-20). The three categories of language—Spanish, Guarani, and both—appear on the horizontal axis, while the vertical axis contains thirty-nine items from her language use questionnaire reflecting combinations of addressee, setting, and speaker's emotional intent. Entries in the columns show the number of respondents in her data sample reporting the use of Spanish, Guarani, or both under the various conditions. Having several variables interspersed on the vertical axis makes it difficult for their interaction to be traced. Unfortunately, limited space does not permit the inclusion of these representational schemes.

Besides clarity and greater number of variables, the LUG also features flexibility in its ability to highlight those variables most significant for a given focus or line of study. Table 2 shows a LUG focusing on more abstract language patterns in the society at large by tracing domains in the horizontal plain rather than the categories of addressee in Table 1. If, for instance, the focus was variation within a given speech community, it might be more useful to plot the several variables under examination along the horizontal axis and to reduce domains to two broad categories (probably formal versus informal) that could be represented by letter designations within each entry on the grid. Table 3 shows a sample legend for such a horizontal axis plotting the four variables of sex, age, education, and rural-urban residence. In such a LUG, entries in the boxes could compare degrees of usage between two different communities as in Tables 1 and 2, or degrees of use within formal and informal domains within the same community as mentioned above, or whatever contrast was most noteworthy in a given situation.

Table 3
Sample Legend for Horizontal Axis

young								older							
urban				rural				urban				rural			
ed.		uned.		ed.		uned.		ed.		uned.		ed.		uned.	
F	M	F	M	F	M	F	M	F	M	F	M	F	M	F	M

It should be noted that the LUG need not be limited to two entries within each box. Degrees of usage for three or more communities could be stacked so long as the vertical height of the boxes was sufficient to prevent crowding. Similarly, there is nothing inviolate about the three-point scale of usage employed in the LUGs shown here. A two- or four-point scale might be more useful in other cases, and degree of usage might not even be a significant variable in all studies. Table 4 shows a sample box incorporating the four variables of age, social status, sex, and degree of use within a single entry that could appear in LUGs such as those in Tables 1, 2, and elsewhere. The appropriate speaker's key is also provided.

Table 4
Sample Box with Four Variables

	Speaker's Key:
yhm 2	
yhf 3	y: young
ohm 1	o: older
ohf 2	h: high social status
ylm/f 1	l: low social status
olm/f 0	m: male social status
	f: female
	m/f: male and female

Note: Degree of use numbers follow the same key as Tables 1 and 2.

2. Representing Patterns of Code-Switching

In a study of three very diverse bilingual communities— Slovenian-speaking peasants in Austria, urban elite college students in North India, and rising urban Chicanos in California—Gumperz (1977:22) states that "code-switching is used for roughly the same ends [communicative functions] in similar discourse contexts." Though communicative or semantic functions and discourse functions are recognized in this and other recent works on code-switching (cf. Gumperz and Hernandez-Chavez 1972; Pfaff 1979) there has been no systematic attempt either to clearly distinguish the two, or to examine their mutual interaction. Table 5 presents a model employing the LUG format designed to these ends. Since role and setting and other social factors such as age, status, and the like in general remain constant in the interactions within which switches occur, these were omitted from the model.

The assignment of particular functions to the categories of communicative functions and discourse functions (on the vertical and horizontal axes respectively) represents my own preliminary attempt and is certainly subject to revision. Limitations of space proscribe all but the briefest summary treatment of them here. The ranking into generic versus specific communicative functions is also my own. The majority of the functions were culled from Gumperz and Hernandez–Chavez (1972) and Gumperz (1977). The Solidarity subfunction of accommodating to the wishes or views of an interlocutor and the two Speaker's Intent subfunctions of introducing comic effect and demonstrating competence in another variety came from Di Pietro (1977). One of the Solidarity functions was not specifically stated by the author, but is my own inference from Gumperz and Hernandez–Chavez (1972), example 28, showing one's license to criticize.

Table 5
Code–Switching LUG

Communicative Function	Discourse Function			
	Signaling New information	Fore-grounding of message	Marking sequence as an aside	Authenti-cation of quotes and reports
Solidarity Stressing common ethnicity				
Accommodation to views or wishes of interlocutor	E–S5 E–E3			
Showing one's license to criticize			E–S1 S–E0	
Stressing that no nonethnics present				
Speaker's Intent Showing emotional involvement				
Showing detachment				
Amplify or reinforce already stated intent				
Qualify previous statement				

Introduce comic effect			
Momentary inclination			
Topic-related functions			
Ethnic/cultural content			
Ethnicity of third person referent			
Private or confidential			
Nature of message			
Personal appeal			
Warning			
Personal opinion			
Generally known fact			
Casual remark			
Personal feeling			
Linguistic competence of speaker			
Incomplete control of variety of use			
Slip of tongue			

Switching key: E-S, English to Spanish switch
                   S-E, Spanish to English switch

NOTE: numbers are hypothetical occurrences in a corpus.

The inclusion of Linguistic Competence of Speaker as a category of communicative function may, initially, seem ill founded, but in the light of Gumperz's (1977) remarks about the importance of background identity for deriving like interpretations and of the ability of participants to derive considerable information about the background of other interlocutors from their switching behavior, it does have a place here.

In terms of the sources of the various discourse functions,

Signaling New Information is mentioned both in Gumperz and Hernandez-Chavez (1972) and in Pfaff (1979). Foregrounding appears in the former, while Marking of a Sequence as an Aside appears in the latter (Pfaff 1979:309). Authentication of Quotes and Reported Speech can be found in both Gumperz (1977) and Pfaff (1979:309).

Several of the semantic or communicative functions, particularly under Nature of Message, represent two opposites or endpoints on continua that Gumperz (1977:30) characterizes as "metaphoric extension of the we/they code opposition." According to this dichotomy, the "we" code (ethnic language) connotes the casualness, privacy, and intimacy of home and peer group relations while the "they" code (dominant language) connotes the formality, publicness, and detachment of outgroup relations. Richards (forthcoming) uses these and other oppositions as coincident with the alternatives of the rhetorical versus the communicative norms, terms first used by Haugen (1953) to describe two functionally differentiated varieties of Norwegian as spoken by immigrants to the United States. The rhetorical versus the communicative norm as used by Richards in his interesting paper equates to the difference between the standard versus the colloquial varieties of the indigenized Englishes in places such as Fiji (Moag and Moag 1977) and Singapore (Platt 1977). It would also seem to equate to the "careful-casual" style opposition as used by Labov and others in reference to monolingual groups. All of these distinctions would seem to connote the same set of semantic oppositions.

Two variables are plotted in the sample entries in the boxes in the code-switching LUG; Direction of Switch (Spanish to English or English to Spanish), and Frequency of Occurrence of Switching. The latter is expressed here in terms of hypothetical number of occurrences in a corpus, but could be rendered in rough usage categories as in Tables 1 and 2 or in percentages. The model cites only two directions for switches, as data-based studies to date have recognized only two languages or dialects between which speakers alternated. Di Pietro (1976) rightly points out that some Italian-Americans actually have four codes between which alternation is possible—standard Italian, Italo-American koine, Standard American English, and pidginized English—switches to each having distinctive connotations relating to speaker's background, intent, and other factors. Gumperz (1977) refers to multivarietal competence of some Chicanos, but includes no data on multivarietal switching. Such could be accommodated in the LUG by entries similar to those shown in Table 4.

Table 6 shows the legend for the horizontal axis of a LUG that would compare the code-switching behavior of speakers of varying linguistic competence within two separate communities. These categories are based on stages 2-4 of the scale of acculturation proposed in Di Pietro (1976) and will be self-explanatory by heading. This eliminates from the data sample essentially monolingual speakers of either language who have only a few frozen phrases in the other.

Table 6
Legend for Horizontal Axis of a LUG

Communicative Function	Code-Switching LUG					
	Chicanos			Italo-Americans		
	Eng. Dom.	Span. Dom.	Full Bil.	Eng. Dom.	Itln. Dom.	Full Bil.

3. Plotting Linguistic Variables

It should be clear from the preceding how the LUG format could also be adapted to plot variable linguistic features such as the five significant phonological variables in New York City English (Labov 1966) or others. The variables would likely be on the horizontal axis, social factors on the vertical axis, and degrees or percentages of use in formal versus informal styles within the boxes.

4. Conclusion

The LUG has been shown to be a notational device capable of representing complex bodies of data on language use/choice, code-switching, and the distribution of linguistic variables. Its strength lies not only in its ability to plot the interaction of five or more significant variables within the basically two-dimensional framework of the printed page, but as well in its flexibility permitting foregrounding of whatever variables are most significant in a given instance. Applied linguists, particularly those responsible for the planning of programs, must have at their fingertips synopses of complex sociolinguistic situations in a compact and usable form. The LUG provides an improved tool for this purpose.

REFERENCES

Di Pietro, Robert J.   1976.   Language as a marker of Italian ethnicity. Studi Emigrazioni (Rome) 42:203-18.
_____.   1977.   Code-switching as a verbal strategy among bilinguals.   In Current themes in linguistics; bilingualism, experimental linguistics, and language typologies, ed. Fred R. Eckman, pp. 3-13. New York: John Wiley and Sons.
Gumperz, John J.   1977.   The socio-linguistic significance of conversational code-switching. RELC Journal 8:1-34.
Gumperz, John J., and Hernandez-Chavez, Eduardo.   1972. Bilingualism, bidialectalism, and classroom interaction.   In Functions of language in the classroom, ed. Courtney B.

Cazden, Vera P. John, and Dell Hymes, pp. 84-108. New York: Teachers College Press. Also in: A pluralistic nation; the language issue in the United States, ed. Margaret A. Lourie and Nancy Faires Conklin, pp. 275-93. Rowley, Mass.: Newbury House.

Haugen, Einar. 1953. The Norwegian language in America: A study in bilingual behavior. Philadelphia: University of Pennsylvania Press.

Labov, William. 1966. The social stratification of English in New York City. Washington, D.C.: Center for Applied Linguistics.

Moag, Rodney F. 1978. Standardization in pidgin Fijian: implications for the theory of pidginization. In Fijian language studies: borrowing and pidginization, ed. Albert Shutz. Bulletin of the Fiji Museum 4:68-90. Published in revised form in Proceedings of the second international conference on Austronesian linguistics. Pacific linguistics, pp. 1444-84.

Moag, Rodney F. and Louisa B. Moag. 1977. English in Fiji, some perspectives and the need for language planning. Fiji English Teacher's Journal 13:2-26. To be reprinted in Occasional Paper Series, Singapore: Regional Language Center.

_____. 1978. Plotting language use patterns, an added tool for teachers and materials writers. Workshop presented at TESOL 1978, Mexico City.

Pfaff, Carol W. 1979. Constraints on language mixing: intrasentential code-switching and borrowing in Spanish/English. Language 55:291-318.

Platt, John T. 1977. A model for polyglossia and multilingualism (with special reference to Singapore and Malaysia). Language in Society 6:361-78.

Richards, Jack C. Forthcoming. Rhetorical and communicative norms in the new varieties of English. In The new Englishes, ed. J. B. Pride. Rowley, Mass.: Newbury House.

Rubin, Joan. 1968. Bilingual usage in Paraguay. In Readings in the sociology of language, ed. Joshua A. Fishman, pp. 512-30. The Hague: Mouton.

Stewart, William A. 1968. A sociolinguistic typology for describing national multilingualism. In Readings in the sociology of language, ed. Joshua A. Fishman, pp. 530-45. The Hague: Mouton.

15. Verbal Communication and Role-Taking: An Analysis of the Use of Deictics

NANCY J. SPEKMAN
University of Maryland

Introduction

Children and adults participate daily in a large number of communication activities. School classrooms, for example, provide opportunities for communicating with different audiences, for various purposes, and under differing contextual constraints. Children are expected to communicate with teachers, other adults, and peers. Communications may be intimate or formal. They may be social in nature or academic, such as working on group projects or presenting ideas to a class. With each change in communication activity and audience typically comes a concomitant change in the language used.

Successful verbal communication requires much more than mastery of the rules of the phonological, syntactic, and semantic systems of a language. It requires also that the speaker identify his/her interlocutor and the needs of that individual, determine the objective of the communication, assess various situational or contextual circumstances, and know the rules regarding cooperation, turn-taking, sequencing, violations and repairs, and other responsibilities (Ervin-Tripp 1964; Garvey and Baldwin 1970; Grice 1975; Hymes 1971, 1972; Schegloff 1972; Schegloff, Jefferson, and Sacks 1977). Linguistic selections, thus, are seen as both socially and cognitively determined.

The purpose of this paper is to focus on that aspect of verbal communication that has to do with taking the perspective of another, i.e., role-taking, and more specifically, with adapting one's language to reflect that perspective. An analysis of deictic usage is recommended herein as a method for gaining insight into a speaker's ability to make these adaptations linguistically. This paper will discuss the relationship between deictics and communication success and present a framework for deictic analysis. Examples from dyadic interactions will be presented to demonstrate the role played by deictics in communication.

Review of Literature

Communication can be defined as one form of social interaction involving both the establishment of interpersonal contacts and the subsequent exchange of information. Extant communication literature lends strong support to the notion that a "sense of audience" is an essential component of successful communication. Rommetveit (1974), for example, speaks of the need to establish a "temporarily shared reality" between or among participants.

This ability to successfully assume more than one perspective—i.e., to assume a point of view other than one's own—is frequently referred to as role-taking. Role-taking skills have been shown to increase with age in a variety of contexts including tasks of a perceptual, conceptual and/or communicational (or social) nature (Feffer 1970; Flavell et al. 1968; Garvey and Baldwin 1970; Krauss and Glucksberg 1969; Looft 1972; Piaget 1926; Rubin 1973). According to Flavell (1971:71-72), successful interpersonal inference requires not only the awareness that a particular situation requires inferential activity, but also the awareness of the inferential activity itself and its application in subsequent behavior. Thus, a speaker must assess the needs of his/her audience based on knowledge of the individual(s) and knowledge of the communication context, and then utilize this information in the preparation of messages. The nature of the language used should reflect this process.

Deictic Usage as a Measure of Role-Taking Skill. The existence of role-taking abilities during communication tasks has been measured or inferred through a variety of means such as task success or failure, content of messages, and modification of messages in response to questions. The methodology presented herein represents an attempt to measure role-taking abilities in specific linguistic terms through an analysis of the use of deictics.

According to Ryan (1974), Habermas posits the existence of certain "dialogic constitutive universals," mastery of which is essential for the establishment of intersubjectivity or shared perspective. These universals allow for the "interlacing of perspective between speakers, for the relating of speakers to the referents of conversation, and for the other pragmatic aspects of the speech situation" (Ryan 1974:187). These universals are expressed in dialogue by certain linguistic elements, such as deictics, and thus represent an intersection of linguistic and social abilities, i.e. the use of linguistic means to a social end. Bar-Hillel (1954), Bloom and Lahey (1978), Fillmore (1975), Rommetveit (1974), and others share this notion on the importance of deictics in communication.

Weinreich defines deictics as "signs used for referring without designation" (Weinreich 1963:145); they involve "a reference to the act of speech in which they are used" (Weinreich 1963:154). Similarly, deictics are defined by Fillmore (1975:39) as "the name given to those formal properties of utterances which are determined by, and which are interpreted by, knowing aspects of the communication act in which the utterances in question can play a role." Deictics are linguistic elements that make reference to, or stand for, people, things, places and time; their interpretation is dependent upon or presupposes the existence of another element either within the discourse itself or within the context of the discourse. They indicate relationships between participants and the content of the message and they contribute to the internal cohesion and external ties of a discourse (Halliday and Hasan 1976). Examples of deictics include personal pronouns, demonstrative pronouns (this, that), terms of location (here, there) and of time (before, after, then), and certain verbs (come, go, bring, take). The purpose of deictic usage is to utilize information that is assumed to be common knowledge between the participants. The correct/incorrect usage of deictics would thus appear to reflect an individual's ability to establish this shared perspective. For example, imagine a listener's confusion were he to hear the following in which the referents, or things referred to, are not identifiable:

> ... and it's not exactly it ... it's when you put it beside it ... it's not it ... you put it under that.*

In recent years, considerable research has addressed the appearance of deictics and their subsequent development in terms of correct comprehension and usage in the language of young children. Studies have focused on the use of personal pronouns (Bloom, Lightbown, and Hood 1975; Chipman and deDardel 1974; Huxley 1970), demonstrative pronouns (deVilliers and deVilliers 1974; Webb and Abrahamson 1976), terms of location (Bloom, Rocissano, and Hood 1976; Charney 1979), and deictic verbs (Clark and Garnica 1974; Richards 1976). With respect to these research studies, Bloom and Lahey (1978:225) note that with each of these forms

> ... acquisition continues often well into the school years and involves the very complex interplay between children's opportunities for using and hearing others use shifting reference and their linguistic, conceptual, and social development. As a result, none of the existing studies are complete; at best they document the earliest stages when children begin to use alternative forms to take account of the shifting relations between

---

*Double underlining indicates deictics here and throughout the paper.

age ranges and across communication situations, both experimental and natural, and which is not limited to only one or two deictic terms. Fillmore (1975) has presented the framework for such a system, one which can evaluate the use of deictics based on both the types of deictics used and the ways in which they are used by the speaker to establish shared knowledge.

Fillmore (1975) has identified five types of deictics that are defined according to the nature of what is being referenced. Person/Thing deictics make reference to the individuals involved in a communication act (you, me), other persons (he, she, they), or to physical objects within or external to the communication setting (it, that, this). Spatial deictics make reference to the location(s) in which individuals or objects are positioned (here, there, top). Time deictics make reference to times (then, now, before). Discourse deictics make reference to the matrix of the discourse itself within which the utterance has a role—i.e. the preceding and following parts of the discourse. For example,

> . . . in the <u>above</u> paragraph.
> . . . and the terms will be defined <u>below</u>.

Social deictics refer to the social relationships of the participants that determine the choice of honorific, polite, or insulting speech levels. For example,

> Bob, Robert, Mr. Spekman, Professor Spekman

In order for deictics to be interpreted correctly the identity of the objects, persons, times, or locations being referenced must be shared or understood by the participants in the communication. The establishment of this point of common knowledge is accomplished by using deictics in three ways, identified as deictic functions. The Gestural function refers to the situation in which the interlocutors are monitoring some shared aspect of the physical setting. For example, in

> Put <u>this there</u>.

the listener must identify the what and the where by monitoring the speaker's point, eye movements, or the like. Symbolic deictics are those whose interpretation involves a shared knowledge of certain aspects of the speech situation, regardless of how this knowledge is obtained (direct perception, previous experience, etc.). For example, in

> When will you be <u>here</u>?

the listener would identify the location as the place at which the speaker is presently located. Anaphoric deictics, in contrast, make reference to shared information that was established previously in the discourse. For example,

John went to the store. There he bought some milk.

The various deictic functions form a continuum that reflects the degree to which correct interpretation is dependent on the speech situation and the language used. To illustrate, gestural deictics are interpreted primarily through the physical and contextual setting; symbolic uses rely more on the language itself, yet are still dependent on some implicit knowledge of the context; and finally, anaphoric uses are interpreted entirely linguistically, based as they are upon preceding linguistic input.

In summary, deictics are common, frequently occurring terms of reference that are interpreted, as Fillmore (1975) states, by knowing something about the communication act in which they occur. In other words, the user must have the needs of the listener in mind and their interpretation is dependent upon the existence of this shared knowledge based between or among interlocutors.

Methodology

Fillmore's framework was operationalized and then applied in an experimental communication task involving pairs of 4th- and 5th-grade boys, separated by an opaque barrier, who were expected to exchange verbally and pool their information in order to achieve a shared goal. Each was given a set of attribute blocks varying on two dimensions of the attributes of color, shape, size, and thickness. One half of the blocks of one child (the speaker) were arranged into a pattern and he was instructed to tell his partner (the listener) how to arrange his blocks so that they looked exactly the same. The dyad members communicated about the designs under three conditions that varied the channels available for information exchange by changing the height of the barrier and by controlling the availability of feedback between the dyad members. The various conditions permitted the analysis of language changes resulting from different contextual constraints. The communication performances were audio-tape-recorded and fully transcribed. For a complete description of this research, see Spekman (1978).

A major issue involved in operationalizing deictic usage was the establishment of criteria for success. With deictics the primary criterion has to do with the interpretability of the terms used; i.e., is the referent readily identifiable? Ideally, this decision should be determined by the listener to whom the information is addressed. It is logical to expect a listener to express some confusion when receiving an ambiguous message (e.g., by requesting repetition or clarification, by using a quizzical facial expression or gesture) or to indicate acceptance of a clearly stated message (e.g., "okay," "I understand"). Unfortunately, this approach did not prove most useful when working with children since their ability to tolerate or even to recognize ambiguity varies so much. Ironsmith and Whitehurse (1978), Markman (1977), and Peterson, Danner, and Flavell (1972) have demonstrated changes with age in the ability to recognize ambiguity and to seek clarification. Even among the 4th- and 5th-graders studied here, the ability of many to tolerate high levels of ambiguity was surprisingly high.

It was necessary, therefore, for the scorer to assume the role of listener and to make judgments accordingly. As the scorer had not directly participated in the communication act, it was necessary for her to rely on knowledge of the physical context (e.g., whether participants could see each other) and/or knowledge of the preceding discourse (e.g., speaker has already provided unambiguous information regarding the referent.) Unfortunately, certain problems were still evident with the scorer assuming this role and with making decisions at a time later than the performance. For example, the scorer's repeated access to preceding discourse and full knowledge of the correct solution created a situation unlike that which the typical listener experienced; further, the scorer, functioning without a video record, could not always determine whether a necessary gesture had really been given by the speaker and seen by the listener. However, this approach was felt to be significantly more reliable and sensitive than using the responses made by the original listener.

The following discussion presents examples of the types and functions of deictics used by the 4th- and 5th-grade boys during task performance and presents specific scoring issues.

Deictic types. Three of Fillmore's five deictic types were examined in this study.[1] Person/Thing deictics were defined as those making reference to the interlocutors or participants in the communication situation, other persons, or to physical objects within or external to the communication setting. For example,

> I told you to do your yellow square.
> Take the blue square and put it in the upper corner.
> Get that.
> Put this down below it.

Spatial deictics were defined as those referring to the identity of places in which objects or individuals are located.[2] For example,

> Put the square here.
> At the top of the paper . . . put it there.

In order for many spatial deictics to be used appropriately they must be anchored or tied to the speech situation in which they occur. Fillmore (1975) refers to this as "deictic anchorage." Consider the following:

1.a.   At the top of the page put . . .
  b.   At the top put . . .
2.a.   On the left side of the little blue triangle you put . . .
  b.   On the left side you should put a . . .

In each pair, it is obvious that the (b) statements lack the precision and information that is found in the (a) statements. The location in each (b) statement is not "anchored" or tied to the context and the listener is left asking, the top of what? the page? the triangle? the left side of what?

Time deictics are those which identify the time at which the communication act takes place, including the time at which the message is sent and/or received. For example,

Now get the blue square
Then take the blue triangle.
The one I told you before.

Deictic functions. The three deictic functions described by Fillmore (1975) were used in the study. Gestural deictics are those which require that the interlocutors share and visually monitor some physical aspect of the communication situation in order for correct interpretation to occur. For example,

It's about this far away.
Put it here. Take that.

The linguistic terms must, therefore, be utilized in conjunction with hand gestures, eye movements, or the like. If no shared visual input between the speaker and listener is possible, such as when they are separated by a high opaque barrier, those gestural deictics utilized must be considered uninterpretable and thus inappropriate.

Unfortunately, the scoring in this area was not always this straightforward and was complicated by other methodological limitations. For example, in one communication condition the children were separated by a low barrier that blocked viewing of the task materials yet permitted the participants to view each other's faces and raised hands. It was thus possible that gestural deictics could be used appropriately. Accurate scoring necessitated a visual record accompanying the audio such that the pairing of the gestural deictic with the required visual information would be evident, as well as the listener's attention to the gesture. Without this information (as in the present case), considerable sensitivity in the scoring is lost. For example, it was frequently noted by the experimenter that some children used gestural deictics and the necessary gestures in the low barrier condition, but that they kept their gestures below the level of the barrier, thus nullifying the effect of the gesture.

The symbolic use of deictics requires that the interlocutors share some knowledge of the communication situation, but this knowledge need not be established by current perception. Thus, for example,

> Put your square at the top of your paper on the left side.

The interpretation of the pronouns is possible because the participants know they are the only individuals involved. The spatial locations, given with reference to the paper, were interpretable since the participants were aware that their work surfaces were the same. Without this previously established shared knowledge base, such interpretation might not be possible.

The final deictic function examined is the anaphoric use, a backward reference, which requires that the referent be established or given within a previous portion of the discourse. Two conditions are necessary for the correct interpretation to be made. First, the referent must be given. Any communication without shared visual input that begins with "Pick it up and put it there" would create confusion. Second, the deictic term must exist in some proximity to the referent. It was impossible to determine a degree of distance that consistently rendered the term uninterpretable; the interpretation appeared to vary depending on the nature of the intervening dialogue. Yet it was evident that typically with increasing distance incorrect usage also increased. An example of a minimal distance follows:

> Take the triangle . . . put it directly under the blue block. Straight down from it.

Deictic Type and Deictic Function. Decisions regarding correct deictic usage were based upon simultaneous consideration of deictic type, deictic function, and communication context (presence or absence of shared visual input). The examples of correct/incorrect usage presented in Table 1 should serve to illustrate this.

Table 1
Examples of Correct and Incorrect Uses of Deictics

Correct	Incorrect
GESTURAL DEICTICS	
a. Person/Thing Get the block that looks like this. (speaker traces a shape in the air that can be seen by the listener)	Put this at the top. (no shared visual input possible)

b. Spatial

About this far apart
(speaker) demon-
strates a distance
of few inches with
his fingers)

Put it over here . . . on
this side of the
paper (speaker
indicates location
by pointing and eye
movements)

Take a small yellow
one . . . thick . . .
and put it on the
right side . . . about
an inch away from
the triangle . . . you
know . . . about
here (no shared
visual input
possible)

c. Time

No examples

No examples

SYMBOLIC DEICTICS

a. Person/Thing

And next, it will be a
yellow, small skinny
square block which
you should put . . .
(forward or cata-
phoric reference;
participants share
knowledge
regarding materials
and objective of
task)

I want you to get your
big blue triangle.
(only two parti-
cipants involved)

Hey, she told us not to
do that. (experi-
menter had given
instructions to both
children and was
only other person
present during the
task)

It's going to be a
square (listener
unable to identify
whether speaker
referring to next
block, arrangement
of all blocks, or
something else)

b. Spatial

On the top of the
paper, put a little
square (anchored or
tied to the paper,
known to be shared
by the participants

Now put the blue small
fat square about 4
inches away from
the top. Then take
the yellow big thick
square and put it
two inches from the
top. (location not
anchored).

Go about two inches to
the <u>left</u> of the
small thin yellow
square (speaker
assumes partner has
placed small thin
yellow square and
anchors new
location to previous
block)

c. Time   <u>Next</u>, get another   No examples
                            small yellow block
                            but make it a
                            triangle.

                            <u>Now</u>, go to the very
                            middle of the paper
                            and put the big, thick,
                            blue triangle there.

ANAPHORIC DEICTICS

a. Person/Thing   Get the big, thick, blue   Put the blue square
                   square and put <u>it</u>   under <u>it</u> (speaker
                   about an inch below   did not provide
                   the yellow triangle   identity of referent
                   (speaker clearly   in preceding
                   establishes   discourse)
                   described square as
                   referent of <u>it</u>)

b. Spatial   Go to the top left   Go to the left . . . no
                   corner of the paper   not really the left
                   and put the square   . . . but you know
                   <u>there</u> (speaker   what I mean . . .
                   clearly establishes   put it <u>there</u>
                   location as   (speaker has not
                   referent)   clearly established
                                                 a location as
                                                 referent)

c. Time   On top of the one we   Get one like the one I
                   <u>just</u> did (speaker   told you <u>before</u>.
                   referring to time   (speaker not clearly
                   immediately   establishing
                   preceding)   previous time
                                                 referred to).

Results and Discussion

   The following discussion presents some of the general findings
of a study that utilized Fillmore's framework to explore the
relationship of deictic usage to communication success. While the
extant literature suggests a positive relationship, the finding here of
a highly significant correlation coefficient (r=.31, p=.004) between
deictic usage and a measure of overall task success provides
statistical support. Further, an analysis of the transcripts provides
numerous examples illustrating this relationship, with incorrect
deictic usage frequently seen as contributing to disruptions in the
flow and success of communication.
   All of the children involved in the communication task used
deictics frequently. As would be expected with children of this age,
none showed any evidence of difficulties with syntactic structures
involving these terms. However, their use in a communicative sense
varied considerably. Since the children were able to use deictic
types and functions correctly at least some portion of the time, the
errors found were interpreted not as an inability to take the
perspective of another, but more as a failure either to recognize the
need, make the appropriate inference, or the appropriate application
consistently. That is, the speakers did not continuously have the
perspective of the listeners in mind. The problems would thus seem
to fall within Flavell's (1970) category of production inefficiencies
and to be indicative of a skill within a child's repertoire yet still in
the developmental stages. This supports Garvey and Baldwin's (1971)
finding that while the communication skills of fifth-graders were
significantly better than those of younger children, they were not
yet equivalent to those of adults.
   The problems with deictic usage in the present study for some
children were quite pronounced and even when a listener indicated
confusion, some speakers could not understand or identify the source
of this confusion and/or could not modify messages as needed for
clarification. For example, in a task with no shared visual input,

   It's a circle. It's like a
       circle. It goes like
       this. Okay?

                          Huh? A circle? What
                             do you mean?

   Good. Okay. It's a circle.

   Looking specifically at deictic types, the children were seen to
have the most difficulty with the correct use of Spatial, followed by
Person/Thing, and then Time deictics. The most obvious error in the
use of spatial deictics was the failure to anchor the terms to the
immediate context. This resulted in messages seen as incomplete
and ambiguous. For example,

At the <u>left</u> put a yellow
square.

Huh?

At the <u>left</u>.

The left of what?

Oh yeah! The <u>left</u> . . . put it
to the <u>left</u> of the big
thick blue triangle.

References to persons were primarily limited to the communication participants themselves and caused no difficulty within this dyadic situation. For example,

<u>I</u> told <u>you</u> to do the yellow square.

It is likely that under other circumstances and as more people (both present and absent become involved as participants and/or topics, the probability of confusion would increase. References to the objects involved in task solution caused considerably more trouble due to failure to identify the referent entirely or to ambiguous reference. For example,

Get the big blue thick square and the tiny yellow thin triangle. Put <u>it</u> below the big yellow triangle.

Time references were used least frequently and typically involved terms used for sequencing task steps. For example,

<u>Now</u> get a blue square and put it in the very middle of the paper. <u>Then</u> get a yellow big thick square and put
. . .

Those attempts to refer to times in the past, however, caused more difficulty and confusion. For example,

Get the small fat square . . . blue and put it like you put that blue one <u>before</u> . . . you know, <u>before</u> . . .

The speaker was referring to the placement of a blue block in a preceding task and the listener's response of "Which one? When?" reflected this inappropriate reference.

A look at deictic functions permits insights into the ways the children tried to establish the shared knowledge and their sensitivity to the constraints placed by the communication situation. Most children were sensitive, at least to some degree, to the differences between the high and low barrier conditions, yet many problems were evident. For example,

Put the square on <u>this</u> side.

> What side? I can't see
> your paper.

I know. Put it on <u>this</u> side.

> What side?

<u>This</u> side. No <u>that</u> side.

The listener's confusion is obvious here, with clarification possible only with shared visual input or increased precision in the language used.

As would be expected, gestural deictics, requiring shared visual input for their interpretation, were used significantly more frequently under the low barrier condition. Frequently, however, the deictic terms were not given in conjunction with any gesture, facial expression, or the like. Further, many children who did use gestural deictics in combination with the necessary gesture or visual signal under this condition, did so even though the listener could not or did not see the gesture, e.g., the gestures were given below the level of the low barrier or were given despite visual inattentiveness of the listener. Some children even continued to use gestural deictics under the high barrier condition when no shared visual input was possible.

Symbolic deictics seemed to cause problems because the speakers tended to assume the listeners had the same level of task-related knowledge. Whereas some children began by describing the overall design and setting up the solution logically, e.g.,

> There are eight blocks and they are all arranged in the
> shape of a triangle. At the top point . . . top of your
> page in the middle . . . put a little blue thin square . . .,
> etc.

others began by assuming more shared knowledge than existed, e.g.,

<u>It</u>'s a triangle.

> Huh?

<u>It</u>'s a triangle.

> What is?

Oh . . . the whole thing . . .
  <u>it</u>'s going to look like a
  triangle.

> Okay.

Anaphoric deictics, relying entirely on previous discourse for their interpretation, were used incorrectly by many children and created considerable confusion. Speakers frequently used deictics as if they were referring backwards when in fact no referent had been given. For example, a speaker began a task with

First, put a fat big yellow triangle at the bottom of <u>it</u>.

Others tried to establish a referent, yet did so in an ambiguous fashion. For example,

> . . . match your hand up about . . . wait . . . match your hand up about where your end of the palm . . . the bottom of the palm . . . where it meets the long . . . where your arm meets the palm and . . . all the way up to . . . your middle finger to the . . . to the top bend . . . you know? Well . . . put it <u>there.</u>

A major contributor to ambiguity was also the distance between the intended referent and the deictic reference. While it was impossible to determine a maximum acceptable distance, it did become clear that as the distance increased so did the likelihood of confusion. One child made reference to a block that had been mentioned nineteen messages earlier and that had been poorly described initially.

It is hoped that this discussion has demonstrated the significance and role played by deictics in influencing the success or failure of communication messages and the value of utilizing a framework such as that suggested by Fillmore. As deictics are terms that appear early in the language of children and continue to be used, such a system for analyzing their communicative use can be applied appropriately across all age groups. Further, its use is appropriate in experimental and natural communication activities alike. This is especially important as attention shifts increasingly to concern for language in use—i.e., the way language is used to fulfill a certain purpose within a certain context. Whenever information is exchanged verbally, it is essential that the language used be appropriate to the needs of an audience. In all communication situations, the partners need to identify the purpose for their interaction and the informational needs of the other(s), and adapt their messages to meet those needs. The analysis of deictic usage provides one system for evaluating this ability to take successfully the perspective of another and may indicate areas for intervention in children with communication problems. It is further recommended that deictic usage be considered in conjunction with other variables also known to contribute to communication success (e.g., information content, response to listener feedback, etc.).

NOTES

1.   Discourse and Social deictics appear to be superimposed on and

absorb aspects of the other three types. Further, as the dyads were composed of fourth and fifth-grade peers, social distinctions marked in language were not considered to be of interest and were not expected, other than a few denigrating remarks (e.g., "You dummy!"). Discourse deictics would become more important in extended oral narratives and in written language.

2. Fillmore presents an important discussion relating to the fact that certain terms identified as Spatial deictics may be used either deictically or nondeictically. Deictic use requires that the speaker adjust his message in light of differing perspectives. For example, to the left of the blue block is a yellow triangle. Here the location in space of the two participants is absolutely essential to correct understanding. In contrast is an example of nondeictic usage, Mary sat to the left of Joe. Here, the locations of both the speaker and listener at the time of the speech act are irrelevant to understanding, since Joe's left side is always the same.

REFERENCES

Bar-Hillel, Y. 1954. Indexical expressions. Mind n.s. 63:359-79.

Bloom, L., and Lahey, M. 1978. Language development and language disorders. New York: John Wiley and Sons.

Bloom, L.; Lightbown, P.; and Hood, L. 1975. Structure and variation in child language. Monographs in Social Research in Child Development 40.

Bloom, L.; Rocissano, L.; and Hood, L. 1976. Adult-child discourse: developmental interaction between information processing and linguistic knowledge. Cognitive Psychology 8:521-52.

Charney, R. 1979. The comprehension of "here" and "there." Journal of Child Language 6:69-80.

Chipman, H., and deDardel, C. 1974. Developmental study of the comprehension and production of the pronoun "it." Journal of Psycholinguistic Research 3:91-99.

Clark, E., and Garnica, O. 1974. Is he coming or going? On the acquisition of deictic verbs. Journal of Verbal Learning and Verbal Behavior 13:559-72.

deVilliers, J., and deVilliers, P. 1974. Competence and performance in child language: Are children really competent to judge? Journal of Child Language 1:11-22.

Ervin-Tripp, S. M. 1964. An analysis of the interaction of language, topic and listener. American Anthropologist 66:86-102.

Feffer, M. 1970. Developmental analysis in interpersonal behavior. Psychological Review 77:197-214.

Fillmore, C. 1975. Santa Cruz lectures on deixis, 1971. Indiana University Linguistics Club. Bloomington, Ind.

Flavell, J. 1970. Developmental studies of mediated memory. In Advances in child development and behavior, ed. H. W. Reese and L. P. Lipsett, 5:181-211. New York: Academic Press.

_____. 1974. The development of inferences about others. In Understanding other persons, ed. T. Mischel, pp. 66-116. Totowa, N.J.: Rowman and Littlefield.

Flavell, J.; Botkin, P.; Fry, C.; Wright, J.; and Jarvis, P. 1968. The development of role-taking and communication skills in children. New York: John Wiley and Sons.

Garvey, C., and Baldwin, T. 1970. Studies in convergent communication: I. An analysis of verbal interaction. Baltimore, Md.: Johns Hopkins University Press. ERIC No. 045 647.

_____. 1971. Studies in convergent communication: III. Comparisons of child and adult performance. Baltimore, Md.: Johns Hopkins University Press. ERIC No. 047 293.

Grice, H. P. 1975. Logic and conversation. In Syntax and semantics. Vol. 3, Speech acts, ed. P. Cole and J. L. Morgan. New York: Academic Press.

Halliday, M.A.K.; and Hasan, R. 1976. Cohesion in English. London: Longman.

Huxley, R. 1970. The development of the correct use of subject personal pronouns in two children. In Advances in psycholinguistics, ed. G. B. Flores d'Arcais and W. J. M. Levelt. New York: American Elsevier.

Hymes, D. 1971. Competence and performance in linguistic theory. In Language acquisition: Models and methods, ed. R. Huxley and E. Ingram. New York: Academic Press.

_____. 1972. Models of the interaction of language and social life. In Directions in sociolinguistics: the ethnography of communication, ed. J. Gumperz and D. Hymes. New York: Holt, Rinehart and Winston.

Ironsmith, M., and Whitehurst, G. J. 1978. The development of listener abilities in communication: How children deal with ambiguous information. Child Development 49:348-52.

Krauss, R., and Glucksberg, S. 1969. The development of communication: Competence as a function of age. Child Development 40:255-66.

Looft, W. 1972. Egocentrism and social interaction across the life span. Psychological Bulletin 78:73-92.

Markman, E. M. 1977. Realizing that you don't understand: a preliminary investigation. Child Development 48:986-92.

Peterson, C.; Danner, F.; and Flavell, J. 1972. Developmental changes in children's response to three indications of communicative failure. Child Development 43:1463-68.

Piaget, J. 1926. Language and thought of the child. New York: Harcourt, Brace.

Richards, M. 1976. Come and go reconsidered: children's use of deictic verbs in contrived situations. Journal of Verbal

Learning and Verbal Behavior 15:655-65.

Rommetveit, R. 1974. On message structure. New York: John Wiley.

Rubin, K. 1973. Egocentrism in childhood: a unitary construct? Child Development 44:102-10.

Ryan, J. 1974. Early language development: towards a communicational analysis. In The integration of a child into a social world, ed. M. P. M. Richards. Cambridge: At the University Press.

Schegloff, E. 1972. Sequencing in conversational openings. In Directions in sociolinguistics: the ethnography of communication, ed. J. Gumperz and D. Hymes. New York: Holt, Rinehart and Winston.

Schegloff, E.; Jefferson, G.; and Sacks, H. 1977. The preference for self-correction in the organization of repair in conversation. Language 53:361-82.

Spekman, N. J. 1978. An investigation of the dyadic, verbal problem-solving communication abilities of learning disabled and normal children. Ph.D. dissertation. Northwestern University, Evanston, Ill.

Webb, P., and Abrahamson, A. 1946. Stages of egocentrism in children's use of "this" and "that": a different point of view. Journal of Child Language 3:349-67.

Weinreich, U. 1963. On the semantic structure of language. In Universals of language, ed. J. H. Greenberg. Cambridge, Mass.: MIT Press.

Part III:

L_1/L_2 Transfer, Contrastive Analysis, Error Analysis, and L_2 Acquisition

16. A Computer-Assisted Study of Spanish-English Transfer

JUDY B. McINNIS
University of Delaware

This paper reports the results of a study of the translingual application of traditional grammar. The basis of the study was established through a 100-item examination of grammatical terms related to English sentences. [1] The subjects were 139 University of Delaware Spanish students. The purpose of the study was to arrive at some measure of the relationship between students' abstract knowledge of English grammar and their performance in intermediate Spanish courses. Computer programs were used for scoring and compiling results of the English examination, for assessing its reliability, and for determining the correlation between students' scores on the examination and their final numerical averages in the Spanish courses. Two groups of students participating in the project received instruction in basic English grammar through a computer-assisted instruction program.

The study focused on students in the third semester course, which during the project term was devoted largely to acquisition of the subjunctive mood. Students spent two weeks on review of Spanish grammar, eight weeks on chapters 18-25 of Turk and Espinosa's <u>Foundation Course in Spanish, Third Edition</u>, 1974, and four weeks on a cultural reader. Eighty percent of the final course grade reflected reading, writing, and listening skills measured by tests that required written responses to oral questions, translation from English to Spanish, or completion of Spanish sentences with appropriate verb forms, idioms, etc. Abstract grammatical knowledge of Spanish was never tested: that is, students were not directly required to cite grammatical rules or to identify the grammatical function of sentence elements. Twenty percent of the final grade was based on knowledge of the content of the cultural reader and on oral performance in class.

Teaching methodology followed the deductive approach used in the grammar text. Explanation of grammatical rules with exposition of similarities and differences between Spanish and English preceded oral and written exercises exemplifying the rules. The organization of the course and the nature of the material to be covered mandated this approach. Since classes met only three hours a week and there was no required laboratory session, the audio-lingual approach was not feasible. An inductive grammatical approach did not seem compatible with the complex structural analysis used by Turk and Espinosa. In his survey, Jelinski (1977:326) found the same approach in the most popular grammar textbooks currently in use at the university level.

Structural analysis assumes the learner's ability to recognize types of clauses and to classify the principal verb in sentences with noun clauses, the antecedent of adjective clauses, and the subordinating conjunctions of adverbial clauses into subjunctive- or indicative-triggering classes. In recent years linguists employing the techniques of generative grammar have attempted to formulate one or two rules that would encompass all uses of the subjunctive. Although they have not reached a consensus on the governing concepts,[2] such systems as Berger's [+ reservation] and Lozano's [+ optative] and [+ dubitative] do supply philosophical underpinning that can be incorporated in the introduction of the subjunctive in elementary Spanish classes. These systems do not obviate the need for understanding grammatical structure since the student must still distinguish independent and dependent clauses. Illustration of the abstract single or double rule usually entails return to the concrete particulars of the structural approach.

Ability to analyze the structure of complex sentences constituted requisite knowledge for learning the use of the subjunctive in the Delaware program. Previous experience teaching Spanish 3 had convinced me that many students lacked this ability. Once outside the confines of a pattern drill, they were as likely to use subjunctive verb forms in the independent as in the dependent clauses of complex sentences.[3] Classroom performance contradicted the textbook's assumption that a student need only have his memory gently prodded to recall and transfer to Spanish grammatical principles learned in elementary and secondary English classes.

To gain a clearer perception of the extent of students' conceptual knowledge, I devised a multiple-choice examination that required students to apply grammatical terms to underlined words, phrases, and clauses appearing in the context of English sentences. All but three items on the examination permitted direct transfer of grammatical terms between languages. The examination was given in English rather than Spanish in order to assess the students' knowledge of concepts not yet studied in Spanish, as well as those acquired in previous courses. The examination included 40 items on the part of speech of single words, 15 items on types of dependent clauses, 10 items on person and number of the subject, 10 items on the transitive-intransitive aspect of verbs, 10 items on active-passive voice, and 15 items on the mood of simple sentences or dependent clauses.

Table 1 shows the performance of students who took the examination upon entrance to Spanish 3 in the spring semesters of 1977, 1978, and 1979. For purposes of comparison, the examination was also given to 48 students entering Spanish 2 in spring semester, 1978.

While not surprising, the results of the examination were discouraging. The range of scores indicated wide variation in

Table 1
Performance on Grammar Examination on Entrance to Course

	Mean	Median	Range
Spanish 3 Students			
(A) 1977—39 students	64	64	25-97
(B) 1978—33 students	61	61	29-95
(C) 1979—19 students	61	57	42-86
Groups A, B, C—91 students	62	60	25-97
Spanish 2 students			
1978—48 students	59	59	22-85

students' knowledge of grammar; the low mean scores revealed that most students had only a tenuous grasp of grammatical principles; the falling median scores of the Spanish 3 groups forewarned that the situation would worsen with each passing year.

Computer-assisted analysis of performance on specific questions and sections of the examination provided a profile of the students' strengths and weaknesses. The examination forms were submitted to a Pennsylvania State University item-analysis program, which supplied data on the difficulty and discrimination of each question. In addition to assessing the reliability of the examination (.89 on the Kuder-Richardson 20 Index), the program facilitated the interpretation of correct and incorrect responses.[4]

Table 2 summarizes mean performance on the sections and subsections of the examination.

Spanish 3 students demonstrated a more sophisticated knowledge of grammar than Spanish 2 students. In the section testing parts of speech, more than 80% of both groups correctly identified simple adjectives (intelligent, handsome, tallest), coordinating conjunctions (and, but), and simple nouns (girls, books). The success rate dropped to the 50-60% range for verbal adjectives, to the 30-40% range for verbal nouns, and to the 15-20% range for subordinating conjunctions. Superior to the Spanish 2 group in recognition of these more difficult items, the Spanish 3 group still resisted the idea that a word's function may vary. Sixty-two failed to distinguish the conjunctional from the prepositional use of after. Fewer than 20% of the students could recognize the function of that when used as a conjunction or relative pronoun rather than as a demonstrative adjective or pronoun. However, the Spanish 3 students did make more intelligent errors than the Spanish 2 students. For example, in the incorrect identification of verbal adjectives, a larger percentage of the Spanish 3 group chose the option verb. The Spanish 3 students also performed better on sections that required recognition of verb function—transitive-intransitive, active-passive, and mood.

Performance was tied to exposure to grammar in the Spanish

Table 2
Mean Performance of Spanish 3 and Spanish 2 Students on
Parts of English Examination

	Spanish 3	Spanish 2
Part I. Parts of Speech	66.3	65.8
Nouns	64.3	57.8
Pronouns	68.7	70.8
Verbs	75.8	75.0
Adjectives	65.9	66.3
Adverbs	59.4	57.3
Part II. Parts of Speech	58.2	55.9
Adjectives	68.8	67.4
Conjunctions	49.0	45.4
Prepositions	72.0	81.3
Pronouns	55.0	49.2
Part III. Person and Number	84.9	85.8
1 person singular	97.8	100.0
2 person singular	75.8	88.6
3 person singular	79.1	81.2
1 person plural	93.4	87.5
3 person plural	89.7	83.3
Part IV. Transitive and Intransitive	46.14	40.84
Transitive	45.9	39.6
Intransitive	46.3	40.9
Part V. Active and Passive	76.2	72.3
Active	83.2	75.0
Passive	71.6	72.3
Part VI. Clauses	50.6	49.6
Noun	44.4	39.2
Adjective	56.3	59.4
Adverb	52.0	51.7
Part VII. Mood	57.1	44.0
Indicative	66.5	50.7
Imperative	61.2	52.1
Subjunctive	45.8	33.4

N.B.:   The mean score on the entire examination for the 91 Spanish
3 students was 62 (s.d. 12.52). The mean score for the 48
Spanish 2 students was 59 (s.d. 11.42).

program and to the recency of that exposure. Spanish 3 students
were more successful in recognition of demonstrative pronouns, a
topic covered in the second semester course, but Spanish 2 students
outperformed them in recognition of predicate adjectives and
personal, interrogative, and indefinite pronouns—topics covered in
the first semester course. In person and number recognition the
Spanish 2 group was superior in the identification of singular

subjects, the Spanish 3 group in the identification of plural subjects, especially compounds (Tom and I, Jane and Mary).

Greater exposure to Spanish made the Spanish 3 group more susceptible to erroneous transfer of Spanish principles to English. The most striking example was the identification of you where an apparent analogy with Ud. resulted in Spanish 3 students falling thirteen percent below the Spanish 2 students. In the sentence Joe was tired, 5% of the students identified tired as a noun, a false transfer based on the misconception that the Spanish sentence would use the tener + noun construction. Furthermore, this 5% was made up of students who achieved scores well above the mean of the group on the entire examination. Of sociological interest was the fact that twice the number of Spanish 3 students who believed she was a second-person singular noun so classified he. Unfortunately, the computer was not programmed to supply data on the sex of students choosing these options so I cannot report of the ratio of men and women suffering these delusions.

The prototype that emerged from this analysis was a Spanish student who could recognize the most obvious instances of grammatical categories but who lacked conceptual understanding of the categories themselves. At least one-half of the students appeared to have no more knowledge of grammar than that gained through the Spanish program, and even that was not held securely. When 50% of the students dutifully exemplified the adage "To err is human" by identifying human as a noun, one could assume they would have difficulty distinguishing noun and adjective clauses.

The importance of knowledge of grammar to achievement in the Spanish course was determined by statistical analysis of the correlation between scores on the English grammar test and final course grades. Of the 91 Spanish 3 students who began the course, 73 completed it with a final course average of 79 (SD 10) and an entrance English grammar examination mean of 64 (SD 12.4). The correlation coefficient of the two measures was .54 ($p < .00005$). I judged this a high correlation in view of the fact that the examination tested abstract knowledge of English grammar and the final course grade reflected functional knowledge of Spanish vocabulary and grammar as well as cultural content of the reader. The mean score of these students on the English grammar examination was two points above that of all students entering the course, a further indication of correlation since most students who dropped the course to avoid failing were low performers on the grammar examination. As a predictive instrument the examination was most easily used to identify extremes. Only three students who scored one standard deviation below the mean rose above D level in the course; conversely, only one student who scored one standard deviation above the mean fell below the B level.

The pedagogical justification of this project was to diagnose grammar competence so that classroom instruction could be adapted to the needs of the class and to identify students who might need special help. After seeing the scores of the first group of students in 1977, I concluded that nearly all students could profit from Culley's A Review of Grammar, University of Delaware Plato Project, 1977. Written for students of foreign languages with Latin-derived grammars, the program teaches parts of speech, mood, voice, tense, case, number, and syntax. It makes effective use of graphics on a display screen to reinforce grammar concepts. Heavy use of the touch panel to record student responses reduces dependence on typing skill, a drawback of many CAI programs. Running time varies from one to six hours, depending on the user's prior knowledge of the concepts reviewed. The advantages offered by this form of instruction were: (1) it permitted a more intensive review than could be conducted in class; (2) it required the student's active participation, and (3) it allowed the student to work at his own pace. The novelty of the form of instruction is a definite asset in teaching material that many students regard as inherently boring.   Such students tend to "tune out" classroom review of grammar because they already know the material, they think they know it, or they believe themselves incapable of learning it. By requiring students to demonstrate mastery of concepts, the computer program engages their full attention.

In the first year of the project the students in Group A were urged to complete the grammar review. Two-thirds of them had some exposure to the program during the first two weeks of the semester. In the second year (Group B), all students were required to work on the program until they achieved a score of 85% on its cumulative quiz. It took the students an average of three hours at the computer terminal to complete this assignment. In the third year (Group C), students had no exposure to the grammar review. At the end of each semester the English grammar examination was administered again. Due to absences on the testing dates my sample was reduced 20%. Table 3 shows the performance of the 58 students who took the examination on both occasions, the final numerical average for the Spanish course, and the correlation (r) between final grade and mean scores on the English examination.

Group B, with the benefit of monitored exposure to the grammar review program, advanced 12% on the English grammar examination; Group A, with some exposure, improved 4% and Group C with no exposure rose only 1%. Beginning the course with mean and median scores closest to those of the lowest group, students of Group B surpassed those of the highest group at the end of the semester. The only student who failed to improve in Group B scored 95% on the pretest and 91% on the posttest. Most encouraging were the marked improvement of students with low initial scores and the consequent reduction of the range of grammar competence in the class.   In Group C the opposite occurred. The range of scores increased from 42 to 86 at the beginning of the semester, to 38 to 85 at the end of the semester with a corresponding increase in the standard deviation. The mean score scarcely improved at all, but

Table 3
Correlation of Spanish 3 Grades with Scores on Pre- and Post
Examinations on English Grammar

	Spanish Average		Grammar Pretest				Grammar Posttest			
	Mean	S.D.	Mean	Md.	S.D.	r	Mean	Md.	S.D.	r
1977-79 73 students	79	10	64	61	12.4	.54				
1977-79 58 students	80	10.3	65	62	12.4	.48	71	73	13.3	.60
Group A 22 students	82	10.2	68	69	11.9	.43	72	73	11.3	.57
Group B 19 students	80	10	64	61	12.2	.62	76	76	10.8	.66
Group C 17 students	76	10	62	59	13.3	.40	63	67	15.3	.53

the median rose 8 points. The split of the mean and median scores reveals the division that occurred in the class. One-half of the students showed marked improvement; the other half either showed no change or fell below their initial scores. The five students who earned D as their final letter grade were also those who suffered the heaviest losses on the grammar examination. Entering the class with low-level understanding of grammar, these students failed to assimilate the necessarily brief classroom presentation of types of dependent clauses and the further complexities of contrastive structures in English and Spanish. By the end of the semester they were even less sure of basic grammatical principles than at the beginning.

Table 4 shows the performance on Groups A, B, and C on the various parts of the grammar examination.

Parts V, VI, and VII tested material most emphasized in the Spanish course. The mean score of Group C improved in the parts testing recognition of active-passive and mood but declined in Part VI, which tested recognition of types of dependent clauses. This decline paralleled a decline in recognition of parts of speech in Part I. Item analysis revealed that students in Group C had great difficulty distinguishing imperative from subjunctive constructions even in complex sentences. From these data it appeared that one-half the students in Group C never mastered the structural method for distinguishing subjunctive usage in Spanish. Nevertheless, they gained enough familiarity with subjunctive structure during pattern drill to pass the course with a low grade. Groups A and B showed a more consistent pattern of simultaneous improvement in recognition of clause type and mood. Although the effect of the preparatory English grammar review must be measured on a larger sample before final judgment, the dramatic improvement of Group B attests that

Table 4
Comparison of Groups A, B, and C on Parts of the Pre- and Post
Examinations on English Grammar

	Group A	Group B	Group C
Part I. Parts of Speech			
Pretest	72	69	68
Posttest	75	75	64
Part II. Parts of Speech			
Pretest	65	60	52
Posttest	66	60	54
Part III. Person and Number			
Pretest	91	81	83
Posttest	91	92	78
Part IV. Transitive-Intransitive			
Pretest	49	47	53
Posttest	57	76	52
Part V. Active and Passive			
Pretest	76	82	76
Posttest	84	84	83
Part VI. Clauses			
Pretest	61	50	54
Posttest	67	76	53
Part VII. Mood			
Pretest	66	61	55
Posttest	72	78	64

its use improved comprehension of the contrastive analysis used in the text and in classroom instruction throughout the semester. The correlation between performance in class and performance on the English grammar examination corroborates that transfer of grammatical knowledge between languages occurred in all three groups. The results of the study also indicate that the amount of transfer varied according to the degree to which it was emphasized and encouraged by the teacher.

Although signs of revision are appearing,[5] rejection of the deductive grammatical method has characterized educational research of the last thirty years. In the article "Modern Languages" in the 1960 edition of the Encyclopedia of Educational Research (p. 879), Birkmaier concluded: "Investigations of the value of training in formal English grammar as a preparation for the study of a modern language, and of the carry-over within the same language of work in formal grammar to ability in reading, writing, or speaking, have shown that there is very little transfer."[6] Searles and Carlsen (1960:461) reached the same conclusion in the article "English." The data collected in my study do not support this conclusion. Rather, analysis of the data confirmed that there was a significant correlation between knowledge of English grammar and performance in Spanish once the student reached the level of complex structures. The study also documented the wide variation of students' command of traditional grammar and identified the low level of conceptual understanding held by most students. Further, the study indicated that computer-based instruction in English grammar improved understanding of grammatical terms and concepts covered in the Spanish course. Finally, the results of the study validated the method used in its completion: computer-assisted analysis of pre- and posttests in English on grammatical concepts to be learned in the Spanish course.

NOTES

1. I refer to traditional grammar, but the student exposed to transformational grammar as outlined in the pedagogical approach of Thomas (1967) and Roberts (1964) was at no disadvantage. The basic grammatical terms tested in my examination appear in both systems.
2. The heated debate between Lozano (1975) and Bolinger (1976) that surfaced in the pages of Hispania exemplifies the lack of consensus. Berger (1978:218-21) supplies an excellent overview of recent studies of the Spanish subjunctive.
3. Shawl (1975:323) observed a similar phenomenon with his students and attributed it "to a lack of understanding of the syntactic structure involved."
4. Gilboa (1976:133-36) provides a useful model for this type of analysis.
5. Carroll (1970:869) cautioned that results of experiments comparing the audiolingual and the traditional methods "have never been strikingly favorable to either method." He also pointed out that since teachers tend to use eclectic methods, true comparisons are difficult. Ney (1975:426) summarizes studies that demonstrate that a student performs better when he can relate items in the foreign language to English. Lindstrom (1976:473) urges teaching students to make intelligent transfers from English to Spanish. Hammerly (1977) presents the results of an experiment that demonstrated that the ser-estar distinction was best taught through a deductive approach.
6. Birkmaier cited the experiments of Hamilton and Haden (1950). It is worth noting—though Hamilton and Haden did not—that the difference between the performance of students in Program D (traditional grammatical approach) and those in Program E (deemphasis on grammar) increased in the second semester to the advantage of Program D. (p. 92). Presumably, this was the semester when the subjunctive was introduced.

REFERENCES

Berger, John L.   1978.   One rule for the Spanish subjunctive. Hispania 61:218-34.
Birkmaier, Emma M.   1960.   Modern languages. In Encyclopedia of Educational Research, ed. Chester W. Harris, 3d ed., pp. 861-88. New York: Macmillan Co.
Bolinger, Dwight.   1976.   Again—one or two subjunctives?   Hispania 59:41-49.
Carroll, John B.   1969.   Modern languages. In Encyclopedia of Educational Research, ed. Robert L. Ebel, 4th ed., pp. 866-78. London: Macmillan Co.
Culley, Gerald R.   1977.   A review of grammar.   University of Delaware PLATO Project, Newark, Delaware.
Gilboa, Carolyn Chiterer.   1976.   Computerized diagnostic testing in remedial English.   In Proceedings of the 1976 Conference on Computers in the Undergraduate Curricula CCUC/7, ed. Theodore C. Willoughby, pp. 133-36. Binghamton, N. Y.: State University of New York at Binghamton.
Hamilton, David, and Haden, Ernest.   1950.   Three years of experimentation at the University of Texas.   Modern Language Journal 34:85-102.
Hammerly, Hector.   1977.   The teaching of ser estar by a cognitive audiolingual approach.   Hispania 60:305-8.
Jelinski, Jack B.   1977.   A new look at teaching the Spanish subjunctive.   Hispania 60:320-26.
Lindstrom, Naomi, Eva.   1976.   Good errors and bad errors: an insight into growing semantic astuteness.   Hispania 59:469-73.
Lozano, Anthony.   1975.   In defense of two subjunctives.   Hispania 58:277-83.
Ney, James W.   1975.   Toward a synthetization of teaching methodologies for second languages.   Hispania 58:424-29.
Roberts, Paul.   1964.   English syntax: a book of programmed lessons. New York: Harcourt, Brace and World.
Searles, John R., and Carlsen, G. Robert. English. In Encyclopedia of Educational Research, ed. Chester W. Harris, 3d ed., pp. 454-70. New York: MacMillan Co.
Shawl, James R.   1975.   Syntactic aspects of the Spanish subjunctive.   Hispania 58:323-29.
Thomas, Owen.   1967.   Transformational grammar and the teacher of English. New York: Holt, Rinehart and Winston.
Turk, Laurel M., and Espinosa, Aurelio M. Jr.   1974.   Foundation course in Spanish, 3d ed. Lexington, Mass.: D. C. Heath and Co.

17. Two-Pronged Error Analysis from Computer-Based Instruction in Latin

GERALD R. CULLEY
University of Delaware

I would like to describe a new technique for error analysis in Latin instruction and share some examples to illustrate its use. The technique is embodied in a set of computer lessons on the morphology of Latin verbs, nouns, and adjectives, but it need not be limited to these applications, nor even to Latin instruction. The significance of this technique will be more evident if I briefly put it into the context of computer instruction in languages.

These Latin lessons were developed over the past three years for use on the University of Delaware PLATO system. PLATO was itself developed at the University of Illinois at Champaign-Urbana and consists of a Control Data Corporation Cyber 173 computer supporting up to 600 student terminals. The terminals are equipped with display panels capable of high-speed display of text, complex graphics, and animation effects. Student input can be made by a typewriter-style keyset or by the touch-sensitive display panel. Despite the number of simultaneous users, response time is about one-eighth of a second and students, when they are running well-designed lessons, are drawn into a highly visual, highly interactive learning experience. The potential for computer-assisted instruction generally is very great, and PLATO is in my opinion the most sophisticated system available, but any computer instruction can be only as good as its courseware. In languages, the quality of lessons has not been high.

Too often, computer language lessons are primitive devices that are little better than automated flashcards. Usually the programmer must encode each question and its answer, a dull, time-consuming process that, if it is to include a broad enough range of material, must entail the writing of many lessons using large amounts of computer memory. A curriculum of exercises to accompany the first year of instruction in a language may easily extend to forty or fifty lessons and a quarter of a million words of memory space. Here is a typical question from such a program: "Type the dative singular of puer bonus." A wrong answer will usually get the response, "No. Try again." Sometimes the programmer will offer a bit more, like "No, look again at the question. Remember that puer is a second declension noun." Such a comment may help, but it is a shot in the dark. The student's error may spring from any of several sources. He may be trying to use the wrong case (genitive for dative) or the wrong number (plural for singular); he may have one word of the phrase wrong and the other right; he may even have typed gibberish. To all of these very different errors the computer would have to make the same response. Small wonder that many teachers have become disillusioned with computer instruction.

What is needed is a "smart" lesson, one that—in effect—knows the language and can thus comment intelligently on a student's answer. For this reason I developed computer routines to conjugate Latin verbs and to decline nouns and adjectives. The benefits exceeded my expectation.

First, efficiency and variety. The computer, provided with a set of noun and adjective bases, can combine those bases with case endings to produce correct Latin forms. One noun base and one adjective base can produce ten phrase, since Latin has five major cases and two numbers. By using a pool of eighty nouns and forty adjectives and combining noun with adjective at random, one can obtain 40,000 distinct practice phrases. A lesson can thus have thousands of question-answer sets in it without the need to program each one individually. Moreover, a single lesson can have the effect of many lessons at a great saving in computer memory. One noun-adjective phrase lesson such as I have described serves my students for the entire first year as they are learning the five Latin declensions. A student can begin using it when he begins the first declension by setting it to ask him only about first declension nouns. As he progresses he can include more and more forms in his practice until he is using all five declensions. The difficulty of the lessons increases as the term continues, and the material studied is both appropriate and unique at each session.

But it is the second benefit—error analysis—that is the theme of this paper. If the computer can decline nouns, it can also analyze a student's typed response according to the rules of Latin case formation. In a word, we can have a "smart" lesson. Suppose we return to that same example, the dative singular of <u>puer bonus</u>. These are some responses the "smart" lesson might make to various student attempts:

Table 1
Typical Responses of a "Smart" Lesson

Student types:	Computer responds:
puer	two words, please.
pure bunk	noun base is wrong
	adjective base is wrong
puero bonus	adjective ending is wrong
pueri buena	noun ending is wrong
	adjective base is wrong
puero bono	ok

This is the first form of error analysis that can be done with a lesson capable of inflecting the forms; incorrect answers receive much more helpful feedback. It should be noted as well that the student is being encouraged to think structurally, to see the noun or adjective as consisting always of a base plus a case ending; or to see the verb as composed of stem, tense/mood sign, and personal ending. The logical system underlying the forms is being presented to him over and over again.

A second, more detailed kind of error analysis can be done from the data the computer collects on student errors. To take only one example, the instructor may collect the number of errors students make in Latin verb forms. The computer can distinguish errors in the stem from those in the tense/mood sign or the personal ending, so a study of the relative frequency of such errors can be done, with obvious advantages for pedagogy. Table 2 shows a preliminary result of such a study. Since the study is not complete, I use these figures only to illustrate the potential of the technique.

Table 2
Relative Frequencies of Errors (in Percentages) in Stem,
Stem Vowel with Tense/Mood Sign, and
Personal Ending of Latin Verb Forms

Exercise ( ) number	Typical ( ) forms	Stem	Stem vowel & ( ) t/m sign	Personal ( ) ending
1	laud/a/t	19.5	14.5	66.0
2	laud/abi/t	15.0	32.0	53.0
3	duc/i/t	17.7	32.0	50.3
	duc/e/t			
4	aud/i/t	7.0	30.0	63.0
	cap/ie/t			
5	laudav//it	23.0	18.0	59.0
	laudav/era/t			
	laudav/eri/t			
6	laud/aba/t	37.0	30.0	33.0
7	laud/a/tur	17.5	13.5	69.0
	laud/aba/tur			
	mon/ebi/tur			
8	laudat//us est	49.0	13.0	38.0
	laudat/us era/t			
	laudat/us eri/t			
9	duc/i/tur	20.0	33.0	47.0
	aud/ieba/tur			
	ca/ie/tur			
10	laud/e/t	15	31	54
	laud/e/tur			
11	laud/are/t	15	28	57

	laud/are/tur			
12	laudav/eri/t	52	17	31
	laudav/isse/t			
13	laudat//us sit	40	15	45
	laudat/us esse/t			

Note how difficulty with a component follows the introduction of new material in that component; for example, the introduction of the perfect stem more than triples stem problems between exercises 4 and 5, and the introduction of the perfect passive stem in exercise 8 has the same effect. The first appearance of passive personal endings in exercise 7 doubles the error rate there. Even in this first stage of data collection it is possible to see areas of difficulty that call for more careful treatment in the classroom.

The above figures will be more valuable when they have been augmented by another year of student use but I personally am convinced that this technique, refined and expanded, will yield valuable results in the study of error patterns—not only in Latin morphology but in other inflected languages as well.

18. Some Empirical Evidence on the Nature of Interlanguages

FRED R. ECKMAN
University of Wisconsin-Milwaukee

Introduction

One of the more interesting hypotheses to be put forth in the field of second-language acquisition in recent years is the interlanguage (IL) hypothesis (Selinker 1972). This hypothesis states that when acquiring a second language (TL), the learner internalizes a system of rules that may be distinct from both the target language and the native language (NL). The claim that such a system is distinct from both the TL and NL is of particular interest since it posits a process of "creative construction" (Dulay and Burt 1974) in second-language acquisition, rather than a process of simple transfer from the TL. Therefore, part of the interest of the IL hypothesis is that it makes it possible to raise a number of interesting questions concerning the nature of ILs.

The first such question that immediately comes to mind is the extent to which ILs can be said to be distinct or independent. The evidence presented so far essentially concludes that utterances produced by second-language learners belong neither to the class of TL utterances nor to the class of NL utterances and, therefore, must be governed by a system that is neither a grammar of the TL nor a grammar of the NL. That is, the grammar governing a learner's TL utterances must be an independent system.

While this type of evidence and argumentation is highly plausible, it is not what could be called an empirical argument. In order to show on empirical grounds that ILs are independent, one must present facts about second-language—learner utterances that necessitate the postulation of some construct as part of the IL of a given learner, where this construct is part of neither the grammar of the TL nor the grammar of the NL.

The second interesting question raised by the IL hypothesis is the extent to which stabilized ILs are similar to (or different from)

I would like to thank Dan Dinnsen for the valuable comments on an earlier version of this paper. I have also benefited from discussing this topic with Edith Moravcsik and Jessica Wirth. This research was supported in part by a grant from the UWM Graduate School, whose support is gratefully acknowledged.

languages that are learned as first languages. If ILs are composed only on rules transferred from the learner's NL, then such a question would lack interest. However, since it is proposed that ILs are independent systems, the possibility is open that ILs differ from first languages in significant ways.

The purpose of this paper is to present evidence from phonology that will shed some light on each of the above questions. Specifically, evidence will be presented to show that it is necessary to postulate at least one phonological rule in the interlanguage of some English learners that is not evidenced in either the TL or the NL. Such evidence argues for the independently motivated conclusion that ILs are independent systems. In addition, it will be shown that the rule that one must postulate in the above-mentioned ILs is one motivated for numerous grammars of languages that are acquired as a first language.

Evidence

Before actually presenting the facts that motivate our conclusion, we should evaluate the type of evidence that we are proposing. Put somewhat differently, we need to consider whether our motivation for postulating a given rule as part of a speaker's IL is strong on methodological grounds.

Consider a rule that has been proposed for a number of first languages and is thought to be very well motivated. Notice, for example, the forms in (1), which are taken from German.

(1) a. [tak]   day   e. [grat]   degree
     b. [tagə]   days   f. [gradə]   degrees
     c. [dɛk]   deck   g. [kalp]   calf
     d. [dɛkə]   decks   h. [kalbəs]   calf's

Although there are only a few forms here, they are representative of the facts in question about German. Specifically, we see that in final position in German, all obstruent consonants are voiceless. Thus, German has no voice contrast in word-final position.

Moreover, some word-final voiceless obstruents alternate with a medial voiced obstruent, as in (1a and b). However, since some word-final voiceless obstruents do not alternate with medial voiced obstruents, German does have a voice contrast in medial position.

Generative phonologists have accounted for these facts by postulating the underlying representations shown in (2), along with the rule of terminal devoicing shown in (3).

(2) a. /tag/   e. /grad/
     b. /tagə/   f. /gradə/
     c. /dɛk/   g. /kalb/
     d. /dɛkə/   h. /kalbəs/

(3) [-sonorant] → [-voice] /_____#
     (Word-final obstruents are voiceless)

This analysis of these facts of German is considered to be very well motivated for the following reasons: (1)   the   underlying representations are justified on the basis of the alternations and the existence of a voice contrast in medial position; (2) the rule of terminal devoicing accounts for the observed alternations and expresses a phonetically true generalization about word-final obstruents in German, namely, that they are all voiceless.

What is important in this example for our purposes is the nature of the evidence for both the underlying representation and the formulation of the rule. It is the observed alternation along with the medial voice contrast that motivates the postulation of underlying voiced segments where only voiceless ones occur superficially.

The above methodology for the establishment of the existence of a rule must be contrasted with that in some of the literature on IL phonology. For example, W. Dickerson (1976) argues for a wave model analysis to account for the acquisition of English /1/ by a number of Japanese speakers. The purpose of Dickerson's wave model, which makes use of the variable rule in (4), is to give a systematic account of what might otherwise be considered variable performance.

$$(4)\quad /\ell/ \;\rightarrow\; /<[\ell]>/ \left\{ \begin{array}{l} \alpha\;[-\text{cons}] \\ \beta\;[+\emptyset] \\ \gamma\;[-\text{high}] \end{array} \right\} \quad\underline{\qquad}\quad \left\{ \begin{array}{l} \delta \left| \begin{array}{l} -\text{high} \\ +\text{low} \end{array} \right| \\ \varepsilon \left| \begin{array}{l} -\text{high} \\ -\text{low} \end{array} \right| \end{array} \right\}$$

That Dickerson is postulating this rule as part of the IL of the speakers in question is clear from the following statement:

(5)   The input to the rule [in 4] is the (1) word class of Japanese English. The output is the target variant which is enclosed in angle brackets to indicate variability, i.e. sometimes [1] is produced, and sometimes another variant (p. 225).

The problem with the rule in (4) is that Dickerson gives no evidence to motivate such a rule as part of the ILs in question. That is, Dickerson presents no forms to show the necessary contrasts or alternations that would justify the postulation of the English phoneme /1/ in the underlying representation of the interlanguage forms. In the absence of such evidence, a rule like (4) represents the relationship of the IL of the speaker in question to the grammar of English.   More specifically, perhaps, the rule provides a way of mapping TL forms onto IL forms. In any event, it is clear that, under the circumstances, a rule like (4) is not motivated as part of an IL.

Having considered the type of data necessary to motivate a rule, I will now present some experimental evidence that motivates a rule of terminal devoicing for some interlanguages. It will also be shown that such a rule must be considered independent because it is not possible to motivate such a rule for the TL or the NLs involved.

Procedure

The data on which the proposed analysis is based was obtained from four students enrolled in the English as a Second Language Intensive Program at the University of Wisconsin-Milwaukee during the academic year 1978-79. These students were between the ages of eighteen and twenty-eight. All of them had studied English in their own country before coming to Milwaukee and all were placed in advanced-intermediate or advanced levels based on overall English proficiency. One of the students, a male, is a native speaker of Cantonese Chinese; and the rest, two females and one male, are native speakers of Colombian Spanish.

The data were obtained in three separate personal interviews where the subjects met individually with the investigator. Each interview lasted approximately one hour, during which time the subject's speech was tape-recorded. The tapes were then transcribed by the investigator and again independently by a research assistant. A reliability check was then run on the transcriptions. If there was a difference in transcription of any forms between the investigator and the research assistant—where either person transcribed the form as a correct TL form—the subject was given the benefit of the discrepancy and the form was scored as a correct TL form. In cases where there was a disagreement in transcription and neither person transcribed the IL form as a correct TL form, the word was discarded altogether. Thus, only those IL forms on which there was complete agreement were used.

During the interviews, different speech styles were elicited from each subject by means of a number of different tasks that he or she was to perform. The directions for each task were given both in writing and on tape and were then followed by a practice, or warm-up, to ensure that the subject understood what he or she was to do.

The first task required that the subject listen to and repeat a list of randomly ordered words that were recorded on tape. The subject first listened to a word, immediately repeated it, then listened to another word, repeated it, and so on.

The next task was designed to elicit alternations from the subject. This was accomplished by having the subject read a word from a three-by-five card and then produce a related form of this word. In each case, the related form was derived by the addition of one of the following morphemes: comparative, superlative, diminutive, or agentive. These forms were elicited by means of a cue written on the reverse side of the card. Thus, for example, the subject was to read aloud the word red, which was typed on a card. The subject then was to flip the card over and on the reverse side would be typed, for example, comparative, whereupon seeing this cue, the subject was to say redder.

This particular exercise is designed to elicit any alternations between word-final and word-medial consonants that a subject may exhibit. Each subject was instructed by questioning in the use of the morphemes before the exercise and his or her understanding of the task involved was determined by means of a practice session where the task was performed on a different set of words. A similar exercise using related forms derived by adding certain prefixes was run to elicit any alternations that the subject might exhibit between word-initial and word-medial consonants.

Each subject was also given, as the third task, a modified cloze reading test. This consisted of a passage of approximately 500 words with a blank in every second or third sentence. The blank was to be completed with one of the two forms that were provided adjacent to it. The purpose of the cloze test was to distract the subjects somewhat from paying close attention to their pronunciation. It was felt that, in this manner, a speech style that was less careful than reading style would be elicited.

For the final task, the subjects were asked to solve and discuss a riddle or logical anecdote. The riddle was presented to each subject both in written form and aloud from a tape. The actual solution to the riddle was, of course, immaterial. It merely provided a common topic and impetus for conversation.

Analysis

From the data in Table 1, we can see that T.C., a native speaker of Cantonese, produces a number of IL forms that have voiceless obstruents in word-final position where the corresponding TL forms have voiced obstruents. It is clear from Table 3 that though the actual number and percentage of this type of IL form varies from exercise to exercise, this type of IL form nonetheless shows up throughout the different speech styles elicited. In addition to this fact, we can also see that some of the IL forms manifest alternations between word-final voiceless obstruents and word-medial voiced ones. The final fact that we need to note is that these IL forms exhibit a voice contrast word-initially, -medially, and -finally, since both voiced and voiceless obstruents occur in all of these positions.

These data parallel closely those discussed above for German in that the IL forms in question exhibit a voice contrast medially and a voice alternation between some medial and final obstruents. However, the IL data depart from this parallelism with German in that the IL manifests a voice contrast finally whereas German does not.

Table 1
Chinese

Subject	Repetition from tape		Reading		Free Conversation		Alternations	
	IL	TL Gloss	IL	TL Gloss	IL	TL Gloss	IL	TL Gloss
T.C.	tæk	tag	lɛk	leg	bəkɔs~bəkɔz	because	fris	freeze
	tæp	tab	bæk	bag			frizər	freezer
	rɛt	red	wʌs	was	hɪs	his	bap	Bob
	gəraʒ	garage	,bɛt	bed	dis	these	babi	Bobby
	ˌlʌf	love	ˌjɔb	job	gɔt	god	pɪk	pig
	pisəs	pieces	ˌʃɛf	shave	ɔf~ɔv	of	pɪgi	piggy
	friz	freeze	bef	bathe			smuf	smooth
							smuvər	smoother
							rɛt	red
							rɛdər	redder
							wɛt	wet
							wɛtər	wetter
							sɪk	sick
							sɪkəst	sickest
							flɪp	flip
							flɪpər	flipper
							kros	close
							krosəst	closest

	from tape		from tape		Conversation			
	IL	TL Gloss	IL	TL Gloss	IL	TL Gloss	IL	TL Gloss
F.C.	tæg	tag	ɔf	of	gɔt~gɔd	god	bɔp	Bob
	rap	rob	bɛt	bed	bɪk~bɪg	big	bɔbi	Bobby
	bʌt	bad	wʌs	was	sɛt~sɛd	said	rɛt	red
	fayf	five	ðɛf	shave			rɛðər	redder
	briθ	breathe	lɪf	live			bɪk	big
	son	zone					bɪgər	bigger
	fʌsi	fuzzy					brɛf	brave
	fris	freeze					brɛvər	braver
	dɛk	deck					prawt	proud
	sop	soap					prawd~ast	proudest
	sɪk	sick					wɛt	wet
	biɣər	bigger					wɛtər	wetter
							sɪk	sick
							sɪkəst	sickest

	from tape		from tape		Conversation			
	IL	TL Gloss	IL	TL Gloss	IL	TL Gloss	IL	TL Gloss
S.O.	tæg	tag	lɛk	leg	gɔt~	god	bɔp	Bob
	bæd	bad	bɛt	bed	sɛt~	said	bɔbi	Bobby
	pig	pig	əgrit	agreed	sɛd		rav	rob
	get	gate			bɪk~	big	ravər	robber
	rɛð	red			big~		smuθ	smooth
	tap	top			biɣ		smuðər	smoother
	tæb	tab					rɛθ	red
							rɛðər	redeer
							prawθ	proud
							prawð~əst	proudest
							du	do
							riðu	redo
							bek	bake
							priβek	prebake
							wɛt	wet
							wɛtər	wetter
							flip	flip
							flipər	flipper
							sef	safe
							sefəst	safest

Table 2 con'd

Subject	Repetition from tape		Reading		Free Conversation		Alternations	
	IL	TL Gloss	IL	TL Gloss	IL	TL Gloss	IL	TL Gloss
V.M.	brit	breathe	disaydət	decided	gɔt	god	rɛt	red
	garaʒ	garage	lɛk	leg	bik	big	rɛðər	redder
	bæd	bad	bɛt	bed	ʌf	of	bɔp	Bob
	pig	pig	sef	shave			bɔbi	Bobby
	rab	rob					gref	grave
	tap	top					grevər	graver
	dɛk	deck					pix	pig
	get	gate					pigi	piggy
							det	date
							priðet	predate
							pe	pay
							pripe	prepay
							tek	take
							ritek	retake
							sef	safe
							sefəst	safest
							hat	hot
							hatəst	hotest

Table 3

Substitution of Voiceless Segment for Voiced Segment

Subject	Repetition from tape				Reading				Free Conversation				Alternations			
	Medially		Finally		Medially		Finally		Medially		Finally		Medially		Finally	
	No.	%	No.	%	No.	%	No.	%	No.	%	No.	%	No.	%	No.	%
T.C.	1/13	8	13/15	87	0/31	0	34/69	49	0/19	0	22/41	54	1/14	7	12/12	100
F.C.	1/12	9	9/15	60	0/21	0	15/69	22	0/25	0	16/45	36	0/14	0	10/12	83

To account for the observed alternations and medial voice contrast, we postulate the forms in Table 4 as underlying representations in T.C.'s interlanguage. The IL forms exhibiting voiceless segments where the corresponding TL forms have voiced segments are accounted for by assuming that the IL in question contains a rule of terminal devoicing as in (3). The problem with postulating a rule like (3) as part of this IL is that there exist forms which are counterexamples to this rule, namely, those IL forms with word-final voiced obstruents. Thus, if we are to maintain a rule like (3) in view of the direct counterexamples cited, we must assume that such a rule, as part of this IL, has a different status from that as part of the grammar of German.

Table 4
Underlying Representations for T.C.'s Interlanguage

Underlying form	Gloss	Underlying Form	Gloss
/ t æ g /	tag	/ kros /	close
/ t æ b /	tab	/ lɛg /	leg
/ rɛd /	red	/ bæ g /	bag
/ gəraž /	garage	/ wʌz /	was
/ lʌv /	love	/ bɛd /	bed
/ pis ɨ z /	pieces	/ jɔb /	job
/ friz /	freeze	/ šev /	shave
/ bab /	Bob	/ bev /	bathe
/ pɪk /	pig	/ bəkɔz /	because
/ smuv /	smooth	/ hɪz /	his
/ flɪp /	flip	/ diz /	these
/ wɛt /	wet	/ gɔd /	god
/ sɪk /	sick	/ ɔv /	of

It seems plausible that this status difference can be attributed to the generally held notion that ILs are variable or somewhat unstable. Therefore, a rule like (3) as part of an IL would represent a variable rule rather than a rule whose application is obligatory. In addition, this rule would represent a prediction about the directionality in which a learner will make errors, rather than representing a phonetically true generalization, as is the case with German. This interpretation is in keeping with the widely-held idea that language-learning errors are systematic rather than random. The systematicity expressed by a rule like (3) being part of   IL is that errors in word-final position will always be in the direction of substituting a voiceless segment for a voiced one, and never the opposite.

The situation is somewhat similar when we consider the data summarized in Table 2, which was elicited from the three Spanish subjects. These IL forms show some of the same properties as those in Table 1. Specifically, many of the IL forms in Table 2 have a word-final voiceless consonant where the corresponding TL form has a voiced consonant. Furthermore, many of the forms exhibit alternations between final voiceless and word-medial voiced obstruents. Along with this alternation, we note that the IL forms in question exhibit a voice contrast in word-medial and word-final positions.

In addition to these shared properties, the IL forms in Table 2 exhibit an alternation between either an initial or final stop and a medial fricative. In some cases, this final stop is voiceless and in other cases it is voiced. The initial stops and medial fricatives involved in this alternation are always voiced.

To account for these facts, we postulate the underlying representations shown in Tables 5-7 as part of the ILs in question, along with a rule of terminal devoicing like (3), and a rule of postvocalic spirantization formulated as in (6):

Table 5

Underlying Representations for F.C.'s Interlanguage

Underlying form	Gloss	Underlying form	Gloss
/ t æ g /	tag	/ lɪv /	live
/ rab /	rob	/ gɔd /	god
/ bæ d /	bad	/ bɪg /	big
/ fayv /	five	/ sɛd /	said
/ briʒ /	breathe	/ bɔb /	Bob
/ son /	zone	/ rɛd /	red
/ fʌsi /	fuzzy	/ big /	big
/ dɛk /	deck	/ brev /	brave
/ sop /	soap	/ prawd /	proud
/ sɪk /	sick	/ wɛt /	wet
/ ɔv /	of	/ wʌz /	was
/ bɛd /	bed	/ čev /	shave

Table 6

Underlying Representations for S.O.'s Interlanguage

Underlying form	Gloss	Underlying form	Gloss
/ t æ g /	tag	/ sɛd /	said
/ bæ d /	bad	/ big /	big
/ pig /	pig	/ bɔb /	Bob
/ get /	gate	/ rab /	rob
/ reʒ /	red	/ smuʒ /	smooth
/ tap /	top	/ sef /	safe
/ t æ b /	tab	/ prawʒ /	proud
/ lɛg /	leg	/ du /	do
/ bɛd /	bed	/ bek /	bake
/ agrid /	agreed	/ wɛt /	wet
/ gɔd /	god	/ flɪp /	flip

Table 7
Underlying Representations for V.M.'s Interlanguage

Underlying form	Gloss	Underlying form	Gloss
/ brid /	breathe	/ rɛd /	red
/ gəraž /	garage	/ bɔb /	Bob
/ bæd /	bad	/ grev /	grave
/ pig /	pig	/ det /	date
/ rab /	rob	/ pe /	pay
/ tap /	top	/ tek /	take
/ dɛk /	deck	/ sef /	safe
/ get /	gate	/ hat /	hot
/ disayd + d /	decided	/ gɔd /	god
/ lɛg /	leg	/ big /	big
/ bɛd /	bed	/ ʌv /	of
/ sev /	shave		

(6)   Postvocalic spirantization

$$\begin{vmatrix} -son \\ +voice \end{vmatrix} \rightarrow [+continuant] \; / \; V\underline{\hspace{2cm}}$$

Voiced obstruents become continuants after vowels

The motivation for rules like (3) and (6) as part of the Spanish subjects' interlanguage is essentially the same as that used to motivate (3) as part of T.C.'s interlanguage. These rules and underlying representations can account for the observed contrasts and alternations, and in addition make it possible to predict the direction in which errors will be made. Thus, a rule like (6) predicts that the Spanish speakers in question will always err in the direction of substituting a voiced fricative for a voiced stop in postvocalic position in TL words. Since such a rule obviously does not express an exceptionless generalization about IL forms, it must be assumed to be a variable, or optional, rule.

Discussion

Given these analyses of the data, the question arises as to the relationship between these interlanguages and the respective NLs. We can ask this question from two perspectives: first, what is the relationship between a learner's IL and his or her NL; and second, what is the relationship between a learner's IL and first languages in general?

To answer the first part of this question, we can show that the relationship between ILs and NLs in this study is different in the case of the rule of terminal devoicing than it is in the case of postvocalic spirantization. Insofar as the latter rule is concerned, it is reasonable to assume that this rule was transferred directly from the respective NL, since Spanish clearly evidences such a rule. Thus, for example, a rule like (6) is necessary to account for the alternations shown in (7).

(7)   a.   [donde]   'where'   c.   [laɣata]   'the cat (f)'
      b.   [deƏonde]   'from where'   d.   [boɣa]   'vogue'
      c.   [gata]   'cat (f.)'   e.   [laβoɣa]   'the vogue'

On the other hand, it is equally reasonable that a rule of terminal devoicing represents a truly independent rule as part of these ILs, since this rule is not motivated for either the TL or the NLs in question. That a rule like (3) is not motivated for the TL is clear from the fact that English has a voice contrast in initial, medial, and final positions and that English exhibits no regular voice alternations between final and medial obstruents. In order to show that terminal devoicing cannot be a part of the grammar of Cantonese or Spanish, we will consider the facts from each of these languages in more detail.

Chao (1969) points out that Cantonese has no voice contrast in obstruents anywhere. Thus, even though Cantonese has both voiced and voiceless obstruents, they are distributed so that they are mutually noncontrastive, with voiceless obstruents occurring initially and finally and their voiced counterparts occurring medially. This means that there is no medial voice contrast in Cantonese, and, therefore, no motivation for a rule of terminal devoicing. T.C.'s interlanguage forms are significantly different from Cantonese forms in that the IL forms exhibit a voice contrast and that some forms show a voice alternation between medial and final obstruents. On the basis of this evidence we conclude that a rule like (3) could not have been transferred directly from Cantonese.

The facts concerning voice contrast in Spanish also support the conclusion that a rule of terminal devoicing could not have been transferred from the NL to the IL. Spanish has no superficial voice contrast in either medial or final position (Bowen 1960). While there are a few Spanish words with final voiceless stops, there are no words in Spanish with word-final voiced stops. The situation is similar for medial position: there are medial voiceless stops in Spanish, but there are no superficial voiced stops intervocalically. Rather, all underlying voiced stops in postvocalic medial and postvocalic final position become fricatives by means of a spirantization rule. Spanish also has no superficial voice contrast in fricatives. This is true because, of the Spanish fricatives shown in (8), [s] and [z] occur in mutually exclusive environments and are therefore noncontrastive, while the others have no voiceless or voiced counterpart in the language with which to contrast.

(8)   [s]   [β]

[z]   [ð]
[f]   [ɣ]
[x]   [θ]*

*Continental Spanish only

Given these facts, it is clear that there are no alternations between final voiceless and medial voiced consonants that would motivate a rule of terminal devoicing.   Consequently, such a rule is clearly independent for the ILs in question, and the IL forms produced are clearly distinct from NL forms.

The conclusion that a rule of terminal devoicing could not have been transferred to the ILs in question from the respective NLs does not mean that such a rule has no rationale or explanation. On the contrary, such a rule is explainable on the basis of a comparison of the NLs and TL involved, along with certain principles of second language acquisition.

It has already been pointed out that both Cantonese and Spanish differ from English in that the latter has a voice contrast in initial, medial, and final position, whereas Cantonese has no such contrast and Spanish has only an initial contrast.   Therefore, a learner with one of these languages as an NL must learn to produce a voice contrast in final position as he or she progresses in the direction of acquiring the TL.   Now if we assume that it is more difficult to acquire a voice contrast in final position than in medial position, as argued on independent grounds in Eckman (1977), and further, if we assume that a learner will acquire those less difficult aspects of the TL before acquiring those more difficult ones, then it is reasonable to expect a learner to acquire a voice contrast medially before doing so finally.   This situation will produce IL forms like those shown in Tables 1 and 2 where the learner correctly produces the contrast medially, but errs finally. Such a situation, as we have seen, motivates a rule like (3).

If we accept this conclusion, then it is possible to reflect on the type of systems that ILs are and the constraints that they are subject to.   On the one hand, we see that it is possible for ILs to contain rules that have been transferred directly from the NL, as with spirantization. On the other hand, we see that it is possible for ILs to have rules independent of both the NL and TL, as with terminal devoicing.   What is particularly interesting in this latter case is that the rule that is shown to be independent is one necessary for the grammars of numerous first languages, such as Catalan, German, Polish, Russian, and others.   Consequently, this evidence would support the conclusion that interlanguages are not only systematic, but that they are systematic in at least some of the important ways that first languages are.

Finally, we should point out that some of the universal constraints on first languages also seem to hold for interlanguages. For example, it has been pointed out in Dinnsen and Eckman (1978) that a language will have a voice contrast in final position only if this language has a voice contrast in medial position; and a language has such a contrast medially only if it has this contrast initially. However, a language may have a voice contrast in medial position without having such a contrast finally.

These same constraints seem to hold for the ILs discussed in this paper. The learners in question made many more voice contrast errors in final position than in medial position. This indicates that the constraint that a language may have a voice contrast in final position only if it also has a voice contrast in medial position holds for both first languages and interlanguages.

In conclusion, this paper has presented data from four interlanguages, involving a single IL and two NLs. It has been argued that the data presented necessitate the postulation of a rule of terminal devoicing as part of the ILs in question. Such a rule is motivated for neither the TL nor the NLs in question, leading to the conclusion that this rule is indeed independent for these interlanguages. Finally, at least some of the rules that are necessary for ILs are the same rules necessary for first languages, and that these rules obey many of the same constraints proposed for NL rules.

REFERENCES

Bowen, D. 1960. Patterns of Spanish pronunciation. Chicago: University of Chicago Press.
Dickerson, W. B. 1976. The psycholinguistic unity of language learning and language change. Language Learning 26:215-31.
Dinnsen, D., and Eckman, F. 1978. Some substantive universals in atomic phonology. Lingua 48:1-14.
Dulay, H., and Burt, M. 1974. A new perspective on the creative construction process in child second language acquisition. Language Learning 24:253-78.
Eckman, F. 1977. Markedness and the contrastive analysis hypothesis. Language Learning 27:315-30.
Selinker, L. 1972. Interlanguage. IRAL 10:209-31.

19. Contrastive Analysis Revisited

MARCEL DANESI
University of Toronto

I wish to state at the very outset that I do not subscribe to any one theory of language methodology. I believe, as Halliday (1979: 241) puts it, that "really effective language teaching is not tied methodologically to any one interpretation of the teaching process or of the learning process." My purpose is not to defend or condemn contrastive analysis (CA), but to attempt an assessment of CA in the light of recently expressed criticism.

During the fifties and sixties, CA was hailed as perhaps the major accomplishment of applied linguistics. Even today CA is assumed (at least tacitly) to be the normal approach to second-language teaching; and it is still used (secretly, of course, by those who no longer deem it fashionable) as a heuristic pedagogical procedure. Teachers know all too well by hard experience that the most common errors are caused by the student's "thinking" in his native language. As Agard and Di Pietro (1965:2) observe, the student "sees the structure of the foreign language through the filter of his in-built native habits." More recently, Di Pietro has expressed this tendency in transformational terms (1971:160): "If transfer and interference are psychologically valid notions, many errors committed by the language learner can be traced back to precisely this matter of applying language-specific rules which are not found in the target language." Common questions such as "How do you say x in foreign language y?" testify to the fact that students approach the foreign language with the telescope of their native language. The hybrid code that emerges characteristically during the learning process is called appropriately interlanguage by Selinker (1969). This interlanguage is particularly evident in free speech situations that require the student to use the foreign language without reference to a fixed grammatical or lexical perimeter (as in the case of exercises on a specific grammatical or lexical topic).

The supporters of CA claim that it allows the teacher, as Pit Corder (1973:293) states, "to understand the source of errors so that he can provide the appropriate data and other information, sometimes comparative, which will resolve the learner's problems and allow him to discover the relevant rules." The identification of potential error sources does indeed facilitate the teaching process and in some areas has proven to be indispensable. For example, students of Italian frequently commit lexico-semantic errors similar to the following ones:

ERROR TYPE	INTENDED MEANING	CORRECT VERSION
(1) Toscanini era un conduttore famoso	Toscanini was a famous conductor	Toscanini era un direttore d'orchestra famoso
(2) Freud era uno scolaro famoso	Freud was a famous scholar	Freud era uno studioso famoso
(3) Vado alla lettura del professore	I'm going to the professor's lecture	Vado alla conferenza del professore

The errors are caused by the substitution of the different meanings of homologous English lexical items (so-called deceptive cognates). In reality, an Italian would interpret the above sentences as: (1) Toscanini was a famous train conductor; (2) Freud was a famous school boy; (3) I'm going to the professor's reading. Without an explicit knowledge of these lexico-semantic contrasts, the student will probably go on uttering such verbal infelicities. It is in areas such as this one that CA emerges as extremely useful.

This simple illustration demonstrates that CA is an etiological science. As Mills (1977:735) points out, CA has shown the teacher in an overt manner that:

(a) Certain features of the target language are more difficult to learn than others.

(b) These difficulties seem due (in part at least) to differences between the students' mother tongue and those of the target language (negative transfer).

(c) Errors of this kind can be anticipated and eventually eliminated by the use of corrective exercises that focus attention on the differences.

Moreover, as Moulton (1968:38) argues, it would be pedagogically counterproductive not to make use of the insights gained from CA, for students cannot be stopped from translating mentally or from perceiving foreign language structures in terms of native language ones: "It seems to me preferable for us to guide the student's simultaneous use of the two languages rather than permit him to flounder in it."

The confident climate of the fifties and sixties vis-a-vis CA has disappeared in the seventies. The question that immediately comes to mind is the following one: If it is common pedagogical experience that native language interference is a persistent source of student errors, why is the abandonment of CA, even as an ancillary heuristic tool, being suggested and even demanded by some linguists? It is to be noted, in fact, that since the nineteenth annual Round Table Conference at Georgetown University (Alatis 1968) and the publication of Di Pietro's Language structures in contrast (1971)—perhaps the definitive work using transformational grammar as a theoretical basis for CA—no significant statement on CA has been published in North America (at least to the best of my knowledge). On the other hand, the number of studies criticizing CA has been increasing.

One reason for this new critical climate is the Zeitgeist, or spirit of the times. CA was initially associated with audiolingualism and its theoretical progenitor, structuralism; and it has become fashionable to attack anything that smacks of structuralism. As transformational grammar established itself as mainstream linguistics in the last two decades, some linguists adapted CA to this new model of language design, and several important findings emerged. For one thing, it was discovered that the deep structures of languages are very much alike, and that differences occur mainly at the surface level. But probably because of its early association with structuralism, the criticism of CA has not abated. Maybe what is wrong with CA is what is wrong with linguistics in general. As Wardhaugh (1974:185) puts it: "Uncertainty is obviously piled upon uncertainty in making contrastive analyses. Such uncertainties arise from inadequacies in existing linguistic theories."

Another reason for the negative attitude toward CA may stem from the tendency to apply it too inflexibly. To quote Mills (1977:736):

> As always happens with new approaches, the pendulum has a tendency to swing too far and we begin to experience the bandwagon syndrome. We hear claims rather reminiscent of a certain airline company to the effect that "this is the ONLY way to learn a language," that it is an indispensable tool and so on; but it was and still is too readily forgotten that the raw findings of contrastive analysis are not for classroom consumption, but for the applied linguist, the textbook writer or the curriculum specialist.

One of the original tenets of CA was that the goal of foreign-language instruction was error-free speech. This is, of course, an impossibility and probably counterproductive. As Hendrickson (1978:388) states, foreign-language teachers "should expect many errors from their students, and should accept those errors as a natural phenomenon integral to the process of learning a second language. When teachers tolerate some student errors, students feel more confident about using the target language than if all their errors are corrected." Critics of this practice should, however, bear in mind that it is not a theoretical consequence of CA per se, but a result of its zealous implementation. A more reasonable goal would be successful, rather than perfect, communication.

Another reason for the disenchantment with CA stems from its tendency to focus almost exclusively on native-language interference. There exists considerable empirical evidence (e.g., George 1972; Burt 1975; Hanzeli 1975) that indicates that interference errors are only one of many error types. Such tendencies as overgeneralization, simplification, incorrect rule selection, etc., all play a role in the production of errors (e.g. Hamp 1968; Gradman 1971; Richards 1971). From this research, a new technique known as Error Analysis (EA) has emerged. However, rather than viewing it as a substitute for CA, it seems more logical to consider EA as a pedagogical complement of CA, since both aim to identify error-producing mechanisms. CA and EA are just two components that should be integrated into a comprehensive theory of foreign-language learning.

EA is not, however, without weaknesses. As da Rocha (1975:58) observes, the most vulnerable aspect of EA is the explanation and classification of errors: "they are not always traceable to a particular linguistic area. As can be expected, this leads to debatable, if not arbitrary, classifications to which no solution is yet envisaged." Probably for this reason, Bell (1974) has voiced one of the strongest criticisms of EA. Using logical argumentation, Bell dismisses EA as a pseudoprocedure. The gist of Bell's case against EA is found in the following statement (1974:48):

> Were Error Analysis to consist of a technique for the full description of the communicative competence of an individual or a group of individuals at a particular point in time in a language which they were learning and if such a description were instantaneous, then it would not be a pseudo-procedure which it undoubtedly is. Since a full description of communicative competence has never been achieved for any individual language user and since no description of such magnitude could ever be instantaneous, Error Analysis stands exposed as a pseudo-procedure of the "impossible in principle" type.

Is Bell implying that unless a scientific procedure is capable of accounting for all the range of observable phenomena within its domain, then it is a pseudoprocedure? This would mean that astrophysical procedures, for example, should be abandoned because they cannot as yet account fully for the nature of the moon (even in this age of moon travel), or that psychology is a pseudoscience because it does not fully explain human behavior, and so on.

Another radical criticism of CA is put forward by Nemser and Slama-Cazacu (1970), who point out that the concept of interference was borrowed from psychology and has been misunderstood by applied linguists. According to these two scholars, interference does not refer to incongruous matches between L_1 and L_2 but to the contact of languages as it occurs within the learner. However, as Jackson (1976:18) emphasizes: "Since CL Contrastive Linguistics is not an integral component of language learning theory, but an autonomous branch of general linguistics, any criticisms of language learning theory, or attempts to include it in such a theory . . . do not of themselves strike at the basic presuppositions of CL."

In my opinion, the strongest objection to CA is that it is grammar-based—i.e., that it is limited to matters of form. Since languages are communicative instruments, differences are bound to occur in nongrammatical domains, such as verbal strategies. As Di Pietro (1976b:35) says: "To learn a new language is not the equivalent of learning the grammar of that language. It is not a special case of data processing, as some linguists might claim. It is much more."   Given this lacuna in the practice of CA, it is not surprising to find that Di Pietro has recently turned his attention to the pedagogical aspects of verbal strategies (e.g., 1975, 1976a, 1978, 1979).

An example of the need to extend CA to the study of verbal strategies is the following one.   An Italian speaker, as Di Pietro (1979:3-4) points out, has at least three ways of saying "Good morning":

(1)   Buon giorno Good morning';

(2)   Hai dormito bene?   Have you slept well?';

(3)   Vuoi caffè?   Do you want coffee?'

The first expression is the general one.   The other two are reserved for members of the family who have spent the night under the same roof.   Contrasts in this area are major sources of communicational difficulty.   Think of the embarrassing position a student of Italian would be in if he went up to a policeman in Italy and greeted him with "Hai dormito bene?"

In conclusion, it appears to me that many of the criticisms of CA do not undermine its basic pedagogical function, i.e., the identification of sources of error.   One of the more interesting incorporations of CA into the modus operandi of language teaching has been proposed by Fischer (1979). According to Fischer, when the foreign language rule is similar to the native language one, or dissimilar but simpler, then an inductive approach in which comparison is made with the native language is used. If the foreign language rule is dissimilar and as complex as, or more complex than, the native language rule, then a deductive approach is more feasible (with no reference to the native language). This pedagogical model may be schematized as follows (FL = foreign language, NL = native language):

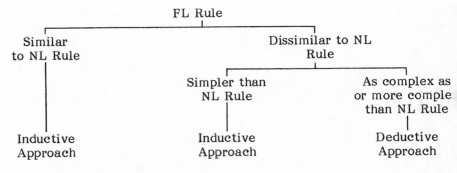

But it must be emphasized that CA is only one of many classroom techniques available to the teacher. As suggested in this paper, CA should be extended beyond the sentence level to sociocultural and psycholinguistic domains (such as the strategic use of language). It is in such domains that language instruction can become a truly meaningful experience for both teacher and learner.

REFERENCES

Agard, Frederick B., and Di Pietro, Robert J. 1965. The sounds of English and Italian. Chicago: University of Chicago Press.

Alatis, J., ed. 1968. Georgetown Monograph series on Language and Linguistics, no. 21. Washington, D.C.: Georgetown University Press.

Bell, Roger. 1974. Error analysis: a recent pseudoprocedure in applied linguistics. International Review of Applied Linguistics 25-26:35-49.

Burt, Marina K. 1975. Error analysis in the adult EFL classroom. TESOL Quarterly 9:53-63.

da Rocha, Fernando J. 1975. On the reliability of error analysis. International Review of Applied Linguistics 29:53-61.

Di Pietro, Robert J. 1971. Language structures in contrast. Rowley, Mass.: Newbury House.

_____. 1975. Speech protocols and verbal strategies in the teaching of Italian. Canadian Modern Language Review 32:25-38.

_____. 1976a. Contrasting patterns of language use. Canadian Modern Language Review 33:49-61.

_____. 1976b. Language as human creation. Washington, D.C.: Georgetown University Press.

_____. 1978. Verbal strategies, script theory and conversational performances in ESL. in TESOL, ed. C. Blatchford and J. Schachter, pp. 149-57. Washington, D.C.: TESOL.

_____. 1979. Verbal strategies in the modern language classroom. The Bulletin 57:3-10.

Fischer, Robert A. 1979. The inductive-deductive controversy revisited. Modern Language Journal 63:98–105.

George, H. V. 1972. Common errors in language learning. Rowley, Mass.: Newbury House.

Gradman, Harry L. 1971. The limitations of contrastive analysis predictions. Working Papers in Linguistics 3:11–16.

Halliday, M.A.K. 1979. The teacher taught the student English: an essay in applied linguistics. In Linguistic and literary studies in honor of Archibald A. Hill, ed. M. A. Jazayery; E. C. Polomé, and W. Winter, 2:233–42. The Hague: Mouton.

Hamp, Eric P. 1968. What a contrastive grammar is not, if it is. In Georgetown University round table on languages and literature, ed. J. Alatis, pp. 137–47. Washington, D.C.: Georgetown University Press.

Hanzeli, Victor E. 1975. Learner's language: implications of recent research for foreign language instruction. Modern Language Journal 59:426–32.

Hendrickson, J. M. 1978. Error correction in foreign language teaching: Recent theory, research and practice. Modern Language Journal 62:387–98.

Jackson, H. 1976. Contrastive linguistics—what is it? International Review of Applied Linguistics 32:1–32.

Mills, Geoff. 1977. Contrastive analysis and translation in second language teaching. Canadian Modern Language Review 33:732–45.

Moulton, W. G. 1968. The use of models in contrastive linguistics. In Georgetown University round table in languages and literature, ed. J. Alatis, pp. 27–38. Washington, D.C.: Georgetown University Press.

Nemser, W. and T. Slama-Cazacu. 1970. A contribution to contrastive linguistics. Revue Roumaine de Linguistique 15:101–28.

Pit Corder, S. 1973. Introducing applied linguistics. London: Penguin.

Richards, J. C. 1971. A noncontrastive approach to error analysis. English Language Teaching 25:204–19.

Selinker, L. 1969. Language transfer. General Linguistics 9:671–92.

Wardhaugh, R. 1974. Topics in applied linguistics. Rowley, Mass.: Newbury House.

20. Transference in Child Speech: A Sociolinguistic Phenomenon

ALVINO E. FANTINI
School for International Training

Introduction: Evolution of a Concept

Extensive use of the word transference these days belies a change in our understanding of a phenomenon previously labeled interference. It was only a little more than two decades ago when the term interference was widely used by linguists (Weinreich 1953; Haugen 1956) who had proposed a notion of what happens when two languages interact.

When applied to second-language learning, the concept resulted in numerous contrastive analyses of learners' native tongues and target languages. Given the differing structures of two linguistic systems, interference was considered a rather predictable outcome. However, teachers soon discovered that not all linguistic predictions actually materialized in the classroom. Also, some applied linguists, like Selinker (1972) proposed that learners go through stages of linguistic accommodation as they attempt to approximate items of the second language. In such a case, there was no direct collision necessarily between two distinct language systems, but rather gradual and progressive stages of adjustments.

Even though the concept of interference was immediately useful, there was also some lingering uneasiness with it. One question asked the minimal unit of interference; and conversely, its outer extensions. Haugen attempted to clarify this by proposing three stages of linguistic diffusion: intergration, interference, and switching (Haugen 1956:40). However, these divisions eventually led to the possibility of others and scholars grappled with the full continuum, not always able to distinguish clearly what was interference and what was a full and complete switch in codes. Another aspect that Weinreich dealt with was the difference between interference in language (in a historical sense) and interference in speech (momentary influences due to the presence of a second language; Weinreich 1953:11). Even this distinction, although useful, leads to consideration of another possible continuum—one through time. In other words, bilinguals often undergo language shifts over a period of time. Shift is especially dramatic and easily visible in children since their acquisition, or dissolution, of a second tongue often occurs within a short period. Consequently we are forced to view transference as a process that tends to obliterate any clear distinction between synchronic and diachronic aspects. The synchronic, in other words, becomes the momentary manifestation of the broader diachronic phenomenon through time.

Other linguists were unhappy with possible social implications of the term interference (i.e., deviation from a norm that carried social judgments). As more studies concentrated on this phenomenon, along with code-switching, researchers increasingly pointed to the fact that bilingual speakers did indeed have a heretofore unexpected control over their dual language systems. This being the case, interference, code-mixing, and code-switching all seem related to factors other than the conflicts in linguistic structures.

Indeed, Weinreich had earlier alluded to "extralinguistic" factors. However, his detailed analysis of interference was admittedly concerned with structural causes (Weinreich 1953:3). In the past few years, thanks to the research of sociolinguists, we now have a more explicit understanding of the interrelationship of language and context, and along with that, a clearer notion of just how social factors affect transference. Recent studies have examined the social (as well as linguistic and psychological) factors that trigger the overlapping (intentional or otherwise) of one language on another, which dramatizes the control that bilinguals have over this process. If mixing is indeed under one's control and is produced for a variety of reasons, it would be important to consider the positive as well as negative aspects of transference. Padilla (1977) attempted to include both by coining the terms interpolation and intercalation. Many others have preferred the label transference. Yet both terms may still be necessary, reserving interference for mixing that is beyond the speaker's control and attributable entirely to structural linguistic differences; transference, on the other hand, might be mixing controlled by the speaker (on a conscious or subconscious level) and which is traceable to environmental and social factors. Both linguistic and sociolinguistic terms may be of continued use in connoting this distinction and are used in this way in this paper.

Having referred to nonstructural (i.e., social) causes of transference, one might now ask how social conditions affect transference across languages; for example:

1. What specific social variables affect transference?

2. Is transference a predictable outcome of languages in contact, or can it occur only in specific instances in relation to varying social factors?

3. In what direction does transference occur? Can it go in either direction across languages?

4.   In what aspect of language does transference
     occur?

5.   Does it occur in some aspects more than in
     others?   Are some aspects subject to greater
     control by the speaker than others?

6.   What positive dimensions of transference are there
     in the speech of bilingual children?

Transference and the Bilingual Child: Some Special Considerations

Despite increased study of adult bilinguals and their use of two
languages, much work is yet to be done with very young children.
Bilingual children, in fact, present additional complexities that must
be considered when transference is being examined. First of all, one
must consider to what extent the child is really undergoing
concurrent and dual language acquisition, or when he is more like
the second-language learner. One needs only to reflect on the great
variety of exposure and acquisitional patterns of bilingual children
who have been described in the literature. Truly concurrent and
equal exposure appears to be more hypothetical than real. Many
children, for example, are exposed to a home language in greater
amounts initially than to the language of the larger society. When
they are older and begin to interact outside the home, the second
language may have caught up. By school age, the second language
often becomes the principal language of the child. Even in cases in
which each parent used a separate language (Ronjat 1913; Leopold
1939-49; and others), it is easy to imagine that exposure must have
varied in kind and in degree, contingent on the interaction and role
function each parent performed. Truly simultaneous and equal
exposure is probably easier to conjecture than to find in reality.
Bilingual acquisition, therefore (like bilingualism itself),
includes a great variety of acquisitional patterns. This is important
to keep in mind as I discuss transference in the "bilingual" child, who
most probably has one dominant language. In addition, Mackey
(1970:554) pointed out that with all bilinguals, we must acknowledge
not only language dominance but also dominance in relation to
various domains of experience. Language dominance configurations
are therefore also critical to this view of transference.
Second, several researchers have suggested that the child
exposed to two languages at a very early age may in fact have only
one linguistic system.   Swain (1972), for example, speaks of
"bilingualism as a first language," suggesting that the differentiation
of the single code occurs only later as a result of the social need to
create two distinct linguistic sets. Padilla, Lindholm (1976:98), and I
(1974:248-49) came to the same conclusion through our own
research. If this is the case it might be accurate to speak not of
interference, but of language separation—a gradual process of

language differentiation. What has been called interference may be the residue of an incomplete process. Yet the bias is clear since one almost always speaks of bilingual behavior with interference, rather than of unilingual behavior with linguistic separation. How we view the process affects in part our understanding of dual language development. In either case, nonetheless, it is <u>differentiated</u> language use that one recognizes as bilingual behavior. And differentiated behavior comes about in response to the demands of a social context that fosters or inhibits transference or separation. Again, the influence of social context cannot be dismissed in considering either phenomenon.

Third, although the adult bilingual speaker theoretically already possesses two fully developed languages, the child exposed to two systems is involved in the process of developing his first mode of communicating. Consequently it is difficult to ascertain which of his deviations in speech are attributable to transference because of the coexistence of two language systems within the same speaker, and which are deviations normal in child speech—that is, those deviations commonly present at the various developmental stages in the speech of even monolingual children of comparable ages. Sorting one from the other is a most challenging task. Once again the developmental question reminds us that we are necessarily concerned with a process, subject to change and evolution.

It is also interesting to note that several sociolinguists are of the opinion that all speakers—bilinguals and monolinguals alike—possess more than one variety of speech, and, in this respect, they are quite alike. Whereas the speaker of Spanish and English behaves in two very discrete manners, he is nonetheless not much different from the monolingual speaker who is capable of varying a single code in differing social circumstances, and who, under some conditions, may be just as prone to transfer elements of one variety to another. The difference resides primarily in the fact that the varieties within a single code are often less noticeable, yet they operate in the same way as two distinct codes in that the choices are often socially motivated. In this respect transference is a phenomenon common to <u>all</u> speakers.

Whatever the case, recent studies have refuted the arbitrariness with which speakers supposedly invoke one form of speech or another. Labov (1966, 1972) documented the interrelationships of specific linguistic elements under varying circumstances in the speech of monolinguals. Hernandez (1975), Valdes-Fallis (1976), and others have likewise recorded and analyzed similar patterns in the speech of bilinguals. Whether one is concerned with code-switching, code-mixing, style-shifting, or transference, most speech modifications have plausible explanations that are often—but not always—rooted in the social circumstances surrounding the speech event. Language use, then, is as systematic as language structure itself. The very young child must learn both language structure as well as the sociolinguistic norms for language use (Bergman 1976). Transference may occur potentially in either area, leaving the linguist-observer to ponder in which area the child deviated. This is a formidable challenge for the observer of very young children.

Case Studies of Two Bilingual Children

To find evidence relevant to questions raised earlier, I examined the speech diaries of two bilingual children. Both children were speakers of Spanish and English. In both cases, Spanish was the sole language of the home; English was a slightly later acquisition, commencing just past the second year. The siblings—Mario and Carla—were subjects of a longitudinal study; the former from birth to age nine, and the latter from birth to her then age of five. Data were examined for evidence of transference with attention on the social circumstances in which it occurred.

Phonological Data. Both children had not quite completed their acquisition of Spanish phonology when they also began active production of English words. Their first words of English were couched within the existing phonemic systems based on Spanish that was available to them at that time. Consequently they lacked several sounds needed for the proper pronunciation of English. For example:

Child's Word	Phone Substitution	Standard
/bilị/	ị → i	Billy
/soš/	j → s	George
/ápo/	ae → a	apple
/tis/	ə → t	this

Only a few months later, however, they acquired the additional phones needed. Nonetheless, phonological interference persisted (although continually diminishing) in Carla to her then age of five and in Mario almost to age seven.

Primary sources of deviance were: (1) underdifferentiation of two phonemes in English (for example, the /b/~/v/ distinction, (2) an inability to produce the sounds /θ/~/ð/ and rr/~/r/, and (3) the influence of Spanish allophonic rule variations upon English (for example, certain consonants in intervocalic and word-final positions). The children's late acquisition of the Spanish /rr/r̃/ and English /ð/θ/ were characteristic also of the late acquisitions of other children and therefore may be counted for our purposes. Interference proceeded primarily from Spanish to English and gave the children's English a slightly foreign quality. The same still holds for Carla at age five; however, this foreign quality totally disappeared from Mario's speech by the time he was seven. Although in the first grade, for example, he was singled out for speech therapy (which he never pursued) by an inexperienced therapist, and by eight years old his third-grade teacher had no inkling that he spoke any language other than English.

Conversely, interference from English to Spanish was rare and almost never occurred. A few unusual and sporadic instances where interference was noted, for example, involved the addition of aspiration:

Age	Child's Pronunciation	Standard Spanish	English Translation
3:1	/se kʰae/	se cae	he falls down
4:2	/pʰepʰito/	Pepito	Pepito (dog's name)
9:6	/tʰio Larry/	Tío Larry	Uncle Larry

and phone borrowings from cognate words:

3:8	/elicátʌ /	helicóptero	helicopter
3:9	telebišyón/	televisión	television

Interference in Spanish was so limited that it was almost never detected by other Spanish speakers.

In any case, the production of sounds seemed to be an area of language that was primarily attributable to the developmental process and largely beyond the conscious control of the children. One indication of this is that it was generally uniform, occurring usually in the same direction and in the same areas regardless of context (except the few rare examples of aspiration of certain Spanish consonants listed above). The children either perceived and were capable of articulating certain sounds, or they were not. There was no clear relation to external social factors. In this sense, one may speak primarily of an evolving phonological system or systems to meet the needs of a rapid lexical growth, or, if one is impatient, of phonological interference across languages. Because their sound systems were still in development, the same might not necessarily be true for the older speaker. However, Mario, who has now fully completed his acquisition of both sound systems, shows virtually no interference in either language. Although phonology seemed less linked to environmental factors, the same cannot be said of other areas of language.

Lexical Transference.   Unlike phonology, lexical borrowing was frequently influenced by social circumstances. The greatest transference of words occurred when interlocutors were also bilinguals. In such cases, Mario and Carla were more inclined to draw upon both language sources. Even so, borrowing was kept in check by the strong attitude of the children's parents against mixing. Borrowing of "culturally bound" words that often had no adequate synonyms was permissible, as for example:

snacks	blueberries
applesauce	peanut butter
popcorn	line-leader (a school term)
school bue	tinker toys

Other "foreign" terms that the children used were also employed by their parents and therefore formed part of the language norm as for example:

ciao	Scotch tape
O.K.	mamma mia (Italian)
baby	mangia (Italian)
nonno	chiacchierone (Italian)

These constitute examples of transference in language, but not in the children's speech, according to Weinreich's distinction (1968:11). Setting also affected transference to some degree since word borrowing increased during stays with English-speaking relatives in Philadelphia, during attendance at nursery school in Austin, Texas, and during attendance at kindergarten.

Transference was definitely most pronounced in the area of the lexicon, possibly reflecting the children's direct experiences through each language fostering vocabulary growth in separate languages. From a developmental point of view, it is interesting to note that transference usually ceased when a synonym was acquired that replaced the borrowed item in the appropriate language. In cases where no equivalent was learned, the borrowed item persisted in the child's speech as exemplified by the many culturally bound expressions. Nonetheless the children usually demonstrated an awareness when using borrowed words by setting those off with "verbal quotation marks"—i.e., a slight pause before saying the word, often a different intonation, and the retention of the phonetic aspects of the word as pronounced in the source language.

The possibility of word borrowing into either language is potentially quite great. It is often a convenient and easy habit to acquire. Yet surprisingly the family attitudes apparently were sufficient to keep lexical borrowings to a minimum. In Mario's case, increasing specialization through four years of schooling caused lexical borrowing when certain topics of conversation are discussed. Yet, even in these cases, insertion of the equivalent in Spanish by either parent is normally sufficient to cause the borrowed word to be dropped.

Grammatical Transference.   Again, amazingly little interference was evidenced in the speech data taken from both Mario and Carla within the realm of grammar. Although four of the types identified by Weinreich were noted, two others did not occur at all (e.g., a change in function of "indigenous" morpheme or category, and "abandonment of obligatory categories") (Weinreich 1968:64–65).

Examples were:

Can you <u>desentie</u> (untie) this?	Transfer of morphemes
I have too many<u>s</u> cars. (unnecessary plural agreement)	Transfer of grammatical relations
Glue put mamá.	Word positioning
I'm <u>saking</u> (from Spanish "sacar" –to take out)	Integration of loan-words

In all, transference into English of the type shown above was slight and transference into Spanish was almost nonexistent. One rare example in Spanish was:

¿Cuántos años <u>eres</u>? (instead of <u>tienes</u>)	Modeled on the English: How old <u>are</u> you?

In grammar, as in phonology, the children experienced greater transference from Spanish to English. However, in the lexical area the exact reverse was true. All systems, of course, were still under development with Spanish dominance in all areas at least until age five. Since both phonology and grammar are relatively closed systems (in that they contain limited numbers of elements to be acquired) and vocabulary is an open one, the first two are relatively complete by age five, whereas the lexicon continues to expand throughout life. This may account in part for transference occurring usually from the direction of the dominant system to the less dominant one in grammar and phonology, whereas the open lexical system is developed in accordance to immediate situational needs.

Phonological interference was largely beyond the children's control and at any stage of development was invariant in all contexts. Grammatical transference was somewhat more controllable but primarily at a subconscious level because the children were often not aware when they had transferred grammatical elements except when called to their attention. Vocabulary, on the other hand, seemed to involve the most conscious act of borrowing and as such, was also most susceptible to influence from the social context.

Regardless of the area of language affected, transference increased in the speech data during periods approaching equal contact and exposure to both languages. It decreased when language use was almost exclusively Spanish or English during a prolonged period. It increased in the presence of bilinguals and decreased significantly in the presence of monolinguals.

<u>Other Areas of Transference</u>. Aside from phonology, the lexicon, and grammar, transference may also occur in other areas of communicative behavior. Evidence in these areas is often less

visible than that found in structure. Yet transference occurs across dual systems at the stylistic, interactional, and conceptual levels, leading naturally to the larger context of cross-cultural differences.

One source of evidence of transference at the conceptual level is reflected through time expressions. For example, Mario invariably prefers to express time in English even when conversing normally in Spanish: "Mamá, no tenemos classes on Monday." Most other time expressions are likewise stated in English: "in the fall", "at 4:00 P.M.", "on Saturday." At first glance this might be construed as code-mixing or lexical borrowing. However, the motivation is more certainly derived from the manner in which Mario has learned all his notions about time. When one considers that Mario was socialized, insofar as time concepts are concerned, through an English-speaking world that involved school hours and days, television schedules, and the learning of days, dates, months, and seasons primarily in the classroom, it is easy to understand his preference to express time notions through English. To date, he still doubts the reliability of Spanish equivalents even though he can usually produce these upon request. The fact remains that he feels more natural, more precise, and more certain when time statements are said in English.

At the interactional level (i.e., those strategies for interacting and relating to others), in many ways Mario seems to operate in a mode more appropriate to Spanish speakers than to English speakers. Most assuredly he has copied this as well as other interactional behavior from his models at home. Yet there is evidence that such behavior patterns are utilized even when operating in English and result in transference. Comments from his teachers—beginning in kindergarten through to the present—indicate that his voice control and participation in group conversation are not entirely suited to the school situation. "He still has a lot to learn about the give and take of conversation," said one teacher, alluding unwittingly to underlying differences in conversational strategies between monochronic and polychronic cultures (Hall 1976:14). In addition, both children continue to greet visitors to the home by extending their hand. When retiring at night, they kiss all guests, female and male alike, often surprising many men unaccustomed to being kissed by a boy of nine. At school, Carla still greets her kindergarten teacher with an embrace and kiss in spite of the fact that virtually no other child in the class acts similarly.

It is at the interactional and also stylistic levels where many bilinguals entering school probably encounter problems. Labov speaks of "language in the inner city" and the styles of speech that black students use in school settings (1972). In similar fashion, Mario seems to have transferred speech styles used with a Bolivian maid to his first schoolteacher. It was obvious enough to cause his teacher to remark on one occasion "My student teacher assistant seems to think you must have a maid at home." When asked why she inquired, the teacher referred to the way Mario requested things of her and others as though they were in a caretaker role. Fortunately the child eventually sensed the differences in his new situation and made the necessary stylistic adjustments.   However, until adjustments are made in interactional strategies or speech styles, in interactional strategies or speech styles, inappropriate transference can often result in misunderstanding between elementary school teachers and bilingual-bicultural children in various stages of development or transference.   It was noted, conversely, that in Spanish he persisted in using tu uniformly with all persons, including an elderly priest who gave him religious instruction. This appears to be a transfer of the ubiquitous English you into Spanish, which leveled out a stylistic and sociolinguistic distinction critical to Spanish.

I have spoken earlier of positive aspects of transference. In part these are instances when the child transfers elements across languages consciously and purposefully to accomplish some specific end. Positive transference in most cases may be useful when dealing with other bilinguals.   In such cases the child may employ to communicative advantage all elements available to him from his dual language systems, which permits a greater range of expression than when restricted to only one system. Obviously this type of transference can only work when dealing with other bilinguals with the same repertoire. In the wrong circumstances, the same behavior would result in the negative, interfering aspects of transference since the interlocutor would not be capable of partaking properly in the interaction. In the right situation, however, it is obvious that the child has a potentially greater expressive range enriched further by the added communicative dynamics that often result from the stylistic and linguistic interplay of two codes.

In fact, the children were often observed using to advantage elements from both systems as a repetitive device or to provide emphasis, to convey a more precise definition, to quote a word or phrase in the original, or to create certain effects (humor, amusement, shock, surprise) as marked speech often does. The above is accomplished through intentional transference at all levels. Depending on the unit of speech involved, we may encroach upon language mixing, or if an even larger unit of speech, code-switching. Once again we face another possible continuum of which transference forms a part.

Other derivatives of the ability to effect positive transference were instances when the child used knowledge of one language to expand knowledge of the second. Often this involved creative and imaginative language use based on an ability to compare and analyze language systems. For example, it is probably not too common for a nine-year-old to know the word intervene, yet Mario used this word by analogy with the Spanish interviene. Both children increased their lexicons significantly by just such comparisons. The same attempt to create the Spanish word migeto (for enano) was less productive when created by analogy with the English word midget.

Positive transference or negative interference?—the answer probably depends on the result. Yet positive aspects of transference permitted a degree of language sophistication to the extent that both children have fair comprehension of similar languages like Portuguese and Italian. They have demonstrated interest, as well, in other forms of communication (Aymara, German, the Greek alphabet, and secret codes). They are surprisingly comfortable, tolerant and interested in persons of other linguistic and cultural background.

Especially noteworthy was Mario's approach to learning to read. Given the inconsistencies of sound-letter correspondence in English, he relied heavily on the more regular sound-letter correspondence of Spanish when decoding the written page. Many times he was observed sounding English words using Spanish phonology. Having heard aloud his Spanish "reading," he was able to recognize the word, which he then adjusted to the proper English pronunciation. In other words, he utilized sound-letter correlations extant in Spanish to learn how to read in English—a feat that he did amazingly well. This is an interesting example of transference being used to advantage in learning word attack skills.

At this point it may seem that we have wandered considerably afar from the original notion of interference, yet transference might legitimately account for all of the phenomena described above in the behavior of bilingual children. Used consciously, to advantage, and in the appropriate circumstances, one may speak of positive transference; when uncontrolled and inapropriate, one might speak of interference. Both are possible in the speech of bilingual speakers, and the children studied in this report demonstrated their ability to deal with these processes even at a very early age.

Summary and Conclusions

Contrastive analyses serve only as a theoretical index to potential interference. However, social factors are the principal determinant as to whether transference will occur at all. Indeed, it would seem natural for bilinguals to avail themselves of all of the communicative devices they possess, particularly when conversing with other speakers acquainted with the same systems. Yet other social conditions may constrain their linguistic choices and inhibit transference to varying degrees. Such was the case of the children examined in this study to the extent that they exhibited amazingly little transference over many years of longitudinal observation.

Returning to the questions posed above, allow me to posit some tentative conclusions suggested by this study:

1. Whereas interference was structurally derived, transference was socially motivated. Social conditions were clearly responsible for most incidents of transference in both children's speech, except phonological interference recorded while the

children were still developing their sound system. Some of the factors affecting transference were: their own pattern of socialization, attitudes favoring language separation, specific settings, certain topics of conversation, and various aspects of their interlocutors.

2. Transference must be viewed as a process—appearing or disappearing, increasing or decreasing, and reversing directions—always in response to changing contexts in which the children found themselves at the moment of speech.

3. Transference varied in direction—from Spanish to English and vice versa. However, certain social conditions affected the direction of transference differently. In addition, phonology, grammar, and lexicon were affected in different ways.

4. Transference occurred in various aspects of the communicative act. It was not restricted solely to structural aspects like phonology, morphology, and syntax. Transference occurred as well across speech styles, interactional strategies, and at the conceptual level.

5. The children exercised surprising control over their dual language systems. When transference was allowed to occur at all, it was for calculated reasons related to language use: social identification, marked speech, emphasis, and so forth. Whatever the reasons, the children were normally aware and sensitive to circumstances that demanded monolingual speech and to those which permitted the utilization of elements from two systems. Positive aspects of this ability to transfer elements were also evidenced.

I have cited reasons that necessitate a broader view of the processes occurring across languages and across registers within the same code. I have noted the impact of specific social correlates on transference and on language use. I have extended the notion of transference beyond structural linguistics to other aspects of communicative acts. I have note the control that even very young speakers exercise over coexistent language systems. And, observing that transference may occur in either, I have emphasized that language acquisition involves both linguistic competence and sociolinguistic norms for use.

In conclusion, transference is a complex and interesting phenomenon. It is probably characteristic of monolingual speakers (when registers and styles are considered) in ways similar to the bilingual's utilization of two codes. And although linguistically manifest, it has its roots, like other aspects of language, in the social environment. Indeed, transference can only be properly understood as a sociolinguistic phenomenon.

REFERENCES

Bergman, C. R. 1976. Interference vs. independent development in infant bilingualism. In Bilingualism in the bicentennial and beyond, ed. G. D. Keller et al. New York: Bilingual Press.

Fantini, A. E. 1976. Language acquisition of a bilingual child: a sociolinguistic perspective. Brattleboro, Vt.: The Experiment Press.

Hall, E. T. 1976. Beyond culture. New York: Anchor Press.

Haugen, E. 1956. Bilingualism in the Americas: a bibliography and research guide. University, Ala.: University of Alabama Press.

Hernandez-Chavez, E. et al. 1975. El lengua je de los chicanos. Arlington, Va.: Center for Applied Linguistics.

Labov, W. 1966. The social stratification of English in New York City. Washington, D.C.: Center for Applied Linguistics.

_____. 1972. Language in the inner city: studies in the black English vernacular. Philadelphia: University of Pennsylvania Press.

Leopold, W. F. 1939-49. Speech development of a bilingual child. 4 Vols. Evanston, Ill.: Northwestern University Press.

Mackey, W. F. 1968. The description of bilingualism. In Readings in the sociology of language, ed. J. A. Fishman. The Hague: Mouton.

Padilla, A. M., and Lindholm, K. 1976. Acquisition of bilingualism. In Bilingualism in the bicentennial and beyond, ed. G. D. Keller et al. New York: Bilingual Press.

Padilla, R. 1977. Language intercalation. Paper read at the National Association of Bilingual Education, New Orleans, La.

Redlinger, W. E. 1976. A description of transference and code-switching in Mexican-American English and Spanish. In Bilingualism in the bicentennicl and beyond. ed. G. D. Keller et al. New York: Bilingual Press.

Ronjat, J. 1913. Le développement du langage observé chez un enfant bilingue. Paris.

Selinker, L. 1972. Interlanguage, IRAL 10:3.

Swain, M. 1972. Bilingualism as a first language. Ph.D. dissertation. University of California, Irvine.

Valdés-Fallis, G. 1976. Social interaction and code switching patterns. In Bilingualism in the bicentennial and beyond, ed. G. D. Keller et al. New York: Bilingual Press.

Weinreich, U. 1968. Languages in contact. The Hague: Mouton.

21. **Contrastive/Error/Performance Analyses: A Comparison Applied to the Interlanguage of an Older Child Acquiring English**

ANNA UHL CHAMOT
The American University

Introduction

Studies of the difficulties encountered by learners of second languages provide useful information for both teachers and curriculum writers. Controversy about the optimal method of analyzing these difficulties and about the merits and shortcomings of contrastive analysis (Schumann and Stenson 1974:2-3) and error analysis (Schachter and Celce-Murcia 1977:445-47) has often obscured the fact that along with the many indubitable difficulties, the second-language learner also experiences some successes and that the ratio between incorrect and correct utterances is a shifting one (Chamot 1978b:8,10).

In this paper, three methods of analysis are applied to the same data and the results are compared. First, contrastive analysis is used in its strong or predictive version (Wardhaugh 1974:12-14) to isolate a group of structures chosen for their frequency of occurrence in English and for the dissimilarities of their expression in the languages involved in the study. Second, an error analysis of the data at three longitudinal points is presented to ascertain whether the predictions of difficulties are borne out. Finally, a performance analysis scrutinizes the structures studied as they occur in their entirety at the three longitudinal points, and a comparison of correct and incorrect utterances is made.

The discussion of the three methods of analysis argues that learner communication strategies can best be captured through study of the complete data (as suggested by Corder 1974:107). A total performance analysis of language samples at different points in a longitudinal study can also provide insights into strategies preferred at the beginning and at more advanced stages of the acquisition process.

Background of Study. The original study (Chamot 1972) providing the data for the present one consisted of an error analysis of a total of 3,495 utterances of a fourth grade boy during his first school year in the United States.

The subject, J-M, was born in Bolivia of French-speaking parents and was in the habit of using French as the language of home and Spanish as the language of school and play. Shortly before his tenth birthday, J-M moved to Austin, Texas, where he continued to speak French with his father and Spanish and eventually English with his new stepmother (the author). He was exposed to English only at school and play during the nine months of the study.

A total of twenty-two tapes of spontaneous dinner table conversation was made during J-M's first school year in the United States. Tapes selected for the present study were at one month after arrival (Tape A), at the fifth month or midpoint of the study (Tape B), and at the end of the study (Tape C).

The morphological and syntactic structures selected for emphasis in this study are the following: verb forms (simple present, present continuous, past, present perfect); noun forms (plural, possessive); do-insertion questions and negations. These structures were chosen because they meet two criteria. First, they occur frequently in English and their incorrect use is easily perceived by most native speakers of English. Second, the Spanish and/or French renditions of the semantic intentions that these structures express differ significantly from English in their surface form, making them candidates, according to contrastive analyzers (see Stockwell, Bowen and Martin 1965:282-85), for predictable second-language learner errors.

Contrastive Analysis

A comparison of some grammatical structures of French, Spanish, and English shows that the first two share many points of similarity, while English has certain unique features that could cause learning difficulties for the French or Spanish speaker. Whether these learning difficulties are intensified in the case of a bilingual speaker of French and Spanish is a question that, intriguing though it is, lies outside the scope of this paper.

Two features of the English verb system were selected for contrasting with French and Spanish, the present continuous (be + V$_{ing}$) and the simple past. These verb forms occur frequently English and are taught early.

The present continuous in English indicates an ongoing or immediate action, and as such is widespread in conversation:

I am writing a letter (now). I am going to the movies tonight.

But the French and Spanish have somewhat different patterns:

Je suis en train d'écrire une lettre. Je vais au cinema ce soir. Estoy escribiendo una carta. Voy al cine esta noche.

Although Spanish uses a parallel construction to English present continuous to indicate ongoing present action, French has to employ a special phrase <u>in the act of</u> to indicate this semantic intention. Neither Spanish nor French use the present continuous to indicate an action expected in the near future. In view of this, contrastive analysis could reasonably predict difficulties in the appropriate use of the English present continuous.

<u>Prediction #1:</u>   Simple present will be used for present continuous. The simple past of English is straighforward except for the morphology of irregular past forms; modulations of meaning are expressed through auxiliaries and modals.   English and Spanish express simple past in parallel ways:

I talked with Mary.   Hablé con María.

In French, however, the simple past is restricted to the written language, and in the spoken language the idea of past is expressed through the passe compose, equivalent in form to the English present perfect:

J'ai parlé avec Marie.

Since the subject's father sometimes used the present perfect for the simple past in English, this error was considered a good candidate for prediction.

<u>Prediction #2:</u>   Present perfect will be used for simple past. All three languages have noun plurals that contain an -s in their written form, but their pronunciation varies. In English the plural morpheme, depending on its environment, can be /s/, /z/ or /ə z/, whereas in Spanish it never can. Moreover, in French the plural -s is silent, and plurality is distinguished orally by the determiner that precedes the noun. A similar situation exists in those dialects of Spanish in which the plural /s/ is aspirated, losing not only its characteristic sound but also even its perceptual salience in the process.

<u>Prediction #3:</u>   English plural -<u>s</u> will be omitted (or perceived as omitted).

The possessive inflection for nouns is a feature of English that differs from the other two languages. In written form as an -'s and in spoken form identical to the plural renditions of /s/, /z/ or /ə z/, the English possessive is completely different from the Spanish and French possessive constructions of N + <u>de</u> + N. Thus:

David's car   el carro de David   la voiture de David

<u>Prediction #4:</u>   English possessive constructions will be rendered by N + <u>of</u> + N.

English questions requiring the insertion of the auxiliary <u>do</u> differ markedly from their French and Spanish counterparts:

Where do you live?   Où habites-tu?   ¿Dónde vives?

Does she have two sisters?   A-t-elle deux soeurs?
¿Tiene dos hermanas?

Not only is an apparently redundant auxiliary added to this type of English question, but this auxiliary also carries the markings for person and tense that are carried by the main verb in the other languages.

Prediction #5:   The auxiliary do will be omitted from English questions requiring it.

English negations containing an auxiliary other than do are only slightly different from their Spanish and French renditions:

She has swum.   He has not swum.
Ella ha nadado.   El no ha nadado.
Elle a nagé.   Il n'a pas nagé.

However, when no auxiliary is present in the English kernel sentence, the negation, as with questions, requires the insertion of do, whereas Spanish and French follow the same pattern as for other negations:

She swims.   He does not swim.
Ella nada.   El no nada.
Elle nage.   Il ne nage pas.

A logical assumption is that do-insertion for negations can be predicted as an area of difficulty for the French and Spanish speaker.

Prediction #6:   The auxiliary do will be omitted from negations requiring it.

Error Analysis

In examining the actual errors made by J-M during the taped conversations, several of the predictions made by contrastive analysis materialized, while others did not.

An error analysis of grammatical problems (Chamot 1978b:183) demonstrated that the most persistent were found in verb forms, omitted constituents, subordination, preposition and article usage, questions, negations, redundant constituents, and noun forms. Fewer errors in later tapes were found in the categories of omitted constituents, verb forms, subordination, and negations, thus indicating approaching acquisition of these structures.

Prediction #1 (present continuous will be used for simple present) did not account for many errors.   This error occurred infrequently even at the beginning stages, and by the sixth month of the study, the present continuous was not only acquired, but even occasionally overgeneralized.

Prediction #2 (present perfect will be used for the simple past) was not borne out at all.   Acquisition of past forms followed a predictable pattern in that initially the base form was used for the past, and then gradually certain past forms began to appear. Only two occurrences of the present perfect were found in the tapes and both were correct. In spite of his father's occasional incorrect models of French transfer, J-M did not use present perfect for simple past.

Prediction #3 (noun plurals will be omitted) did foresee a serious problem for this subject. Whether his rather frequent use of singular forms for plural was due to a process of simplification or to transfer of pronunciation habits from French and/or his dialect of Spanish cannot be ascertained. Even in the last tape there were errors in noun plurals:

Are there any school?

Prediction #4 (possessives will be rendered by N + of + N) had some occurrences in the beginning states, but not after the midpoint of the study. In the first three months of the study, there were a few constructions such as:

the sister of Mark   the helper of Mrs. C

But by the end of the study, J-M was producing without difficulty:

that man's cat   in people's houses

Prediction #5 (do will be omitted from questions requiring it) was borne out, and intonation as sole question marker was a preferred strategy from the fourth month of the study. Typical questions were:

Daddy want (vegetables)?   The rock come from a star?

Prediction #6 (do will be omitted from negations requiring it) was borne out during the first part of the study, but correct negations were produced during the final three months. The formula I don't know accounted for many correct negations; typical errors were:

No speak French!   But I no have any book.

Table 1 summarizes the results of the predictions made by contrastive analysis on the data that was submitted to error analysis.

Performance Analysis

A performance analysis examines all occurrences of a given structure, and decisions about correctness are based on the context in which an utterance occurs. In this way, errors are seen in relation to a sampling of the learner's entire second-language output, and the relative significance of individual errors can be judged more accurately than in error analysis alone. A performance analysis can aid the teacher or researcher in determining which structures are

Table 1
Error Analysis: Validity of Predictions

Prediction	Not Valid	Valid Infrequently	Valid Early Stages Only	Valid Throughout Study
1		x	x	
2	x			
3				x
4		x	x	
5				x
6			x	

Prediction 1:   Simple present substituted for present continuous.
Prediction 2:   Present perfect substituted for simple past.
Prediction 3:   Noun plural omitted.
Prediction 4:   Possessive noun inflection omitted.
Prediction 5:   Do omitted in do-insertion questions.
Prediction 6:   Do omitted in do-insertion negations.

being avoided, which are in an active acquisition phase with both correct and incorrect renditions occurring, and which may be fossilized errors (see Selinker 1974:118-19) because their error rate remains constant over a period of time.

     The performance analysis of some of the main structures used by J-M during his nine-month exposure to an English-speaking environment provides clues about his learning strategies, successful and unsuccessful. The present performance analysis deals only with tapes at the beginning (Tape A), midpoint (Tape B), and conclusion (Tape C) of the study, and is limited to those five structures shown by error analysis to have been validly predicted through contrastive analysis.

     Table 2 compares the correct and incorrect productions of the structures examined in Predictions 1, 3, 4, 5, and 6 (Prediction 2 did not account for any errors in this study).

Discussion.   As indicated in Table 2, J-M had some correct productions of most of these structures from the beginning of the study, after only one month's immersion in English. Yet, at that time, the view of his parents and teachers was that his ability to speak English was practically nonexistent. Our impression was that his language was error-ridden, perhaps because we listened for errors more than for correct forms. Progress was obscured by the often-frequent occurrence of certain errors (such as omission of plural marker, use of base verb form for past, etc.) that we found particularly irritating. With hindsight it is easy to see that a more supportive atmosphere in which errors were tolerated rather than always corrected might have been more conducive to the learning process.

Table 2
Preformance Analysis: Five Structures

	Prediction				
	1	3	4	5	6
Tape A					
Start of Study					
Sample Size	5	14	5	6	47
Correct	20.0%	57.0%	0.0%	33.3%	76.6%
Incorrect	80.0%	43.0%	100.0%	66.7%	23.4%
Tape B					
Midpoint					
Sample Size	6	26	4	32	38
Correct	50.0%	65.0%	50.0%	31.3%	94.7%
Incorrect	50.0%	35.0%	50.0%	68.7%	5.3%
Tape C					
End of Study					
Sample Size	8	16	2	29	24
Correct	87.5%	81.0%	100.0%	58.6%	100.0%
Incorrect	12.5%	19.0%	0.0%	41.4%	0.0%

Prediction 1:   Simple present substituted for present continuous. Limited frequency of occurrence.

Prediction 3:   Noun plural omitted.

Prediction 4:   Possessive noun inflection omitted. Very limited occurrence in all tapes.

Prediction 5:   Do omitted in do-insertion questions. Limited occurrence in first month. Sample for Tape C taken from Month 8, since Month 9 contained only 2 do-insertion questions (1 correct, 1 incorrect).

Prediction 6:   Do omitted from do-insertion negations. See Table 4 for explanation of large samples. Sample for Tape C taken from Month 8, as Month 9 contained only 6 do-insertion negations (all correct).

Prediction #1 (use of present continuous):

Although use of simple present for present continuous did occur throughout the study, there were some correct usages from the beginning:

Mother, where are you going tomorrow?

There were errors as well:

Now I go (to take) my bath.

Toward the end of the study there were a few overgeneralizations of the present continuous:

I would keep it, so when we are going to Africa . . .

Correct use of the present continuous ranged from only 20% of obligatory contexts at the beginning of the study to 87.5% by the end. Apparently this structure was being actively acquired in spite of its differences in usage from Spanish and French. In this instance, frequency of the English model as input seemed a more powerful influence than did interference from patterns of the previous languages.

Prediction #3 (omission of noun plural ending):

Ommission of plural markers occurred throughout the study:

| (first tape) | Twelve page. |
| (last tape) | Well, I read the direction. |

Although this error seemed to persist and was a feature of J-M's speech that was constantly noted and corrected by his parents, the performance analysis indicates that even at the beginning of his exposure to English, he used plurals correctly in 57% of obligatory contexts and by the end of nine months was using them correctly 81% of the time. Whether this gain is average or not can only be ascertained by comparison with longitudinal studies of similar subjects; Butterworth and Hatch (1978:245) state that their thirteen-year-old Spanish-speaking subject did not learn plurals during the period of their study, so it may be that J-M's progress was more satisfactory than it first appears.

Prediction #4 (use of 's to indicate possession):

At the very beginning of the study there were no occurrences of possessive constructions of the N + 's type, but by the end of the first month a few were being attempted, though without success. Some errors were due to the use of the French or Spanish pattern, N + of + N, as:

the gym of Mr. S   the helper of Mrs. C

Others merely omitted the possessive marker:

| Mother: | Whose eraser? |
| J-M: | Steve eraser. |

Still others utilized double possessive markings:

Tommy of Mrs. C's

This structure was acquired by the end of the study, ranging from no correct instances in the first month (due perhaps to an avoidance strategy that ensured few attempts), to 50% correct at the midpoint of the study and 100% correct by the end.

The apparent ease of acquisition of the possessive 's is in sharp contrast to the continuing difficulties with the plural -s, yet both are noun inflections and follow the same morphophonemic rules. This situation parallels that of Hakuta's (1978:143) five-year-old Japanese-speaking subject. He attributes it to the influence of the first language, which has no plural marker, but does have a possessive marker for nouns. The case of J-M is just the opposite, for Spanish and French both have plural markers but not possessive inflections for nouns.

Prediction #5 (do-insertion questions):

Omission of do where required occurred in many questions, and error analysis indicated that this was a major problem that improved only slightly over the course of the study. Typical examples are:

Where you put them?   It make a hole in the earth?
Why you go in your home?   If an airplane fall, it burn too?

However, many cases of do omission produced acceptable questions in the context of conversation:

You remember the cheese in the restaurant?

Since many yes/no questions in spoken English omit do habitually, whereas it is obligatory in WH-questions, a new classification of these questions was made. Table 3 separates WH-questions and yes/no questions with obligatory do-insertion; do omissions that sounded natural in the context are excluded from this new analysis because there is no satisfactory way to decide if their apparent correctness masks an inability to perform a do-insertion or merely reflects the disinclination to do so where not obliged.

No do-insertions were attempted in yes/no questions at the beginning of the study, but by the end, almost as many of this type as of WH-questions were attempted. By the end of the study, only 60% of J-M's yes-no questions requiring do were produced correctly. This contrasts with his progress in production of WH-questions, which ranged from 66.6% correct in the first month of the study to 90.9% correct by the end.

Prediction #6 (do-insertion negations)

Omission of do in negations accounted for errors mainly in the first part of the study. Examples are:

I no use the machine.   Me no put the milk in the floor.

By the midpoint of the study there were few incorrect do-insertion negations, and some instances of double marking occurred:

I didn't saw her.

Table 3
Performance Analysis: Yes/No and WH-Questions
(Excluding Acceptable DO Omissions in Y/N)

| | Question Type | |
	Yes/No	WH-
Tape A — Start of Study		
Sample Size	0	3
Correct	0.0%	66.7%
Incorrect	6	13
Tape B — Midpoint		
Sample Size	6	13
Correct	66.7%	46.2%
Incorrect	33.3%	53.8%
Tape C — End of Study		
Sample Size	10	11
Correct	60.0%	90.9%
Incorrect	40.0%	9.1%

Note: Most Yes/No questions were of the type in which do omission was acceptable in the context, and few do-insertion yes/no questions were attempted until the latter part of the study. Although few WH-questions requiring do-insertion were attempted in the first month, the number had increased significantly by the middle of the study.

By the end of the study the insertion of do in appropriate negations was evidently acquired, as no further instances of do omission occurred.

The information in Table 2 indicates a high percentage (76.6%) of correct do-insertion negations from the very beginning of the study. However, as with do-insertion questions, a closer look at the data calls for reclassification. The formula I don't know was learned early and used often, thus accounting for many of these correct usages.   Table 4 separates these formulas from instances of a productive use of do in negations, and, following the example of Cancino, Rosansky, and Schumann (1978:210), this expression is eliminated from further analysis.

By ignoring the repeated use of the useful formula I don't know, the analysis in Table 4 indicates that while no do-insertion negations were produced correctly during the first month of the study, this structure was in an active acquisition phase during the midpoint of the study with more do-insertions attempted and few errors, and was acquired by the end of the study.

In comparing acquisition of the do-insertion process in both questions and negations, the order of difficulty for J-M seems to be:

Easiest—Negation (no do omissions by end of study)

Next most difficult—WH-questions (9.1% omissions by end of study)

Most difficult—yes/no questions (28.6% omissions by end of study)

The sequence of acquisition for these types of questions and negations appears in general to follow that found for the Spanish-speaking subjects of Cancino, Rosansky, and Schumann (1978:229-30).

Table 4
Performance Analysis: Negations
(Excluding Formula I don't know)

Tape A — Start of Study
Sample Size	11
Correct	0.0%
Incorrect	100.0%

Tape B — Midpoint
Sample Size	30
Correct	93.3%
Incorrect	6.7%

Tape C — End of Study
Sample Size	10
Correct	100.0%
Incorrect	0.0%

Note: More than twice as many formulas (I don't know) were found in the first month of the study as in the last month (34 versus 14).

Summary and Conclusion

This study presents three methods of analysis of the language data of a child learning English as a new language. The subject, J-M, was a ten-year-old French/Spanish bilingual who learned English through exposure of an English-speaking school and neighborhood environment. Recordings of his spontaneous dinner table conversation were made during the first nine months of his residence in the United States, and tapes from the first, fifth, and final months of the study were used for the analyses.

Contrastive analysis of French, Spanish, and English was used to determine English structures that could be expected to cause learning difficulties for J-M. Although many contrasts between the three languages could have been studied, six were selected based on criteria of frequency and of variance between the English pattern and the Spanish and/or French ones.

Six predictions of areas of difficulty were made on the basis of contrastive analysis:

Prediction #1:   The simple present will be substituted for the present continuous (French and/or Spanish transfer).

Prediction #2:   The present perfect will be substituted for the simple past (French transfer and father's model).

Prediction #3:   Noun plurals will be omitted, or perceived as omitted (phonological transfer from French and/or subject's dialect of Spanish).

Prediction #4:   The possessive noun inflection will be omitted and a possessive construction of N + of + N will be preferred (transfer from French and/or Spanish).

Prediction #5:   The auxiliary do will be omitted from do-insertion questions (no French or Spanish equivalent).

Prediction #6:   The auxiliary do will be omitted from do-insertion negations (no Spanish or French equivalent).

An error analysis of the data was then made to ascertain whether the predictions were borne out in fact, and if so, whether they seemed to hold for all or only part of the time period studied.

The results of the error analysis showed varied strengths in the six predictions:

Prediction #1 (present continuous) was valid infrequently and only at the beginning of the study.

Prediction #2 (simple past) was not valid.

Prediction #3 (noun plurals) was valid throughout the study.

Prediction #4 (noun possessive inflection) was valid infrequently and only at the beginning of the study.

Prediction #5 (do-insertion questions) was valid throughout the study.

Prediction #6 (do-insertion negations) was valid in the early part of the study only.

A performance analysis then examined all occurrences of the five structures identified by error analysis as having been, in some degree at least, valid predictions of contrastive analysis. This final analysis indicated a fluctuating ratio of correct to incorrect production of the five structures identified in Predictions 1, 3, 4, 5, and 6. The range of correct productions in obligatory contexts from the first to the last month of the study was:

Prediction #1 (present continuous): from 20% to 87.5% correct.

Prediction #3 (noun plurals): from 57% to 81% correct.

Prediction #4 (noun possessive inflection): from none attempted to 100% correct.

Prediction #5 (all do-insertion questions): from 66.6% to 76.2% correct.

Prediction #5a (do-insertion in yes/no questions): from none attempted to 60% correct.

Prediction #5b (do-insertion in WH-questions): from 66.6% to 90.0% correct.

Prediction #6 (do-insertion negations excluding I don't know): from none attempted to 100% correct.

The performance analysis provides insights into J-M's learning strategies that are absent from the error analysis. Two of the most significant indications are that an avoidance strategy apparently operated on some structures at the beginning of the study, and that when a structure was once attempted, at least some correct productions were found side-by-side with incorrect ones.

This type of information can be of use to both teacher and researcher in pinning down the actual difficulty of some structures and the ratio of correct to incorrect productions that can reasonably be expected at different stages of second-language learning. The teacher especially could profit from viewing the learner's interlanguage not so much as a morass of errors to be eliminated, but rather as a developing mosaic through which correct productions are at first scattered thinly, and then gradually increasing until they surpass incorrect ones. More attention to the learner's correct productions can reassure both student and teacher that progress is taking place and can help make the learning situation a cooperative endeavor instead of a disheartening undertaking in which the learner commits all the errors and the teacher makes all the corrections.

Although a performance analysis of a second-language learner's total output would be extraordinarily time-consuming, an analysis of the specific problems revealed by error analysis can provide insights that are not possible through contrastive analysis or error analysis alone.

REFERENCES

Butterworth, Guy, and Hatch, Evelyn. 1978. A Spanish-speaking adolescent's acquisition of English syntax. In Second language acquisition, ed. Evelyn Marcussen Hatch, pp. 231-45. Rowley, Mass.: Newbury House.

Cancino, Herlinda; Rosansky, Ellen J., and Schumann, John H. 1978. The acquisition of English negatives and interrogatives by native Spanish speakers. In Second language acquisition, ed. Evelyn Marcussen Hatch, pp. 207-30. Rowley, Mass.: Newbury House.

Chamot, Anna Uhl. 1972. English as a third language: its acquisition by a child bilingual in French and Spanish. Austin, Tex.: University of Texas. ERIC No. #ED060770.

_____. 1978a. Grammatical problems in learning English as a third language. In Second language acquisition, ed. Evelyn Marcussen Hatch, pp. 175-89. Rowley, Mass.: Newbury House.

_____. 1978b. Development of English sentence formation in a Spanish/French bilingual child. Paper read at 2d Annual Los Angeles Second Language Research Forum, Los Angeles, California.

Corder, S. P. 1974. Idiosyncratic dialects and error analysis. In New frontiers in second language learning, ed. John H. Schumann and Nancy Stenson, pp. 100-113. Rowley, Mass.: Newbury House.

Hakuta, Kenji. 1978. A report on the development of the grammatical morphemes in a Japanese girl learning English as a second language. In Second language acquisition, pp. 133-47. Rowley, Mass.: Newbury House.

Schachter, Jacquelyn, and Celce-Murcia, Marianne. 1977. Some reservations concerning error analysis. TESOL Quarterly 2:441.51.

Schumann, John H., and Stenson, Nancy. 1974. Introduction to New frontiers in second language learning, pp. 1-10. Rowley, Mass.: Newbury House.

Selinker, Larry. 1974. Interlanguage. In New frontiers in second language learning, ed. John H. Schumann and Nancy Stenson, pp. 114-36. Rowley, Mass.: Newbury House.

Stockwell, Robert P.; Bowen, J. Donald; and Martin, John W. 1965. The grammatical structures of English and Spanish. Chicago: University of Chicago Press.

Wardhaugh, Ronald. 1974. The contrastive analysis hypothesis. In New frontiers in second language learning, ed. John H. Schumann and Nancy Stenson, pp. 11-19. Rowley, Mass.: Newbury House.

22. Second-Language Acquisition and Language Universals

SUSAN GASS
University of Michigan

Traditionally, second-language-acquisition studies have had considerable influence from linguistic theory. This paper is an attempt to view the relationship from a slightly different perspective. It is an investigation of the role of second-language acquisition as it bears on linguistic theory. The theoretical construct under consideration is the Accessibility Hierarchy (AH) proposed by Keenan and Comrie (1972; 1977; and 1979), which is perhaps the most influential study of universals of relative-clause formation (RCF).

Based on an investigation of nearly fifty languages, Kennan and Comrie found that natural languages differ with regard to which NP positions can be relativized. They further found that these differences are not random in that there is a clear relationship between the NPs that any given language can relativize. Based on constraints on relativizable sentence constituents of these languages, they proposed a universal hierarchy to express the dependency relationship. This hierarchy, known as the accessibility hierarchy, is presented in Table 1. Also in Table 1 are the various relative clause types discussed in this paper.

Table 1

SU > DO > IO > OBL > GEN > OCOMP [1]

Relative-Clause Types

a. Subject
The boy who kissed Mary

b. Direct Object
The boy who(m) Mary kissed

c. Indirect Object
The girl that Mary sent a letter to

d. Object of Preposition
The desk that I told you about

e. Genitive
The teacher whose course I took

249

> f.   Object of Comparative
>   The girl that Mary is taller than

Briefly, the interpretation of the hierarchy is such that if a language allows relativization out of a position, it also allows relativization out of all positions higher on the hierarchy (listed to the left of that position). However, it does not necessarily allow relativization on lower positions. A further constraint demands that relative-clause formation strategies operate on adjacent segments of the hierarchy. What differentiates languages of the world is the lowest position that may be relativized.

Although the hierarchy was established on the basis of data from approximately fifty languages, it is claimed that all languages obey the constraints of the hierarchy. Keenan (1975) further suggests that in addition to the universal implications of the hierarchy, "there is a sense in which the subject end of the CH [AH] expresses the 'easiest' or most 'natural' positions to relativize" (p. 138). Thus, within any given language, the higher end appears to be easier to relativize than the lower end. If this is the case, there is intralinguistic validity as well as universal validity to the hierarchy. In an attempt to substantiate this hypothesis, Keenan investigated variation in English by collecting samples of relative clauses (RCs) in various written materials, finding that the frequency with which positions are relativized conforms to the AH in the sense that the higher end has more RCs than the lower end. Secondly, he showed that authors, who were independently judged to use relatively simple styles, used proportionately more RCs on the higher end of the hierarchy than did authors with a more complex syntactic style. An additional hypothesis, as yet unconfirmed, predicted that there is a tendency in authors with simple styles to convert "underlying DO's into superficial subject position (e.g., by PASSIVE) under relativization" (1975:145).

I shall present here data from second-language acquisition that bear on the claims made by Keenan. More specifically, I shall investigate the production of RCs by students learning English as a second language whose native languages are typologically diverse with respect to their relative clause frequency (RCF) strategies, including the positions on the AH that they can relativize. Yet despite the differences in the RCF strategies of their native languages, the students were found to follow the Keenan-Comrie hierarchy in their production of English RCs according to the following three parameters:

> a.   the frequency with which different positions are relativized
>
> b.   the accuracy of the positions relativized
>
> c.   the most actively avoided positions

    d.   the amount of transfer from the native language in
the form of pronoun retention

If, as Keenan suggested, there is psychological reality to the
AH—that is, if language use reflects its ordering principle, a strong
test case would come from second-language acquisition data,
particularly from students representing typologically diverse native
languages. This is especially the case when none of the results can
be predicted (or explained) from grammatical analyses of the
students' native languages (NLs), but rather are found to be due to
universal constraints.

    The research reported on in this paper deals with the
acquisition of English relative clauses by seventeen intermediate to
advanced adult learners. Table 2 gives the native languages of the
subjects, along with a list of the relativizable positions in their
languages.

Table 2
Native Languages of the Subjects

Language	Positions relativizable
Arabic	SU—OCOMP
Chinese	SU—GEN
French	SU—GEN
Italian	SU—GEN
Japanese	SU—GEN
Korean	SU—GEN
Persian	SU—GEN
Portuguese	SU—GEN
Thai	SU—IO

All students were enrolled in an English-language training program
at Indiana University with many taking graduate courses
concurrently.

    The data were gathered by administering two tasks given six
times over a four-month period. For the first task, subjects were
given approximately forty-five minutes to write compositions, with
a minimum of three choices of topic at each testing session. Second,
the subjects were asked to combine two sentences so that the
resulting structure was a relative clause. In this task, the subjects
were presented with twelve pairs of sentences and were told to
combine them to form one English sentence, with the instructions
such that other forms of combination were precluded. To test
notions of universality of RCF, sentences representing the types in
Table 3 were included. The first symbol represents the grammatical
position in the first sentence of the noun that is identical in both
sentences, and the second symbol is the grammatical relation of the
NP in the subordinate sentence.

Table 3
Sentence types for the combining experiment

a.	SU	SU	example: The boy fell. The boy came.
b.	SU	DO	example: The girl ran away. I hit the girl.
c.	SU	IO	
d.	SU	OPREP	
e.	SU	GEN	
f.	SU	OCOMP	
g.	DO	SU	
h.	DO	DO	
i.	DO	IO	
j.	DO	OPREP	
k.	DO	GEN	
l.	DO	OCOMP	

As an example, consider k (DO GEN). The NP that is identical in those two sentences is in direct object position in the matrix sentence and a genitive in the sentence to be embedded, as in these sentences:

I saw the man. The man's son works at the drugstore.
I saw the man whose son works at the drugstore.

Four native speakers of English were also given the same task in order to ensure that the errors of nonnative speakers were due to their lack of proficiency rather than to the task itself. In the forty-eight sentences that the native speakers produced, there were only four errors, three of which were adjacency errors, of the type such as:

?* The man was working whose son went to school.

As was mentioned, both tasks were given to all subjects six times over a four-month period. For the combining task the lexical items differed but the syntactic structure was held constant from one testing session to another. Since statistical analyses failed to detect significant differences between the testing sessions, the results discussed below are based on the total score across all of a subject's tests.

Figures 1 and 2 give the results of the written compositions for language groups, as well as for all subjects together.[2] We see that the frequency distributions of RCs does in fact conform to the AH. That is, in this sample of 203 RCs, there were more formed on the higher positions of the hierarchy than on the lower end. These results differ from Keenan's in two ways. First, RCs formed on lower positions were even less common in this study. Second, in Keenan's sample there was a smaller percentage of RCs on subjects than in the present study. However, Keenan's data came from

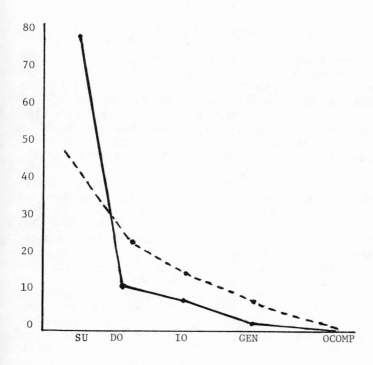

Fig. 1. Percentage of Total Relative Clauses in Free Compositions.
The dotted line represents Keenan's data.

SU	DO	IO OPREP	GEN	OCOMP	
86	12	2	0	0	(Arabic)
91	5	0	5	0	(Chinese, Japanese, Korean)
75	16	8	0	0	(Thai)
70	16	13	2	0	(Romance)
71	23	6	0	0	(Persian)

Fig. 2. Distribution of Relative Clauses in Free Compositions by Language
Groups (in Percents)

native speakers of English. Furthermore, he divided his subjects into two groups, one of which was independently judged to use syntactically simpler sentences than the other. It was found that the group using a simpler style also had a higher percentage of RCs on the higher end of the hierarchy than did the other group. The second-language learners of this study can clearly be classified as having simple styles in English. Hence, the high frequency of subject relatives among these subjects can be correlated with the syntactic simplicity of their compositions.

The second task required the subjects to form specific types of relative clauses. Detailed instructions were given as to what syntactic pattern to use and in what way to utilize the two sentences presented to the subjects. Keenan hypothesized that authors with simple styles tend to move underlying direct objects into subject position under relativization, but it is difficult to prove the presence of such a process in a psychologically real sense when using uncontrolled data. In the present study it was found that there was indeed a marked tendency to avoid relativizing on positions that were low on the hierarchy. This was done by changing a part of one of the sentences in order to relativize on a higher position than the intended one or by not following task instructions. This active avoidance does indicate a psychologically real process. This means of avoidance was seen primarily in one of four ways:

1. Substitution of one lexical item for another (usually the opposite)
   Example: The woman danced. The man is fatter than the woman.
   Changed to: The woman that is thinner than the man danced. (Persian and Chinese)

2. Switching the order of the two sentences so as to embed the sentence that was intended to be the matrix
   Example: He saw the cat. The dog jumped on the cat.
   Changed to: The dog jumped on the cat that he saw. (Arabic)

3. Changing the identical NP in order to relativize on a different noun
   Example: He saw the woman. The man is older than the woman.
   Changed to: He saw the man who is older than the woman. (French)

4. Changing the syntactic structure of the second sentence
   Example: He saw the woman. The man kissed the

woman.
Changed to: He saw the woman who was kissed by
the man. (Arabic)

The results presented in Figures 3 and 4 show that with the exception of the genitive, relative clauses formed on lower positions of the AH were avoided more frequently than those formed on higher positions.   There was considered to be an instance of avoidance any time an NP was relativized in such a way that the resultant RC was based on a position other than the intended one. In all but two instances the new position was higher than the intended one and in most cases was either a subject or a direct object.

Still another important measure to consider when dealing with second-language learners is the percentage of correct responses per position. If the AH is indeed easier on the higher end, we would expect a higher percentage of correct responses to RCs on subjects than to RCs on low positions on the hierarchy. Looking at Figures 5 and 6 we see that in fact, again with the exception of the genitive, this measure does conform to the orderings of the hierarchy.

We have seen then that several facts concerning the acquisition of RCs by second-language learners correlate with the orderings of the AH.   However, in each case the genitive proved to be an exception. There were more correct responses to the genitive and fewer cases of its avoidance than would have been predicted by a consideration alone of its position on the hierarchy. There must, therefore, be certain structural language-specific features of the genitive that give it increased prominence.[3] One possibility is that this position has the only relative marker that is uniquely coded for case/grammatical relation in English.   Moreover, there are no variants such as that or which that can be used. The fact that whose is uniquely coded and that there are no variants may serve to make it the most salient of the English RC markers, thereby rendering it easily perceivable by the second-language learner.   A second possibility is that the learners of this study may have interpreted the genitive marker plus the following noun phrase as a unit that was then treated as a subject or direct object of the verb. For example, in the phrase "The man whose son just came home . . .", it is possible that whose son was treated as a unit, the subject of the verb came (J. Wirth, personal communication). In the corpus of this study all instances of the genitive in this view were either subjects or direct objects, positions high on the hierarchy. This would then explain its relatively high number of correct responses.

The evidence presented here constitutes support for the hierarchy being a hierarchy of psychological accessibility. However, despite its universality and its active role in second-language learning, its modification by intralingual features is indeed possible, as was seen by the preceding discussion regarding the genitive. In addition, the interaction between the AH and the native language of the second-language learner can also be found.

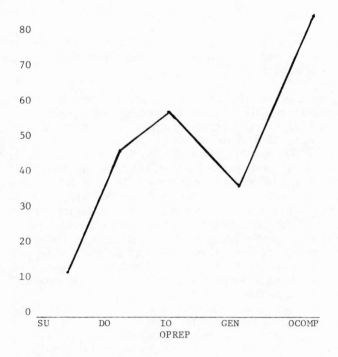

Fig. 3. Percentage of Sentences Avoided on Combining Task (all groups)

SU	DO	IO OPREP	GEN	OCOMP	
38	25	46	23	53	(Arabic)
8	38	58	10	93	(Chinese, Japanese, Korean)
8	68	53	52	88	(Thai)
18	62	64	58	88	(Romance)
7	36	38	30	58	(Persian)

Fig. 4. Percentage of Sentences Avoided by Language Groups

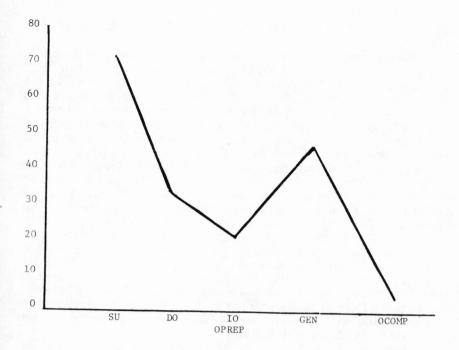

Fig. 5. Percentage of Sentences Correct on Combining Task (all groups)

SU	DO	IO OPREP	GEN	OCOMP	
48	28	27	47	10	(Arabic)
78	60	28	88	0	(Chinese, Japanese, Korean)
90	30	25	30	13	(Thai)
68	28	17	33	0	(Romance)
70	20	18	38	4	(Persian)

Fig. 6. Percentage of Sentences Correct by Language Groups

Besides considering which positions can be relativized, we find that languages of the world differ in other aspects of their RCF strategies. Among the most important are: (1) adjacency to the head noun; (2) retention or omission of the relative clause marker; (3) ordering of the relative clause with respect to the head noun; (4) case markings on the relative marker (variable vs. invariable); and (5) pronoun retention or omission. In an investigation of syntactic transfer, Gass (1979) found that of these possible differentiating factors, there was only one for which transfer effects could be determined. That variable was pronoun retention. He determined that speakers of languages that have pronominal reflexes in RCs also use them in English to a significantly greater degree than do speakers whose languages do not have pronoun retention in RCs.[4] For this study I formed two groups of learners on the basis of whether or not their languages had or did not have pronomial reflexes in relative clauses. I compared the two groups in their use of or lack of use of pronominal reflexes in English relative clauses. Then t tests were run to determine significant differences between the groups. I found that instances of transfer had to be viewed in relation to the AH, since significant differences were not found for all positions, as can be seen in Table 4.

Language transfer can only be found in the upper section of the hierarchy. Keenan and Comrie (1977) claimed that it is more common to retain pronouns in the lower positions than in the higher ones. Therefore, the use of pronouns by all subjects in genitive and object of comparative positions suggests a universal strategy used to deal with complex structures, independent of language background. From these data it is impossible to determine whether for speakers of languages with pronominal reflexes the use of pronouns in these lower positions reflects their own native language or natural orderings of difficulty.

In conclusion, I have shown that several facts about RCF by second-language learners correlate with the orderings of the accessibility hierarchy as proposed by Keenan and Comrie:

a. the frequency with which different positions were relativized

b. the accuracy of relativization on the different positions

c. the active avoidance of RCs formed on lower positions

d. the difference in positions for which there is evidence of transfer in the form of pronoun retention

In so doing, I have provided additional evidence in support of its

Table 4
Transfer Effects on Combining Task

Variable		$\overline{x}$	$\underline{t}$ values	probability*
Pron. ret. SU**				
Pron. ret. DO	Grp. 1*** N=8	26.46	2.42	.023
	Grp. 2 N=9	2.03		
Pron. ret. IO	Grp. 1 N=8	28.33	1.9	.045
	Grp. 2	7.04		
Pron. ret. OPREP	Grp. 1 N=8	23.13	2.09	.038
	Grp. 2 N=9	2.04		
Pron. ret. GEN	Grp. 1 N=10	13.8	-.30	ns
	Grp. 2 N=7	16.9		
Pron. ret. OCOMP	Grp. 1 N=8	30.2	1.48	ns
	Grp. 2 N=9	8.7		

* one-tailed test of significance
** none of the languages had obligatory retention in subject position
*** Group 1 = speakers of languages with pronoun retention
Group 2 = speakers of languages without pronoun retention

being a hierarchy of psychological accessibility, and, more importantly, I have shown the relevance of second-language acquisition data for linguistic theory and for the insights they can provide on the nature of language.

NOTES

1. SU = subject
   DO = direct object
   IO = indirect object

OBL   = oblique (in English, object of preposition)
GEN   = genitive
OCOMP = object of comparative
>   = more accessible than

2.   For the purposes of this study, the positions IO and OPREP have been combined. There were three reasons for this: (1) In English they behave in an analogous manner; (2) in Keenan's (1975) study they were combined, so combining them here made it easier to compare the results of this study with his; and (3) the results for the two positions were very close and in many instances identical, so that combining them did not affect the results in a significant way.

3.   It is possible to hypothesize that the ordering found in this study argues against the hierarchy proposed by Keenan and Comrie. The fact that the genitive is out of hierarchical order could be construed to be counter-evidence to their claim. However, since there is strong independent motivation for the existence of the hierarchy as proposed, it is better to account for the one exception than to reject the hierarchy.

4.   An example of a pronominal reflex in a relative clause is "*The man that you saw him jumped into a blue car."

REFERENCES

Gass, S.   1979.   An investigation of syntactic transfer in adult L2 learners.   In Research in second language acquisition, ed. R. Scarcella and S. Krashen. Rowley, Mass.: Newbury House.
Keenan, E.   1975.   Variation in universal grammar.   In Analyzing variation in language, ed. R. Fasold and R. Shuy. Washington, D.C.: Georgetown University Press.
_____.   1977.   Noun phrase accessibility and universal grammar. Linguistic Inquiry 8:63–100.
_____.   1979.   Data on the noun phrase accessibility hierarchy. Language 55:333–51.
Keenan, E., and Comrie, B.   1972.   Noun phrase accessibility and universal grammar.   Paper read at the Linguistics Society of America annual meeting.

23. Theories, Dichotomies, and Synthesis in Second-Language Teaching

H. M. HAMMERLY
Simon Fraser University

Not long ago a student newspaper published a cartoon depicting a widely held view of the relationship between theory and practice. The first frame showed two intellectuals angrily confronting each other as they held signs promoting different theories. The second frame had the two men marching together holding the sign for only one of the theories, the other theory having been completely discarded. Then the two intellectuals came by a peasant woman who held a placard saying "Practice." In the final frame, the three of them were seen happily parading with the "Theory" sign held high and a smaller placard saying "and practice" below it.

This view of the relationship between theory and practice should be considered erroneous on at least two counts. It downgrades practical concerns into a pursuit not worthy of the best minds. More seriously, it makes practice wholly subservient not only to theory in general (which is bad enough) but to a given theory emerging from the struggle between theories. Such slavish submission of practice to a given theory has had negative consequences in many fields of endeavor.

Instead, it would be preferable to view theory and practice in terms of mutual feedback with empirically oriented research interposed between them. Theories with claims to applications in any field should yield testable insights that, if validated, can be translated into more successful procedures of some kind or another in that field. Conversely, the objectively determined success or failure of practice in a field of activity should be explainable by one or more theories within that field or external to it. (In other words, there is nothing as practical as a demonstrably valid theory, and demonstrably successful practice has a theoretical explanation.)

Second-language (L2) is a field of activity that has been following, for too long, the vagaries of theories and views in other fields. While no one would question that many disciplines—as shown on Chart 1—can make a contribution to the L2 field, there is no valid reason why this field should have long been, successively or simultaneously, an appendage of or very closely associated with the classical languages, literature, phonetics, structural linguistics, behaviorist psychology, education, transformational linguistics, cognitive psychology, and psychiatry.

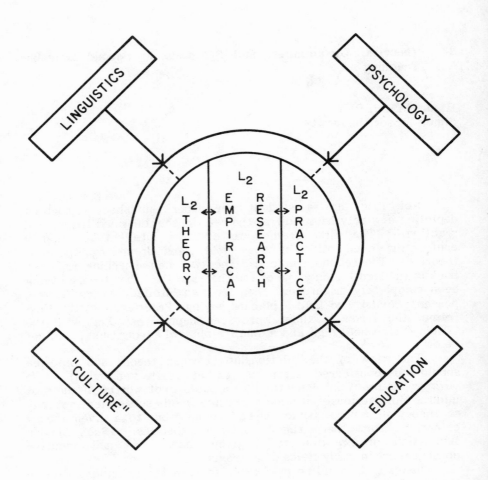

Chart I

Even less is there any valid reason for L2 theory and practice to follow any particular theory in another discipline. To take linguistics as an example, L2 specialists should feel free to draw upon useful concepts in traditional grammar, structuralism, transformational grammar, and all other schools, and to disregard whatever is irrelevant. (Examples of irrelevant issues are native competence, language universals, and ambiguous sentences.) Least of all is there any valid reason, other than faddism, for the L2 field to follow the very latest manifestation of an external theory. Sometimes earlier phases of a theory yield useful concepts—for instance, the concept of kernel sentences, abandoned years ago in transformational grammar, is pedagogically useful.

Since the interests of L2 specialists differ largely from those of linguists, psychologists, education specialists, literature specialists, and others, L2 specialists alone must decide, on empirical grounds, what they will accept or reject from other fields. That is, while one can still refer to the sum of the relationships between a field of knowledge and practical endeavors as its "applied" aspect, it would be desirable for L2 specialists to decide what is "applicable" to their field and to speak in terms of "applicable" rather than "applied" linguistics, psychology, and so forth. To elaborate, the term <u>applied linguistics</u> implies that somehow L2 specialists and scholars in other language-related fields must make an effort to apply to their discipline all of the latest form of linguistic theory, speculative implications included. The phrase <u>applicable linguistics,</u> on the other hand, indicates that L2 specialists (and others) would choose themselves what seems promising, from various linguistic schools (from different times and places), and feel quite free to retain only what actually works, regardless of the preferences of linguists.

In addition to trying to impose their views on practice in even loosely related fields, theorists can perform a disservice by generating slogans. A slogan, almost by definition, overstates a point of view not only by what it says but also by what it leaves unsaid. Thus, some of the linguistics-generated L2 slogans of the forties and fifties (Moulton 1961) were quite misleading. On reading, for example, that "a language is a set of habits," a present-day reader might erroneously conclude that in those days linguists qua pedagogues did not believe in the existence of rules or in the possibility of a potentially infinite number of sentences. The slogan "Language is speech, not writing" gives the definite (and equally false) impression that the written language was ignored. "Teach the language, not about the language" seems to rule out any explanation; yet explanations were given. And because of the slogan "Languages are different," it has been wrongly assumed that those days did not see any generalizations across languages or about languages per se.

More recent linguistics-generated slogans have been equally misleading. For instance, the statement ". . . normal linguistic behavior . . . is stimulus-free . . ." (Chomsky 1966:46), simplified to the slogan that language is stimulus-free, has led many in the L2 field to minimize the importance of learning theory despite the fact that (1) the word stimulus as used above is so narrowly and mechanistically defined that most events psychologists would call "stimuli" are excluded, (2) the statement refers to native language use, not to L2 teaching or learning; and (3) the intelligent conditioning of L2 rules is demonstrably effective. Moreover, the concept of linguistic "creativity" that is a corollary of this slogan has led to the fostering of what we could call "destructive creativity" in the L2 field—the use of the second language too early and too freely, resulting in a very defective interlanguage becoming embedded in the learner.

Conflicting linguistic, psychological, and educational theories have not only generated slogans, they have also produced numerous dichotomies—a few useful, some unnecessary, many misleading—that have resulted in much polarization and confusion in the L2 field that could have been avoided. Only a few of these oppositions will be discussed here. (A caveat is in order. While a "solution" is proposed for each of the dichotomies discussed, it should be kept in mind that the conclusions presented are only partly based on empirical research. They have mostly emerged from years of observation in different capacities, bibliographical research, and analysis of the issues.)

A few of the dichotomies can be useful, provided they are understood correctly and assuming it is recognized that the two elements in opposition are mutually exclusive only at particular points in time, not at all times. Examples of conditionally useful dichotomies are "induction/deduction" and "drill/communication." The claims and counterclaims for deduction and induction tend to disregard the informal evidence that the quality and quantity of practice used to internalize a rule are of far greater importance than the manner of its initial presentation. Also, it seems that both types of presentations are useful. A deductive treatment may be required for rules that are very complex and unlike any native language rule. An inductive treatment can be applied without a major loss in efficiency to the teaching of those rules that are simple and evident. Moreover, an intermediate approach can be used for the numerous rules between the two extremes.

The "drill/communication" dichotomy is useful in bringing out the necessity of communication and the insufficiency of drill. However, this disjunction has led many to the elimination of drill and to exclusive concentration on communication, which, granted, tends to result in some ability to communicate, but very inaccurately. Obviously, if the goals of the L2 program include communication with both fluency and accuracy, neither should be sacrificed for the sake of the other, and both communicative activity and intelligent drill should have a role to play.

Some dichotomies are unnecessary, the result of attempts to discredit existing ideas in order to substitute new ones for them. It is as if proponents of new ideas felt they could secure a place on the land only by displacing earlier homesteaders, regardless of how spacious the land may be. Examples of unnecessary oppositions are "omniscience/know-nothingism" and "contrastive analysis/error analysis."

Beginning in the midsixties, at the time the mentalist revolution in linguistics and psychology began to be felt in the L2 field, it became de rigueur to say that nothing was really known about L2 learning. The implications were that only the new school could eventually yield any genuine knowledge and that any claim to knowledge outside the new school could only be a presumption of omniscience. If we take a broader view above the clashes between schools of thought, however, we can see that knowledge advances joltingly but without interruption, despite such setbacks as the occasional call to move it back to point zero. Thus, much was known about L2 learning before the last time it was claimed nothing was known—and more is known today.

The "contrastive analysis/error analysis" dichotomy is also unnecessary, since the alternatives complement rather than oppose each other. In the course of the development of this dichotomy, however, an exaggerated and easy-to-discredit version of the contrastive analysis hypothesis that hardly anyone proposed, the so-called "strong" version, became part of the error analysis literature. Both types of analysis have considerable explanatory usefulness. Furthermore, contrastive analysis, despite the barrage of criticism against it, is a more than adequate predictive tool to aid in the preparation of new L2 materials for the beginning and intermediate levels. Error analysis can help in the revision, not the preparation, of materials.

Many dichotomies are misleading; among them are "habits/rules" and "linear/integrated." The opposition between linguistic habits and internalized rules is misleading on several grounds. First, it involves a misdefinition of the term habit as the learning of a fixed response to a specific stimulus resulting from mindless repetition. (No wonder so few linguists are interested nowadays in the mechanics of the learning process.) A linguistic habit should be defined, instead, as the behavioral relationship between an internalized rule and accurate, fluent performance. Second, the concept of language as a system of rules has led by extension of the term rule to emphasizing elaborate deductive rule statements in L2 teaching. But if we separate the internalization of a rule from an explicit statement of it, it becomes clear that, while rules must be internalized, how and when a rule is stated, if stated at all, is a pedagogically controllable variable. Finally, the antibehaviorism associated with the view that subconscious rules are preeminent has led to minimizing systematically guided practice in the overt learning of L2 rules. But only through such practice can L2 learners succeed in the gradual internalization of a rule, formation of the intervening linguistic habit, and development of accuracy and fluency in performance—all three of which need to proceed simultaneously (see Chart 2).

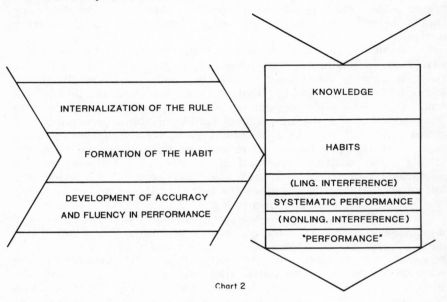

Chart 2

The "linear/integrated" opposition is misleading in that it reflects the view that, since a language is an integrated set of rules, a second language should be learned holistically as opposed to one rule at a time. This is an unrealistic view, since there is no way the human mind can accurately internalize a complex set of rules in toto. For the sake of both efficiency and effectiveness, L2 specialists would do well to channel the efforts of the L2 learner towards the mastery of learning tasks one by one. Exposing beginning students to the integrated set of rules of the most elaborate L2 grammar means starting out with what should be the eventual outcome of many years of L2 study; it leads the learners down the path of communicative semicompetence and structural incompetence. There should be, instead, a succession of increasingly complex L2 grammars as each rule is learned and integrated with those learned earlier.

As seen in the foregoing examples, loyalty-dividing slogans and dichotomies can be explained in such a way that they lose much of their divisiveness. In this manner one can leave behind the positions they represent or misrepresent—which are extremist and unproductive—and carry over from them, into the more productive middle ground, only the aspects that are logically defensible and demonstrably useful.

Such a process of synthesis is very much needed in the L2 field, which for the last one hundred years has been disrupted by major revolutions every two decades and lesser changes every three to five years. No doubt change is essential to progress; however, the kind of frequent and radical change that there has been in the L2 field, not unlike a pendulum gone berserk, while creating the impression of purposeful movement, has been mostly misspent energy leading to confusion.

The need for synthesis, however, should not lead the L2 profession headlong into any haphazard combination of theories and practices, for hasty synthesis can lead to misguided eclecticism, and that would be worse than no synthesis at all. Certain pitfalls must be avoided and certain principles followed.

Misguided eclecticism characteristically shows disregard for some of the evidence, whether factual or logical. It may uncritically accept any procedure that is propounded with sufficient salesmanship. It may combine, from various sources, elements that do not support or even that contradict each other. It may consist of blind compromise, automatically choosing the midpoint between any two views regardless of merit. Lacking principles, it is philosophically close to the ever-present faddism. Clearly, such eclecticism is undesirable.

A better alternative to misguided eclecticism can be called "enlightened eclecticism," a phrase coined earlier in another context (Ornstein, Ewton, and Mueller 1971:64) but good enough for further service. What is "enlightened" (to paraphrase Webster's Third) has been freed from ignorance and misinformation and is based on full comprehension of the problems involved—certainly worthwhile goals. But for enlightened eclecticism to be possible in the L2 field, three essential conditions would have to be met.

The first condition is that the L2 field be viewed as a separate discipline. Only thus will it be able to reject decisively all unacceptable "implications" and inexpedient "applications" of theories in other disciplines. The L2 field needs to be free to develop its own theory and practice unswayed by undue influences or irrelevancies, and to retain only what works.

The second precondition of enlightened eclecticism is an agreement on the goals of L2 study. It may be the least difficult condition to meet—while there can be many programs with many different goals, it seems to be generally recognized that the overall goal of L2 study is "communication plus." This goal can be explained as (1) skill in one or more L2 modalities, plus (2) insight into the second and native languages and into language in general, and (3) understanding of the two cultures and of culture in general.

The third condition for the introduction of enlightened eclecticism is that empirical research in L2 teaching be conducted scientifically rather than attempting to fit a particular paradigm. There is no reason for this field to be a form of philosophy in which data is made to fit speculation. It is by interposing bias-free empirical research between theory and practice that informed views based on observable evidence will again weigh more than subjective theorizing.

Should these three conditions be met, enlightened eclecticism could be established by implementing the principles embodied in the following recommendation. Gather, from all reliable sources, past and present, the best fact-supported elements that can be combined into a harmonious whole, appropriate to all variables, efficient, and effective in reaching the stated goals.

If it becomes a reality, such an enlightened synthesis would terminate a long period of confusion, disharmony, and near-anarchy in the L2 field. By acquiring autonomy, unity of purpose, and a scientific basis, and by proceeding on broad but common ground, the L2 profession would be able to make steadier and surer progress, freed of pressures by other fields, in its search for relevant facts, its development of viable theories, and its pursuit of better practical results.

REFERENCES

Chomsky, Noam. 1966. Linguistic theory. In Language teaching: broader contexts, ed. Robert G. Mead, Jr., pp. 43-49. Washington, D.C.: Northeast Conference Reports.

Moulton, William G. 1961. Linguistics and language teaching in the United States: 1940-60. In Trends in European and American linguistics: 1930-1960, ed. Christine Mohrmann, Alf Sommerfelt, and Joshua Whatmough, pp. 82-109. Utrecht: Spectrum.

Ornstein, Jacob; Ewton, Ralph W. Jr.; and Mueller, Theodore H. 1971. Programmed instruction and educational technology in the language teaching field. In Language and the teacher: a series in applied linguistics, ed. Robert C. Lugton. Philadelphia: Center for Curriculum Development.

24. The Competing-Plans Hypothesis (CPH) Extended to Second-Language Speech Production

HANS W. DECHERT
University of Kassel

The Problem

About thirty years ago contrastive analysis (CA) was used to analyze systematically the origin of second-language learners' errors. Later it was defined "as the method whereby the differences between two or more languages are made explicit" (Di Pietro 1978). Such a comparison and description of linguistic systems, it was thought by many, would lead to an understanding of learners' problems. The successful identification and description of particular structures of the two languages involved and the construction of more effective teaching material based on analyses of interference between the two languages seemed to be only a question of time. Near-native competence attained through systematic prevention of native-language (L1) induced errors seemed to be a realistic teaching objective.

Error analysis (EA) is based on the concept of second-language learners' approximative (Nemser 1971), transitional, and idiosyncratic (Corder 1971) knowledge of the language being learned. This intermediate language has been referred to as interlanguage and is assumed to be systematic, even though fraught with errors (Selinker 1972; Corder 1974a, b, 1975a, b; Dickerson 1975). EA has been applied since the early seventies to help teachers of a second language recognize, describe, and explain learners' errors. Almost exclusively written corpora have been studied.

It is obvious that this new approach implies a different, noncontrastive concept of "error" (Corder 1974b). Errors, according to EA, reflect a stage of development in one's interlanguage. They are not of interest so much as violations of the target language system, but as a means of getting access to the learners' linguistic stage of development and his problems at that stage.

Avoidance. In a number of recent papers (Schachter 1974; Cohen 1975; Perkins and Larsen-Freeman 1975; Swain 1975; Kleinmann 1977, 1978; Seliger 1977; Dechert forthcoming) the strategy of avoidance in second-language production has been discussed as an important issue. Schachter especially has questioned the validity of the a posteriori methodology of EA. Second-language productions are often characterized by the nonappearance of certain "difficult" target language structures. Such productions are, therefore, less erroneous than an a priori CA would predict. In such cases EA may lead to wrong conclusions as to the linguistic competence of the learner in question.

Hence, it is indeed a shortcoming in EA not to take into account the possibility that errors have been avoided by various strategies such as simplification (Bertkau 1974; Levenston and Blum 1977; Blum and Levenston 1978), overgeneralization (whatever that may be!), over- and under-representation (Levenston 1972), violation of level of utility (cf. Brown 1958).

Conclusion. In order to get full insight into their learning and production problems, any adequate analysis of language learners' errors must consider the cultural and linguistic background established by their native languages. The linguistic system they have acquired first continuously influences their way of looking at things, their hypotheses, and therefore, also their second languages.

The merit of CA is that it has provided us with many striking examples of this interference from L1. Strangely enough, we do not know much about the positive transfer of general cognition gained in L1 for the facilitation of L2 production. The interlanguage hypothesis is responsible for a new notion of "error" and has taught us the transitional character of human language, primary as well as secondary. We are now much better prepared to take errors as natural, if not systematic indications of stages within a dynamic development of the learner's ability to express himself. But since the ability to plan and monitor speech not only consists of the knowledge of what to say, but also of what to avoid saying and what to say instead—in L1 as well as in L2—the phenomenon of avoidance strategy requires an unprejudiced treatment far beyond its critical implications for the reevaluation of CA versus EA (Dechert 1979). We also need a theoretical framework with the explanatory power to account for a wide range of planning problems reflected in the incidence of errors or hidden with the help of avoidance strategies. It is the goal of this paper to present such a theory.

Speech Sample

The recording of Barbara's narration was made on December 20, 1976. She was majoring in English. At that time she had had eight years of English at a Gymnasium and four years of language training in various courses taught by native speakers of English at the University of Kassel, Germany. As part of her academic studies she had spent about half a year as an exchange student at a midwestern American college. Her general educational background as well as her contact with English-speaking people must be considered much above average. At the time of the recording, her age was twenty-three.

The recording was made by a student assistant whom she knew well. A cartoon used by Goldman-Eisler (1961) was presented to her in printed form. Neither its title, "Man and girl become engaged," nor any other verbal information was given in order to avoid any intrusion concerning the meaning and structure of the story or the purpose of the elicitation task. A recording of what she said was transcribed afterward and analyzed aurally and instrumentally by three experienced student assistants, each working independently.

Pauses, together with falling intonation, were considered to be the delimiting factors in the assessment of narrative planning units, referred to here as episodic units (Dechert forthcoming). Pauses in connection with "speech errors" (such as slips of the tongue, false starts, repetitions, fusions, blends) and their corrections were assumed to reflect lower-level processes of verbal planning within the chosen narrative schema.

The resulting final transcript (Appendix 1) is intended to demonstrate

— the noncorrespondence between the structure of the presented cartoon (S) and the chosen story structure (E), and

— the occurrence of a large number of "errors" of various origin and nature and Barbara's attempts to avoid or correct them before, during, or after their appearance.

Interpretation of Errors.   Although we are dealing with the production of a rather advanced learner of English, the number and seriousness of her errors were quite remarkable. One must not forget, however, the complexity of the elicitation task under discussion:

— The task has elements of a projective test: a harmless trick of a girl's father is turned into a story verging on infidelity and is expressed almost as a confession.

— Having set up this general framework, Barbara must stick to it and make it as consistent as possible. Several planning problems that arise are due to the misunderstanding of the message.

— Barbara's decision to follow the given story schema only partially puts her in danger of a loss of schematic control and a collision of cartoon and production structure.

— There are a number of properties in the original

cartoon that must be named when producing it verbally; such as the term for a musical instrument and seating arrangements of the figures. If the words for these objects are inaccessible, search processes, pauses, and avoidance strategies are likely to occur. Some passages in Barbara's production are fluent and disclose a near-native competence:

(1.5)   A CANDLE WAS LIT ON THE TABLE

(2.1)   THE ATMOSPHERE BECAME VERY ROMANTIC

(3.1)   HE TOOK MY HAND (—) AND HE LOOKED INTO MY EYES

(4.1)   I LIKED THAT TOO AND I DIDN'T SAY ANYTHING

Fluent passages like these, which are by no means "easier" than others from a contrastive point of view, co-occur with disfluent passages that at first sight would not be expected to cause any planning problem for an advanced speaker. What is it then that makes her speak fluently in one place and have difficulties in other places? This is a question that CA has not been able to answer. The following hermeneutic interpretation points out some answers to this question.

The following passage, beginning in line 5.1, reads

WE WENT

(5.2)   OUT (— — — —)   THE RESTAURANT

(5.3)   OUT OF   THE RESTAURANT

The self-correction OUT OF THE RESTAURANT following immediately the L1-induced form *OUT THE RESTAURANT ('aus dem Restaurant') with a lot of pausing before, during, and after this passage shows intensive planning and monitoring accompanying the repair. Of course, Barbara without any question "knows" the correct English form OUT OF and yet slips into the wrong one at first. Why does she?

Another example of possible interference is a more complicated one (lines 9.5 to 9.8). Again the pauses interrupting the flow of speech reveal planning and mental correction of planning. Why is Barbara not satisfied with the correct version in her mind, as in:

(9.5)   WHEN   WE (—)   ENTERED

(9.6)   MY (— —)   HO me ,

to which she finally comes back anyhow in line 9.8?

Why does she introduce the phrase MY DOOR (line 9.7), stimulated by the cartoon but leading to a syntactically wrong alternative, so that she has to drop and correct it at once in line 9.8? Is it the L1 notion (not necessarily expression, to be sure) of the composite "Haustür" or "Wohnungstür" that is iconically and semantically present that makes her stop in line 9.6 with MY HO and try to add the concept "door" without success? As in the previous case, the existence of more than one notion and the load of processing in connection with the decision to be made seems to be one possible cause of interference.

In lines 1.9 to 1.12 there is another interesting case of L2 planning difficulties caused either by a strange incapability to name the instrument ("violin") properly or an interference.

(1.9)		HE HAD
(1.10)	A (— — —)	GUITAR . NO
(1.11)	A . (em) 5.8)	VIOLIN
(1.12) IN HIS HAND		

That the gypsy's instrument is not a guitar should be perfectly clear to her. But is it really? Or why is there not a positive transfer from the L1 expression "Violine" to "violin"? Instead there is obvious searching, monitoring (demonstrated through the parenthetical remark NO) and an extremely long pause until she finally succeeds in finding VIOLIN. The only explanation I have for this complicated search process is that the only appropriate German composite "Zigeunergeige" (with the two-syllable component "Geige" starting with a "G") is somehow present in the processing system, blocks the transfer of "Violine" and permits the wrong, but phonetically similar word GUITAR to slip in. If this explanation is correct we have a striking example of two different plans in L1 und L2 for the same concept fused into each other on different levels of processing.

Fossilization. A state of anxiety or other excitement on one hand or a state of extreme relaxation on the other have been held responsible for the backsliding of second-language learners into fossilized forms of errors (Selinker 1972). It seems that neither of the fossilizations in this sample can be explained that easily.

(6.1)   BANK for bench (German 'Bank')

(3.3)   HOLD for held (German 'halten, hielt')

That both forms are not uttered without control of the monitor is indicated by the surrounding pauses in line 6.1 and the prolonged and unsuccessful correction in line 3.3. In both cases either the preceding portion of speech (line 3.2) or the following lines (6.1) present additional planning problems, so that it seems to be the overload of planning and decision making that may occasion these fossilizations.

Lexical Search. The most frequent planning problems advanced second-language learners have, as has been stated elsewhere (Schlue 1977; Dechert 1979), result from lexical search. One who does not know the words "gipsy" or "violin," or who has learned them but cannot retrieve them, is not able to verbalize the portion of the cartoon in which they are depicted. It is obvious that many pauses in the transcript are expressions of search processes for proper words and phrases; I have already mentioned a few (for example, line 3.2). Other search processes that are not accompanied by false starts or slips of the tongue disclosing alternatives are hard to identify.

  There are two special examples of search processes in the text worth mentioning:

(1.2)   AND 9— —) WE WENT OUT . TO A (—)
         SPANISH RESTAURANT (— -- — —)

(1.3)   IT WAS VERY

(1.4)   A VERY NICE ONE (— —)

and in lines 2.5 to 2.7:

(2.5)   AND [he] BECAME MORE (— —) (e).

(2.6)   KIND (— —)

(2.7)   KINDLY (— — - —)

Both corrections are grammatical, the first one (line 1.4) changing slightly the meaning, the second resulting in a mistake. As in other instances in this paper the latter version proves to be of little success. In this case they do not present lexical alternatives but an unnecessary and even incorrect grammatical solution to a lexical search problem.

Hypothesis Testing. To understand and speak a language means not only to reproduce linguistic patterns, but also to generate utterances never experienced before. Hypothesis testing is another expression for this way of reconstructing the world anew.

  One of Barbara's problems in doing so is that she misses the point of the cartoon presented to her. She not only fails to grasp its humor but she changes the message: she makes it a story of infidelity. The storyteller cheats on her husband with the young fellow who takes her out to the restaurant, then to the park and, quite consistently, to her apartment.

  The ambiguity of the German expression "Bekannter," which

might be applied in this case, leads Barbara to invent or hypothesize the nonexisting English word *MY ACQUAINTANT and *AN OLD ACQUAINTANT OF MINE. After the park scene and when entering the apartment, he is called MY FRIEND! Barbara's invention can be considered to be a case of hypothesis testing in second-language production.

In line 9.1 the utterance

(9.1)   HE F . (e) (— — —)

obviously is a first indication of the expression HE FOLLOWED ME taken up in lines 9.2 to 9.11 does not add very much but presents a number of corrupted words, phrases, and repetitions. It discloses the attempt to say something other than what is already in the planning process (HE F[ollowed me]). But it is not uttered since the solution of the story (AN ACQUAINTANT vs. MY FRIEND) in the framework of the misunderstood message (MY HUSBAND vs. MY FATHER) must be developed, decided upon and put into words. It does not seem to be an accident that precisely at this point in the production the cartoon structure and story schema diverge again.

The Competing-Plans Hypothesis

The errors in Barbara's narration obviously occur in the neighborhood of various filled and unfilled pauses. They are accompanied by self-corrections and other expressions of monitoring. As the transcript tries to demonstrate graphically, these errors seem to fall into positions that, in the overall outline or frame of the whole narration reveal lower-level routines from which single verbal plans are developed, tested against each other, and finally executed. In other words, it is the competition of verbal plans taking place in positions of high processing load that is responsible for pauses, errors, and their corrections. This phenomenon is called the "competing plans hypothesis of speech production" in L1. It is based on the work of Greene (1972), Mackay (1972, 1977), and Baars and Motley (1976).

The numerous "speed errors" that occur in natural speech, even that of highly competent speakers, are thought to be the result of competing plans. This competition of plans is caused by a potential ambiguity in the speech control system. "Any system faced with solving the problems of speech production will occasionally emit errors. They are the price we pay for our ability to express ourselves so well" (Baars 1978). At present this hypothesis seems to have the most inclusive explanatory power to account for various types of errors in L1, and, as we assume, in L2 as well.

Competing plans in the speech-production system lead to momentary uncertainty, which in turn is reflected in pauses, hesitations, and prolongations. These temporal variables of speech production in connection with errors may be taken as symptoms of intense mental activity in the search, decision, or avoidance procedures inherent in the planning and execution of speech, which is a highly complex process on various levels and sublevels. As is the case with complex executive systems in general, there are many degrees of freedom of choice in the subsystems. Diminished control of the speech production system at its periphery may reflect competition between conflicting plans and so lead to the source of errors.   In other words, when speech is planned, some general context dependent and context constructing notions are retrieved, coined, and fed into the system, establishing a frame of reference. They undergo various coding and recoding procedures at various levels, more and more in danger of getting out of control. This is definitely not a serial process, run through step by step, but a multidetermined evocation of plans. Only one of them can be used in the output part of the system each time. Sometimes, however, more than one plan are executed before or while being decided upon.

In other cases under the pressure of time, inappropriate alternative plans are chosen because of a lack of availability or accessibility of more adequate ones.   Competitive plans are sometimes uttered successively, sometimes blended or fused with each other.   The competition of speech plans is only partly conscious, depending on the degree of linguistic awareness regulating the production.   The activity of a monitor is thus an important part of the speech-production system, its gradual development a necessary component of L1 and L2 language acquisition.

The competing-plans hypothesis provides a comprehensive explanation for the origin of speech errors in L1.   It can be extended, as has been suggested throughout this paper, to an all-encompassing theoretical model for the explanation of errors in L2 as well. Competition of speech plans, representing different stages (notions, concepts, frames, hypotheses) in the interlanguage of the nonnative speaker, taken from L1 and L2, emerges as the source of planning problems and errors, especially when the complexity of the verbalization task or situation brings about a decrease of control at the periphery of the language-processing system.   At present we have very little detail about how the system works.

Conclusion

I began with a few remarks about CA and EA in order to draw a rough sketch of the context in which efforts to explain and understand the planning problems of second-language speakers have developed. Psycholinguistics ought to have an increasing part in a learner-centered (rather than language-oriented) analysis of these problems.   Such an approach, entitled "Contrastive Psycholinguistics," takes up a 1970 proposal by Nemser and Slama-Cazacu called "Contact Analysis."   My intention is to change some of the bathwater and keep the baby, to modify slightly a remark of

Bolinger in his introduction to Di Pietro's Language Structures in Contrast.

REFERENCES

Baars, Bernard. 1977. On eliciting predictable speech errors in the laboratory: Methods and results. Paper read at the 12th International Congress of Linguists, August/September 1977, Vienna.

_____. Forthcoming. The competing plans hypothesis: an heuristic viewpoint on the causes of speech errors. In Temporal variables of speech. Studies in honour of Frieda Goldman-Eisler, ed. Hans W. Dechert and Manfred Raupach. The Hague: Mouton.

Baars, Bernard J., and Motley, Michael T. 1976. Spoonerisms as sequencer conflicts: evidence from artificially elicited errors. American Journal of Psychology 89:467-86.

Bertkau, J. S. 1974. An analysis of English learner speech. Language Learning 24:279-86.

Blum, Shoshana, and Levenston, E. A. 1978. Universals of lexical simplification. Language Learning 28:399-415.

Brown, Roger. 1958. How shall a thing be called? Psychological Review 65:14-21.

Cohen, Andrew D. 1975. Error correction and the training of language teachers. Modern Language Journal 59:414-22.

Corder, S. Pit. 1971. Idiosyncratic dialects and error analysis. IRAL 9:147-59.

_____. 1974a. The elicitation of interlanguage. IRAL Special Issue, pp. 51-63, Stuttgart: Gross.

_____. 1974b. Error analysis. In Techniques in applied linguistics. The Edinburgh course in applied linguistics, ed. J. P. B. Allen and S. Pit Corder, pp. 122-54. Vol. 3. London: Oxford University Press.

_____. 1975a. Error analysis, interlanguage and second language acquisition. Language Teaching and Linguistics: Abstracts 8:201-18.

_____. 1975b. The language of second-language learners: the broader issues. Modern Language Journal 57:409-13.

Dechert, Hans W. 1979. On the evaluation of "avoidance strategies" in second-language speech productions. A psycholinguistic approach. Paper read at the TESOL Summer Meeting in Los Angeles, July 13-14, 1979.

_____. Forthcoming. Contextual hypothesis-testing-procedures in speech production. In Towards a cross-linguistic assessment of speech production, ed. Hans W. Dechert and Manfred Raupach. Bern, Frankfurt, Las Vegas: Peter Lang.

Dickerson, Lonna J. 1975. The learner's interlanguage as a system of variable rules. TESOL Quarterly 9:401-7.

Di Pietro, Robert J. 1978. Language structures in contrast. Rowley, Mass.: Newbury House.

Goldman-Eisler, Frieda. 1961. Hesitation and information in speech. In Information theory, ed. Colin Cherry. London: Butterworths.

Greene, Peter H. 1972. Problems of organization of motor systems. In Progress in theoretical biology, ed. R. Rosen, and F. M. Snell. Vol. 2. New York: Academic Press.

Kleinmann, Howard H. 1977. Avoidance behaviour in adult second language acquisition. Language Learning 27:93-107.

_____. 1978. The strategy of avoidance in adult second language acquisition. In Second language acquisition research, ed. William C. Ritchie. New York: Academic Press.

Levenston, E. A. 1972. Über und Unterrepräsentation-aspekte der muttersprachlichen Interferenz. In Reader zur kontrastiven linguistik, ed. Gerhard Nickel. Frankfurt: Athenäum Fischer Taschenbuch.

Levenston, E. A., and Blum, Shoshana. 1977. Aspects of lexical simplification in the speech and writing of advanced adult learners. In Actes du 5ème colloque de linguistique appliquée de Neuchâtel. Geneva: Droz.

Mackay, Donald G. 1972. The structure of words and syllables: evidence from errors in speech. Cognitive Psychology 3:210-27.

_____. 1977. Speech errors: retrospect and prospect. Paper read at the 12th International Congress of Linguists, August/September 1977, Vienna.

Nemser, William. 1971. Approximative systems of foreign language learners. IRAL 9:115-23.

Nemser, William, and Slama-Cazacu, Tatiana. 1970. A contribution to contrastive linguistics (a psycholinguistic approach: contact analysis). Revue Roumaine de Linguistique 15:101-28.

Perkins, Kyle, and Larsen-Freeman, Diane. 1975. The effect of formal language instruction on the order of morpheme acquisition. Language Learning 25:237-43.

Schachter, Jacquelyn. 1974. An error in error analysis. Language Learning 24:205-14.

Schlue, Karen. 1977. An inside view of interlanguage. In Proceedings of the Los Angeles Second Language Research Forum, ed. Carol Alice Henning, pp. 342-48. Los Angeles: University of California Press.

Seliger, Herbert. 1977. Semantic presuppositions underlying avoidance strategies. CUNY Forum 3:63-81.

Selinker, Larry. 1972. Interlanguage. IRAL 10:209-31.

Swain, Merrill. 1975. Changes in errors: random or systematic? Paper read at the 4th International Congress of Applied Linguistics, Stuttgart. Published in Abstracts, Vol. 86.

SPEECH SAMPLE TRANSCRIPT

S	E	
1	1	
	2	
2		

1.1 (em) . ONE EVENING . I WENT OUT (- -) WITH AN OLD ACQUAINTANT . OF MINE (- -)

1.2 AND (- -) WE WENT OUT . TO A (-) SPANISH RESTAURANT (- - -)

1.3 IT WAS VERY [nice]

1.4 A VERY NICE ONE (- -)

1.5 A CANDLE WAS LIT ON THE TABLE (- -)

1.6 AND WE WERE TALKING

1.7 MY . (e) (-) ACQUAINTANT AND I.

1.8 WE WERE TALKING TOGETHER (- - - -)

1.9 AND (- -) AFTER A WHILE (- -) AN OLD GYPSY . APPEARED . HE HAD

1.10 A (- - -) GUITAR . NO

1.11 A . (em) (5.8) VIOLIN (- - -)

1.12 IN HIS HAND AND HE PLAYED . VERY NICE . SONGS (- - - - -) //

2.1 (em) (3.3) THE ATMOSPHERE BECAME VERY ROMANTIC (- -)

2.2 AND (-) I . RECOGNIZED . THAT

2.3 MY ACQUAINTANT (-)

2.4 MY OLD ACQUAINTANT (- - - - -)

2.5 CHANGED (- - -) AND BECAME MORE (- -) (e) .

2.6 KIND (- -)

2.7 KINDLY (- - - -) //

3	3	3.1	HE TOOK MY HANDS (-) AND HE LOOKED INTO MY EYES (- -)
4		3.2	AND SUDDENLY (- -) HE (- -) SAT QUITE (-) NEAR . TO ME (- -)
		3.3	<u>AND</u> HE HOLD .
		3.4	HE HOLD
		3.5	ME IN HIS ARMS (- - - -) //
4	4	4.1	I LIKED THAT AND I DIDN'T SAY ANYTHING (- - -) //
5	5	5.1	AT THE END OF THE EVENING (- - -) WE WENT
		5.2	OUT (- - -) THE RESTAURANT .
		5.3	OUT OF THE RESTAURANT (- -)
		5.4	<u>AND</u> (- -) WENT TO A PARK (- - -) //
	6	6.1	THERE . I SAT ON A (- - -) BANK (- -)
		6.2	AND (- -) HE CONFESSED (- -) THAT . HE LOVED ME (- - - - -)//
6	7	7.1	I WAS VERY DELIGHTED (smile) (- - -) //
7	8	8.1	<u>AND</u> . WE WENT TOGETHER TO MY HOME (3.3) //
	9	9.1	HE F[ollowed] . (e) (- - -)
		9.2	HE SEEMED TO LIKE THAT TOO (- -)
		9.3	<u>AND</u> HE (- - -)
		9.4	WHEN I .

7	9		
	9.5 WHEN	WE (-) ENTERED	
	9.6	MY (- -) HO[me]	
	9.7	MY DOOR.	
	9.8	MY HOME (- - - -)	
	9.9 I FIRST WENT		
	9.10	IN (-) [the living room]	
	9.11	TO	THE LIVING ROOM (- - - -)
	9.12 AND (- -)	MY ACQUAINTANT FO[llowed]	
	9.13	MY FRIEND.	FOLLOWED ME (- - -) //
8	10		
	10.1 HE WAS VERY SURPRISED SUDDENLY TO SEE MY HUSBAND (- - -)		
	10.2	WHO (- - - -)	
	10.3	WHOM	
	10.4 I INTRODUCED TO HIM //		

KEY TO SYMBOLS

Pauses:

.	up to 300 milliseconds
(-)	up to 500 milliseconds
(- -)	up to 1 second
(- - -)	up to 1,5 seconds
(- - - -)	up to 2 seconds
(- - - - -)	up to 2.5 seconds
(- - - - - -)	up to 3 seconds
(3.8)	3,8 seconds
(em)	filled pause
AND	prolongation
//	unit boundary line
FO[llowed]	anticipated plan
S	scene in the cartoon
E	episode in the narration

Part IV: Language in the Classroom: Pedagogical Implications

25. The Semantics of the French Subjunctive: An Application to the Classroom

EUGENE A. FONG
University of Houston

Tradition has handed down essentially two different ways of viewing the selection of subjunctive or indicative verb forms in sentential complements. The difference between these two approaches is most clearly seen in the analysis of the use of mood in embedded sentences functioning as noun clauses, as in:

(1)　Je me rends compte que René ne vient pas de Bordeaux.
'I realize that Rene does not come from Bordeaux.'

(2)　Je doute que René vienne de Bordeaux.
'I doubt that Rene comes from Bordeaux.'

Following the most common analysis, one can account for the use of the subjunctive verb form in sentence (2) by some sort of classificatory mechanism for matrix verbs or phrases; i.e., douter 'to doubt' belongs to a syntactic and/or semantic class of matrices that require subjunctive verb forms in sentential complements. According to this view, then, the subjunctive forms themselves have no real semantic function; they appear purely on the basis of a cooccurrence relationship that is syntactically determined.

Largely ignored by many linguists, structural and transformational alike, has been another view that the use of the subjunctive or indicative mood corresponds directly to certain basic semantic concepts such as truth value, presupposition, or assertion. According to this hypothesis, the choice of mood in French is directly correlated with what the sentence as a whole expresses about the truth of the proposition included in the sentence. That is, we postulate that the speaker wishes to convey certain information about the truth value of a proposition and that he chooses his syntactic constructions accordingly. Suppose, for example, that the speaker wishes to assert that he believes a certain proposition to be a true statement. He may do so in a number of ways depending on how he wishes to qualify the assertion.

(3)　Les Russes atterriront sur la lune l'année prochaine.
'The Russians will land on the moon next year.'

(4)　J'imagine que les Russes atterriront sur la lune
　　　l'année prochaine.
　　　'I imagine that the Russians . . .'

(5)　Je suis certain que les Russes atterriront sur la
　　　lune l'année prochaine.
　　　'I am certain that the Russians . . .'

(6)　Il est évident que les Russes atterriront sur la lune
　　　l'année prochaine.
　　　'It is obvious that the Russians . . .'

In (3) the speaker merely asserts the proposition to be a true statement. In sentences (4) through (6) the same proposition is asserted, but with some qualification.

The difference between the two positions should be made clear. The first analysis claims that the subjunctive or indicative forms do not function meaningfully because the choice of mood is determined automatically by the phrase type found in the matrix. Hence, this is a syntactically based analysis. Even though the matrices are classified in terms of their meaning, the result is considered to be only syntactic—the mood of the complement verb being merely a morphological reflex of the class of the matrix phrase. The second analysis is semantically based in that it claims that the mood of the complement verb can be freely chosen and thus carries meaning. The hypothesis is that there are several basic attitudes that a speaker can adopt toward a proposition. These attitudes govern the choice of mood and the choice of matrix, one independently of the other. The analysis of mood in French that follows in this paper is based on the semantic hypothesis. The data and the discussion are limited to that class of verbs which admit both indicative and subjunctive complements. Thus, mental-act verbs like <u>croire</u> 'to believe', <u>imaginer</u> 'to imagine', etc., when negative or interrogative, can be followed by an embedded sentence whose verb is in either the indicative or the subjunctive mood:

(7a)　Je ne crois pas que le Prince est tombé amoureux
　　　d'Odile.

(7b)　Je ne crois pas que le Prince soit tombé
　　　amoureux d'Odile.
　　　'I do not believe that the Prince fell in love with
　　　Odile.'

(8a)　Crois-tu que la balène est une mammifère?

(8b)　Crois-tu que la balène soit une mammifère?
　　　'Do you believe that the whale is a mammal?'

Two solutions to this distribution are possible: either (i) we are dealing with verbs that represent two homophonous entries that take different complements or (ii) we must mark semantically in the underlying structure the complement that a matrix verb will take. I show that the semantic property of assertion determines the choice of complement. Further, independent syntactic evidence will show that the complements of this class of matrix verbs are indeed different in underlying structure. Finally, we shall see how such a semantic interpretation of the choice of mood can be applied in order to create exercises that drill the interaction of semantic factors and syntactic constructions.

In any semantic study of sentential complements, the notion of presupposition is important. I accept here the definition advanced by the Kiparskys (1970) and by Keenan (1971). First, the truth of the complement is presupposed by the entire sentence.

(9)   Je regrette que Jean soit parti.
        'I am sorry that John has left.'

The speaker presupposes that the embedded clause expresses a true proposition and makes some comment about the proposition. Further, the truth value of a presupposed proposition will remain constant under the normal processes of negation and interrogation.

(10)   Je ne regrette pas que Jean soit parti.
        'I am not sorry that . . .'

(11)   Regrettez-vous que Jean soit parti?
        'Are you sorry that . . .'

In sentences (10) and (11), although the matrix verb has undergone negative and interrogative transformations, it is still assumed to be a fact that John has left.

When we compare sentences (9), (10), and (11) with sentence (12),

(12)   Gutrune s'est rendu compte que Brünnhilde était
        l'épouse de Siegfried.
        'Gutrune realized that Brunnhilde was Siegfried's
        wife.'

we notice that presupposed propositions can be either in the indicative or the subjunctive mood. The notion of presupposition, then, is not a sufficient condition for the choice of mood in sentential complements. We must look elsewhere.

In this analysis, I accept and apply Hooper's (1973) notions of assertion and nonassertion. An assertion is the proposition expressed in a declarative sentence. More specifically, the speaker or the subject of the sentence has an affirmative opinion regarding the truth value of the proposition. The speaker may express his opinion in a number of ways, depending on whether or not he wishes to qualify the assertion. If there is no qualification, he states the proposition directly.

(13)   La Guerre de Troie n'aura pas lieu.
        'The Trojan War will not take place.'

He may, of course, qualify in various degrees his belief in the truth value of the proposition with the use of the appropriate matrix.

(14)   Il me semble que la Guerre de Troie n'aura pas lieu.
        'It seems to me that . . .'

(15)   Je pense que la Guerre de Troie n'aura pas lieu.
        'I think that . . .'

(16)   Il est certain que la Guerre de Troie n'aura pas lieu.
        'It is certain that . . .'

Note that presupposition that a proposition is true and assertion that it is true are not equivalent. For example, in sentence (17) the proposition that French is easy to learn is being asserted.

(17)   Il est clair que le français est facile à apprendre.
        'It is clear that French is easy to learn.'

However, the truth of this proposition is not presupposed. Thus, the negation of the matrix does affect the truth value of the embedded clause.

(18)   Il n'est pas clair que le francais soit facile à apprendre.
        'It is not clear that French is easy to learn.'

In (18) the speaker does not think and certainly does not presuppose that French is easy to learn.

Using the notions of presupposition and assertion to classify complements, we find the following possibilities:

(19)   Asserted (not presupposed):   Je sais que Beethoven a écrit neuf symphonies.
        'I know that Beethoven wrote nine symphonies.'

(20)   Presupposed (not asserted): Il est bizarre que Jean veuille quitter son poste.
        'It is strange that John wants to quit his job.'

(21)   Neither asserted nor presupposed: Je ne suis pas
        sur qu'Adam veuille la pomme.
        'I am not sure that Adam wants the apple.'

On the basis of the three preceding sentences, it beomces readily
apparent that the indicative mood of the complement correlates
directly with assertion (sentence 19) and that the subjunctive mood
correlates with nonassertion (sentences 20 and 21). This distinction
will be accepted to account for the variation in mood in the
complements of matrix verbs like croire, penser, etc. When the
complement is asserted, its verb will appear in the indicative.

(22)   Je ne pense pas que notre équipe a gagné le
        match.
        'I do not think that our team won the game.'

(23)   Croyez-vous   que   Reagan   est   le   président
        convenable   pour   résoudre   les   problèmes
        nationaux?
        'Do you believe that Reagan is the right
        president to solve the national problems?'

However, if the complement is not an assertion, its verb will be in
the subjunctive.

(24)   Je ne pense pas que notre équipe ait gagné le
        match.

(25)   Croyez-vous   que   Reagan   soit   le   president
        convenable   pour   résoudre   les   problèmes
        nationaux?

The task is now to show that these complements are not dependent
on the matrix and that the two are different one from the other in
underlying structure.

        Verbs of the croire, penser class are verbs that optionally
undergo NEG-raising. Given the three sentences below, the question
to be answered is the following: What is the relationship of (26b)
and (26c) to (26a)? Do both (26b) and (26c) result from NEG-raising
and therefore are both related syntactically to (26a)?

(26a)   Marc croit que Tristan n'est pas amoureux
         d'Iseut.
         'Marc believes that Tristan is not in love with
         Isolde.'

(26b)   Marc ne croit pas que Tristan est amoureux
         d'Iseut.
         'Marc does not believe that . . .'

(26c)   Marc ne croit pas que Tristan soit amoureux
         d'Iseut.
         'Marc does not believe that . . .'

If both (26b) and (26c) are results of NEG-raising, it would mean that
they are both related to (26a), and that the difference in the choice
of mood does not reflect a difference in underlying structure; i.e.,
the complements are identical in underlying structure.

NEG-raising is useful in determining the relationship among
sentences such as the preceding. In order to see how NEG-raising
works, examine the functioning of what Prince (1976) calls negative
polarity items. These are expressions that are grammatical only
when they are constituents of a negated clause in underlying
structure. Consider the following sentences:

(27a)   Guy n'a pas dormi de la nuit.
         'Guy has not slept all night.'

         Fifi n'a pas levé le petit doigt pour m'aider.
         'Fifi has not lifted a finger to help me.'
         Jean ne parle pas un mot d'anglais.
         'John does not speak a word of English.'

(27b)   *Guy a dormi de la nuit.
         'Guy has slept all night.'

         *Fifi a levé le petit doigt pour m'aider.
         'Fifi lifted a finger to help me.'

         *Jean parle un mot d'anglais.
         'John speaks a word of English.'

In complex sentences, we find the same distribution.

(28a)   Mon frère croit que tu ne comprends pas un mot
         de français.
         'My brother believes that you do not understand
         a word of French.'

(28b)   Mon frère ne croit pas que tu comprennes un
         mot de français.
         'My brother does not believe that you
         understand a word of French.'

(28c)   *Mon frère ne croit pas que tu comprends un
         mot de français.

(29a)   Max imagine que sa femme n'a pas dormi de la
         nuit.

'Max imagines that his wife has not slept all night.'

(29b)   Max n'imagine pas que sa femme ait dormi de la nuit.
'Max does not imagine that his wife slept all night.'

(29c)   *Max n'imagine pas que sa femme a dormi de la nuit.

(30a)   Je pense qu'il n'en a du tout pas parlé.
'I think that he has not spoken about it at all.'

(30b)   Je ne pense pas qu'il en ait du tout parlé.
'I do not think that he has spoken about it at all.

(30c)   *Je ne pense pas qu'il en a du tout parlé.

In complex sentences such as (28b), (29b), and (30b), expressions such as un mot de francais, de la nuit, and du tout are grammatical even though the negation appears in the matrix clause. We must therefore conclude that the negation originated in the subordinate clause and was moved to the matrix verb through NEG-raising. The ungrammatical nature of sentences (28c), (29c), and (30c) shows that when the complements are in the indicative and the negation appears in the matrix verb in surface structure, this is not a result of NEG-raising. Instead, the negative transformation has operated on the matrix itself. We conclude that sentences (28a) and (28b), (29a) and (29b), and (30a) and (30b) share a common underlying structure, while the structure that underlies (28c), (29c), and (30c) does not meet the structural index of NEG-raising and is therefore different.

The formation of tag questions and corrective responses in French further show two different underlying clause structures. Affirmative sentences can take either oui or non as a tag, whereas negative sentences admit only non.

(31a)   Hermione est belle, oui/non?
'Hermione is beautiful isn't she?'

(31b)   Hermione n'est pas belle, *oui/non?
'Hermione is not beautiful, is she?'

Now consider the following complex sentences:

(32a)   Je suppose que Georges ne viendra pas, *oui/non?
'I suppose that George will not come, will he?'

(32b)   Je ne suppose pas que Georges vienne, *oui/non?
'I don't suppose that George will come, will he?'

(32c)   Je ne suppose pas que Georges viendra, oui/non?

We conclude from the grammaticalness of the tags that sentences (32a) and (32b) share a common negative underlying structure and are thus related one to the other. That both tags in sentence (32c) are acceptable leads us to believe that the complement was never negative in underlying structure and that the negation belongs instead to the matrix.

Now that we have established a clear semantic distinction between the use of the indicative and the subjunctive moods in sentential complements, let us now turn to practical applications of our analysis.

The vast majority, if not all, of the textbooks approach mood as though it were the subjunctive that must be learned. This approach gives the student the impression that the subjunctive is something odd or unusual. When the subjunctive is introduced, it is often drilled to the neglect of the indicative. Thus, almost no attention is given to the matrix classes that require indicative complements. The results of this approach are particularly evident when the conjunctions that introduce the subjunctive are taught. The student is presented with the list of conjunctions that require a complement in the subjunctive, and these are drilled. The student generalizes, incorrectly, the rule to all conjunctions, producing an ungrammatical sentence such as *Je joue au tennis pendant que mon frère lise un livre 'I play tennis while my brother reads a book.' Such ungrammatical sentences show that it is not the subjunctive that needs to be taught, but rather the distinction between the two moods.

We have seen that the complement may contain the basic proposition of the sentence and that the mood of the complement indicates the speaker's view of the truth value of that proposition. In order to drill this semantic factor, we choose a sentence such as the following as a cue for a pattern drill:

(33a)   Je ne crois pas que mes amis _____
        en France demain.   (partir)

(33b)   Comprenez-vous que Jean _____
        quitter l'université?   (vouloir)

The student is asked to assert the truth value of the proposition:

(34a)   Je ne crois pas que mes amis partiront en
        France demain.

(34b)   Comprenez-vous que Jean veut quitter
        l'université?

or the student is asked to be unassertive about the proposition:

(35a)   Je ne crois pas que mes amis partent en France demain.

(35b)   Comprenez-vous que Jean veuille quitter l'université?

We can extend the preceding type of exercise where the comment on the truth value of the proposition is expressed by the mood of the complement to other types of sentences where the proposition in the complement is commented on or qualified by the matrix. This is by far the more frequent construction. We take a sentence such as <u>Jean viendra te voir.</u> The student is asked to:

(i)   assert it
       (36)   Je suis sûr (certain) que Jean viendra te voir.

(ii)   doubt it
       (37)   Je doute que Jean vienne te voir.
               Je ne suis pas sûr (certain) que Jean vienne te voir.

(iii) comment on it
       (38)   Il faut (il est essentiel, important, etc.) que Jean vienne te voir.
               Je ne regrette pas que Jean vienne te voir.

There is an important observation to be made between the many exercises currently found in textbooks and the types of exercises proposed here. According to the traditional exercises, the use of mood in a sentential complement is viewed as a co-occurrence relationship between matrix and complement. The occurrence of a matrix phrase conditions the occurrence of the indicative or the subjunctive in the complement. Thus, for example, a student learns that être sûr 'to be sure' requires a complement in the indicative while il faut 'it is necessary' requires one in the subjunctive. It is maintained here that the use of a matrix and corresponding mood should not be viewed as a co-occurrence relationship. Instead, the speaker has information that he wishes to convey and certain decisions to make concerning the means of conveying it. First, does the speaker presuppose the truth value of his proposition? If he does, does he wish to report it objectively or does he wish to make a subjective comment about it? If the speaker does not presuppose the truth value of a proposition, does he wish to doubt it or does he wish to influence its realization? These semantic factors are responsible for the choice of matrix and choice of syntactic pattern.

The preceding two exercises encourage the student to

associate matrix choice and syntactic pattern with basic semantic
categories.   This process seems to be closer to the processes
involved in real speech than what is usually found in the dependency
type of drills that require the student to only fill in the blank
mechanically.

Still other exercises can be used at a more advanced level--
e.g., in a third-year or an advanced grammar course. One or both of
the following exercises can be adopted. First, for each member of
the following pair of sentences, the student is asked to furnish a
context that would be semantically appropriate:

> (39a)   Schlesinger admet que le président lui a parlé à
>   ce sujet.
>   'Schlesinger admits that the president spoke to
>   him about this matter.'
>
> (39b)   Schlesinger admet que le président lui ait parlé
>   à ce sujet.

A variation of the preceding exercise consists of a given situation.
For each situation, the student is to choose the appropriate
sentence:

> (40a)   A   reporter   for   the   Washington   Post   is
>   interviewing Schlesinger about the energy
>   crisis. The reporter is aware that the president
>   has spoken to him about it, but Schlesinger is
>   not aware of this.   During the course of the
>   interview, Schlesinger denies that he and the
>   president have spoken about the energy crisis,
>   but finally admits that this conversation has
>   taken place. Which sentence would the reporter
>   write in his notebook?
>
> (40b)   A   reporter   for   the   Washington   Post   is
>   interviewing Schlesinger about the energy
>   crisis.   After having denied several times any
>   conversation with the president, Schlesinger
>   finally informs the reporter that he and the
>   president have talked about this subject; but the
>   reporter is unaware that this conversation took
>   place. Which sentence would the reporter write
>   in his notebook?

In the first case, the reporter would write down: Schlesinger admet
que le président lui a parlé à ce sujet. The reporter is stating that
Schlesinger has finally admitted what he, the reporter, considers to
be the truth.   In the second case, the reporter would write:
Schlesinger admet que le président lui ait parlé à ce sujet. Here, the

reporter is simply reporting what happened but that he himself has no way to evaluate the validity of the confession. He is in no position to assert the truth value of the proposition. It, as in case one, (40a), Schlesinger were interviewed for hours in search of the specific information that the president had spoken to him, the use of a complement in the subjunctive, que le président lui ait parlé, would be totally inappropriate. Only the use of a complement in the indicative, que le président lui a parlé, can convey the reporter's awareness. Note also that the action of Schlesinger is in both cases exactly the same and that he may not be aware of what the reporter already knows or assumes to be the truth.

Another useful exercise would be to choose the appropriate answer to the question.

(41a)   Ne crois-tu pas qu'il fasse beau?
    (a)   Mais si, il fait beau.
    (b)   Oui, je suis d'accord avec toi.

(41b)   Ne crois-tu pas qu'il fait beau?
    (a)   Mais si, il fait beau.
    (b)   Oui, je suis d'accord avec toi.

In this exercise, the student must realize that questions (41a) and (41b) are not paraphrases. In question (41a), the speaker remains neutral, he does not indicate his feelings about the weather's being nice or bad. The student must also remember that NEG-raising has been applied to this question. Thus, an appropriate English gloss for this question would be: 'Is it true that your opinion happens to be that the weather is not nice?' An appropriate answer to this question would therefore be: Mais si, il fait beau 'Of course, the weather is nice.' The speaker may also answer: Mais non, il ne fait pas beau 'No, the weather is not nice.' The sentence: Oui, je suis d'accord avec toi 'Yes, I agree with you,' is a totally incongruous response to the question. In question (41b), the speaker is committed to the truth of the complement. He assumes that the weather is nice and asks if the hearer agrees. Thus, an assertion, il fait beau, is made. Consequently, Oui, je suis d'accord avec toi is the appropriate answer. Many native speakers feel that Je suis d'accord avec toi is too forceful a response to the type of question asked here. They would prefer to answer with Oui, tu as raison, 'Yes, you are right.' This response, although less strong, still indicates that the hearer is in agreement with the speaker about the assertion made in the complement.

We have seen that the choice of mood in the complement in French is not a syntactically based one determined by the matrix, but rather a semantic one based on whether or not the speaker wishes to assert the proposition of the complement. Traditionally, the use of mood has been approached syntactically in the form of co-occurrence type of exercises. Until now, the semantics of the proposition has not been taken into account.

The exercises proposed here can be used to drill not only the choice of mood with the limited group of matrix verbs such as croire, penser, imaginer, admettre, etc., as discussed earlier, but also the choice of mood in other syntactic constructions. The notion of assertion or nonassertion can be used to drill the choice of matrix and appropriate mood in the complement using such verbs and expressions as regretter, vouloir, il faut, étre sûr, savoir, etc. This notion can also be extended to drill the choice of mood after superlative adjectives or in relative clauses, as in Jean est le garçon le plus facile à plaire que je connais/connaisse, 'John is the easiest boy to please that I know,' or Je veux acheter une voiture qui peut/puisse économiser l'essence 'I want to buy a car that saves gas.'

The exercises examined here are consistent with the cognitive code model of language learning. The student's mental activity and cognitive structure are brought into play in performing these exercises.   They provide the student with the opportunity to integrate the knowledge that he has already acquired, in particular: (i) the forms of the indicative and the subjunctive, (ii) the semantic categories of the matrices, and (iii) the particular co-occurrence relationships. It should be further noted that these exercises more closely approximate the competence of the native speaker.

It is not my contention to replace the traditional exercises, for they are indeed needed to drill the forms of the subjunctive; rather, I suggest that they be supplemented by exercises that go beyond the objectives of the traditional methods of drilling the French subjunctive.

REFERENCES

Hooper, Joan B. 1973. On assertative predicates. UCLA papers in syntax 5.   Reprinted in Syntax and semantics, ed. J. P. Kimball. Vol. 4, 1975. New York: Academic Press.

Keenan, E. L.   1971.   Two kinds of presupposition in natural language. In Studies in linguistic semantics, ed. C. J. Fillmore and D. T. Langendoen, pp. 45-54. New York: Holt, Rinehart and Winston.

Kiparsky, Paul, and Kiparsky, C.   1970.   Fact.   In Progress in linguistics, ed. M. Bierwisch and K. Heidolph, pp. 143-73. The Hague: Mouton.   Also in Semantics: an interdisciplinary reader, ed. D. D. Steinberg, and L. A. Jakobovitz, pp. 345-69. 1971. New York: Cambridge University Press.

Prince, Ellen F. 1976. The syntax and semantics of NEG-raising, with evidence from French. Language 52:505-26.

26. Defining the Need for a Pedagogical Grammar: Relative Pronouns in French Textbooks

JEANNETTE LUDWIG
State University of New York at Buffalo

Since the heyday of structuralism and its influence on foreign-language teaching, linguists, psychologists, and classroom teachers have all demonstrated considerable interest in the form and content of pedagogical grammars and second-language syllabi. However, the advent of transformationalism rendered linguistics a much more abstract and theoretical, rather than empirical, undertaking. As a result, linguists were left with the problem of determining whether, if at all, this new construct could be used effectively in the creation of classroom materials. Though Chomsky expressed reservations on the question (1966A), he nevertheless distinguished between the grammar of the linguist, to be used <u>inter pares</u>, and that of the classroom, to be used by teachers and students:

> A grammar describes and attempts to account for the ability of the speaker to understand an arbitrary sentence of his language and to produce an appropriate sentence on a given occasion. If it is a pedagogic grammar, it attempts to provide the student with this ability; if a linguistic grammar, it aims to discover and exhibit the mechanisms that make this achievement possible. (1966b:10)

Thus, if the linguistic grammar tells the specialist what it is and how it works, the pedagogical grammar should be able to tell the student how to understand it and do it too.

The purpose of this discussion is to determine the extent to which contemporary theoretical and applied linguistic insights have found their way into foreign-language materials at the college level. The work outlines the central issues that have dominated recent linguistic thought on pedagogical grammars and analyzes the textbook presentation of relative pronouns in French at the college level. Limiting the scope of the study to a single concept in one of the many target languages taught in the United States today provides a mechanism for making specific, detailed observations about presentation and reinforcement techniques at several instructional levels. These findings can then serve as a basis from which more general statements, as well as suggestions for improvement, can be made.

Though teachers most often use a textbook as the syllabus or plan for a course, Noblitt (1972:316-17) appears to equate the pedagogical grammar with the syllabus, and separates the pedagogical grammar from the textbook:

A PG . . . must not only formulate a series of learning events in terms of specified objectives, it must further determine the contingencies for the most efficient ordering and presentation of these events. As such a PG is not a pedagogical text—it is rather the basis on which a text is constructed. (The underlying PG for a specific language course can only be retrieved by analyzing the total presentation: formal statements, examples, exercises, etc.) A PG is characterized by analyses which purport to integrate at every level the demands of descriptive accuracy and acquisition feasibility.

In a sense, then, the textbook is the concrete manifestation or token of which the pedagogical grammar is the type. Without further belaboring the issue of terminology, we will content ourselves with Allen's definition of the pedagogical grammar, which has simplicity and flexibility as its advantages:

A pedagogic grammar consists of a selection of material drawn from one or more scientific grammars and presented according to principles which are entirely pragmatic and which have nothing to do with the axioms of linguistics. (1974:70)

This definition reflects the contemporary shift toward eclectic selection of linguistic analyses and leaves to the psychologist and the classroom teacher the problems of refining understanding of the principles of learning, including the effects of various presentational or reinforcement schemes.

Though methodological concerns dominated the literature in the 1960s, the issue of the content of the pedagogical grammar has received the most attention recently, particularly in Europe (Currie 1975).   The goal of foreign-language instruction is now generally recognized to be communicative competence; that is, the ability to send and receive messages in the target language that are not only referentially accurate, but also appropriate to specific social or interpersonal situations.   Candlin (1972) described the theoretical background for the development of situation-based pedagogical grammars, while Wilkins (1972) has sparked the greatest interest to date, primarily because his notional grammar takes the interactional needs of the learner into account.

Clearly, the grading or hierarchizing of material should strike a balance between communication priorities on the one hand and intrinsic linguistic or learning difficulty on the other. In this context, Corder used the term <u>surrender value</u> to characterize the student's concept of the importance or meaningfulness of the items in a syllabus. Items of high surrender value are "those speech functions . . . which are most useful to the learner, most central to his needs" (Corder 1973:318). Alert to the practical matter of motivation, Corder observed that "most learners are not going to tolerate doing a lot of work which has only a pay-off after a considerable amount of time" (1973:318).

The concepts just outlined constitute the theorectical aspects of the second-language learning branch of applied linguistics. To determine the extent to which these considerations have been incorporated in contemporary foreign-language materials in the United States, a study was undertaken of recent college-level texts in French. The relative pronoun construction was selected for the purposes of the study for several reasons. First, relatives are well defined in the transformational literature as examples of the principles of embedding, one of the most significant contributions of the Chomsky approach. Second, the acceptable use of relatives in both French and English necessitates an understanding in real language use. Third, the rules for the relative transformation in French involve no new concepts for the English-speaking learner; the process is distinct on formal ground alone.

Though other, more complex and exhaustive analyses of relativization are available (see Chomsky 1965; Reibel and Schane 1969), a simplified restatement of the general principles, adapted from Dubois-Charlier and Leeman (1975:288-93) and Jacobs and Rosenbaum (1968:199-204), will suffice for the present purposes.

Starting from a deep structure of a noun phrase modified by a sentence (Figure A), the following rules apply:

1.   Identification of the redundant element through attachment of the cover symbol WH- (QU- in French) to that element in the embedded sentence (Figure B).

2.   Fronting of the WH- element to the initial position in the embedded sentence (Figure C).

3.   Replacement of the WH- segment by the relative pronoun appropriate to the role of that segment in the deep structure (Figure D).

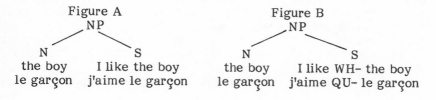

Figure A
NP

N   S
the boy   I like the boy
le garçon   j'aime le garçon

Figure B
NP

N   S
the boy   I like WH- the boy
le garçon   j'aime QU- le garçon

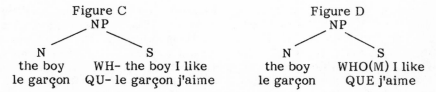

Figure C

NP

N — the boy / le garçon

S — WH– the boy I like / QU– le garçon j'aime

Figure D

NP

N — the boy / le garçon

S — WHO(M) I like / QUE j'aime

As stated earlier, the pedagogical grammar should be able to tell the student how to understand it and do it too. Viewed in this light, the transformational approach to relatives has several pedagogical advantages. Presenting the two sentences—the matrix and the sentence to be embedded—side by side helps the student see that the relative clause is an <u>expansion</u> or <u>modification</u> of a noun in the main sentence. Here too it can be pointed out that relativization is a much more powerful and informative procedure than use of adjectives alone. Because it helps raise the surrender value or importance of the process in the student's eyes, this knowledge is vital if he is to feel the need to use relatives in his own productions. After the redundant item in the second sentence has been identified, and its role in the sentence defined, fronting can then be illustrated. The ultimate step of selecting the appropriate relative to replace the redundant item can then be seen as a process of labeling the item in terms of its function—i.e., <u>qui</u> for subjects, <u>que</u> for objects, <u>dont</u> for objects of a preposition. Stated another way, this sequence serves the dual purpose of a pedagogical grammar, first because it tells the student how to understand it by showing that the relative replaces something (which determines its form) and that it modifies something (which determines its function). Second, it tells the student how to do it too by providing him with a systematic inventory of procedures for arriving at the relative pronoun appropriate to any given set of sentences.

My study of twenty-eight contemporary college texts in French (see the appendix for exact titles) reveals that the explanations for relative formation and use have incorporated few, if any, of the insights that transformational, communication- or situation-based grammars have to offer. The function of relatives and their value in communication is seldom explained, making relatives appear optional or unimportant to students. That relatives serve to link, join, or connect two sentences was overtly mentioned in only three of the ten first-year texts, five of the ten second-year texts, and in one of the eight third-year texts. Moreover, none of the first-year books stated why linking two sentences is desirable. The second- and third-year students hardly fare better, since only one of the ten texts and two of the eight texts, respectively, mention modification, definition, or expansion as functions of relative clauses. Students are forced to accept, with no real rationale or motivation, the fact that sentences can be joined grammatically.

At the level of form, the situation is not much improved. Most texts present relatives by using surface-structure descriptions and examples with the relative already in place in the sentence. Such presentations fail to capture all the information relevant to the process and tell the student nothing about the how or why of getting to an acceptable relative-clause construction themselves. Only four of the ten first-year texts mentioned that the relative pronoun replaces something in the original embedded sentence. The replacement concept is introduced directly in only one of the ten second-year texts and in only one of the eight third-year texts. Fortunately, six of the ten first-year books do show the main sentence and the embedded sentence separately before presenting the relativized equivalent. Examples such as "Le garçon mange du chocolat. J'aime le garçon → Le garçon que j'aime mange du chocolat' are virtually absent from texts at the more advanced levels. Of the second-year texts studied, eight of the ten and all of the third-year texts give relativized sentences alone, choosing instead to <u>describe</u> rather than <u>show</u> how embedding works. Thus, the examples do not serve as conceptual models for the subsequent exercises that require students to link two separate sentences.

If students complain that their language texts are too hard to understand, it is often with good reason. In the present study, the texts using the word <u>antecedent</u> in their description of relativization seldom defined that term. More frequently, the antecedent is put into relief through graphics or by statements such as "In this sentence, XXX is the antecedent." Of the six first-year texts using the word, only four regularly described it or pointed it out in sample sentences. Of the nine second-year texts using the term, only four defined or explained what the antecedent is. All of the eight texts at the third-year level included the word, but only three described its use. Regardless of the linguistic description used as a source for teaching materials, no one has yet proposed that terminology be introduced but not explained. Careless or inadequate descriptions place an extra, unnecessary step between learners and the information they need.

In addition to the general observations made thus far, the relative <u>dont</u> in French deserves closer scrutiny, since it entails an imposing learning problem for students. In French <u>dont</u> functions both as a replacement for prepositional phrases with <u>de</u> and for possessives, as is (1) and (2):

(1)   Le garçon (j'ai parlé du garçon) mange du chocolat.
        Le garçon <u>dont</u> j'ai parlé mange du chocolat.

(2)   Le garçon (nous avons réparé sa voiture) est pauvre.
        Le garçon <u>dont</u> nous avons réparé la voiture est pauvre.

In both cases, the process of fronting and conversion of the redundant element is the same. On the other hand, in English sentences indicating possession, fronting involves the entire possessive noun phrase, as in (3):

(3)   The boy (we fixed his car) is poor.
        The boy <u>whose car</u> we fixed is poor.

As a result, the possessive relative in English exhibits both a change in normal subject-verb-object word order and the elimination of the determiner for the noun in the embedded sentence.

Students who consistently identify items and procedures in French with those in English will need extra help in avoiding erroneous productions such as (4), which involves word order, or (5), which involves the determiner in the embedded sentence:

(4)   *Nous connaissons le garçon dont voiture nous avons réparé.

(5)   *Nous connaissons le garçon dont nous avons réparé sa voiture.

The difficulty of possessive <u>dont</u> is apparent from the results of a translation passage that included the phrase "a family whose son was living in New York." Only two of twenty first-year students tested produced "dont le fils habitait a new York," compared to eight of twenty at the second-year level, and four of twenty at the third-year level. In this sample, the most common means of translating <u>whose</u> was the erroneous use of <u>qui</u>, represented nine times in both the first- and second-year levels, and four times in the third year. In their attempts to use <u>dont,</u> five beginning students and one second-year student produced *<u>dont fils</u>, a direct though inappropriate translation of <u>whose son,</u> paralleling (4) above. Two third-year students gave *<u>dont son fils</u>, which shows a surfeit of determiners and parallels (5) above.

Despite the contrastive difficulty of possessive <u>dont,</u> borne out in this case by empirical data, the textbooks in this study devoted most of their attention to adjective and verb phrases that take <u>de</u>, such as <u>être content de</u>, <u>être fier de</u>, <u>parler de</u>, and <u>avoir besoin de</u>, particularly at the beginning levels. Though all of the ten first-year texts included at least one example of <u>dont</u> indicating possession, only three of them pointed out its significance, formation, or word order peculiarities for the English-speaking student. At the second-year level, all but one of the ten texts either treated the word order and article usage for the possessive <u>dont</u> or provided the English equivalent <u>whose</u> in their explanations. At the third-year level, five of the eight texts mentioned the significance, word order, article usage, or English equivalent in their presentation of possessive <u>dont</u>.

These findings bring up the important issue of the frequency and the difficulty of an item chosen for inclusion in a set of language-teaching materials or textbook. If an item is more difficult and less frequent than another, as is the case for dont and lequel in French, it will be correspondingly harder for the learner to use it correctly himself. On the other hand, simple and relatively frequent items such as qui and que can be acquired without concentrated effort on the student's part, and may well be extended inappropriately for use in other contexts. In spite of these common sense observations, in none of the texts surveyed did dont or lequel individually occupy significantly more explanatory space than qui or que, which were the first relatives presented, nor did the kind and number of exercise differ radically.

If a concept is to be understood and used acceptably, especially a complex or contrastively difficult item like relatives, the material should be reintroduced at several points in the course of study. In his discussion of the need for review in the foreign-language syllabus, Howatt (1974:18) concluded that "the lack of opportunity for constant revision is the most glaring defect in foreign language courses." Apart from the few texts at the first-year level containing brief review chapters, none of the relatives are overtly discussed a second time in any of the materials surveyed. As any classroom teacher can tell, one "dose" or "injection" is not sufficient to anchor any concept in the learner's mind.

Another means of reminding students of the concepts they have already encountered is to break the item down into discrete and manageable bits, each of which is introduced at a different point in the learning sequence. Most of the first-year texts used this spiral syllabus approach to introduce the relatives: seven of the ten texts separate the presentation of qui and que from the rest of the relatives, and three of these seven present the concept in the first half of the text. In contrast, only one text out of ten at the second-year level and one out of the eight at the third-year level presented qui and que separately from the remaining relatives. Thus, over the course of a hypothetical three years of study, a student would be called upon to deal with relativization actively at only three or possibly four points in his coursework. That students do not feel comfortable using relatives is no surprise, given the limited number of opportunities they have to focus on the issue directly.

Finally, consideration must be given to the question of grading materials to suit the specific needs of learners at different levels. Noblitt (1972:322-23) and Allen (1974:72-73) both cited the necessity for developing sequences that are tailored to the purposes and capacities of intermediate and advanced learners. Though the textbook is only one component of any course, it does nevertheless play a very important role in shaping how and what the students learn. This study indicates that third-year students literally repeat the entirety of their second-year course, with perhaps more reading included in the package. With only one or two exceptions, the explanations, examples, and exercises that appeared in advanced texts differ very little from those of their second-year counterparts. It is the exceptional textbook that encourages flexibility of expression and develops a more refined insight into the processes of the target language, by using a "recombinant" or conceptual approach. This type of text includes relativization in a discussion of the various means of linking two sentences, or places it with modification procedures such as adjectives and apposition.

Taken as a whole, the present findings indicate a considerable gap between theoretical and applied linguistics on the one hand and second-language pedagogy on the other. In a sense, the theory of applied linguistics has not yet been applied. That textbooks are often inadequate is not new information; indeed, teachers and students have complained about them for years. This study goes a bit further by pinpointing specific areas where improvement can be made. For example, though relativization is one of the processes best defined and understood using the transformational approach, the concept is still presented in terms of surface structures, much the same as it was fifty years ago. The eclecticism that most applied linguists have called for has yet to materialize. Moreover, the terminology used to describe its form is often lacking in definition or meaning for students. This only frustrates their efforts to comprehend and use the construction.

Setting aside the questions of linguistic description per se, recent work in applied linguistics emphasizes communicative value in selecting and presenting grammatical items. Nonetheless, the present study of relatives in French indicates that the function of a grammatical structure is rarely made clear in teaching materials. Omissions of this sort limit the students' perception of the usefulness of the item, thereby reducing the chances that they will use it in their work.

Psychological issues involving learning theory are also overlooked in many textbooks today. Repetition, review, and recombination are generally assumed to assist the learning process, yet none of the texts examined took concrete measures to ensure that relatives would truly become a part of the learners' active repertoire in French. Teaching sequences did not provide opportunities for intensive work on the contrastively more difficult aspects of the process, and hardly any of the texts afforded a chance for systematic or active review. In the same vein, applied linquists have begun to urge that materials be graded to fit the needs of learners at the beginning, intermediate, and advanced levels of study. The "facts" about a language may be constants, but the significance of those facts and their relation to other processes in the language change as the learner gains experience. Unfortunately, current materials have not yet made substantial progress in this regrd, as this study shows.

The purpose of this work is not to criticize specific texts, but rather to evaluate the internal structure of foreign-language texts in general. Indeed, that students can and do use their foreign languages successfully is a testimony to their linguistic insight, aided in large measure by their teachers ad the textbooks they employ. The fundamental question is not then whether we do the job of teaching foreign languages, but how well we do it. The findings of this study define more clearly the areas we will have to attend to with greater rigor before we reach an ideal pedagogical grammar, one which may in turn be passed on to our students in the concrete form of an effective, stimulating textbook.

REFERENCES

Allen, J. P. B. 1974. Pedagogic grammar. The Edinburgh course in applied linguistics. In Techniques in applied linguistics, ed J. P. B. Allen and S. Pit Corder, pp. 59–92. Vol. 3. London: Oxford Univ. Press.

Candlin, Christopher N. 1972. The status of pedagogical grammars. In Theoretical linguistic models in applied linguistics: 3rd AIMAV seminar; ed. S. Pit Corder and E. Roulet, pp. 55–64. Brussels: AIMAV; Paris: Didier.

Chomsky, Noam. 1966A. Linguistic theory. In Language teaching: broader contexts, ed. Robert C. Mead, Jr., pp. 43–49. Washington, D.C.: Northeast Conference on the Teaching of Foreign Languages.

_____. 1966B. Topics in the theory of generative grammar. The Hague: Mouton.

Corder, S. Pit. 1973. Introducing applied linguistics. Harmondsworth, Middlesex: Penguin.

Currie, William. 1975. European syllabuses in English as a foreign language. Language Learning 25:339–54.

Dubois-Charlier, Francoise, and Leeman, Danielle. 1975. Comment s'initier a la linguistique? Paris: Larousse.

Howatt, Anthony. 1974. The background to course design. The Edinburgh course in applied linguistics. In Techniques in applied linguistics, ed. J. P. B. Allen and S. Pit Corder, pp. 1–23, Vol. 3. London: Oxford University Press.

Jacobs, Roderick A., and Rosenbaum, Peter S. 1968. English transformational grammar. Waltham, Mass.: Blaisdell.

Noblitt, James S. 1972. Pedagogical grammar: towards a theory of foreign language materials preparation. IRAL 10:313–31.

Reibel, David, and Schane, Sanford eds. 1969. Modern studies in English: readings in transformational grammar. Englewood Cliffs, N.J.: Prentice-Hall.

Wilkins, D. A. 1972. The linguistic and situational content of the common core in a unit credit system. Strasbourg: Council of Europe.

Valette, Jean-Paul, and Valette, Rebecca. 1976. Contacts: langue et culture francaises. Boston: Houghton Mifflin.

APPENDIX

First-year texts

Dietiker, Simone Renaud. 1976. Franc-parler. Lexington, Mass.:
D. C. Heath.

Hagiwara, Michio P., and de Rocher, Françoise. 1977. Thème et
variation: a practical introduction to French. New York:
John Wiley and Sons.

Hansen, Terrence L.; Wilkens, Ernest J.; and Enos, Jon G. 1978. Le
français vivant. 2d ed., rev. Julian Kaplow. New York: John
Wiley and Sons.

Harris, Julian, and Lévêque, André. 1973. Basic conversational
French. 5th ed. New York: Holt, Rinehart and Winston.

Jarvis, Gilbert A.; Bonin, Thérèse M.; Corbin, Donald E.; and
Birckbichler, Diane. 1979. Invitation: French for
communication and cultural awareness. New York: Holt,
Rinehart and Winston.

Jian, Gerard, and Hester, Ralph. 1977. Découverte et création:
Les bases du français moderne. 2d ed. Chicago: Rand
McNally.

Lenard, Yvonne. 1977. Parole et pensée: introduction au français
d'aujourd'hui. 3 ed. New York: Harper and Row.

Mondelli, Rudolph, and Francois, Pierre. 1978. Conversational
French one. 3d ed. New York: D Van Nostrand.

Noblitt, James S. 1978. Nouveau point de vue. Lexington, Mass.:
D. C. Heath.

Valette, Jean-Paul, and Valette, Rebecca. 1976. Contacts: langue
et culture françaises. Boston: Houghton Mifflin.

Second-year texts

Balas, Robert, and Rice, Donald. 1979. Qu'est-ce qui se passe?
Conversation/révision de grammaire. Chicago: Rand McNally.

Barson, John. 1975. La grammaire à l'oeuvre. 2d ed. New York:
Holt, Rinehart and Winston.

Bragger, Jeannette D., and Shupp, Robert P. 1978. Chère
Francoise. Révision de grammaire française. Chicago: Rand
McNally.

Brown, Thomas H. 1974. Langue et littérature. A second course in
French. 2d ed. New York: McGraw-Hill.

Carlut, Charles, and Meiden, Walter. 1976. French for oral and
written review. 2d ed. New York: Holt, Rinehart and
Winston.

Comeau, Raymond F.; Bustin, Francine L.; and Lamoureux, Normand
J. 1977. Ensemble: Grammaire. An integrated approach to
French. New York: Holt, Rinehart and Winston.

Dietiker, Simone Renaud. 1978. Enbonne forme. Révision de
grammaire française. 2d ed. Lexington, Mass.: D. C. Heath.

Max, Stephan. 1979. Dialogues et situations. A program for intermediate French conversation, composition, and grammar review. 2d ed. Lexington, Mass.: D. C. Heath.

Mondelli, Rudolph, and Francois, Pierre. 1972. French conversational review grammar. 3d ed. New York: D. Van Nostrand.

Ollivier, Jacqueline. 1978. Grammaire française. New York: Harcourt Brace Jovanovich.

Third-year texts

Barrette, Paul, and Fol, Monique. 1969. Un certain style ou un style certain? Introduction à l'étude du style français. London: Oxford University Press.

Benamou, Michel, and Carduner, Jean. 1971. Le moulin à paroles. Conversation et composition au niveau avancé. 2d ed. New York: John Wiley and Sons.

Breunig, L. C.; Mesnard, Andre; Carlson, Helen M.; and Geen, Renee. 1964. Forme et fond. Textes littéraires pour l'étude de la langue francaise. New York: Macmillan.

Darbelnet, J. L. 1977. Pensée et structure. 2d ed. New York: Charles Scribner's Sons.

Daudon, Rene. 1962. French in review. 2d ed. New York: Harcourt Brace Jovanovich.

Guillou, Jean, and Vitols, Madeleine. 1972. Le français contemporain. New York: Holt, Rinehart and Winston.

Hoffman, Leon-François. 1973. L'essentiel de la grammaire française. 2d ed. New York: Charles Scribner's Sons.

Limouzy, Pierre, and Bourgeacq, Jacques. 1970. Manuel de composition française. New York: Random House.

27. The Notional Functional Syllabus in Adult ESL: Promises and Problems

JO ANN CRANDALL and ALLENE GUSS GROGNET
Center for Applied Linguistics

In former times, languages were studied for their own sake, for the discipline that grammar and translation exercises could provide, as well as for access to other literatures. With the advent of World War II, however, the need arose for more than a reading and writing proficiency. The audiolingual method was developed to emphasize listening and speaking skills, and greater attention was paid to oral proficiency. More recently, with increasing numbers of immigrants and refugees enrolled in adult ESL classes, the need has grown for concentrating more on oral proficiency and for making language teaching more functional.

Structural syllabuses, like those used in most language programs, focus on the language taught, without much analysis of what students need or want to learn of the language or what they want to be able to do with the language after studying it. Situational syllabuses, where the organization of the language material to be taught is by situation, is a step toward more consideration for what students need to do with the language, since each lesson presents a context (for example, going shopping or opening a checking account) and teaches relevant vocabulary and structure within that situational frame. Sociolinguists and ethnographers like Hymes, Paulston, and others emphasize the need for students to acquire more than grammatical competence (where students demonstrate mastery of the structures of the language); they also need communicative competence (to learn to use the language and function competently with it).

A natural outgrowth of the trend to more functional language teaching is the development of the notional/functional syllabus (Wilkins 1976; van Ek 1976). This syllabus organizes the language material by what people do with language, such as give information, request clarification, greet or refuse—i.e. the functions—and by what concepts they express with the language, such as time, quantity, space—i.e., the notions. The notional/functional syllabus reflects the insights of speech-act theorists like Austin (How to Do Things with Words) and Searle (Speech Acts), who pointed out that language is used to do things. The syllabus also reflects the findings of psycholinguists like Gardner and Lambert (Attitudes and Motivation in Second Language Learning) that people (especially adults) can be motivated to acquire a language for what they can do with it (instrumental motivation) as well as for acculturating to the other group (integrative motivation).

Adult-learning theorists have stressed the importance of making adult instruction learner-centered—that is, treating the adult as someone with a complex set of responsibilities, needs, and goals involving various social, political, economic, or religious roles. A functional syllabus can direct the language learning to those needs and roles helping an adult, for example, to acquire a second language to be able to function in a job in that language.

Discourse analysis has also provided insights into the ways language is used and the various functions it plays in our lives. By studying the way both oral and written discourse is structured and by actually recording samples of utterances or texts, discourse analysts (including conversational analysts) have provided some insights into what language the classroom should be teaching. Too many texts in the past taught language in isolation, requiring students to practice grammatical drills that seemed removed from the real world and whose function or usefulness was not immediately obvious. Classroom discourse was too often a discourse style of its own and phrases like "they study accounting" or "he doesn't always wear yellow shirts" would form the basis of classroom practice in structural approaches; these could be more relevant and functional if they were clearly related to a context and were functional. For example, "I'm studying welding" or "He's going to have trouble" or "He doesn't always wear his safety goggles" might be more appropriate for a welder learning English. The early focus was on language as a "thing" (or "artifact" in Di Pietro's terms) rather than on the ways people use the language—i.e., on language as a functional "tool." For linguists, the early emphasis on language form and structure was to be expected, but for language teachers, who are increasingly aware of adult needs, adult reasons for wanting to learn a second language, and adult discourse, the shift in emphasis is from language form to language functions.

People have hundreds of ways that they use the language (functions) and numerous ideas (notions) that they need to express. There have been attempts to categorize broadly these functions and notions by Halliday (1973), Hymes (1972), and most recently, Wilkins in his <u>Notional Syllabuses</u> (1976). Wilkins identifies at least six categories of functions:

> imparting and seeking factual information
> expressing and finding out intellectual attitudes
> expressing and finding out emotional attitudes
> expressing and finding out moral attitudes
> getting things done (suasion)
> socializing

These six represent "what people do by means of language." They are, of course, broken down into numerous subcategories to include such functions as offering help, giving clarification, greeting, etc.

These functions and the notions (such as time, space, or quantity) form the basis of a syllabus for language teaching, with the earliest version being the Threshold Level of the Council of Europe. Wilkins (1976) and van Ek, in the Council of Europe materials (1976), attempt to identify the language functions and notions that an adult would need to be able to participate at a basic level in a range of social situations necessary for everyday interaction if one were visiting a Common Market country. Most of these functions or notions would not surprise anyone, but they are important for the language teacher because they enable teachers to structure their classes around what the adults need to be able to do with the language and to allow learners to focus on the uses of the language that they believe are most important.

For adults studying ESL in the United States, English is needed because adults want to get a job or get into a vocational training program; they want to be able to communicate something through it. As Wilkins puts it, "Languages are not learned for their own sakes but because they enable the learner to communicate something to others or to comprehend what others themselves wish to communicate."

A lesson based on the notional/functional syllabus can take a variety of forms, but it will set out some function such as "requesting clarification" or "offering advice" and then provide linguistic and situational clues for practice using these appropriately in a variety of situations. One of the major strengths of a notional/functional lesson is that it provides a variety of contexts that require different registers; it also provides a series of options from which we choose, both in initiating that function and in responding to it.

For example, in a lesson requesting clarification, which is part of a Clerical (Vocational ESL) Lesson that has been developed at the Center for Applied Linguistics, the following options are provided as acceptable requests for clarifying how many copies of a report are needed:

> Was that 5 copies?
> Did you say 5 copies?
> That was 5 copies, wasn't it?
> Five copies? (with rising intonation)
> I'm sorry, but I didn't get that. How many was that?

The notional/functionl approach recognizes that several different syntactic structures can fill one function (though they may be used under different circumstances). For example, in asking to look at a copy of someone else's book, a child might simply grab it and say "Give me that!" An adult is more likely to say, "Could I see that when you're done with it?"

The notional/functional approach also takes notice of the fact that we can use the same sentence in a variety of ways. If I say, "I'm terribly tired," I could be offering an excuse for not attending a party, an apology for why I am being so difficult to deal with today, or a request for help in some work.

With a notional/functional syllabus, language instruction can also be tailored to meet the specific needs of learners, especially of adults. It is wasteful to require uneducated Vietnamese refugees to study a global English course entailing several years of hard work when their basic need is to acquire enough English to get an entry-level job as an electronics assembler or an auto mechanic. It is equally inefficient to require adults who merely want to study the language for travel purposes or who look at the language class as a social occasion to use a standard (global) ESL text. Scientists or technicians who want access to texts and lectures in English should not be made to sit through an English class that requires them to read American literature or to practice going grocery shopping in English. A competency-based adult education program needs an ESL course that shows an understanding of the Adult Performance Level and that is competency-based and functional. A Spanish-speaking adult in a bilingual vocational program needs an ESL class that recognizes his vocational training. Since the notional/functional syllabus begins by identifying the ways in which people want to use the language, it provides an appropriate framework for creating relevant, efficient language programs. In these programs, adults will still need to master the sound system and structures of English, but they will be presented in a more functional program.

The promise of the notional/functional approach is both exciting and challenging. Although there are a number of texts in the formative and experimental stage, no series exists that has been tested and used long enough to be proven successful. In our experience in developing notional/functional job-related (Vocational ESL) materials for Indo-Chinese programs across the country, we have encountered a number of difficulties or challenges that need to be addressed before the promise of the new approach can become reality.

What Is the Place of Grammar?

The first problem is to determine the place of grammar within the notional/functional lessons. To date, the following approaches have been tried:

1. Assume a mastery of a certain number of structures (perhaps through the conditional) and then after that, use the functional approach. This involves using a more structural approach in the early ESL classes.

2. Present the functions with attention to

grammatical sequencing, limiting the early lessons to basic structures and then returning to these functions later, when students have more command of English. During these later lessons, introduce more difficult structures for these same functions (spiralling).

3.   Divide the course so that one text (and one class hour) is structural or audiolingual and emphasizes grammar, while the other text (and class hour) is functional.

4.   Provide a functional component within a basically structured or sequenced course.

5.   Instruct the teacher to stop and teach the grammatical structures if the students have trouble with them, and perhaps provide a separate teacher's manual or text that provides grammatical explanations and drills for the teacher to use.

6.   Ignore the question of grammar, assuming that people will sort this out from the intake and thus focus on acquisition as more important than learning.

How Do You Sequence Functions?

Linguists and language teachers think they know how to sequence language structures. In comparing six or seven ESL series, one will find general agreement about the sequencing, whether it is theoretically or pedagogically correct. However, it is not easy to sequence functions. Should "offering to help" be taught before or after "responding to criticism"? It is possible to let intuition be the guide as to what is most important, frequent, or of earliest necessity. However, it would be far more useful to students to find out what they want to do with the language and then base the lessons on that. To do so, however, requires an ethnography of communication, a study of native speakers using the language in the same contexts or situations that the learners are interested in.

For example, if the needs of an employee include being able to make small talk with co-workers and the boss on the job so that they can get along with other employees, it is possible to incorporate small talk in early lessons. The inability to talk about the weather, the ball game, the weekend, or the family, in very short conversational chunks (primarily for "phatic communion" or to "keep company") has been a problem for many of the Indo-Chinese. This problem can be interpreted too easily as standoffishness or it can be concluded that the Indo-Chinese don't fit in." The ESL teacher can prevent the problem by providing conversational practice in making small talk. For example:

> Joe: Hi, Vinh. How was your weekend?
> Vinh: Not so good. The rain . . .
> Joe: Yeah, I know. Maybe it'll be better next weekend.

or

> Vinh: The traffic was terrible this morning.
> Joe: I got caught in it, too.
> Vinh: I guess that's a problem all over.

or

> Sally: Isn't the weather lousy?
> Vinh: It sure is. I can't wait for summer.

For job–related language instruction, a task analysis can be done to find out what function language plays (either in receptive or productive skills) in completing a job task. Some of the analysis can be of textbooks or manuals, but it is also important to interview supervisors and vocational instructors, to talk to employees, and actually to verify this information by recording language use on the job. The sequencing, then, is by tasks: these are organized around the various skills that are taught in the vocational program. For more general notional/functional texts, however, the problem of sequencing is much greater.

What Do You Do with Mixed Levels?

We have found that the notional/functional approach is one of the best ways of dealing with mixed levels, since it groups students by what they need to do with the language rather than by mastery of structures. It is difficult to put an advanced student in a beginning level course if the course is grammatically sequenced. However, with common goals with beginners or intermediates since they all need to acquire certain communicative skills. In fact, the advanced learner can serve as a peer teacher for those who still need to master certain structures and join the rest of the students in mastering the functions being studied.

How Do You Test?

Morrow has shown some samples of ways of testing how well someone has mastered a function by setting up situations and asking for a response or by giving a passage and then asking students where it might be said, with whom, under what conditions, and about what topic. If the language function was a written one, it must be tested in writing, and if it was a spoken one, it has to be tested orally. If students have been taught to request a raise in writing, they must be tested in writing as well.

As Morrow (1977) puts it, in the notional/functional approach, the materials are the tests and the tests are the materials. If a student is given a task to do, like requesting help in finding a person or a place, then the only test for mastery of that function is whether they succeed in actually finding that person or place. A functional approach must involve functional tests.

What Is the Role of the First Language?

With the notional/functional approach, the role of the first language becomes more important than with other methodologies. Since this approach focuses on semantic and sociolinguistic considerations, it is often useful to explain or discuss the notion, the meaning, or the functions in the first language if it is possible (if the teacher speaks the student's first language or a bilingual aide is available). The problem is to know when to use the first language and how much of the first language to use in any given class session.

Although there are a few problems with the notional /functional approach, we still believe in its promise. Given the number of non- and limited-English-speaking adults currently in the United States and the number that will be arriving (168,000 Indochinese a year alone), the notional/functional approach gives promise of really providing adults with the linguistic and, to some extent, the cultural coping skills they need to become a part of American life. For us as professionals in the field of language teaching and learning, the challenge in the coming years will be to convert a rational, student-centered syllabus into working texts.

REFERENCES

Austin, J. L. 1962. How to do things with words. London: Oxford University Press.
Crandall, J. A. 1979a. Adult vocational ESL. No. 22 of Language in Education Series. Arlington, Va.: Center for Applied Linguistics.
_____. 1979b. Adapting and creating vocational ESL materials. MS.
_____. 1979c. Practical and theoretical concerns in adult vocational ESL: the characteristics of successful vocational ESL programs. Paper read at 1st Invitational Workshop on ESL and Bilingual Approaches to Academic and Vocational Programs for Adults, Brownsville, Texas.
Fishman, J. 1968. Readings in the sociology of language. The Hague: Mouton.
_____. 1972. Domains and the relationship between micro- and macro-sociolinguistics. In Direction in sociolinguistics: the

ethnography of communication, ed. J. J. Gumperz and D. Hymes. New York: Holt, Rinehart and Winston.

Gardner, R. C., and Lambert, W. E. 1972. Attitudes and motivation in second language learning. Rowley, Mass.: Newbury House.

Gingras, R. C., ed. 1978. Second language acquisition and foreign language teaching. Arlington, Va.: Center for Applied Linguistics.

Grognet, A., and Crandall, J. A. 1978. ESL: vocational/manpower English workshop. Paper read at annual meeting of TESOL, Mexico City.

Halliday, M. A. K. 1973. Explorations in the functions of language. London: Arnold.

Hymes, D. 1962. The ethnography of speaking. In Readings in the sociology of language, ed. J. Fishman. The Hague: Mouton.

_____. 1972. Models of the interaction of language and social life. In Directions in sociolinguistics, ed. J. J. Gumperz and D. Hymes. New York: Holt, Rinehart and Winston.

Knowles, M. 1977. Techniques of evaluation for a notional syllabus. Reading, England: Centre for Language Studies.

Munby, J. 1978. Communicative syllabus design. Cambridge: At the University Press.

Searle, J. 1969. Speech acts. Cambridge: At the University Press.

van Elk, J. 1975. Systems development in adult language learning: the threshold level. Strasbourg: Council of Europe.

_____. 1976. The threshold level for modern language learning in schools. London: Longman.

Widdowson, H. G. 1978. Teaching language as communication. Oxford: At the University Press.

Wilkins, D. A. 1976. Notional syllabus. London: Oxford University Press.

28. Accuracy vs. Fluency Revisited for the Advanced ESL Composition Class

LOUIS A. ARENA
University of Delaware

By tradition, as well as by most scientific criteria of expectation, the English-as-a-second-language (ESL) teacher is primarily a teacher of language usage. Although most ESL teachers are better prepared by their training and experience to teach the listening, speaking, and reading skills, colleagues from all departments will expect the ESL teacher ultimately to teach students how to write. Further, in very few cases does this mean that the ESL instructor must teach his or her students only expository writing. In most cases, the ESL teacher is expected to teach not only expository but also descriptive, narrative, and/or technical writing. In addition, ESL instructors must also be prepared to teach courses in persuasive writing, writing themes about literature, and even more currently, writing themes about the film.

Although the ESL student will be emphasized primarily in this discussion, I include the native American with the foreign student in these beginning comments because both seem to be experiencing unprecedented difficulties in college-level writing courses. This inclusion has a direct relation to the purpose of this paper, however, which is to propose that some of the reasons that American students cannot write in their native language are not really different from the reasons that foreign students cannot write English as their second language. Based on experience at the University of Delaware, I agree with Zamel's observations (1976) that the ESL student who is ready to compose and convey his ideas, thoughts, and emotions on paper is not essentially different from the native American English-speaking student in the regular English composition class. I think that the time has come for us to reevaluate some of the established sets of principles for teaching composition to both kinds of students and for all kinds of writing. One such principle is the traditional premise that accuracy in foreign-language study should come before fluency. In writing courses, this means that the student should write accurately at the sentence level prior to writing fluently at the paragraph and discourse levels.

I propose that this long-followed, valid, and reliable principle for teaching spoken English may not be conducive to creating an atmosphere within which the ESL (or native) students, can fully and spontaneously convey all of their thoughts on paper. Indeed, I

316

maintain that only by fostering fluency along with and even ahead of accuracy in composition courses can the ESL student develop linguistic self-confidence and lose his linguistic self-consciousness. However, this does not mean that compositions should be accepted with numerous mechanical inaccuracies; but fostering fluency prior to accuracy, however, does encourage the ESL student to focus on the meaning of what he wants to write about, not how he must write it, and creates an atmosphere where the student can express in writing all of his ideas on the topic. Once all of a student's ideas are on paper, the job of clearing up inaccuracies still remains to be accomplished—by whatever materials and means the ESL instructor desires. In fostering fluency first, however, both the teacher and the student benefit. On the part of the ESL instructor, there is more written material to observe. The ESL student may gain some much-needed confidence by being able to at least get most of his ideas and meanings down on paper without the linguistic constraints that are often generated by an error-oriented classroom atmosphere.

A brief look at the literature on teaching ESL composition verifies that it is almost totally accuracy and error-oriented in nature. Since 1950, most ESL methodologists maintain that composition is the last of the skills that one masters when learning English as a second language. Writing to inform a reader is the culmination of the other language skills and is therefore dependent upon the previous mastery of the other three language skills. Fries (1964), Lado (1964), Mackey (1967), DeCanay (1967), Finocchiaro (1974), and Rivers (1968), among many other methodologists, all agree that the usual order of learning the four skills is listening, speaking, reading, and writing.

To be sure, I do not argue the validity of the principles of these methodologists for teaching spoken English. Indeed, I maintain that only after the skills of listening, speaking, and reading have been fully mastered, in that order and to that degree, should an ESL student be evaluated beside an American student when learning how to write. Almost all of the literature dealing with teaching ESL composition clearly maintains that in order to learn to write ESL, there is a need for controlled guidance and grammatical exercises that guide the student in constructing complex, compound, or compound-complex sentences. In general, all of the writing materials are based on the common axiom that mechanical inaccuracies are to be avoided in ESL composition courses and that constant correction and revision are standard procedures. Zamel (1976) noted concisely several of the more well-known authors—e.g., Pincas (1962), Dykstra (1964), Spencer (1965), Moody (1965), Rojas (1968), Ross (1968), and Paulston (1972)—who have published materials that clearly reflect and apply the principle of linguistic accuracy prior to fluency in the teaching of composition. In short, most of our current ESL composition materials are primarily error-oriented and attempt to prevent mechanical errors at the preparagraph level of writing.

The practices of the past have indeed produced some visible successes; however, they must also be given some of the credit for producing some invisible failures. If we want the ESL composition class to be successful, it must be designed to extend rather than to constrain the linguistic abilities that the ESL student brings to the classroom. Although a student's speaking abilities may be drawn upon as a first stage in the writing process, I suggested that a directed emphasis on fluency gradually replace the concern for error-free production that has characterized the ESL student's spoken English instruction.

This transition from speech to writing presents a variety of difficulties beyond the obvious ones of symbolizing the spoken language according to the writing system of American English. Perhaps the first of these difficulties is to define clearly and distinguish among the several styles of writing that the ESL student may be asked to produce—e.g., expository, descriptive, narrative, argumentative, and technical compositions, as well as writing about literature and the film. The latter two types of writing may be especially difficult for some ESL students to learn because of cultural reasons that are mentioned later. A second difficulty revolves around the roles of spectator and participant, assumed by both the teacher and the student in the ESL composition class. Britton (1970:123) points out this crucial distinction "between informing people about our experiences (which would be a participant activity) and inviting them to share in the process by which we pay homage to, or celebrate . . . our past experiences—an activity in the role of spectator."

Work in ESL composition falls into both categories. Whether the composition involves exposition, narration, description, or persuasion, the task of students is to inform their readers of important facts, persuade readers to share their views, or cause readers to take some action. This task is made more difficult by the fact that the ESL teacher almost always acts as a spectator who is seldom informed, persuaded, or moved to action simply because he or she does not share his student's culture. In turn, the ESL student knows full well that to involve the teacher as a participant is a culturally difficult if not impossible task. As a result, he is more likely to ask the teacher "How did I do?" (teacher as spectator), rather than "How did you like my composition?" (teacher as participant). For the ESL student to become motivated to involve the teacher as both participant and spectator is an accomplishment of the most inspired teaching and learning.

The difficulty involving these two roles assumed by the ESL student and his writing teacher is especially important in that it directly relates to the development of the student's positive linguistic self-confidence. The more comfortable a student is with his or her teacher as both a participant and a spectator, the less inhibited the student will be in getting ideas down on paper. When a student dispels any linguistic inhibitions, he or she can focus upon fluency and assign accuracy a secondary role. In the advanced, three-credit ESL composition course at the University of Delaware, we have observed that instruction that emphasizes fluency rather than error-free production enhances the ESL student's self-confidence, which in turn results in an extension of his language abilities—both native and second-language.

In emphasizing fluency in the ESL composition classroom, however, there are three potential problems:

1.   Defining and distinguishing among the various kinds of writing assignments in American colleges and universities;

2.   Fostering fluency without having to accept unbridled inaccuracy;

3.   Taking into consideration the differences between the literary devices found in the student's native literature and their American English counterparts.

The latter involves the role of contrastive analysis in helping ESL students to grasp literary experiences (American-British), a topic that is virtually untouched to date except by Di Pietro at the University of Delaware and Kaplan at the University of Southern California.

1.   Identifying and Defining Expository, Narrative, Descriptive, and Technical Writing

I have described elsewhere (1973, 1975a, b) the task of defining and distinguishing among the various kinds of writing, as well as checking for accuracy while focusing upon clause and multiparagraph level constructions. By means of a clause-analysis technique, the structural styles of expository, narrative, descriptive, and technical writing can be objectively identified and defined in terms of the frequency of occurrence of four surface-clause types: transitive, intransitive, equational, and passive. The hypothesis underlying these definitions is that certain patterns of the four clause types can be observed and formulated for the four major styles of writing. After four years of continuous research and clause analyses of published writing, I find that the normal frequency-of-occurrence rates of the four surface clause types in the four writing styles are as follows:

Table 1
Expected Frequency of Occurrence of
the Four Surface Clause Types*

Style of Writing	Transitive	Intransitive	Equational	Passive
Expository	50%	20%	20%	10%
Descriptive	15%	30%	45%	10%
Narrative	20%	45%	25%	10%
Technical	10%	5%	20%	65%

* $\pm$8% maximum variation permitted (Arena 1975b:89)

Defining persuasive or argumentative writing (not listed in the table) can be achieved either by interfacing expository style with the use of any or all of nine propaganda devices, or by considering only the expository presentation as logical persuasive writing. Good, clear, expository writing is, after all, persuasive writing. The nine propaganda devices that are commonly used to effectively but illogically persuade audiences are (1) name-calling and the use of invectives; (2) glittering generalizations; (3) tabloid-type thinking; (4) testimonials; (5) bifurcation; (6) association; (7) identification; (8) bandwagon; and (9) cardstacking. In writing persuasive compositions of the propaganda type, the ESL student must clearly intend to argue his or her topic by consciously misleading the reader by means of the nine propaganda techniques or logical fallacies. The viewpoint of contrastive analysis at Delaware indicates that all of the nine propaganda devices are crosscultural and are seemingly universal that is, all of the ESL students have experienced the devices in their native language and, as such, the meanings of the devices are not new to them.

The other type of writing not listed in the table is that describing or analyzing literature. It is perhaps the most difficult composition class for most ESL students. There are simple reasons for this difficulty. Literary devices, tone, point of view, imagery, and symbolism are often difficult for the native American to either assimilate or to apply in literature compositions; for cultural reasons, however, some of the devices are often demoralizingly difficult for the ESL student to understand and to apply. Because some literary devices may not be universal, many ESL students have much difficulty learning what an American author is trying to communicate by such devices as tone, imagery, and symbol. These devices may be very different in the literary counterparts of the student's native language. For the Japanese ESL student, for example, symbol and image may be sensorial, auditory, and visual, rather than just visual and/or conceptual as they may be for the native American-English speaker. The same is true for the ESL student when asked to write a composition about a film. The elements used in film-making such as motion, angle, and music may be so culturally different for the ESL student that he may not be able to grasp the literary experience that the American filmmaker intended to convey.

Experience at the Writing Center at Delaware suggests that approximately five of the seven kinds of writing may be objectively identified and defined for the advanced ESL composition student without much cultural conflict; (1) expository, (2) narrative, (3) descriptive, (4) technical, and (5) persuasive writing. The ESL teacher's task of defining each kind of writing is indeed an important one to carefully undertake to its finish. Without an objective definition of each kind of writing, the ESL student may confuse one type with another and, for example, may mistakenly write a narrative composition when the assignment calls for a descriptive one.

2.   Fostering Fluency without Accepting Inaccuracy

This second problem area may be handled in two ways in advanced ESL composition courses: (1) by supplemental individualized writing instruction at a university writing center;* and (2) by the use of the clause analysis technique to scan a student's paper for mechanical inaccuracies. After a student has written a draft of a composition, he may receive writing instruction at the writing center before handing in the composition. At such time, the writing center staff member may do one of two things:

1.   After discussing the content and overall organization of the essay with the student, the instructor may ask the ESL student to self-monitor the essay for mechanical faults; or

2.   The instructor may perform a clause-level analysis of the composition (that is, the same clause analysis technique that is used to define the four kinds of writing).

The clause analysis will objectively describe and derive the ESL student's "structural fingerprint" in terms of the type, number, frequency of occurrence of clause types, and the average length and

---

*The University of Delaware Writing Center is an auxiliary facility of the department of English, staffed by a director and faculty, where any registered student may receive individualized writing instruction. Attendance at the Writing Center is not mandatory and there is no cost to the student for any instruction received.

depth of embedding that the ESL student has employed in his writing. Experience over the past six years has shown repeatedly that the summaries of several clause analyses of a student's different compositions correlate so accurately and consistently in terms of the type, number, frequency, and embedding depth that the analyst can describe accurately and objectively the same person's writing that have not been analyzed. Such consistently correlating descriptions of a person's written idiolect constitute what we have come to call a writer's personal "structural fingerprint." Once the "structural fingerprint" has been determined, it is easily found and verified in any of the student's other writings. In this holistic approach, therefore, accuracy is not only closely monitored by both the teacher and student, but is also predicted in the advanced ESL composition course at Delaware. Noted, however, that written accuracy is monitored only after written fluency is permitted to develop.

3.   Contrastive Analyses of Rhetorical Features

The third potential problem area in emphasizing fluency in the advanced ESL composition course is how to take into consideration the differences that exist between rhetorical devices which are used in the literature of the ESL student and those which are used in American and British literature. For the reasons mentioned earlier, perhaps the most difficult writing assignment for an ESL student in which to display fluency is one that asks him to write a theme about a piece of literature. This type of writing assignment often taxes an ESL student's cultural and cognitive capacities to his limit.

It should also be noted that although contrastive analyses may point out differences and similarities between the literary devices found in American literature and those found in the ESL student's native literature, an ESL student's fluency will not be hindered because he or she does not have the language ability to write. An ESL student's fluency will be hindered, however, if he or she does not have control of the content that is denoted by each rhetorical device. I agree with conclusions reached by Lado that the student has not used his native language as a resource (see Lado's contribution to this volume). Once both the American and the ESL student understand the notions conveyed by the devices, both may be motivated to convey their ideas fluently at first and to concern themselves with error-free production after their first drafts.

It is my position that global concerns such as linguistic fluency, total organization, and the ability of an ESL student to interact with his teacher as participant as well as spectator ought to play a significant and early role in the advanced ESL composition class. Unfortunately, the opposite is probably the general rule. Most teachers likely assume that by taking care of the sentences, the larger patterns will take care of themselves. Still others seem to feel that correcting problems in spelling, punctuation, and usage has a prior claim that cannot be denied, even if fluency is sacrificed.

The situation demands some reflection. It is the students' ideas, not their sentences, that are really the basic units of any essay. To treat sentences as if they were the primary elements of an essay omits the larger patterns of fluency, organization, and even the intentions of the student-writer. The primary task of the ESL composition teacher is to motivate his students to develop skills using these larger patterns. To do so, the ESL teacher must honestly acknowledge the important differences between the methodologies appropriate for teaching spoken English and those for written English. Although linguistic accuracy before fluency is important and necessary in the mastery of English as a spoken language, the specter of an ever-watchful teacher, poised to assault any and all writing errors, certainly has to have a detrimental effect on a student's writing ability. Such an error-oriented atmosphere only breeds, if not perpetuates, linguistic neuroses.

The advanced ESL composition teacher can create the atmosphere and situations within which the ESL student may actually learn to like to write. When fluency is fostered prior to accuracy in writing classes, the ESL student not only grows in fluency, but also uses his own language as a resource to extend his mastery of the written language. Only at the last stages of this positive learning situation should error-free production exercises have any place in the class. In fostering fluency first, the instructor acknowledges that his or her primary function is to extend the language of the ESL student and not to purify it.

REFERENCES

Arena, L. A. 1973. Linguistics and composition: a method for "structural fingerprinting." In Meaning: a common ground of linguistics and literature, ed. D.L.F. Nilsen. Cedar Falls, Iowa: University of Northern Iowa Press.

_____. 1975a. A method for improving the writing skills of foreign students in university level expository English composition courses. In New directions in second language learning, teaching and bilingual education, ed. M. K. Burt and H.C. Dulay. Washington, D.C.: TESOL.

_____. 1975b. Linguistics and composition: a method to improve writing skills. Washington, D.C.: Georgetown University Press.

Britton, James. 1970. Language and learning. London: Lungmans.

Brooks, Nelson. 1974. Language and language learning. New York: Harcourt, Brace & World.

Dacanay, F.R., and J.D. Bowen, 1967. Techniques and procedures in second language teaching. Philippine Center for Language Study. Quezon City: Alemar-Phoenix Publishing House.

Di Pietro, Robert J. 1978. Language structures in contrast. Rev.

ed. Rowley, Mass. Newbury House.

Dykstra, Gerald. 1964. Eliciting language practice in writing. English Language Teaching 19:23-36.

Finocchiaro, Mary. 1974. English as a second language; from theory to practice. New York: Regents Publishing Co.

Fries, Charles C. 1974. Teaching and learning English as a foreign language. Ann Arbor, Mich.: University of Michigan Press.

Kaplan, Robert. 1966. Cultural thought patterns in intercultural education. Language Learning 16:1-20.

Lado, Robert. 1964. Language teaching. New York: McGraw-Hill Book Co.

Mackey, William F. 1967. Language teaching analysis. Bloomington, Ind.: Indiana University Press.

Moody, K. W. 1965. Controlled composition frames. English Language Journal 19:146-55.

Paulston, Christina B. 1972. Teaching composition in the ESOL classroom: techniques for controlled composition. Washington, D.C.: TESOL.

Paulston, Christina B., and Bruder, Mary Newton. 1976. Teaching English as a second language: techniques and procedures. Cambridge, Mass.: Winthrop Publishers.

Pincas, Anita. 1962. Structural linguistics and systematic composition teaching to students of English as a foreign language. Language Learning 12:185:94.

Rivers, Wilga. 1968. Teaching foreign language skills. Chicago, Ill.: University of Chicago Press.

Roberts, Edgar V. 1973. Writing themes about literature. Englewood Cliffs, N.J.: Prentice-Hall.

Robinett, Betty Wallace. 1978. Teaching English to speakers of other languages: substance and technique. New York: McGraw-Hill Book Co.

Rojas, Pauline M. 1968. Writing to learn. TESOL Quarterly 2:127-29.

Ross, Janet. 1968. Controlled writing: a transformational approach. TESOL Quarterly 2:253-61.

Spencer, D. H. 1965. Two types of guided composition. English Language Teaching 19:156-58.

Zamel, Vivian. 1976. Teaching composition in the ESL classroom: what we can learn from research in the teaching of English. TESOL Quarterly 10:67-76.

29. **The ESL Performance of Grade 10 Francophones in Quebec: Some Methodological Considerations**

BRUCE BARKMAN and LISE WINER
Concordia University, Montreal

Introduction and Background

This study describes the English-as-a-second-language performance of 27 French-speaking adolescents from middle-class backgrounds at the secondary IV (grade 10) level in a regional high school about thirty miles outside Montreal. The school serves suburban and rural communities and the students' primary exposure to English is in their ESL classroom, with the exception of three individuals who have nativelike skills in English. This class is one of seven that are being observed over a three-year period. The design of the project as a whole (Lightbown and Barkman 1978) allows for cross-sectional study of the interactions among learners, teachers, texts, and methods of ESL instruction of almost the entire period that English typically is taught in Quebec (grades 5-11) and for longitudinal studies of up to three years for individual learners and groups. The initial sample contained 176 students from grades 6, 8, and 10, who were observed in 1977-78. Slightly over 100 of them have been followed during the second year of the study. The frequency of the observational schedule and the degree of cooperation required from the teachers, students, and schools made random sampling impossible, but the classes and schools selected for this intensive study are reasonably typical of the ESL instruction in Quebec public schools.

The learners in the grade 10 class discussed in this study (10-A hereafter) had had about 540 hours of ESL instruction in school, starting in grade 5, before we began to observe and record their ESL classes. During the course of the year, the students received

This research is part of a project funded by grants from the Department of the Secretary of State of Canada to Patsy M. Lightbown and Bruce Barkman, and by a grant from the Social Sciences and Humanities Research Council of Canada to Bruce Barkman and Patsy M. Lighbown. Other financial support has been given by Concordia University and Le Ministère de l'Education du Québec. Nancy Belmore, Clause Faerch, Lili Ullmann, and Anne Barkman provided indispensable assistance.

approximately 100 hours of instruction, in sixty-minute classes that met five times during each seven-day school cycle. Their teacher is a native speaker of English who has a B.A. in English, a B.Ed. degree, and special training and considerable experience in teaching ESL. The materials used were primarily the first Canadian edition of the Lado English Series, Book Four and the accompanying workbook, along with various teacher-prepared materials.

We observed and recorded eleven of these classes at regular intervals throughout the year. Two observers noted individuals' speaking turns and as much of their speech as possible, in addition to the most pertinent features of their nonverbal classroom behavior. This procedure has made it possible to obtain a virtually complete record of classroom speech for all the individual learners as well as for the group as a whole.

The primary data for this study are the transcriptions from these eleven recordings, which have been entered into a computer system. Printouts were made of all utterances for class sessions and also of all utterances for each student, by session. Accurate running word counts, word diversity counts, and other quantitative measures have resulted from the computerized treatment of the data.

The major goals of the study are to obtain detailed longitudinal information on the ESL development of a large group of learners, to describe their ESL classroom interactions, and to attempt to determine the relationships between the learners' developing knowledge of English and their classroom activities.

The Framework for Analysis

Performance-analysis studies in first- and second-language acquisition have used a variety of sometimes quite different and often unclear criteria in describing and analyzing the language events under investigation. Error analysis research has faced a number of theoretical and methodological difficulties, generally centering on the place of errors in relation to total performance, and the definition and classification of error types. Hammarberg (1973) and Schachter (1974), for example, have pointed out the difficulties of approaching errors without considering their context. And, as Svartvik has noted, "Although the study of errors is a natural starting point, the final analysis should include linguistic performance as a whole. Hence performance analysis would seem to be a more appropriate name than error analysis (1973:8)." The notion of error in the present study is generally consistent with the performance-analysis approach of such researchers as Faerch (1978) and Zydatiss (1976).

Specific methodological problems are observable most frequently in the basic area of definition and classification of terms. Richards, for example, in a pioneering attempt to define the parameters of the field of error analysis (1973), described an error-classification scheme that does not always treat as separate categories the linguistic description of errors (for example, the omission of a required article), the assignment of sources to the errors (such as intralingual or interference), and the making of inferences as to what the learner might be doing (i.e. overgeneralizing). Because of these and other methodological difficulties, such as general disagreement on rating the accuracy of syntactic constructions—see Baily, Madden, and Krashen (1974), Anderson (1977), and Dulay and Burt (1974)—it is prudent to state as exactly as possible how the data have been quantified and analyzed.

The Norm Used in Evaluating the Learners' Performance

The goals of ESL instruction in Quebec, as set down in guidelines from the Ministry of Education (1977:88), are to produce people who approximate the skills of adult native speakers of English very closely in a wide range of situations of language use by the end of what is typically a six-year period, with a maximum of 800 hours of instruction. We have therefore taken our own variety of spoken North American English as the norm for evaluation of the learners' utterances. The samples of spoken language obtained from the three nativelike users of English in the class under study demonstrate the need to obtain normative data from matched groups of English-speaking students at the same grade levels on some of the same tasks. (We have, in fact, collected and transcribed such native-speaker data, but have not yet analyzed it.) The general absence of normative observational data in second-language studies is a serious problem and the work of those researchers (Gaies 1977, and Chaudron 1979) who do include baseline data shows how valuable such information can be.

Normative data would be helpful in determining whether what looks like an error actually is one, since it hardly seems reasonable to classify the habitual patterns of language use of native speakers of a standard variety of a language as error-laden. In addition, normative data would provide a baseline for comparisons of the number of words produced, the diversity of words, and other quantitative measures of linguistic performance. In the absence of baseline data, we can only guess at the significance of such measures for second-language acquisition.

General Parameters of Performance Analysis

In order to evaluate linguistic performance of any kind, an analytic procedure must be adopted that takes into account the appropriateness of the verbal behaviors that are used to express discourse functions, the degree to which the linguistic forms correspond to norms of grammatical correctness, both in and out of the linguistic context in which the utterances are produced, and the accuracy of the content expressed through the verbal behaviors.

Then the linguistic distance between L2 learners' utterances and corresponding utterances that conform to the variety being used as the norm must be determined, so that the degree to which their performance approximates the norm can be measured.

Discourse Performance. We have not yet attempted to determine the appropriateness of the linguistic forms used by the learners to express the various discourse functions characteristic of the language classroom. However, in the four secondary school classes that were observed in 1977-78, the use of French was forbidden, and violations of the English-only rule were censured by students and teachers alike. We have therefore classified the use of French as an inappropriate expression of discourse function in those classes. When the analysis of classroom interactions is more advanced (Lightbown and Barkman 1978:71-85), some objective means may be found for deciding whether answers to rhetorical questions, certain patterns of silence, interruption, disruption, overlap, and other linguistic and paralinguistic behavior have unwanted effects on the outcome of the discourse, and for determining when certain discourse functions are appropriate or inappropriate.

Utterance and Discourse Correctness. The first requirement that a linguistically well-formed utterance must meet is that it not violate the rules governing the formation and transformation of sentences of the norm adopted for comparison. When we examined the classroom utterances of the 10-A class in isolation from any larger context, close to 80 percent of these utterances were linguistically well formed. Many others deviated from the norm in various ways. For example, She don't want to disappoint him is easily recognizable as ill-formed. We rated such utterances as linguistically incorrect in the utterance context. While all utterances that are linguistically incorrect in utterance context are also incorrect in the discourse context, the cited form in question is also linguistically incorrect in the discourse context for other reasons. The question that preceded this response was Why did the sheriff permit Mr. Easton to say he was the sheriff?, so the verb form required by the context is didn't, she should be he, and him should be her. The response is linguistically incorrect at three points if both the utterance context and the discourse context are considered, but at one point only if the utterance context alone is considered.

Content Accuracy. The content accuracy of the learners' utterances may be evaluated with respect to knowledge of the world, of the subject matter, and of lesson content. In order to evaluate the content accuracy of the statement Miss Fairchild was an ambassador, we have to know the lesson materials that have been studied, but it is grammatically correct in the utterance context and lexically appropriate, though, not, as it turned out, accurate. Treating content accuracy separately from linguistic correctness makes it possible to study the linguistic features involved in the inaccurate statements.

Linguistic Description of the Learners' Errors

Despite the existence of several schemes for L2 error analysis (Richards 1974, Selinker 1972, Corder 1971, Dulay and Burt 1974), there are difficulties in applying any of them to L2 performance data. Chaudron (1977:25-28) is one of the few researchers who discusses the difficulties he encountered and some of the decisions he made when attempting to determine which linguistic categories applied to errors in the classroom speech of French immersion students. Following his example, we attempt to provide an exact description of our classification of the 10-A learners' errors into broad linguistic categories labeled grammatical, grammatical and lexical, lexical, collocational, and other (which was used for uninterpretable utterances or corrected pronunciation errors). Each of these categories can be subcategorized so that a detailed analysis of particular structures can be performed, and we illustrate this in our analysis of the learners' performance on the Be + V-ing structure.

Units of Error Description

The basic unit of error analysis is a single utterance. If an utterance satisfies the syntactic, lexical, contextual, and discourse conditions already discussed, it is considered correct. If the utterance does not satisfy those conditions, we undertake a linguistic description of the ways it deviates from the evaluators' variety of English that has been used as a norm. Within each utterance, the analytic subunits are the fundamental syntactic functions in use in linguistic descriptions, such as subject, main verb, direct and indirect objects, noun and adjective complements, and adverbials. These functions are realized by the various members of one or more form classes. The form classes may be closed, such as determiners, auxiliaries, prepositions, and pronouns, or open, such as nouns, verbs, adjectives, and adverbs. A given function may be realized by a single word or by strings of words, among which various relations obtain.

The linguistic description of an utterance that contains one or more errors involves a comparison of what was produced with what should have been produced. Since it is possible to correct almost any utterance in more than one way, guidelines have to be set down for choosing one alternative over the others. We decided that a feasible approach would be to make the minimum number of changes (thus eliminating at least some of the alternatives) in the learners' utterance that were required for it to be grammatically and lexically correct in the discourse context. The result of these changes is an utterance that provides the point of comparison for the classification of the errors in the original utterance.

Most of the time we found that a single change sufficed to correct a given structure or syntactic function, as in Miss, I don't understand the part B, which can be corrected by deleting the. We labeled these simple errors. If more than one change was required to correct the main verb, we labeled the error complex, but counted it as one error, as in What means fallen?, which requires the insertion of does and the deletion of -s. We also classified an error as complex if more than one word had to be supplied in order to produce a grammatically and contextually appropriate utterance. For example, Campsite, as a response to the question Where specifically are they in the forest?, has to be expanded. The teacher expanded the student's response to At the campsite. (Simple and complex refer to the number of operations involved in error correction, not to learning difficulty.)

Grammatical Errors

If the addition of an inflectional morpheme or deletion of what looks like one makes that part of the learners' utterance correct, the error is grammatical. Examples are Miss, you have good muscle (add plural), and I have one mistake? (delete -s).

Another type of grammatical error requires changes in word order, as, for example, She has a dress blue (transpose dress and blue), and I think we are late a little bit (transpose a little bit and late).

Finally, an error is classified as grammatical when it involves the addition of a member of a closed class of words (function words) having a single lexeme as its sole member, such as be (aux), have (aux), or when it involves the deletion of a member of a class of function words. Examples are Miss, what hike back? (add be (Copula) and Miss P— is need glasses (delete is, add third singular).

Grammatical and Lexical Errors

When a single word or phrase requires a lexical and a grammatical change, such as the addition of an inflectional ending as well as the lexemic change, it is both a grammatical and a lexical error. Examples are I take my calculator for the test (change take to brought), and I do a mistake (change do to made).

When both syntactic and lexical changes are necessary to correct the incorrect content of an utterance, the error is also considered both grammatical and lexical. Future as a response to the question What's the difference between weather and temperature? obviously requires both grammatical and lexical change.

If an utterance contains a sequence that is semantically uninterpretable in part and that is also syntactically inappropriate in the context, the sequence is classed as a single grammatical and lexical error. For instance, the teacher concluded a discussion on the importance of money with Usually it's the rich who say money isn't important, and a student commented If you don't have money she's not in a tree.

When we coded the 10-A class sessions, we classed the omission of an entire syntactic function such as object or of a function word class containing more than one member such as prepositions, as both grammatical and lexical. Thus, the omission of a preposition in I listen the text was put into the grammatical and lexical category, since more than one preposition, say with or to, might have been appropriately supplied in the context. However, this decision now seems quite arbitrary, since both the lexical and syntactic choices appropriate to the utterance are in fact nonexistent in the learners' utterance, and the learner might equally well have made an appropriate lexical choice if he had supplied the right syntactic category in the first place. We have therefore decided to reanalyze this kind of omission as grammatical only. The only omissions that would still be classified as both grammatical and lexical are those where the omission of the syntactic function or function word class results in an utterance that contrasts in meaning with the corresponding utterance where that class has been supplied. No examples have been found in our data so far, although they are not uncommon in the language, as, for example, He broke the bottle and He broke out the bottle.

Lexical Errors

When the students used French, we classified these utterances as grammatical and lexical errors, provided they were longer than a single word, but made no further linguistic analysis. This procedure seemed justified, even though these utterances were almost always linguistically correct, given the strictures against using the students' L1 in the L2 classroom. If the French utterance contained only one word, we classed it as lexical only, since we considered such utterances to have no obvious syntactic structure. Examples are Tu n'as pas commencé encore? (addressed to another student) and Maudit! The first example is grammatical and lexical and the second is lexical only.

An incorrect word choice from an open or a closed word class is treated as a lexical error. The entire word may have to be replaced, as in I lost the bus (missed), He will catch a rhume (cold). Other lexical errors require various kinds of modifications of the learners' utterances, as in powertive (powerful), calcul mental (mental calculation), smoke car (smoking car), concludive (conclusive), physic course (physics course), and I finished my home (homework), in which derivational affixes and bases are incorrect or have been omitted altogether.

Collocational Errors

A final type of error is collocational.   A collocational error involves the occurrence of two lexemes in a single utterance that ought to be semantically compatible but for some reason are not. This is one of the most common error types among intermediate and advanced learners.   An example from our data is My legs is not too tall (long), where legs and tall do not collocate. We had expected to find far more of these errors than we did, in fact, and have therefore counted them separately from the other kinds of lexical errors, but the overall percentages are so low that we will probably combine them.

Attribution of Sources to the Learners' Errors

Hatch   (1978a:2-10)   reviews   the   theoretical   approaches underlying attempts to attribute sources to learner error.   The attribution of sources to errors, when reduced to the empirical basis on which it must ultimately rest (the performance of the learners), can be characterized as emphasizing intrinsic or extrinsic factors. By intrinsic, we mean that the errors reflect difficulties in learning the second language that are due to the linguistic nature of that language. In English, the modals, auxiliaries, inflections, the use of articles, and the expression of aspect, among other structural features, are problem areas for both L1 and L2 learners of the language, and these difficulties are reflected in L2 performance, regardless of the first-language background of the L2 learners.

Whether one attributes these errors in L2 to a common learning system (Richards 1973), claims similarities of the L2 errors to the normal developmental errors of L1 learners of English (Dulay and Burt 1974) or, as we prefer, simply ascribes them to the nature of the linguistic system of English, makes little difference, so long as one remembers that the basis for attribution resides in the linguistic performance of the learners and comparisons of how their performance deviates from the rules of the system or subsystem the learner is trying to master. We have labeled the source of intrinsic errors English.   Examples are He compared with an ambassador (compared requires an object), and It's not good of the nerves (for, not of).

Extrinsic Errors

It can be argued that almost every error is intrinsic to English, and this may not be an entirely untenable position. However, there also appears to be a number of extrinsic sources for errors, including the learners' mother tongue, the materials used in instruction, and the instructor.   By far the most frequently occurring extrinsic source of error in our data was the mother tongue, with materials-

or teacher-induced errors accounting for less than one percent of all errors.

Transfer and English Errors

We observed that an error could often be attributed to more than one source. Rather than trying to decide which source predominated in such cases, we attributed the error to both sources, such as English and transfer. For example, learners of English from different language backgrounds and children learning English as a mother tongue have difficulty producing the inflectional morpheme for the third singular form of the verb. This is an intrinsic difficulty, because it is the only such regular marker of agreement between the subject and verb in English, and there are very few inflectional morphemes in the language as a whole. When a French-speaking learner says He want find Ron?, however, we considered the failure to supply the third singular morpheme as both an English and a transfer error, since the singular forms of present-tense verbs in French for all persons are pronounced alike and the third-person singular and plural verb forms are also pronounced alike for all regular verbs. The lack of a two-way contrast between third singular and all other present-tense verb forms in French makes it more than likely that both intrinsic and extrinsic (the mother tongue in this case) factors contribute to such errors from French speakers.

Transfer Errors

Besides errors attributable to English alone and to both English and the mother tongue, we found that many errors could be attributed to the mother tongue alone. We have called these transfer errors, rather than interference, because we wish to emphasize that the learners' attempts to use the forms and structures of one language in the utterances of another (Haugen 1953, 1956; Mackey 1962) are a prominent characteristic of the language-learning process (at least for languages as closely related and with such prolonged periods of contact as English and French). Such attempts, when successful, in the sense that the resultant utterances are error-free, are usually unobservable.

When the structures of L1 and L2 do not coincide, a learner's attempt to transfer an L1 structure to L2 results in a set of language events that does not conform to the norms of the language being learned, but that corresponds in precisely statable ways to the structures of the mother tongue. Integrated loanwords or structures are thus not counted as negative transfer. Although most of the examples of negative transfer in the classroom data involved only the lexicon, as in We came by pouce (from faire du pouce' to hitchhike' or disparition ('disappearance'), any part of the linguistic system may be involved.

A detailed framework for the analysis of transfer has been

developed by Mackey (1976), who also gives precise methods for quantifying what he calls the interlinguistic distance between pairs of semantically equivalent expressions in two languages. Haugen (1953) describes transfer along an importation–substitution scale depending on the amount of L1 material used, with pure loanwords, such as <u>pouce</u> at the importation end of the scale and at the substitution end expressions like <u>Things are the things</u> (<u>Les affaires sont les affaires</u> 'Business is business', but <u>affaire</u> in Canadian French is often used in contexts where the English equivalent is 'thing'). We have used Mackey's and Haugen's frameworks, applying them as described below.

A French utterance was counted as a single transfer error, as were French words incorporated into otherwise English utterances, such as <u>Some boy and girl go to fête</u>, where the context requires <u>birthday party</u>. When an utterance contained what looked like a possible transfer error, we translated the utterance into French to see if the linguistic description that applied to the utterance was attributable to transfer only or if the learner had modified the syntax of the French equivalent when transferring it to English. Levenston (1971) describes a similar procedure. If modifications had been attempted, we attributed the error to transfer and English. For example, <u>I have hungries</u> is obviously modeled on <u>j'ai faim</u> (literally 'I have hunger'). However, the French noun appears to have first been changed to the appropriate adjective equivalent in English and then modified again, perhaps idiosyncratically, or following a regular pattern of English, as in <u>I have measles</u>. Since the French and English equivalents do not show a perfect syntactic correspondence, we attributed the complex error <u>have hungries</u> to transfer and English, rather than to transfer alone. Where the correspondence between the English and French expressions is exact, we classified the error as transfer only. Examples are <u>Protection of the wind</u> (<u>protection du vent</u>) and <u>He look the world</u> (<u>il regarde le monde</u>).

Teacher- and Materials-Induced Errors

While our classroom data included practically no teacher- or materials-induced errors, there are some classrooms where such attributions would be frequent. In the 10-A class, we found that three errors could be attributed to the materials and two to the instructor. It did not seem fruitful to attempt to define these error types except by example, since they are so infrequent in our data.

Indeterminate Sources of Error

There are some errors whose source cannot be determined with any certainty. We have labeled these indeterminate, and generally we called student utterances that had the wrong content indeterminate, since we did not know why they gave the wrong answer. For instance, student 21 says that <u>Miss Fairchild was an ambassador</u> in response to a question concerning the reason for comparing the position of sheriff to that of an ambassador. Any reasons we might advance would be highly speculative, so we preferred to say that the attribution of a source was indeterminate. Table 1 presents examples of the error classification scheme discussed above.

Performance Analysis of 10-A

In this study, we give results for the group as a whole (N=27), with the nativelike users of English excluded (N=24), or for the 16 nonnative users who continued to study English in grade 11 and for whom we have collected data over a two-year period. We first present and discuss some global measures of their ability and then a detailed description and discussion of their performance on the <u>Be</u> + V-ing construction.

Correct and Incorrect Utterances in the Classroom Data

The first measure of performance we obtained is the proportion of correct utterances to number of utterances in the classroom sessions, by individual and group totals and means. We chose the semester rather than the individual class sessions as the time unit for longitudinal comparisons of the learners' performance because of the small amounts of data obtained from individuals in each session. The mean number of utterances obtained from each individual per session was nine in the first semester and nineteen in the second. While the increase is striking enough, there are still not enough data, even in the second-semester sessions, to make meaningful comparisons session by session for a range of grammatical structures. The choice of the semester as a time unit seemed a natural one, considering both the academic organization of the school and what we knew about accuracy rates for various structures over time, namely that there are large fluctuations in these rates over the short term (exacerbated by having only small amounts of data) that can be minimized if data obtained on several occasions are grouped and treated as a single time period.

Table 2 presents the results for individuals and the group by semester and for the year. Excluding the three nativelike users of English, the rate of increase in the proportion of correct utterances in the second semester is 3.0 percent, and this group (N=24) produced 1.8 times as many utterances in the second semester.

In the first semester, half of the students got 70 percent or more of their utterances correct, using the discourse, content, and other linguistic conditions described above. In the second semester, three-fourths of the students got 70 percent or more of their utterances correct.

TABLE 1

Examples of Error-Classification Coding

UTTERANCE	DESCRIPTION						LING COR		ERROR CATEGORY					ATTRIBUTION						TYPE	
		1	2	3	4	5	6	7	8	9	10	11	12	13	14	15	16	17	18	19	20
1. The dog is looking at him.		6	+	+	+	0	+	+	+											+	
2. Miss, I don't understand the part B.	delete the	7	+	+	+	1	-	-		+				+		+				+	
3. Today we are going to visit a new house that was announced in the newspaper.	announced =advertised	15	+	+	+	1	-	-		+				+	+						+
4. What means fallen?	add does, delete -s	3	+	+	+	1	-	-	+					+						+	
	transpose fallen/mean					2			+							+					+
5. Campsite	add at the	1	-	+	+	1	-	+	+					+						+	
6. Miss, you have good muscle.	add -s	5	+	+	?	1	-	-			+					+				+	+
7. I'm get along French not too bad.	add -ing	7	+	+	+	1	-	-	+					+						+	
	add in					2	-	-			+			+						+	
	add -ly					3	-	-						+						+	
8. She has a dress blue.	transpose dress/blue	5	+	+	+	1	-	+		+					+						+
9. Miss, what hike back?	add is	4	-	+	?	1	-	+	+					+						+	
10. I take my calculator for the test.	take =brought	7	+	+	?	1	-	-		+	+			+	+					+	+
11. I see you the next dance.	add will	6	+	+	?	1	-	-			+			+						+	
	add at					2	-	-			+			+						+	
12. Tu n'as pas commencé encore?	French	5	+	-	?	1	/	/		+					+					+	
13. He will catch a rhume.	French	5	+	-	+	1	/	/		+					+					+	
14. Ron dead.	add is	2	-	+	-	1	-	-	+					+						+	
	dead=lost					2	-	-		+									+	+	
15. My legs is not too tall.	is=are	6	+	+	?	1	-	-	+					+						+	
	tail=long					2	-	-		+							+			+	
16. (Miss Fairchild believed that Mr. Easton was___) a butterfly.	a Western sheriff	2	-	-	-	1	-	-				+					+				+
17. /tænly/	tone	1	-	+	+	1	-	+					+	+						+	

Col. 1 = number of words; Col. 2 = subject and main verb; Col. 3 = discourse function appropriate; Col. 4 = content accurate;
Col. 5 = error number; Col. 6 = discourse context; Col. 7 = utterance context; Col. 8 = grammatical; Col. 9 = lexical;
Col. 10 = grammatical and lexical; Col. 11 = collocational; Col. 12 = other; Col. 13 = English (intrinsic); Col. 14 = transfer;
Col. 15 = English and transfer; Col. 16 = materials; Col. 17 = instructor; Col. 18 = indeterminate; Col. 19 = simple;
Col. 20 = complex; LING COR = Linguistic correctness.

The mean number of correct utterances per session for the second semester is significantly greater than that mean for the first semester, to the .001 level, applying a one-tailed t-test for related groups.

Other General Measures of Linguistic Performance

In order to obtain a rough notion of the complexity of the learners' language, we determined the proportion of utterances that had a subject and a main verb (following the definition developed by Fries 1952:176 , rather than the T-Unit approach proposed by Hunt 1965 , which cannot unambiguously be applied to our data) by semester and for the year, the difference in the proportions between semesters, the rate of change, and the mean length of utterance in words. This information is displayed in Table 3, which also shows the total number of words produced by each student during the recorded sessions. We thought that the mean length of utterance measure would give us some idea of the learners' fluency. With the exception of student 23, who certainly was fluent, the learners with a mean length of utterance of between 4.4 and 5.2 seemed to be more fluent than those who had either higher or lower means. Those with higher means tended to have them because they read aloud or recited from memory quite often and those with lower means appeared to be more hesitant in speaking, produced utterances with no apparent syntactic structure more often, and seemed generally less fluent.

The ranges in use of subject and verb for the twenty-four non-native users are 33.3-81.5 in the first semester, 41.0-76.7 in the second semester, and 41.3-76.6 for the year. The reasonably fluent learners used subjects and verbs about half the time, which seems appropriate for the kinds of language activities that occurred in their classes. Once again, we underline the necessity for normative data from native speakers, because the group proportions for utterances with subject and main verb are higher for the nonnative users than for the entire class.

While analyses of a range of syntactic structures remain to be done, we think that such analyses will be more revealing of the learners' ability than the admittedly crude comparison of utterances with and without subjects and main verbs. The preliminary diversity of word counts that have been done for the 10-A sessions and the class sessions of a generally less proficient class, 10-B, indicate that 10-A produced about twice as many different words as 10-B. If the preliminary results are borne out, we think that group and individual diversity of word counts will probably provide one of the best comparative measures of overall ability.

Table 4 presents the number and percentage of correct and incorrect utterances, number of errors, and percentages of error by linguistic category and by attribution. We calculated ratios for the grammatical, lexical, and grammatical and lexical error categories,

TABLE 2

Number of Correct Utterances (CU), Number of Utterances (U), and Percentage of Correct Utterances (%C) in Classroom Data for Students in 10-A, by Semester and School Year

STUDENT ID	SEMESTER 1 (SESSIONS 1-6)				SEMESTER 2 (SESSIONS 7-11)				SCHOOL YEAR (SESSIONS 1-11)			
	CU	U	NO. SESSIONS IF LESS THAN 6	%C	CU	U	NO. SESSIONS IF LESS THAN 5	%C	CU	U	NO. SESSIONS IF LESS THAN 11	%C
01	20	27	(5)	74.1	28	37		75.7	48	64	(10)	75.0
02	21	33		63.6	42	69		60.9	63	102		61.8
03 [1]	97	111		87.4	153	168		91.9	250	279		89.6
05	41	56		73.2	55	97		56.7	96	153		62.7
06	23	33		69.7	229	316		72.5	252	349		72.2
08	17	20	(5)	85	31	36	(3)	86.1	48	56	(8)	85.7
09	41	59		69.5	34	45	(3)	75.6	75	104	(9)	72.1
10	26	39		66.7	92	141		65.2	118	180		65.6
11	141	228		61.8	106	198	(4)	53.5	247	426	(10)	58.0
12	20	28	(5)	71.4	38	43		88.4	58	71	(10)	81.7
13	14	21	(4)	66.7	6	8	(2)	75.0	20	29	(6)	69.0
14	15	27		55.6	47	63		74.6	62	90		68.9
15	2	5	(3)	40.0	23	32		71.9	25	37	(7)	67.6
16	36	52	(5)	69.2	41	56	(4)	73.2	77	108	(10)	71.3
17	14	16		87.5	41	48		85.4	55	64		85.9
18 [1]	13	14	(4)	92.9	46	48		95.8	59	62		95.2
19	16	26	(4)	59.2	25	44	(4)	56.8	41	70	(10)	58.6
20	58	85		68.2	204	244		83.6	262	329		79.6
21	82	95		86.3	107	134		79.9	189	229		82.5
22	10	18	(4)	55.6	33	43		76.7	43	61	(9)	70.5
23	180	245		73.5	228	309		73.8	408	554		73.6
24	9	12	(4)	75.0	7	10	(1)	70.0	16	22	(5)	72.7
25	13	18	(4)	72.2	64	84		76.2	77	102	(9)	75.5
26	39	63		61.9	62	93		66.7	101	156		64.7
27	39	51		76.5	87	118	(4)	73.7	126	169	(10)	74.6
28	26	36		72.2	47	63		74.6	73	99		73.7
32 [1]	23	25		92.0	32	36	(4)	88.9	55	61	(10)	90.2
Group Totals N=27	1036	1443		71.8	1908	2583		73.9	2944	4026		73.1
N=24²	903	1293		69.8	1677	2331		71.9	2580	3624		71.2

1. Subject has nativelike skills in English;
2. Excluding 03, 18, and 32.

TABLE 3

Number and Percentage of Utterances with Subject and Main Verb and Mean Length of Utterance in Words
for Students in 10-A, by Semester and Year

STUDENT ID	1	2	SEMESTER 1					SEMESTER 2					SCHOOL YEAR						
			3	4	5	6	7	8	9	10	11	12	13	14	15	16	17	18	19
01			22	27	81.5	8.1	218	27	37	72.9	8.6	317	49	64	76.6	8.4	535	-8.6	-10.6
02			13	33	39.3	4.8	159	38	69	55.1	7.0	483	51	102	50.0	6.3	642	15.8	40.2
03[1]			55	111	49.5	4.5	498	69	168	41.1	3.6	600	124	279	45.1	3.6	1098	-8.4	-17.0
05			37	56	66.1	6.5	365	55	97	56.7	6.7	647	92	153	60.1	6.6	1012	-6.0	-9.1
06			15	33	45.4	4.0	131	164	316	51.9	3.8	1196	179	349	51.3	3.8	1327	6.5	14.3
08	5	3	8	20	40.0	5.1	101	21	36	58.3	5.0	180	29	56	51.8	5.0	281	18.3	45.8
09		3	21	59	35.6	3.9	230	28	45	62.2	6.0	269	49	104	47.1	4.8	499	26.6	74.7
10			17	39	43.6	4.1	161	78	141	55.3	4.6	650	95	180	52.8	4.5	811	11.7	26.8
11	5	4	127	228	55.7	4.5	1025	102	198	51.5	4.1	813	229	426	53.8	4.3	1838	-4.2	-7.5
12	5		11	28	39.3	5.6	156	29	43	67.4	7.1	307	40	71	56.3	6.5	463	28.1	71.5
13	4	3	8	21	38.1	3.4	71	4	8	50.0	5.8	46	12	29	41.3	4.0	117	11.9	31.2
14			15	27	55.6	5.2	141	42	63	66.7	6.1	386	57	90	63.3	5.9	527	11.1	20.0
15	5	4	4	5	80.0	6.8	34	23	32	71.9	8.1	258	27	37	73.0	7.9	292	-8.1	-10.1
16	5		33	52	63.5	6.2	322	34	56	60.7	7.0	393	67	108	62.0	6.6	715	-2.8	-4.4
17			9	16	56.3	5.3	85	34	48	70.8	6.4	307	43	64	67.1	6.1	392	14.5	25.8
18[1]			2	14	14.3	4.9	68	34	48	70.8	6.4	308	36	62	58.1	6.1	376	56.5	395.1
19			15	26	57.7	5.7	149	31	44	70.5	8.5	376	46	70	65.7	7.5	525	12.8	22.2
20	5		40	85	47.1	3.8	327	100	244	41.0	3.9	943	140	329	42.6	3.9	1270	-6.1	-13.0
21			41	95	43.2	3.5	328	66	134	49.3	4.3	581	107	229	46.7	4.0	909	6.1	14.1
22		4	10	18	55.6	5.5	99	33	43	76.7	5.8	249	43	61	70.5	5.7	348	21.1	37.9
23			104	245	42.4	3.6	871	163	309	52.7	3.7	1132	267	554	48.2	3.6	2003	10.3	24.3
24	4	1	4	12	33.3	5.2	62	6	10	60.0	10.6	106	10	22	45.5	7.6	168	26.7	80.2
25	4		8	18	44.4	5.1	91	46	84	54.8	4.5	382	54	102	52.9	4.6	473	10.4	23.4
26			26	63	41.3	5.5	346	43	93	46.2	4.7	435	69	156	44.2	5.0	781	4.9	11.9
27		4	32	51	62.7	6.4	327	57	118	48.3	5.1	596	89	169	52.7	5.5	923	-14.4	-23.0
28			16	36	44.4	4.5	162	38	63	60.3	4.8	303	54	99	54.5	4.7	465	15.9	35.8
32[1]		4	10	25	40.0	4.4	111	20	36	55.6	5.4	196	30	61	49.2	5.0	307	15.6	39.0
N=27			703	1443	48.7	4.6	6638	1385	2583	53.6	4.8	12459	2088	4026	51.9	4.5	18097	4.9	10.1
N=24			609	1293	47.1	4.6	5961	1262	2331	54.1	4.9	11355	1898	3624	52.4	4.5	16316	7.0	14.9

Col. 1 = number of sessions in semester 1 if less than 5; Col. 2 = number of sessions in semester 2 if less than 5; Col. 3 = utterances with subject and main verb; Col. 4 = number of utterances; Col. 5 = percentage of utterances with subjects and main verbs; Col. 6 = mean length of utterance (in words); Col. 7 = number of words; Col. 8 = utterances with subject and main verb; Col. 9 = number of utterances; Col. 10 = percentage of utterances with subject and main verb; Col. 11 = mean length of utterance (in words); Col. 12 = number of words; Col. 13 = number of utterances with subject and main verb; Col. 14 = number of utterances; Col. 15 = percentage of utterances with subject and main verb; Col. 16 = mean length of utterance; Col. 17 = number of words; Col. 18 = percentage difference for subject and main verb between semester 1 and 2; Col. 19 = rate of change in percentage of utterances with subjects and main verbs.

1. Subject has nativelike skills in English.

since the vast majority of errors fell into one of these three categories. Three students made more lexical than grammatical errors, including two of the nativelike users. Six students had approximately equal proportions of grammatical and lexical errors. Eight students had approximately one-and-a-half times as many grammatical as lexical errors, and nine made at least twice as many grammatical as lexical errors. We assume that this reflects a developmental trend, with the ratio of error types moving from higher grammatical to higher lexical as the learners become more proficient in English, because we know that students 03 and 18 have a nativelike command of English. This assumption will be tested with the less proficient 10-B group and the classes in the lower grades, as well as with the students in 10-A who continued to study English in grade 11. We will also examine the correlation of error-type ratios with other measures for these individuals and groups.

Columns 17 and 18 of Table 4 display percentages of errors attributed to English and transfer and English combined and those attributed to English and transfer and transfer combined. We suspect that one of the reasons for the great disparity in the percentages of transfer errors reported in the literature may be that other researchers have not allowed for the possibility that an error can meet the criteria for inclusion in both the English and the transfer attribution categories. Instead of creating a third class, they may have decided to put them in one or the other, with the results favoring either intrinsic (column 17) or transfer (column 18) sources, according to the theoretical position favored by the analyst.

Performance on the Be + V-ing Construction

We have tested our analytical framework for ESL performance on a particular syntactic construction, Be + V-ing, with data obtained from class sessions and two administrations of a picture card description task.

The picture card task, based on a technique used by Upshur (1971), is fully described in Lightbown and Barkman (1978:34-37). The student chose one of a set of four picture cards that differed from each other minimally and described it so that the interviewer could guess which of the four he had. Every picture card provided an appropriate occasion for the use of the Be + V-ing construction. We analyzed only the data that derive from the seven picture card sets used on both administrations of the task, given a year apart in April and May.

An entire syntactic construction, rather than a part of one, is evaluated, first in terms of its use in an appropriate or inappropriate context (see Table 5). We did not find any instance of Be + V-ing in an optional context, but there may conceivably be some, if not for Be + V-ing, then for other constructions, so we prefer the word "appropriate" to "obligatory." Such an approach makes it possible to keep track of inappropriate uses of the correct or partially correct

TABLE 4

Number and Percentage of Correct and Incorrect Utterances, Number of Errors,
Error Percentage by Linguistic Category and by Attribution, for Students in 10-A

STUDENT ID	CLASS DATA					ERROR PERCENTAGE BY LINGUISTIC CATEGORY & ATTRIBUTION												
	1	2	3	4	5	6	7	8	9	10	11	12	13	14	15	16	17	18
01	48	75.0	16	25.0	20	75.0	15.0	10.0			30.0		60.0			10.0	90.0	60.0
02	63	55.9	39	44.1	53	60.4	26.4	5.7		7.5	22.6	7.5	52.8			17.0	75.4	60.3
031	250	89.6	29	10.4	28	17.9	46.4	28.6	7.1		39.3	25.0	17.9			17.9	57.2	42.9
05	96	62.7	57	37.3	69	42.0	43.5	11.6		0.3	39.1	14.5	27.5	1.4		17.4	66.6	42.0
06	252	72.2	97	27.8	119	44.5	33.6	21.0		0.8	41.2	17.6	33.6			7.6	74.8	51.2
08	48	85.7	8	14.3	11	45.4	45.4		9.0		63.6	9.0	18.1			9.0	81.7	27.1
09	75	72.1	29	27.9	44	52.2	29.5	15.9			29.5	13.6	40.9	2.2	4.5	14.6	70.4	54.5
10	118	65.6	62	34.4	.70	55.7	31.4	12.9			40.0	7.1	40.0		1.4	11.4	80.0	47.1
11	247	53.5	179	46.5	214	44.4	29.0	24.8		1.4	37.9	20.1	34.6			5.6	72.5	54.7
12	58	81.7	13	18.3	16	56.3	31.3	6.3	6.3		31.3		43.8			25.0	75.1	43.8
13	20	69.0	9	31.0	10	40.0	50.0	10.0			50.0	30.0	20.0				70.0	50.0
14	62	68.9	28	31.1	36	38.9	33.3	13.9	5.6	8.3	38.9	5.6	41.7	8.3		5.6	80.6	47.3
15	25	67.6	19	51.4	19	47.4	31.6	15.8	5.3		52.6	5.3	31.6			10.5	84.2	36.9
16	77	71.2	31	28.8	36	66.7	19.4	8.3	5.6		50.0		44.4			5.6	94.4	44.4
17	55	85.9	9	14.1	5	55.6	33.3	11.1			56.6	22.2	11.1			11.1	67.7	33.3
181	59	95.2	3	4.8	5	20.0	40.0	40.0			80.0					20.0	80.0	
19	41	58.8	29	41.2	51	56.9	23.5	17.6	2.0		33.3	5.9	49.0			11.8	82.3	54.9
20	262	79.7	67	20.3	80	36.3	27.5	31.3	5.0		28.8	27.5	27.5			15.0	56.3	55.0
21	189	82.5	40	17.5	39	38.5	25.6	35.9			25.6	28.2	23.1			5.1	48.7	51.3
22	43	70.5	18	29.5	21	57.1	33.3	4.8	4.8		47.6	4.8	19.0			28.6	66.6	23.8
23	408	73.6	146	26.4	180	50.6	27.2	18.3	0.6	3.3	42.8	16.7	18.3			11.7	61.1	35.0
24	16	72.7	6	27.3	7	28.6	28.6	42.9			57.1	29.0	28.6			14.3	85.7	28.6
25	77	75.5	25	24.5	31	45.2	22.6	32.3			29.0	29.0	35.5	3.2		3.2	64.5	64.5
26	101	64.7	55	35.3	79	54.4	31.6	7.6		6.3	35.4	17.7	29.1			17.7	64.5	46.8
27	126	74.6	43	25.4	48	33.3	35.4	31.3			29.2	14.9	66.7			10.4	95.9	81.6
28	73	73.7	26	26.3	41	58.5	26.8	14.6			36.6	14.6	36.6			12.2	73.2	51.2
321	55	90.2	6	9.8	6	33.3	16.7			50.0	100.0						100.0	
Group Totals N=27	2944	73.1	1082	26.9	1342	47.6	30.2	18.9	0.75	2.46	37.9	16.8	41.0	0.37	0.01	10.9	78.5	57.8
N=24	2580	71.2	1044	28.8	1303	48.4	29.9	18.6	.61	2.30	37.4	16.8	41.8	0.38	0.02	10.7	76.9	58.6

Col. 1 = number of correct utterances; Col. 2 = percentage of correct utterances; Col. 3 = number of incorrect utterances;
Col. 4 =percentage of incorrect utterances; Col. 5 = number of errors; Col. 6 = grammatical; Col. 7 = lexical; Col. 8 =
grammatical and lexical; Col. 9 = collocational; Col. 10 = other; Col. 11 = English (intrinsic); Col. 12 = transfer; Col. 13=
English and transfer; Col. 14 = materials; Col. 15 = instructor; Col. 16 = Indeterminate; Col. 17 = English and transfer +
English; Col. 18 = English and transfer + transfer.

1. Subject has nativelike skills in English.

form as well as of correct and incorrect forms in appropriate contexts. Then the entire utterance is evaluated for linguistic correctness in the utterance and discourse contexts. This serves the same purpose for the entire utterance as the appropriate context evaluation for the construction under study.

Next, the various parts of the construction under study are evaluated. When Be + V-ing must be supplied, there are three ways that the learner can produce an incorrectly formed utterance. He can omit Be altogether, fail to make the proper agreement between Be and the subject, or omit -ing.

Finally, the construction under study is evaluated for correctness of form and correctness of use. In columns 7 and 8 of Table 5, the third example contains an instance of a correctly formed construction, wrongly used, since the context was What does he do first? (displaying picture of a little boy getting out of bed).

The learner's performance on the Be + V-ing construction for the different types of data is displayed in Table 6. There is considerable variation in individual performance depending on the type of data. Group correctness and error patterns also vary over time. The 17.6 percent difference between the first and second administrations of the picture card task, with increased correct use of the construction, is quite striking. More interesting to second-language researchers are the error percentages in the various categories for both administrations. Omission of Be with an -ing inflected verb accounts for a very small percentage of errors. The use of the right form of Be with an uninflected verb where Be + V-ing is required is more than double that percentage on both administrations of the picture card task. The change from the first to the second administration suggests that these learners are moving directly from the use of an uninflected form where the construction is required to correct use of the construction.

The much higher percentages of correctness in the classroom sessions suggest that when attention is more focused on form and when the task is clearly presented, correctness of form results.

Although we have collected and partially analyzed other types of data, including standardized grammar and listening tests, cloze tests, and a grammaticality judgment test, among others, we have not reported on these measures here. This is because the statistical tests have not yet been completed. However, preliminary treatment of the comparison data indicates that a variety of measures, taken longitudinally, provides the best picture of variability and uniformity in second-language development.

In conclusion, we would like to state that although other investigators may choose not to use the analytical framework we have developed, it should at least prove useful in the interpretation of our work.

TABLE 5
Sample Coding, <u>Be</u> + <u>V=ing</u>

UTTERANCE	APPROPRIATE CONTEXT	LINGUISTIC CORRECTNESS				CONSTRUCTION CORRECT		
		D	U	Be	Agr	Ing	Use	Form
1. I'm taking dental hygiene.	+	+	+	+	+	+	+	+
2. She's holding three balloon red.	+	-	-	+	+	+	+	+
3. He's getting up.	-	-	+	+	+	+	-	+
4. He touch the table.	+	-	-	-	-	-	-	-
5. They try to talk about the accident.	+	-	+	-	-	-	-	-
6. I taking English.	+	-	-	-	-	+	-	-
7. He is get up.	-	-	-	+	+	-	-	-
8. It's rain.	+	-	-	+	+	-	-	-
9. They going in the school.	+	-	-	-	-	+	-	-
10. Six persons who are run.	+	-	-	+	+	-	-	-
11. The boys is sitting.	+	-	-	+	-	+	-	-

D = in discourse context; U = in utterance context; Agr = agreement.

TABLE 6

Be + V=ing Performance by Students in 10-A on Different Types of Data*

STUDENT ID	+ Be + Agr + Ing			+ Be + Agr - Ing			+ Be - Agr + Ing			+ Be - Agr - Ing			- Be - Agr + Ing			- Be - Agr - Ing		
	I	II	III	I	II	III	I	II	III	I	II	III	I	II	III	I	II	III
01	1	7	6														3	1
05	3	–	1		2										1		9	4
06	–	1	2					1					1				4	3
08	1	–	1										1	3			4	
09	4	5	5										1				4	1
10	5	1	2		1	1											3	
12	1	5	1		1	1											1	1
14	2	8	5		1	1									2		4	
16	5	–	1													1	1	2
17	2	2	4		1	1		1									7	3
20	4	3	7	1	2	1											1	2
22	4	3	5		1	3									1		1	1
23	5	9	51			1												
25	3	1	31			1											3	
26	5	6	6		1								1			1	4	2
28	1	–	3	1									1				7	3
N = 16 NO. CORRECT	46	51	57	2	10	10		2					5	3	4	2	56	23
% OF TOTAL	83.6	41.8	59.4	3.6	8.1	10.4		1.6					9.1	2.6	4.2	3.60	45.9	24.0

* Data types:

I   Class sessions, 55 instances
II Picture card task, 1st administration, 122 instances
III Picture card task, 2d administration, 96 instances

1. In addition to these totals, these individuals supplied one formally correct instance of the construction in an inappropriate context, accounting for 2.1% of the total number of instances.

REFERENCES

Anderson, Roger W. 1977. The impoverished state of cross-sectional morpheme acquisition/accuracy methodology (or: the leftovers are more nourishing than the main course). Proceedings of the Los angeles Second Language Research Forum, ed. Carol Alice Henning, pp. 308-19. Los Angeles: Department of English, University of California at Los Angeles.

Bailey, Nathalie; Madden, Carolyn; and Krashen, Stephen D. 1974. Is there a "natural sequence" in adult second language learning? Language Learning 24:235-43.

Chaudron, Craig. 1977. Teachers' priorities in correcting learners' errors in French immersion classes. Working Papers in Bilingualism 12:21-44.

_____. 1979. Complexity of ESL teachers' speech and vocabulary explanation/elaboration. Paper read at the Thirteenth Annual TESOL Convention, Boston, Massachusetts.

Corder, S. Pit. 1971. Idiosyncratic dialects of error analysis. IRAL 9:2. Reprinted in Error analysis: perspectives on second language acquisition. (1974), ed. Jack C. Richards, pp. 158-71. London: Longman.

Dulay, Heidi C., and Burt, Marina K. 1974. Natural sequences in second language acquisition. Language Learning 24:37-53.

Faerch, Claus. 1978. Performance analysis of learner's language. Papers from the fourth Scandinavian conference of linguistics, ed. Kirsten Gregerson. Odense, Denmark: Odense University Press.

Fries, Charles C. 1952. The structure of English. New York: Harcourt, Brace & World.

Gaies, Stephen J. 1977. The nature of linguistic input in formal second language learning: linguistic and communicative strategies in ESL teachers' classroom language. In TESOL '77: teaching and learning English as a second languate, ed. H. Douglas Brown, Carlos A. Yorio and Ruth H. Crymes, pp. 204-12. Washington, DC: TESOL.

Gouvernement du Quebec, Ministere de l'Education. 1977. L'enseignement primaire et secondaire au Quebec, Livre vert. Quebec: Editeur officiel du Quebec.

Hammarberg, B. 1973. The insufficiency of error analysis. In Errata, ed. Jan Svartvik. Lund, Sweden: Gleerup.

Hatch, Evelyn. 1978. Second language acquisition: a book of readings. Rowley, Mass.: Newbury House.

Haugen, Einar. 1953. The Norwegian language in America. 2 vols. Philadelphia: University of Pennsylvania Press.

Haugen, Einar. 1956. Bilingualism in the Americas: a bibliography and research guide. Publication of the American Dialect Society 26. University, Alabama: University of Alabama Press.

Hunt, Kellogg. 1965. Grammatical structures written at three grade levels. Research Report No. 3. Champaign, Ill.: National Council of Teachers of English.

Lado, Robert. 1972. Lado English series, book 4. Montreal: Centre educatif et culturel.

Levenston, E. A. 1971. Over-indulgence and under-representation—aspects of mother tongue interference. In Papers in contrastive linguistics, ed. Gerhard Nickel, pp. 115-21. Cambridge: At the University Press.

Lightbown, Patsy M., and Barkman, Bruce. 1978. Interaction among learners, teachers, texts and methods of English as a second language. Report to the Language Programs Branch, Department of the Secretary of State of Canada. Montreal: TESL Centre, Concordia University. ED 166 981.

Mackey, William F. 1962. The description of bilingualism. Canadian Journal of Linguistics 7:51-85.

_____. 1976. Bilinguisme et contact des langues. Paris: 2 Klincksieck.

Nickel, Gerhard. 1971. Papers in contrastive linguistics. Cambridge: At the University Press.

Oller, John W. Jr. and Richards, Jack C., eds. 1973. Focus on the learner: pragmatic perspectives for the language teacher. Rowley, Mas.: Newbury House.

Richards, Jack C. 1973. A non-contrastive approach to error analysis. English Language Teaching 25:204-19. Reprinted in Focus on the Learner: pragmatic perspectives for the Language teacher, ed. John W. Oller, Jr. and Jack C. Richards, pp. 96-113. Rowley, Mass.: Newbury House.

Richards, Jack C., ed. 1974. Error analysis: perspectives on second language acquisition. London: Longman.

Schachter, Jacquelyn. 1974. An error in error analysis. Language Learning 24:205-14.

Svartvik, Jan, ed 1973. Errata. Lund: Gleerup.

Upshur, John A. 1971. Objective evaluation of oral proficiency in the ESOL classroom. TESOL Quarterly 5:47-59.

Zydatiss, Wolfgang. 1976. Learning problem expanded form—a performance analysis. IRAL 14:351-71.

30.   Patterns of Teacher/Child Interaction In Preschool Settings

BETH HASLETT
University of Delaware

Introduction

Language development has been a subject of study by philosophers, linguists, and psychologists for many years. Developmental psycholinguistics has shifted from a narrow focus on syntax to include semantic and cognitive aspects of language development. The study of the acquisition of linguistic competence has also been expanded to include the development of communicative competence: that is, understanding the functions as well as the form of utterances is now believed to be essential for constructing a model of how a child acquires language and communication skills (Hymes 1972; Searle 1969; Williams 1970). The acquisition of language and communication skills is the focal point of study in the relatively new field of sociolinguistics, the study of the interactions of speaker, listener, and topic. Many sociolinguists have argued that the language and communication skills a child acquires are determined by the functions language performs in the social context in which that child lives.

Differential Communicative Competencies

With the emphasis on differences in language and communication skills across children, researchers focused on such variables as the child's linguistic experience, cognitive-perceptual development, the context in which utterances occur, etc., and their impact on the child's developing communicative competencies (Bloom 1970). Bloom, Lightbown, and Hood (1975) examined variation in children's early language development. Although the children talked about the same kinds of things and followed the same developmental sequence, they utilized different linguistic means to communicate the same information. Nelson (1975) explored the structure and strategies children use in learning how to communicate. According to the model she posited, integration of the child's preverbal concepts, his acquisition strategies, and parental-acceptance patterns are necessary for understanding the development of a child's communication skills. Shatz and Gelman (1973) explored four-year-old children's abilities to adjust to a listener: remarks addressed to two-year-olds contained more short, simple utterances and more attention-getting utterances than remarks addressed to peers or adults. Peers were treated like adults with regard to utterances addressed to them. A study by Cowan, Weber, Hoddinott, and Klein (1976) found that the topic of conversation influenced the child's language production.

Bloom, Rocissano, and Hood (1976), analyzing two-and-a-half and three-year-old children's conversations with adults, found that children's speech became more topically related to adults and, in turn, adults directed more questions to those children whose comments were linguistically related to the adult utterances. Furthermore Bloom et al. concluded that discourse rules (e.g., speaking when spoken to) functioned independently of the cognitive processes involved in speaking and understanding.

Interaction in Preschool Settings

A growing number of studies have focused upon communication patterns of young children in preschool settings. Such settings contribute to one's understanding of the social influences on speech, the relationship between comprehension and production, and how differences in context contribute to differneces in speech production. Beyond this, however, are two additional reasons for the special importance the preschool setting has in developing children's communicative abilities: (1) the role of the preschool teacher in providing a model for adult/child interaction and (2) the role of the preschool in providing important communicative experiences that aid the child in future social encounters.

In addition to the teacher's role as a "significant other" in providing another model for adult/child interaction, teachers have been found to play a significant role in the development of a child's self-concept (Ausubel 1954; Jaurard and Remy 1955; Heist and Webster 1960; Green 1969) and his expectations of himself and his academic achievement (Coleman 1966; Rosenthal 1973). Bernstein (1970), Hymes (1970), and others have detailed the importance of school and peer relationships in the socialization process.

The importance of a child's communicative style for academic achievement has been documented by William's research (1970) on the "stereotype hypothesis." Williams found that teacher's expectations of a pupil's performance corresponded closely to the extent to which that child's speech deviated from the standard dialect. Children, as well as adults, act according to their expectations of others and these expectations are derived from stereotypes based on an individual's speech patterns. As Williams states:

> the teacher's image of a low-status or disadvantaged child was one whose speech they would rate in the direction of being non-standard and ethnic and whose general performance may seem somewhat unsure and reticent to them . . . the suggestion is that upon hearing

a very brief portion of the child's speech a stereotype
was elicited in the teacher and she used this [as a basis
for judging the child]. (1970:388-89; bracketed addition
is mine.)

It seems clear that teacher/child and child/child interactions
are important aspects of a child's intellectual, social, and emotional
growth. As M. A. K. Halliday (1973) observes:

there may be differences in the relative orientation of
different social groups towards the various functions of
language in given contexts and towards the different
areas of meaning that may be explored within a given
function. . . . When these differences manifest
themselves in the contexts that are critical for the
socialization process they may have a profound effect
on the child's social learning; and therefore on his
response to education, because built into the
educational process are a number of assumptions and
practices that reflect differentially not only the values
but also the communication patterns and learning styles
of different sub-cultures. (1973)

Communicative Studies in Preschool Settings

An indepth study of the preschooler's interpersonal speech-
usage by Schacter et al. (1974) found three stages of communication
development. Using the instrument they developed on the basis on
analyzing 2,000 statements from 100 preschoolers observed during
free play periods, Schacter uncovered an initial state of primary
socially interdependent speech, followed by the development of
secondary social patterns, and last, tertiary socialized speech.
Before three years of age, the preschooler's speech consisted mainly
of desire implementation, reports on one's self and things, self-
referring statements and word naming (learning the implementing
category). This stage contained the greatest amount of speech
directed at adults. This pattern of speech, the primary socially
interdependent speech, seems very well suited for insuring mutual
gratification during the close interdependent state between child
and adult. Schacter and her associates found a major developmental
change occurring at age three, when children's speech functions
showed increasing self-other differentiation. Ego-enhancing,
boasting statements increased substantially; peer-directed
collaborative statements and joining statements began to increase
with age. This stage was called secondary sociable speech. From
four-and-one-half to five-and-one-half years of age, speech patterns
emerged that demonstrated communicative adjustments to various
listeners: this stage was labeled tertiary socialized speech. As the
child developed a less egocentric orientation and increased self-

other differentiation, his or her speech patterns began to accommodate to the needs of the listener. Females were found to address significantly more statements to adults than did males. Middle-class blacks and whites scored consistently higher than disadvantaged blacks in modulations (explanations, justifications, etc). Advantaged subjects scored consistently higher in asserting desires to adults. Schacter suggests that disadvantaged children may have suffered a basic loss of trust in adults, and therefore, even at a very early age, do not talk much to them.

While this study contributes to the understanding of how children communicate, it suffers from some major weaknesses. First, the coding categories developed are very difficult to discriminate and do not appear, in some cases, to be mutually exclusive. Second, the research focus is clearly on the speaker's utterances rather than on the social negotiation of conversation in which the participants are engaged. Furthermore, as Cazden observes in her review of this study, changing the context in which the interaction occurs may change the communication patterns observed. Cazden suggests that future research explore the context variables and that it include speech that is a response to others.

Although much research has been done in preschool settings, very little analysis has focused upon teachers' utterances or the teacher-child dialogue. The purpose of the present study is: (1) to analyze the functions of teacher-student dialogue, particularly from an interactive perspective, (2) to assess differences in teacher-talk across class levels, and (3) to assess differences in children's responses to teachers as a function of age and sex of the child.

The Flander's Interaction Analysis Categories (FIAC) were utilized to assess teacher-child interaction. The FIAC are designed to evaluate teacher talk, examining the functions of teacher utterances, categories of questions, and the degree of teacher control of the classroom (or dialogue). Although the FIAC have not been used as an instrument for evaluating preschool teachers, it was believed that the FIAC would provide a useful set of functional categories. (See Appendix A for FIAC categories.) The use of the FIAC interaction matrix, in view of its heavy emphasis on time measurements as an index of teacher control, did not seem useful to apply since the preschool environment is not as tightly structured as most elementary, high school, or college classrooms. (Teachers talking to the entire class or a substantial portion one-third of the class were the exception rather than the rule among preschools; most of the instruction is carried out in a dyad (teacher-pupil) or by teachers talking with two or three children at some activity center).

Method

Data Collection

Subjects. Forty-one preschoolers at a daycare center served as subjects in the study. This preschool offered a good cross-section of economic backgrounds, parental educational levels, and ethnic origins. Subjects included 10 three-year-olds (5 females, 5 males), 18 four-year-olds (11 males, 7 females), and 13 five-year-olds (8 males, 5 females). Eleven teachers served as subjects also.

Sampling Strategy. The experimenter recorded the children and teachers over a seven-month period, observing subjects in varied play activities in the mornings. The classroom teaching style was informal; that is, teachers circulated through the classroom at various activity stations set up for the day (e.g., reading corner, painting area, puzzle and small toy area, etc.), helping children, talking with them, settling disputes, and so forth. The teachers interacted with the children primarily when the children were involved in tasks they had selected to do, and the teachers atempted to facilitate this activity in a number of ways (instruction, asking questions, explaining, etc.). Each teacher made efforts to circulate in the classroom. Thus it was believed that tracking "target teachers" insured coverage of all children in the classroom, and therefore a representative sample of teacher/child interaction was included in the corpus. Since each teacher served as a "target teacher" for six weeks of the six-month data collection period, this was believed to also ensure adequate sampling across all teachers and all children. One child who had delayed speech was excluded from the sample. Although there were "group times" with a teacher discussing events/ideas with a group of children, such instances were not included in the corpus since they were essentially teacher monologues interspersed with questions/responses by the children. (Also, these "group times" represented only thirty minutes per day of teacher/child dialogue. This balance is probably unique to preschool settings or to open classrooms.)

Approximately three to four hours of observations were collected each week. Each observation session averaged approximately fifteen minutes. Since running notes on the activity and general setting were being taken, it was thought that longer sessions would be too exhausting. The experimenter recorded subjects with a portable stereo cassette taperecorder concealed in a shoulder bag. The experimenter controlled the recording by a remote control microphone concealed in the bag's side compartment. The experimenter's observations of the first month were discarded since this period served as a time for both children and teachers to become accustomed to the experimenter's presence in the classrooms and to work out recording/coding strategies. The children as well as the teachers soon became accustomed to the experimenter's presence and did not pay much attention to the experimenter.

All recording was done between 9:30 and 11:30 A.M. Since all the children were observed to be most active and involved during this period. For each day, a "target teacher" was selected in each class; over the period of time in the study, each teacher served as a primary target for five to six weeks.

Data Analysis

Tape Transcription. Each tape was transcribed and marked for episodes. A communicative episode was defined as conversational sequences that maintained a common topic or focus of attention and that accomplished some interactional purpose (Dore 1977b). Those utterances that were unintelligible or uninterpretable were deleted from the data sample.

Coding System

Flanders Scale. The Flander's Interaction Analysis Categories (FIAC) were selected as the coding categories for teacher/pupil interaction. The FIAC scales are particularly suited for analysis of teacher utterances since they deal with types of questions, techniques for building upon pupil's comments, and other specific task concerns for teachers. The categories also include an analysis of the cognitive level of the questions asked by teachers and the cognitive level of responses by pupils.

Coder Training and Reliability. The experimenter trained a graduate research assistant to use these coding systems on previously collected data. Ground rules were established for coding each category, especially when disagreements over interpretation were found. This training took place over a three-week period. The research assistant then analyzed the data collected for the present study. The experimenter separately coded every fifth episode in the data sample (approximately 25% of the data) as a reliability check. Agreement between the research assistant and the experimenter was .76.

Data Sample. The data analyzed was collected as part of a larger study that analyzed child/child and teacher/child interaction. The present study analyzed only teacher/child interaction. 2,269 utterances reflected teacher/child interaction (994 teacher utterances and 1,275 child utterances).

Results

Teacher Talk

FIAC. Teachers differed significantly with respect to types of statements made. Teacher-initiated remarks were more frequent (480 statements) than teacher responses to pupils (303 utterances). least frequent utterances were content questions (168 questions) (χ^2 = 777; p < .0001). The most frequent teacher-initiated remarks were lecturing statements (20% of all teacher remarks), then commands (9%) and justificatory statements (9%), least frequent were directions (7%). The content questions were recall in nature (15% of all teacher utterances) rather than open-ended (2% of all teacher questions). Teacher responses differed significantly across response categories and over strategies within each response category. Developing pupil ideas was the most frequent teacher response (18% of all teacher utterances), and praising/encouraging pupils was done about 12% of the time. (See Table 1 for differences in response categories and techniques within categories).

Table 1
FIAC Strategies Across All Teachers and Classes*

FIAC Strategies	Teacher Class Level			
	Twos	Threes	Fours	Fives
Responses				
1. Accepts feelings	5.9			
2. Superficial encouragement	7.0		5.3	
3. Emphasizes reasons for praise	6.2		9.2	8.2
Responses Using Pupil Ideas				
1. Repetition, superficial acknowledgment	6.6		7.0	7.4
2. Pupil's idea developed in light of teacher perception				4.9
3. Pupil's idea developed in terms of a teacher's question		7.0		13.9
Content Questions				
1. Narrowly focused questions, emphasizing recall.	23.0	14.5	13.0	9.0
Teacher-Initiated Remarks				
1. Lecturing	18.0	21.0	12.6	26.2
2. Commands	9.0	9.1	10.4	
3. Explains directions	5.0	5.4	10.9	
4. Criticizing, justifying authority		14.0	11.3	

*All response and initiated strategies are given in percentages of overall utterances within each class level. Differences across strategies within each class level were significant at the p = .0001 level (χ^2 tests). Differences across all teachers over class levels and strategies was significant at p = .0001 level.

Cognitive Level of Questions/Lecturing Statements. Cognitive levels of teacher utterances were analyzed according to whether they involved concrete objects or events, the mental operation of grouping, or the mental operation of inferring. Content questions and utterances coded as lecturing were analyzed in this way. All teacher-talk, if it could be appropriately analyzed in those dimensions, centered upon the level of concrete objects and events (573 teacher utterances were not capable of being analyzed in this manner).

Differences among Teachers. Teachers' utterances were analyzed across the different age groups (teachers of two-year-olds contrasted with teachers of three-year-olds, etc.) and across functions.

Teachers of Five-year-olds. FIAC. The major portion of teacher-talk consisted of responses to their pupils (32% of all utterances) and initiating remarks (25% of all utterances, N = 127). (See Table 1 for all strategies accounting for more than 5% of the total teacher statements for that age group). Lecturing by narrowly focused statements and asking questions that further developed the pupils' ideas were the single most frequent techniques (40% of all teacher-talk). Differences across teacher-talk strategies were significant (χ^2 = 456, p < .0001). Some inferential or grouping statements (N = 12) made were by these teachers; all other content questions (N = 13) and lecturing statements (N = 30) involved the level of concrete objects and events.

Teachers of Four-year-olds. Teacher strategies differed significantly across all general response categories (χ^2 = 1,278, p < .00001). Teacher-initiated remarks constituted 44% of all teacher talk, with strategies being equally split across lecturing, explaining directions, commanding, and providing justification for behavior. Twenty percent of teacher talk was responding to pupils, and the most frequently used strategy was to strongly praise/encourage pupils. All content questions and lecturing remarks were at the cognitive level of concrete objects/events.

Teachers of Three-year-olds. Teacher-talk strategies varied significantly across response categories (χ^2 = 564, p < .00001). Teacher-initiated remarks comprised 49% of all teacher utterances with lecturing being the most frequent strategy. Narrowly focused questions were the next most frequent category (N = 27) and occurred as frequently as utterances justifying behavior (N = 26). Teacher response strategies were to comment briefly on the pupil's remark or to raise a question about the remark. Cognitive level of statements also varied significantly ($\chi^2 = 267$, p < .0001). Interestingly, 12% of teacher remarks involved the mental operation of inferring, but the predominant tendency was to discuss concrete objects and events.

Teachers of Two-year-olds.   Flander's response categories and strategies differed significantly across teachers ($\chi^2 = 659$, p < .0001).   Teacher-initiated remarks were most common (32%) and lecturing was the most frequent technique. Highly focused content questions were the most frequently utilized teacher-talk strategy (23% of all utterances).   Praise of students was the most common teacher response to pupils' remarks. Questions and lecturing were done on the concrete level of thought.

Teacher Comparisons across Class Levels.   Teacher talk was contrasted across class level. FIAC categories differed significantly as a function of class level ($\chi^2 = 13.3$, p < .05). Teacher-initiated utterances were the most frequent category of utterances, followed by teacher's responses and then questions. Only among teachers of the five-year-olds is there a balance between teacher-initiated remarks and teacher responses. The percentage of content questions decreased with increasing pupil age.   Lecturing was the most frequently used teacher-initiation utterance, while praise of student and development of student ideas were the most frequent response strategies.

Children's Talk with Teachers.   Children's dialogues with teachers were analyzed according to FIAC response categories and cognitive level of utterances.   Responses were analyzed as a function of age and sex of the child.

Overall Children's Responses.   Children initiated talk with teachers (N = 60) about twice as much as they responded to teachers (N = 333) with the remaining comments being coded as uninterpretable in view of those categories (N = 273; this reflects statements that continue the conversation, $\chi^2 = 673$, p < .0001). Of those utterances capable of being coded for cognitive level of utterance (N = 994, 97% involved concrete objects and events rather than grouping or inferring ($\chi^2 = 1,896$, p < .00001).

Five-year-olds.   FIAC categories differed significantly across five-year-olds, with children initiating remarks about three times more than responding to teacher talk ($\chi^2 = 55$, p < .0001). No significant sex differences occurred across FIAC categories.   Children's utterances were coded as being on the concrete object/event level.

Four-year-olds. FIAC categories differed significantly across the fours, with children initiating remarks about four times more often than they responded to teacher-talk ($\chi^2 = 407$, p < .00001). No significant sex differences were found across FIAC categories.

Three-year-olds. FIAC categories varied significantly across the threes, with slightly more responses than initiating statements made ($\chi^2 = 91$, p < .0001). No significant sex differences were found across FIAC categories.

Two-year-olds. FIAC categories varied across the twos, with twice as many responses as initiating remarks ($\chi^2 = 88$, p < .0001). No significant sex differences were found across FIAC categories.

Discussion

Teacher-Talk

Overall, teachers used more initiating than responding utterances and asked questions least frequently. Almost all teacher utterances were on the level of referring to concrete objects and events; this confirmed other research demonstrating that children's concepts and verbal strategies center upon concrete referents, as Piagetians suggest. The greater percentage of teacher-initiating utterances reflected teacher control of the interaction. Interestingly, the percentage of teacher-initiated remarks decreased as class level (and child age) increased. Teachers of the five-year-olds made more responding (32%) than initiating utterances (25%), whereas teachers of two-, three- and four-year-old children made two to three times more initiating than responding remarks. It was thought that this reflected teachers' accommodation to a major communicative shift by children at four-and-a-half to five-and-a-half years of age as found by Schacter and her associates (1974). Schacter found that children at this age demonstrated communicative adjustments to listeners; the teachers of the fives may be responding to these communicative skills by instituting a balanced dialogue between teacher and child rather than the earlier teacher-controlled interaction (as measured by percentage of teacher-initiated remarks). Further evidence to support this would be the decrease in regulatory statements by teachers as a function of increasing child age. Responses by teachers also increased with increasing age of the child. Such findings demonstrated that teachers were sensitive to the developing cognitive and communicative skills of the preschoolers.

Analysis of the teachers' talk also confirmed that teachers, even on the preschool level, were incorporating the standard teaching interact documented by Bellack (1966) and others. "Teacherese" consists of a teacher's probe, followed by the student's response and subsequent teacher evaluation of the student response. Teachers' questions were narrowly focused recall or informative questions and teachers' responses to children's replies were evaluative.

Another common teacher-initiated utterance was regulatory and designed to control/channel student behavior. These regulatory remarks decreased as student age increased. Lecturing or presenting information was also a frequent teacher-initiated remark. Questions declined in use as child age increased. Generally, lecturing and regulatory remarks reflected the two primary teacher functions of instructing and socializing children.

Teachers gave praise frequently in response to students, especially to two- and three-year-old children. Around four years of age, children's ideas were developed by the teacher as a means of responding to children and this tactic was a more frequent response strategy than overt praise. When children were five, teachers were using development of pupil ideas four times more frequently than praise as a teacher response strategy. This communicative shift by the teachers seems to mirror the developing cognitive skills of the child.

Children's Talk with Teachers. Overall, children initiated remarks (N = 660) twice as frequently as they responded to teacher remarks (N = 333). The remarks all reflected concern for or with concrete objects or events. Interestingly, children did not use many expressive remarks ("ouch,", "ow", "gosh," etc). when talking with teachers, although this is common in peer interaction. Many children's utterances were made with forcefulness (e.g., as an exclamation rather than a statement); thus, expressiveness may be conveyed paralinguistically by the child when interacting with adults, whereas in child/child interaction expressiveness may be conveyed by conventional exclamations such as "ouch," etc.

Two- and three-year-olds responded more than they initiated remarks; this trend was dramatically reversed among the four- and five-year-olds. At three years, children are beginning to shift from parallel play to more social, interactive play; during this period, parallel conversational skills seem to be developing. At four, the child can assume control over and initiate a dialogue with an adult quite comfortably.

As has been found in other studies, no significant sex differences were found among preschoolers' communication. However, the FIAC categories may not be appropriately sensitive measures for assessing such differences.

Teacher-Child Dialogue. The study's findings revealed a sensitive interplay of communicative strategies. With an increase in child age, teachers' control of the dialogue decreased; teachers' responses increased, and children initiated more talk. At four and five years of age, children appeared to be quite comfortable with initiating and maintaining dialogue. There appears to be real mutual engagement and dialogue among preschoolers and teachers: this appears to be more similar to parent-child interaction than teacher-child interaction (as found in studies of teacher-child interaction among older children). Children who attend preschool undoubtedly find the adjustment to school less traumatic than children without such experience because of the socialization and communicative skills learned in preschool settings. Teacher-child dialogue in preschools appears to be a transition from "motherese" in the home to the "teacherese" they will encounter in most traditional school settings. "Motherese" has been found to use repetition and expansion as communicative strategies; teachers used repetition through brief reiterations of student remarks and expanded pupil utterances by raising further questions about their pupils' remarks. "Teacherese," the teacher probe, student response, and teacher evaluation cycle, was also demonstrated in the present study, particularly with four- and five-year-olds.

Future Research. More research in this area is needed since there is a lack of basic information about communicative development, particularly from an interactive viewpoint. Future studies could explore teacher-pupil dialogue on a episode-by-episode basis, rather than by focusing on broad trends, as did the present study. In addition, different levels of functional analyses are needed, particularly in adult-child interaction where the context of such interaction is so varied.

REFERENCES

Bellack, A.; Kliebard, H.; Hyman, R.; and Smith, F., Jr. 1966. The language of the classroom. New York: Teachers College Press.
Bernstein, B. 1970. A sociolinguistic approach to socialization: with some reference to educability. In Language and poverty, ed. F. Williams, pp. 25-62. Chicago: Markham Press.
Bloom, L. 1970. Language development. Cambridge, Mass.: MIT Press.
Bloom, L.; Hood, L.; and Lightbown, P. 1974. Imitation of language development: if, when and why. Cognitive Psychology 6:380-420.
Bloom, L.; Rocissano, L.; and Hood, L. 1976. Adult-child discourse: developmental interaction between information processing and linguistic knowledge. Cognitive Psychology 8:521-52.
Cazden, C. 1966. Subcultural differences in child language: an inter-disciplinary view. Merrill-Palmer Quarterly 12:185-219.
Dore, J. 1977. Children's illocutionary acts. In Discourse production and comprehension, ed. R. Freedle. Hillsdale,

N.J.: Erlbaum Associates.

_____. 1978. Variation in preschool children's conversational performances. In Children's language, ed. K. Nelson. Vol. 1. New York: Gardner Press.

Dore, J.; Gearhart, M.; and Newman, D. 1978. The structure of nursery school conversation. In Children's language, ed. K. Nelson, pp. 337-96. Vol. 1. New York: Gardner Press.

Flanders, N. 1970. Analyzing teaching behavior. Reading, Mass.: Addison-Wesley.

Garvey, C. 1977. Play with language and speech. In Child discourse, ed. S. Ervin-Tripp and C. Mitchell-Kernan. New York: Academic Press.

_____. 1979. Contingent queries and their relations in discourse. In Developmental pragmatics, ed. E. Ochs and B. Schieffelin. New York: Academic Press.

Haliday, M. A. K. 1973. Forward to Class, codes and control, ed. B. Bernstein. Vol. 2. London: Routledge and Kegan Paul.

Hymes, D. 1972. On communicative competence. In Sociolinguistics, ed. J. Pride and J. Holmes. Harmondsworth, Middlesex: Penguin.

Labov, W. 1972. Language in the inner city. Philadelphia: University of Pennsylvania Press.

McDermott, R.; Gospodinoff, K.; and Aron, J. 1976. Criteria for an ethnographically adequate description of activities and their contexts. Paper read at the annual meeting of the American Anthropological Association, Washington, D.C., November.

Schacter, F.; Kirshner, K.; Klips, B.; Friedricks, M.; and Sanders, K. 1974. Everyday preschool interpersonal speech usage. SRCD Monographs 39:3.

Shatz, M., and Gelman, R. 1973. The development of communication skills. SRCD Monographs 38:3.

Searle, J. R. 1969. Speech acts. New York: Cambridge University Press.

_____. 1975. Indirect speech acts. In Syntax and semantics, ed. P. Cole and J. Morgan, Vol. 3. New York: Academic Press.

Soskin, J.; and John, V. 1963. The study of spontaneous talk. In The Stream of Behavior, ed. R. Barker, pp. 228-82. New York: Appleton-Century-Crofts.

Williams, F. 1970. Language, attitude and social change. In Language and poverty, ed. F. Williams. Chicago: Markham Press.

APPENDIX
FLANDER'S INTERACTION ANALYSIS CATEGORIES

Teacher Talk

A. Teacher responses to pupils:

1. Accepts feeling. Accepts and clarifies an attitude/feeling of a pupil in a nonthreatening way.

2. Praises or encourages. Praises, encourages pupil action or behavior.
    a. encouragement is superficial, like "um-hm," "good."
    b. provides reasons for praise, or gives special emphasis.

3. Uses pupil's ideas. Clarifying, building or developing ideas suggested by the pupil.
    a. merely repeats, very brief summaries, superficial response.
    b. pupil's idea is developed in terms of teacher perceptions
    c. pupil's idea is developed in terms of his own, or another pupil's idea mentioned previously
    d. similar to a or b, except phrased as a question

B. Teacher's content questions:

1. Narrow, factual questions emphasizing recall: what, when, where

2. Broad, open questions which permits flexibility in answering

C. Teacher-initiated utterances

1. Lecturing. Teacher gives facts, opinions about content, procedures and activities; expresses teacher's own views or explanations.
    a. narrow, factual focus; restricted concepts and purposes
    b. negative comments, disagreement without comments or explanation

2. Giving Directions. Directions, orders or commands to which a pupil is expected to comply.
    a. commands to which compliance can easily be judged, absence of reasons or explanations
    b. explains direction, how and why something is to be done
    c. provides alternatives, gives pupil some choice in making decisions

3. Justifying authority/behavior. Statements designed to change pupil behavior from unacceptable to acceptable, criticizing other's behavior, scolding, stating why the teacher is doing what he is doing.

D. <u>Pupil talk</u>:

1. <u>Pupil response.</u> Remarks in response to a comment by teacher, soliciting a response from the pupil.
2. <u>Pupil-initiated remarks.</u> Talk by pupils that they initiate; developing own ideas, developing a new topic, freedom in pursuing new ideas, etc.